Strategic Capabilities and Knowledge Transfer Within and Between Organizations

Strategic Capabilities and Knowledge Transfer Within and Between Organizations

New Perspectives from Acquisitions, Networks, Learning and Evolution

Edited by

Arturo Capasso
University of Sannio, Italy

Giovanni Battista Dagnino
University of Catania, Italy

Andrea Lanza
University of Calabria and SDA Bocconi Business School, Italy

With a foreword by Sidney G. Winter

Edward Elgar
Cheltenham, UK • Northampton, MA, USA

Published by
Edward Elgar Publishing Limited
Glensanda House
Montpellier Parade
Cheltenham
Glos GL50 1UA
UK

Edward Elgar Publishing, Inc.
136 West Street
Suite 202
Northampton
Massachusetts 01060
USA

A catalogue record for this book
is available from the British Library

ISBN 1 84376 945 X

Printed and bound in Great Britain by MPG Books Ltd, Bodmin, Cornwall

Contents

v

Contributors

Jay B. Barney, Ohio State University, USA

Carlo Boschetti, University of Bologna, Italy

Sebastian Bruque-Camara, University of Jaen, Spain

Arturo Capasso, University of Sannio, Italy

Armando Cirrincione, Bocconi University, Italy

Raffaele Corrado, University of Bologna, Italy

Giovanni Battista Dagnino, University of Catania, Italy

Valentina Della Corte, University of Naples 'Federico II', Italy

Maria Chiara Di Guardo, University of Cagliari, Italy

Consuelo Dolz, University of Valencia, Spain

Pierre Dussauge, HEC School of Management, France

Simone Ferriani, University of Bologna, Italy

Marco Galvagno, University of Catania, Italy

Maria Iborra, University of Valencia, Spain

Andrea Lanza, University of Calabria and SDA Bocconi Business School, Italy

M. Teresa Martìnez-Fernàndez, University of Castellon 'Jaume I', Spain

José A. Medina-Garrido, University of Cadiz, Spain

Olimpia Meglio, University of Sannio, Italy

Will Mitchell, Duke University, USA

F. Xavier Molina-Morales, University of Castellon 'Jaume I', Spain

Stefano Pace, Bocconi University, Italy

Miguel Rivera Santos, Babson College, USA

José Ruiz-Navarro, University of Cadiz, Spain

Mauro Sciarelli, University of Naples 'Federico II', Italy

Harbir Singh, Wharton School, University of Pennsylvania, USA

Denise Sumpf, European Business School, Germany

Maurizio Zollo, INSEAD, France

Foreword

For some time now, the phenomenon of organizational knowledge has been a major focus of attention for a wide range of academic researchers and business practitioners. The attention is well deserved. Few topics indeed present such a diverse range of interesting puzzles and problems. Many of these are fascinating by virtue of their intellectual depth and challenge; others suggest opportunities for major improvements in business performance – and only a few combine both of these attractive features. Although a good deal has been learned about these problems, satisfying conclusions remain elusive in many cases. Assuredly, a central lesson from the research and experience to date is that these problems are harder than they look, but no less important. While the popularity of individual approaches may wax and wane, and other concerns certainly compete for attention, there is little sign that interest in organizational knowledge problems is going to fade away anytime soon.

The chapters in this book address in particular the links between knowledge and strategic capabilities. A major theme is that the ability to address knowledge problems effectively is itself a strategic capability. Like the more straightforward capabilities in production, marketing or distribution, the various types of knowledge management capabilities – such as diffusing superior practices internally, or learning from alliance partners, or accessing complementary knowledge through a network – rest fundamentally on specific organizational knowledge. Such knowledge always derives in significant part from the organization's experience with the class of problems. In the knowledge domain, however, 'experience' is generally multi-faceted and its meaning often ambiguous. Substantial elements of novelty distinguish this month's problem from the similar one encountered last month – the degree of 'similarity' is largely a matter of cognitive framing, not of objectively ascertainable fact. Hence, the manager who perceives the similarity and seeks to apply learning from the past may well be advantaged by so doing, but can also encounter the hazards of giving too little weight to the differences. For example, a string of acquisition or alliance experiences is, as several of the papers here attest, a considerably more subtle and challenging learning context than the production lines that were originally featured in the literature of 'learning by doing'.

Another strikingly recurrent theme of these chapters is the problematic nature of what might be termed 'the knowledge boundaries of the firm'. While no one seems to challenge the basic proposition that the firm is a significant entity in the creation and retention of knowledge, these authors explore a rich variety of elaborations, qualifications extensions and amendments of this basic idea. Thus, for example, firms have in principle many opportunities to gain by moving knowledge internally, but such transfer is no trivial matter – significant resources and capabilities are required. At the same time, a firm embedded in a network and/or located in an industrial district faces related challenges (but distinctive strategic hazards) in managing knowledge flows in both directions across the boundaries conventionally defined by ownership and control. Again, when ownership relations are changed one day by an acquisition, it is quite clear that the old knowledge boundaries are not much changed by the next morning, though they are now in part an internal feature of a larger firm. It takes deliberate effort and capabilities to accomplish the knowledge integration component of the total post-acquisition integration process, thereby to realize the knowledge-related promise of the acquisition.

Overall, the chapters in this impressive book advance a strongly dynamic perspective on the relationship of knowledge to competitive advantage. Peter Drucker's famous proposition that knowledge is now the dominant source of competitive advantage stands intact, but this book provides an important gloss on it. Durable advantage (if achievable at all) ultimately depends on strength at the meta-level of organizational knowledge, the knowledge required to manage knowledge effectively. The studies reported here are a valuable platform for future research on this key proposition.

Sidney G. Winter

Wharton School, Philadelphia

February 2005

1. Introduction: strategic capabilities and knowledge transfer within and between organizations

Arturo Capasso, Giovanni Battista Dagnino and Andrea Lanza

BACKGROUND TO THE BOOK

This book focuses on strategic capabilities intended to facilitate mechanisms of knowledge transfer and key processes for knowledge generation and organizational learning and evolution. The book is the imaginative outcome of the collected efforts of several international strategy scholars who undertake original research on the broad relationship between strategic capabilities and knowledge transfer at both intra- and inter-organizational levels and from various viewpoints.

Since this collection of papers has a pretty intriguing story, it is probably worth recalling its onset. The book is in fact the outgrowth of a conference-track with basically the same title that two of the present editors have organized within the EURAM (European Academy of Management) Conference hosted in Milan by the SDA Bocconi Business School in May 2003.

The towering quality and quantity of the papers received and selected by the convenors and then presented at the venue, together with the spirited discussions that have generally sparked out from presentations and discussants' reports, prompted us to explore a few possible follow-ups to the above stimulating EURAM pursuit. One of the ideas that materialized almost immediately in the editors' minds was that of preparing an edited book containing a revised and refined version of the best papers presented in the conference-track. The present book is the outcome of this initial vision. In order to assure continuity to a successful venture, subsequent to the first one, we convened a second conference-track with the same title within the EURAM Conference held in St. Andrews, Scotland, in May 2004. Surprisingly enough, should we combine the two EURAM conference-tracks

1

(that is, Milan and St. Andrews), the papers and abstracts received from practically all over the world total the remarkable figure of 69, while the total number of papers that have been presented in the two venues is 42.

THE UNIFYING THREADS OF THE BOOK

As with all edited collections of papers, this book basically contains the miscellaneous efforts of several different contributors. It is thus important to identify one or more common threads that unify in some way the chapters presented henceforth, which may be regarded as the book's *fils rouges*. In our understanding, the first unifying thread that links the contributions contained in this book is the fact that, as a whole, it significantly contributes to the growth of knowledge in this research area, pushing its boundaries forward and challenging the existing wisdom. What gives originality to this endeavor is that all the papers contained in this book are written with the unequivocal aim of exploring the role that strategic capabilities play in allowing (or preventing) knowledge transfer in firm and inter-firm environments. Accordingly, as regards the relationships between strategic capabilities and the transfer of knowledge, the book encompasses different levels of analysis (such as, the firm, the inter-organizational network, the industry), different theoretical lenses (the resource-based view, the knowledge-based view, the evolutionary perspective, transaction cost economics, cognitive theory, and so forth), and different methodological stances. We now explain the motivation of this study.

In recent years, drawing on seminal works in the evolutionary perspective of the firm (Nelson and Winter, 1982, 2002; Tushman and Romanelli, 1985), thinking and practice in strategic management have both devoted increasing attention to issues gathered together under the broad label of 'knowledge management' (Hedlund, 1994; Teece, 1998). Moving from the shared assumption that knowledge production and exploitation is strategically significant for firms (Winter, 1987), a new research agenda has emerged, unveiling the importance of investigating how firms develop, integrate and organize knowledge (see the pioneering contribution of Hayek, 1945). In this vein, a growing body of literature in the last decade has focused on the processes of knowledge generation, knowledge sharing, knowledge identification and knowledge transfer within and between firms.

The focus on knowledge transfer relates to three apparently distinct but nonetheless complementary research perspectives in the strategic organization agenda. First, it recalls the *strategic capabilities* perspective (Amit and Schoemaker, 1993; Teece *et al.*, 1997; Dosi *et al.*, 2000; Eisenhardt and Martin, 2000), appreciating firm capabilities as the organizational and managerial systems supporting the learning processes necessary in intra- and inter-organizational knowledge transfer. Second, it links up to the burgeoning *knowledge-based theory of the firm* (Kogut and Zander, 1992; Grant, 1996; Porter-Liebeskind, 1996; Nonaka *et al.*, 2000; Eisenhardt and Santos, 2002; Grant, 2003), which regards the firm as a repository of knowledge and a knowledge-creating entity. Third, it takes into account the *strategic networks* perspective (Gulati, 1999; Gulati *et al.*, 2000; Hansen, 2002) claiming the relevance of inter-firm relationships as platforms of inter-organizational learning and evolution.

The strategic capabilities perspective is based on a set of 'needed-to-win' capabilities; that is, the ability of firms to integrate resources, to learn and to reconfigure their businesses. Capabilities building and renewal lie, in this view, at the very basis of the firm competitive advantage and value creation (Teece *et al.*, 1997; Helfat and Peteraf, 2003). The strategic network perspective on organizational learning and development explores how knowledge is acquired from the parent company by joint ventures, managed in international joint ventures, transferred across partners and integrated and developed in a network of inter-organizational cooperative relationships (Dyer and Singh, 1998; Dyer and Nobeoka, 2000), while also paying attention to the role of social capital in inter-firm knowledge integration-oriented relationships (Porter-Liebeskind *et al.*, 1996; Nahapiet and Ghoshal, 1998). The knowledge-based view of firms virtually strives both to deconstruct the black box of the firm's production function into its more basic components and interactions and to reconstruct the resource-based theory (Barney, 1991; Peteraf, 1993; Mocciaro Li Destri and Dagnino, 2003) by providing a platform for a new view of the firm as a dynamic system of knowledge generation, diffusion and application (Langlois and Robertson, 1995; Nonaka and Toyama, 2002). According to this idea, the firm's knowledge repository and its ability to generate, enrich or replicate knowledge lie at the very core of a sound strategic theory of the firm based on capabilities and capabilities evolution.

Whereas, as earlier noted, a good many efforts have been made in this direction and we have an emerging body of studies as regards the issue of strategic capabilities and knowledge transfer, we acknowledge that we are far from reaching a conclusive point: under-researched areas and inconsistencies still remain, providing opportunities for further empirical and theoretical research. These may be expressed in the following research questions to which we have tried to respond, at least in part, by offering this volume to the wide global community in the field of strategy and management.

What does firm and inter-firm knowledge transfer mean? Is complete knowledge transfer really possible? What kinds of knowledge transfer are feasible? What capabilities need to be activated in order to transfer knowledge and learning within a firm? And between or among firms? How do partner-specific characteristics and knowledge-specific characteristics affect knowledge transfer and learning in an alliance context? How are different forms of cooperation related to the learning results? How are organizational mechanisms and institutional arrangements related to knowledge transfer and learning between partners? How is knowledge transferred during post-acquisition processes, either by human resources bilateral redeployment or by administrative systems, routines and best practices transfer? How can this transfer be embedded in organizational routines or best practices? What kind(s) of stickiness may impede or delay the transfer of best practice within or between firms? How can social capital either help inter-firm knowledge integration success or mitigate inter-firm knowledge integration failure? How can the risk of opportunism and conflicts, on one hand, and the interest to acquire knowledge from a partner and learn, on the other, be balanced and managed? How are high-performance strategic knowledge networks managed?

WHY A BOOK ON STRATEGIC CAPABILITIES AND KNOWLEDGE TRANSFER?

In our view, the subject of this book is pretty appealing in current times and is acquiring a foremost status in strategy literature (where several books now focus on knowledge management at theoretical, empirical and managerial-applied levels). Notwithstanding that, since the exploration of the relationships between firm capabilities and knowledge transfer is at the beginning of its life cycle, we cannot list any published monographic studies which are fully dedicated to it. In our view, the key distinctive feature of this volume consists in its being the very first book exploring systematically the crucial relationship between strategic capabilities and knowledge transfer. Therefore it appears truly unique in its objective and scope.

A second distinctive feature is that the volume is the product of the collected efforts of several international strategy scholars, with various geographical roots and cultural and ecological backgrounds, who have unambiguously decided to undertake original research on the relationships between strategic capabilities and knowledge transfer at both intra- and inter-organizational levels from several viewpoints (that is, acquisitions, networks, learning and evolution). Although it is composite in nature, the book shows a high degree of coherence and consistency, since all the authors – driven by substantial common interests and aims – are conducting conceptual and empirical research in the same directions, have already experienced an intense dialogue among themselves (especially during the two EURAM conferences earlier recalled), and generally show consistent results. For the reasons above, the book significantly contributes to the growth of knowledge in this research area, pushing its boundaries forward and opening avenues for future research.

In addition, one of the most important results achieved by the book has been the fact that it gathers together several academic scholars who focus their research interest on topics related to strategic capabilities and knowledge transfer so as to continue shaping and growing a *scientific community* primarily dedicated to this subject. We are thus confident that it is possible to consolidate further this community, stimulating additional investigation on an issue so relevant to current strategy investigation.

We also emphasize the originality, freshness, and innovativeness of the approach proposed in the book as well as the fact that it brings together several perspectives on the issue of strategic capabilities and knowledge transfer within and between organizations, as concerns, respectively, acquisitions, networks, learning and evolution. Since, as already mentioned, the book is the outcome of the collective effort of several international scholars, the single chapters embrace various methodological approaches; for example, conceptual, empirical, case-based, or a combination of these. In our understanding, as it comprises a variety of approaches applied to the very same broad theme of investigation, this characteristic is a self-reinforcing feature of our proposal. Truly, one of the strengths of strategic management has traditionally been the multiplicity of basic disciplines (for example, economics, sociology, psychology, history) from which it has drawn the ensuing richness and fertility of its methodological and epistemological stances.

STRUCTURE OF THE BOOK

The book is organized as follows: after the introduction, there are thirteen chapters divided into three parts and, finally, the concluding chapter.

As regards the first part 'Strategic capabilities and knowledge transfer: perspectives from firm and industry heterogeneity', comprising Chapters 2–5, the contributions shed light on the broad and intertwined nexus of relationships linking firms and industry heterogeneity, as well as on capability development and knowledge transfer in different contexts, ranging from the tourism industry to Hollywood filmmaking and industrial district dynamics. In Chapter 2, 'Managing heterogeneity, allocative balance, and behavioral and technology concerns in competitive and cooperative inter-firm relationships', Andrea Lanza maintains that firms select their partners among competitors aiming at two main goals: acquiring knowledge for a non-immediate innovation purpose, which mainly relies on knowledge sharing, and to a minor extent on knowledge creation, and whose main outcome is future technology development; and developing knowledge for a rapid innovation and a fast market entry with new products and services. Knowledge sharing and creation processes constitute difficult activities, whose accomplishment entails the identification of some critical factors: heterogeneity in each partner's knowledge base; allocation trade-offs between sharing and creating activities; and behavioral concerns related to partners' commitment and rent appropriation attempts.

In Chapter 3, 'Digital economy and sustained competitive advantage in the tourism industry', Jay B. Barney, Valentina Della Corte and Mauro Sciarelli's aim is to identify the main sources of sustained competitive advantage in the new economy. In order to reach this objective, they try to answer these questions: can e-commerce and digital economy be a source of competitive advantage? can this logic be applied in the tourism industry? The authors examine firms operating in the tourism industry for several reasons. Tourism is regarded as a very attractive industry, whose economic trends show its importance in the general economy. Several firms try to enter and are extremely interested in this sector, even in the logic of conglomerate diversification.

In Chapter 4 'Transferring organizational capabilities across transient organizations: evidence from Hollywood filmmaking', Simone Ferriani, Raffaele Corrado and Carlo Boschetti highlight how the increasing need for flexibility and the shrinkage of firms' time frames have fostered the development of project-based forms of organization. Some of the organizational features of project-based organizations appear at odds with resource- and capability-centered perspectives on the firm. While a key assumption of these conceptions of organizational functioning is that firms develop path-dependent organizational processes shaping their conduct, project-based organizations exhibit no ostensible history-based path to build upon their organizational behavior and capabilities. A project-based enterprise is a transient form of organization that ceases to exist as soon as its single target is achieved. This apparent paradox prompts various intriguing questions as to the organizational mechanisms that allow these temporary systems to integrate their highly mobile knowledge assets into a valuable and consolidated set of capabilities. Using the Hollywood motion picture industry as empirical grounding for their reasoning, the authors show that, in a project-based environment, firm disbanding does not necessarily imply the termination of collaborative interactions established during single projects.

Chapter 5, 'Knowledge transfer as a key process for firm learning: the role of local institutions in industrial districts', by F. Xavier Molina-Morales and M. Teresa Martinez-Fernàndez, is concerned with social networks, geographical proximity of firms and local institutions. In particular, this chapter reviews the ideas streaming from the industrial district literature by analysing the role that local institutions play as a factor that can account for the competitive advantage and the capacity to create the economic value observed within the district. The chapter draws on an analysis based on a comparison of district members and non-members. The empirical findings suggest a positive association between district membership, contribution of local institutions, and value creation as measured by innovation.

Part two, 'Strategic capabilities and knowledge transfer: perspectives from evolution, learning and networks', comprising Chapters 6-9, combines insights from evolutionary and network views on learning, knowledge development and innovation. Chapter 6, 'Coupling combinative and relational capabilities in interorganizational best practice transfer: an evolutionary perspective', written by Giovanni Battista Dagnino, points out that current strategic management studies usually couple the intensification in the globalization of best business practices with the growing of the specific capabilities needed to transfer business knowledge between or among firms and to implement those practices locally. Whereas the management and transfer of best practices has grown up basically in relation to the 'large firms' environment, both the literature and the practice of strategy have devoted much less consideration to networks and systems of firms. Therefore the aim of the chapter is to show why and how systems of firms – intended as efficient modes of organizing and networking strategic resources and capabilities – are able by coupling combinative and relational capabilities to produce superior economic and knowledge value in transferring best business practices inside and outside their borders.

In Chapter 7, 'Heuristics and network position: a cognitive and structural framework on innovation', Armando Cirrincione and Stefano Pace propose a basic distinction between an approach that bases innovation on internal capabilities and an approach that focuses on the network to which the firm belongs. In the first approach, innovation is seen as originating within the firm thanks to its capabilities, primarily cognitive ones, since innovation is linked to new knowledge. At the other end of the spectrum, innovation is considered a network-based phenomenon: new knowledge is created through exchanges among partners of a network (that is, distributed innovation). Knowledge does not reside in a single subject or organization, but is network-based. The aim of this chapter is to couple together the network and the cognitive arguments. The hypothesis suggested is that a broker firm – a firm that holds a structural hole position within a network – has the advantage of being exposed to different cognitive heuristics (above all when the network is formed by nodes belonging to different industries). While this chapter acknowledges the relevance of structural position in a network, it adds the heuristics concept to explain the innovative process: the broker firm is more innovative since it can share many heuristics, thanks to its structural hole occupation. In this view, the structural and the cognitive arguments are considered to be deeply intertwined.

Chapter 8, 'Developing dynamic capabilities with IT', by José A. Medina-Garrido, José Ruiz-Navarro and Sebastian Bruque-Camara, observes that the organizations of the 21st century may use the notion of dynamic capabilities as a way to adapt more promptly to a changing economic world. In this chapter, the authors analyze the relationship between information and communications technology (ICT) and the creation process of dynamic capabilities. They propose a model for the creation of dynamic capabilities in which they define the role that ICT may play: (1) identifying the firms nexus of capabilities (over time and space); (2) maintaining a capabilities catalogue; (3) assisting the transformation of existing capabilities and the internal transfer of new synthesized capabilities throughout the organization.

In Chapter 9, 'On the relationship between knowledge, networks, and the local context', Chiara Di Guardo and Marco Galvagno point out that the external environment confronted by individual firms within a network may differ in significant reaspects from the environment faced by similar firms outside that network. In particular, they explore how the environment shapes and influences the performance of an aggregate of interacting firms, drawing upon studies of local business networks and regional clusters. Additionally, they focus their attention on the process of value creation within local business networks, observing that in a local business network the locus of value creation is usually found within the local context and its ability to create a network of knowledge exchange relations among the various (local) agents.

The third part of the book, 'Strategic capabilities and knowledge transfer: perspectives from mergers, acquisitions and alliances' (Chapters 10–14), puts emphasis on the integration process that follows inter-organizational dynamics such as mergers, acquisitions and alliances. In Chapter 10, 'Knowledge transfer in mergers and acquisitions: how frequent acquirers learn to manage the integration process', Arturo Capasso and Olimpia Meglio underscore that, according to the academic literature on M&A performance, acquiring firms, on average, do not manage to create value from their deals but, notwithstanding the aggregate performance, some acquirers perform better than others in handling acquisitions and manage to create economic value via acquisitions. A possible explanation, provided by the authors, is that some of the acquiring firms, and in particular those firms that can be described as frequent acquirers, could achieve better than average performances in their acquisitions as a result of a distinguished capacity to learn from previous experience, transferring knowledge within their organizations from one deal to another. Consequently, they analyze the main issues of the post-acquisition integration process and propose a conceptual framework of the integration capability, prior to presenting an empirical investigation based on a few comparative case studies.

In Chapter 11, 'Merger and acquisition integration: the influence of resources', Maria Iborra and Consuelo Dolz analyze the integration process in acquisitions. First, the authors define the integration process through the integration level and the integration approximation. Second, they analyze the variables that determine the integration level and the integration approximation. Third, they explore the impact of the integration level and approximation on integration performance. On the basis of a sample of 80 Spanish acquisitions between 1992 and 1999, Iborra and Dolz show that integration processes differ in level and approximation; they also show how the resources that allow value creation influence both the integration level and the integration approximation. Lastly, these two dimensions of integration type (level and approximation) are related to acquisition performance.

In Chapter 12, 'Acquisition-integration at Siemens Mobile Phones: applying a resource-based perspective', Denise Sumpf posits that, although M&As have been a fact of organizational life and a constant managerial challenge over the last decades, an effective way to integrate two firms has not been put forth and is not evident yet. However it seems that several key success issues, for instance culture, vision and strategy, in addition to risk management, heavily determine the outcome of most transactions. Some firms prove to have better integration capabilities then others, which leads to the assumption that the design of the integration elements (vision and strategy, culture, communication, and so on) is a unique capability in the view of the resource-based theory. This chapter highlights the basic conditions of the resource-based theory and follows methodically a single-case-study approach to examine whether or not the elements of an integration strategy fulfil the requirements of capabilities that warrant sustainable competitive advantage. It critically examines the individual post-merger-integration effort/strategy, emerging in the course of the acquisition of Bosch Telecom (which has sites in Germany and Denmark) through the Siemens' business unit Information and Communication Mobile (ICM) in Munich, in the light of the resource-based view.

Chapter 13, 'The determinants of inter-partner learning in alliances: an empirical study in e-commerce', by Miguel Rivera-Santos, Pierre Dussauge and Will Mitchell, maintains that a firm's capacity to control the transfer of resources in alliances is driven by two essential abilities: learning ability and protection ability. To explain learning in alliances, previous research has focused on a wide range of factors, such as the firm's alliance experience, its knowledge base, its intent to learn, the alliance content and governance, and the tacitness and embeddedness of the targeted resource. Rivera-Santos, Dussauge and Mitchell argue that many of these factors overlap and that a shift to the micro-level of analysis is necessary to realize that they are components of one or both abilities. The micro-level components they identify are either specific to the firm (interface, experience and intent) or specific to each alliance (alliance characteristics, personnel characteristics and governance structure).

Chapter 14, 'Deliberate learning in corporate acquisitions: post-acquisition strategies and integration capability in US bank margers', by Maurizio Zollo and Harbir Singh, focus on acquirers' variation in performance and examine how learning processes specific to the management of the post-acquisition phase affect it. Zollo and Singh provide a theoretical argument and an empirical test for the performance implications of post-acquisition integration decisions, as well as the interaction between these decisions and some resource- and capability-based antecedent. Their focus on the acquiring firm, instead of the target or the combined entity, is influenced by the observation that learning processes and post-acquisition decisions are housed primarily within the acquirer's corporate development department or its relevant business unit. The US banking industry, where the study is positioned, is a good example of a particularly turbulent environment, where the tight coupling of deregulation, disintermediation, and technological evolution have generated an unprecedented wave of acquisitions in a relatively short amount of time. It thus provides a good laboratory for testing whether different acquirers' approaches to post-acquisition management and different levels of expertise in managing the integration process are systematically associated with different performance outcomes.

ACKNOWLEDGMENTS

The editors wish to thank all the individuals and institutions who in different ways have supported them in the conception and preparation of this book and also in the organization of the EURAM conference-track that has been the cradle in which it has found nourishment. Since no book can be better than its content, the first mention goes to all the contributors who have contributed their time and efforts matching scientific wisdom with emotional involvement. Donatella Depperu, who served as the chair of the 2003 EURAM Conference held in Milan-Bocconi, deservers a special mention. Sid Winter is to be recognized for a couple of relevant reasons: first, for immediately encouraging this endeavor when one of the editors walked into his office at the Wharton School in Philadelphia asking for his advice;

second, for kindly accepting to write the book's Foreword. Jay Barney, Will Mitchell, Joan Enric Ricart and Maurizio Zollo have accepted with no hesitation to buttress our idea when we asked their personal participation to arrange a symposium on the book's theme on the occasion of the 2005 Academy of Management Meeting in Honolulu, Hawaii. Our home institutions, the University of Sannio, the University of Catania, the University of Calabria and SDA-Bocconi Business School, have provided generous support for our annual EURAM journeys. By constantly supporting the preparation and rielaboration of the book's successive drafts, Stefania Corigliano, Vincenzo Gasparro, Paola Merendino, Giacomo Pascarella, Zaira Spena, and Matteo Rossi have significantly helped us to navigate through the rough waters of the demanding editorial work. Last but not least, for their continuous assistance and extreme kindness we are particularly grateful to Karen McCarthy, Alexandra Minton, Francine O'Sullivan of Edward Elgar Publishing and to the copyeditors and proofreaders. We feel that this undertaking has been greatly facilitated by the sympathetic encouragement and the friendly involvement of all these people. A final word of affection is left for our families, who have always been warmly supportive during our absences for preparing the book.

REFERENCES

Amit, R. and P.J-H. Schoemaker (1993), 'Strategic assets and organizational rent', *Strategic Management Journal*, **14**.
Barney, J.B. (1991), 'Firm resources and sustained competitive advantage', *Journal of Management*, **17** (1).
Dosi, G., R.R. Nelson and S.D. Winter (eds) (2000), *The Nature and Dynamics of Organizational Capabilities*, New York: Oxford University Press.
Dyer, J.H. and H. Singh (1998), 'The relational view: cooperative strategy and sources of interorganizational competitive advantage', *Academy of Management Review*, **23**, 660–79.
Dyer, J.H. and K. Nobeoka (2000), 'Creating and managing a high-performance knowledge-sharing network: the Toyota case', *Strategic Management Journal*, Special Issue **21** (10–11), 345–69.
Eisenhardt, K.M. and J.A Martin (2000), 'Dynamic capabilities: what are they?', *Strategic Management Journal*, Special Issue **21** (10–11), 1105–21.
Eisenhardt, K.M. and F.M Santos (2002), 'Knowledge-based view: a new theory of strategy?' in A. Pettigrew, H. Thomas and R. Whittington (eds), *Handbook of Strategy and Management*, Thousand Oaks, CA: Sage.

Grant, R.M. (1996), 'Towards a knowledge-based theory of the firm', *Strategic Management Journal*, Winter Special Issue **17**, 109–22.

Grant, R.M. (2003), 'The knowledge-based view of the firm', in D.O. Faulkner and A. Campbell (eds), *The Oxford Handbook of Strategy*, New York: Oxford University Press.

Gulati, R. (1999), 'Network location and learning: the influence of network resources and firm capabilities on alliance formation', *Strategic Management Journal*, **20** (5), 397–420.

Gulati, R., N. Nohria and A. Zaheer (2000). 'Strategic networks', *Strategic Management Journal*, Special Issue **21** (10–11), 203–15.

Hansen, M. (2002), 'Knowledge networks: explaining effective knowledge sharing in multiunit companies', *Organization Science*, **13**, 232–48.

Hayek, F.A. (1945), 'The use of knowledge in society', *American Economic Review*, **35** (4), 519–30.

Hedlund, G. (1994), 'A model of knowledge management and the N-form corporation', *Strategic Management Journal*, **15**, 73–90.

Helfat, C.E. and M.A. Peteraf (2003), 'The dynamic resource-based view: capability lifecycles', *Strategic Management Journal*, Special Issue **24** (10), 997–1010.

Kogut, B. and U. Zander (1992), 'Knowledge of the firm, combinative capabilities, and the replication of technology', *Organization Science*, **3** (3), 383–97.

Langlois, R.N. and P. Robertson (1995), *Firms, Markets and Economic Change: a Dynamic Theory of Business Institutions*, London and New York: Routledge.

Mocciaro Li Destri, A. and G.B. Dagnino (2003), *The Resource-based Firm Between Value Creation and Value Appropriation*. Paper presented at the INSEAD–AiSM Conference, Fontainebleau, 24–26 August, and at the Strategic Management Society Annual Conference, Baltimore, 9–12 November.

Nahapiet, J. and S. Ghoshal (1998), 'Social capital, intellectual capital and the organizational advantage', *Academy of Management Review*, **23**, 242/66.

Nelson, R.R. and S.G. Winter (1982), *An Evolutionary Theory of Economic Change*, Cambridge, MA: Belknap Press.

Nelson, R.R. and S.G. Winter (2002), 'Evolutionary theorizing in economics', *Journal of Economic Perspectives*, **16** (2), 23–46.

Nonaka, I. and R. Toyama (2002), 'A firm as a dialectical being: towards a dynamic theory of a firm', *Industrial and Corporate Change*, **11** (5), 995/1009.

Nonaka, I., R. Toyama and A. Nagata (2000), 'A firm as a knowledge-creating entity: a new perspective on the theory of the firm', *Industrial and Corporate Change*, **9** (1).

Peteraf, M.A. (1993), 'The cornerstones of competitive advantage: a resource-based view', *Strategic Management Journal*, **14**.

Porter-Liebeskind, J. (1996), 'Knowledge, strategy and the theory of the firm', *Strategic Management Journal*, Winter Special Issue **17**.

Porter-Liebeskind, J., A.L. Oliver, L. Zucker and M. Brewer (1996), 'Social networks, learning and flexibility: sourcing scientific knowledge in new biotechnology firms', *Organization Science*, **7**, 428–43.

Teece, D.J. (1998) 'Research directions for knowledge management', *California Management Review*, **40** (3), 289–92.

Teece, D.J., G. Pisano and A. Shuen (1997), 'Dynamic capabilities and strategic management', *Strategic Management Journal*, **18** (7), 509–33.

Tushman, M.L. and E.R. Romanelli (1985), 'Organizational evolution: a metamorphosis model of convergence and reorientation', in L.L. Cummings and B. Staw (eds), *Research in Organizational Behavior*, Vol. 7, Greenwich, CT: JAI Press.

Winter, S.G. (1987), 'Knowledge and competence as strategic assets', in D.J. Teece (ed.), *The Competitive Challenge*, Cambridge, MA: Ballinger pp. 185–220

PART ONE

Strategic Capabilities and Knowledge Transfer:
Perspectives from Firm and Industry
Heterogeneity

2. Managing heterogeneity, allocative balance, and behavioral and technology concerns in competitive and cooperative inter-firm relationships

Andrea Lanza

INTRODUCTION

Scholars in the management field consider knowledge a fundamental source of competitive advantage (Winter, 1987; Cohen and Levinthal, 1990; Kogut and Zander, 1992). This is witnessed by a number of contributions in the resource-based (Wernerfelt, 1984; Barney, 1991) and knowledge-based (Spender, 1996; Conner and Prahalad, 1996) views of the firm, which acknowledge scarce and unique competences and knowledge as valuable resources (Winter, 1987).

A *sine qua non* for knowledge to be valuable is its tacitness (Polanyi, 1967; Nonaka, 1994), conceived of as its social embeddedness within the firm (Kogut and Zander, 1992). According to this perspective, a firm's valuable knowledge is represented by the bundle of skills and expertise embedded at a collective level (Nelson and Winter, 1982; Nahapiet and Ghoshal, 1998). The construction of this bundle requires time and this, along with the casual ambiguity linking valuable knowledge to competitive advantage (Reed and DeFillippi, 1990), preserves it from observation and imitation (Barney, 1991).

Nevertheless it has been noted that contemporary hyper-competitive environments impel firms to strengthen their competencies, and to broaden the array of capabilities required to maintain the pace of innovation (D'Aveni, 1994). Given the nature of valuable competencies and capabilities, this represents a trade-off, for firms often lack time to internally develop such kinds of resources while simultaneously broadening them (Nagarajan and Mitchell, 1998). To cope effectively with this trade-off, firms often pursue competitive and cooperative strategies simultaneously (Lado *et al.*, 1997), through the integration of their competencies with competitors' complementary ones (Brandenburger and Stuart, 1996). Especially when an industry's knowledge base advances rapidly, it is virtually impossible for a firm to maintain the pace of innovation solely relying on its internal knowledge sourcing via in-house R&D (Burgelman and Rosenbloom, 1989; Ireland *et al.*, 2002). Thus seeking for external partners via non-equity collaborative efforts (Arora and Gambardella, 1990) becomes a viable solution for complementing a firm's internal knowledge endowment (Nicholls-Nixon and Woo, 2003).

Developing new knowledge along with competing partners is increasingly adopted in order to gain a competitive advantage through product quality enhancement and innovation (Dyer and Nobeoka, 2000). Yet it represents a very difficult and risky task. In fact, such a knowledge developmental process is made up of two different, yet related, phases: the sharing phase and the creating one. More precisely, sharing knowledge with competing partners is a fundamental step for effective knowledge creation activities (that is, for effectively competing in the marketplace). Peteraf and Bergen (2003) effectively stress this point, linking a firm's resource and capability endowment to the functions it serves, that is, to the customer needs it aims to satisfy. Accordingly, prior to entering a knowledge-based co-opetitive partnership, firms should have identified their co-opetitors, choosing one of the following as the main goal to pursue:

- acquiring and co-developing knowledge for a non-immediate new product development, which mainly relies on knowledge exchange and sharing, whose main outcome is future technology development;
- acquiring and co-developing knowledge for a rapid market launch, aiming at knowledge creation, whose main result is a fast market entry with new products and services.

The former puts emphasis on knowledge sharing; the latter points out new created knowledge exploitation and related rents appropriation. (See Figures 2.1a and 2.1b.)

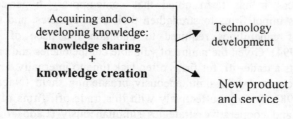

Figure 2.1a   Co-opetition goal

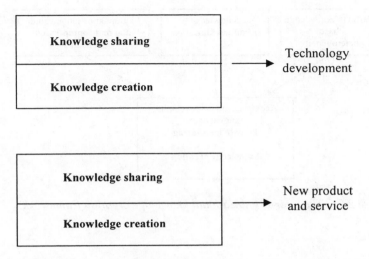

Figure 2.1b   Co-opetition choices

The management of knowledge sharing and knowledge creation processes requires a multidimensional approach as regards handling heterogeneity in partners' knowledge endowment, efficient and effective allocation of knowledge between sharing and creating activities, and behavioral concerns related to partners' orientation towards the outcome of the partnership. Thus the goal of this chapter is to develop a framework for co-opetitive inter-firm knowledge sharing and knowledge creation strategies, with respect to the following issues: knowledge base heterogeneity, knowledge allocation balance, and behavioral and future technology value concerns. It is argued that partner-firms should pay attention to these issues in order to identify effective inter-organizational practices for knowledge sharing and creation processes and then to lower the risk of a failure in the co-opetitive activity. (See Figure 2.2.)

The chapter is organized as follows: the next section develops the theoretical background of the argument and its relevance in the strategic management field; the following section deals with the theoretical background of knowledge governance dimensions; then propositions are developed; finally a model for resource allocation management is presented and discussed.

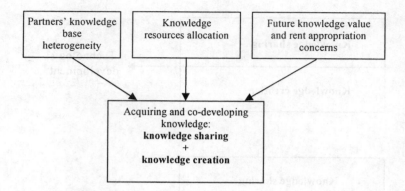

Figure 2.2   The inter-organizational knowledge creation framework

THEORETICAL BACKGROUND

The Inter-organizational Knowledge Development Process: Heterogeneity, Allocative Balance, and Technology Value and Behavioral Concerns

While in the past a competitor's collaborative goals were seen as an imitation attempt, and therefore as a threat (Porter, 1980), in the present competitive landscape this is no longer the case (Hamel *et al.*, 1989; Mody, 1993). Rather, allying with a competitor is an effective way to address uncertainties and costs of radical technological change (Nagarajan and Mitchell, 1998; Dussauge *et al.*, 2000).

Consequently, in recent years an increasing body of studies has shed light on the issue concerning the role of collaboration between competing partners (Hamel *et al.*, 1989; Anand and Khanna, 2000). In this vein, it has been argued that the best partner in a strategic collaboration is a strong competitor (Hamel, 1991); while the study of knowledge co-development between competing partners has become one of the major goals of inter-organizational relationships (Khanna, 1998; *Strategic Management Journal*, 2000).

Yet, as noted above, the process leading to the inter-organizational development of new knowledge requires an appropriate alignment concerning partners' extant knowledge, which is crucial for effectively carrying out the knowledge sharing, and consequently the knowledge creating, processes. The need for alignment stems from the heterogeneity characterizing what has been labeled the partners' knowledge base (Kale and

Singh, 1999; Anand and Khanna, 2000), or intellectual capital (Nahapiet and Ghoshal, 1998). Thus, in order to perform an effective inter-organizational knowledge creation process, partners have first to accurately align their knowledge bases during the knowledge sharing process.

Besides handling the heterogeneity problem, once the partnership is set up, firms have to cope with two other issues: knowledge allocation on sharing and creating activities, and behavioral concerns regarding partners' orientation towards the future value of jointly created technology. With respect to the first issue, partners should manage appropriately the sharing–creating balance, the risk being that of committing too many resources to knowledge sharing, and hence performing poorly in knowledge creation, and vice versa. The second issue concerns partners' orientation towards the exploitation of the new jointly created knowledge, which if driven by opportunism may lead to a waste of value, given the non–recoverable and idiosyncratic nature of the knowledge resources committed to the partnership (Makhija and Ganesh, 1997; Lane and Lubaktin, 1998). Further, as noted above, each firm represents a heterogeneous base of knowledge socially embedded at the organizational level. Thus, the more partners' knowledge bases overlap, the easier the sharing effort will be and the faster the knowledge creation is expected to be; conversely, the more heterogeneous knowledge bases are, the more difficult the knowledge sharing process will be, and the slower and more difficult the knowledge creation process may be.

Inter-organizational knowledge sharing and knowledge creation processes also entail allocative and behavioral concerns. That is, partner-firms first have to determine how to effectively allocate their knowledge to both these processes in order to avoid negative outcomes from the collaboration; then they have to understand what the orientation of the other partner is towards the outcome of the collaboration and the exploitation of its results. Similar (that is, lowly heterogeneous) competing partners are likely to be fierce competitors aiming at a fast exploitation of their collaborative efforts. On the other hand, heterogeneous competing partners are likely to be interested in joint future technology development. Hence they will be aiming more at knowledge acquisition mainly done through a deep knowledge sharing activity than at jointly developed knowledge exploitation. The following sub-sections address these aspects.

Knowledge Base Heterogeneity

Heterogeneity in a firm's knowledge endowment has two roots: the composition of its knowledge base (Winter, 1987; Kogut and Zander, 1992; Lane and Lubaktin, 1998) and the levels of analysis in knowledge and knowing (Spender, 1996; Nahapiet and Ghoshal, 1998).

Studies in the knowledge-based view of the firm (Winter, 1987; Kogut and Zander, 1992; Spender, 1996) highlight the existence of two main types of knowledge, variously labeled. The first refers to experience-based and practical knowledge. The second concerns theoretical and abstract knowledge. Scholars have defined these types of knowledge in different ways: procedural and declarative (Ryle, 1949); knowledge and information (Nelson and Winter, 1982; Kogut and Zander, 1992); tacit and explicit (Polanyi, 1967; Nonaka, 1994); contextual knowledge and general and abstract knowledge (Arora and Gambardella, 1994).

Levels of analysis in knowing are also crucial in understanding knowledge base heterogeneity, for knowledge can be held either at the individual (Simon, 1991) or at the collective/social (*routine* – Nelson and Winter, 1982) level. Spender proposes a 2 x 2 matrix using 'types of knowledge' (tacit/explicit) and 'levels of analysis' (individual/social) as dimensions. This four-cell matrix provides a useful articulation highlighting the composition of a firm knowledge base.

The existence of a valuable knowledge base is what allows a learning partner to pursue a knowledge exchange. Yet in order for this exchange to effectively take place partner firms have to manage the heterogeneity of their respective knowledge bases. Dussauge *et al.* (2000) refer to this concept, distinguishing between link and scale alliances. The former are those partnerships where allies contribute different capabilities, the latter where allies contribute similar capabilities. Their findings support the view that link alliances are more suitable for learning and capability acquisition than scale alliance. Yet this point is quite entangled. In fact, on the one hand, Stuart (1998), dealing with crowding (technology shared by many firms) and prestige (distinctive and highly qualified knowledge base) technological positioning within an industry, argues that heterogeneity in the technological position of potential competing partners increases opportunities for alliance formation. On the other hand, Dyer and Singh (1998: 685) argue that effective knowledge exchange between strategic partners '*is a function of the extent to which partners have developed overlapping knowledge bases*'; and Lane and Lubaktin (1998) argue that a firm has the greatest potential to learn from partners with similar knowledge bases, although holding different specialized knowledge. The point is thus to separate complementarity of partners' strategic resources from heterogeneity in partners' knowledge resources, for complementarity and heterogeneity are not overlapping concepts.

Extending the absorptive capacity concept (Cohen and Levinthal, 1990) on an inter-organizational base, a firm's learning is effective when the new knowledge to be acquired is related to the firm's existing knowledge base (Mowery *et al.*, 1996; Dyer and Singh, 1998). Since the point is how to internalize the knowledge created at the inter-organizational level, it follows that, if a firm wishes to learn from its competing partner, its internalizing ability will result in an immediate innovative potential if both partners have similar knowledge bases. Otherwise, in the case of a heterogeneous knowledge base they will have to concentrate on knowledge base alignment, the goal of their knowledge creation activity generally being the development of either a new technology or a new standard, rather than a new product development race (Lane and Lubaktin, 1998).

Therefore it is important to ascertain whether competing partners are heterogeneous or not, with respect to the predominance of either tacit or explicit knowledge in their knowledge base. Predominance of the same type of knowledge (either tacit or explicit) in both partners will result in low heterogeneity, or similarity. Conversely, if each competing partner experiences differences in the predominance of the type of knowledge (either tacit or explicit) characterizing its knowledge base compared to the partner's one, there will be high heterogeneity.

Knowledge Allocation Balance

Even if knowledge is ultimately exchanged at the individual level (Simon, 1991), competing partners have to manage this exchange at the collective level (Liebeskind *et al.*, 1996), through knowledge sharing and knowledge creation activities. Therefore knowledge sharing and knowledge creation processes require the analysis of how individuals deploy their knowledge in inter-organizational contexts (Cohen and Levinthal, 1990; Kale and Singh, 1999), and how firms harness the learning effect of knowledge deployment (Lane and Lubaktin, 1998; Dyer and Singh, 1998). These aspects, in turn, require an accurate balance as to how partner firms allocate their knowledge endowment to the two main collaborative processes noted above, knowledge sharing and knowledge creation.

Firms own at a given moment a certain knowledge endowment, developed over time through learning (Dierickx and Cool, 1989). This holds true also on an inter-organizational basis. That is, knowledge is developed in an inter-firm context, over time, through a learning process (that is, by means of knowledge sharing and knowledge creation activities). Nohria and Eccles (1992b) argued that the integration of competencies in innovation networks requires *face-to-face* interaction, and Doz (1996) has demonstrated that successful partnerships have an evolving structure that takes place through sequential learning cycles. Both face-to-face interaction and sequential learning cycles represent patterned processes specific to the inter-organizational context (either a team or a division), by means of which partner-firms develop a common base of knowledge. Changes in these patterned processes (whether for replication or adjustment purposes), especially when they are ineffectively carried out owing to inappropriate deployment of resources, seldom prove effective and are often costly (Winter, 1995).

This view is consistent with the concept of *routine* (Nelson and Winter, 1982; Winter, 2003), in an inter-organizational perspective (Dyer and Singh, 1998). When two competitors contribute to founding a partnership, they provide their own knowledge. However , this knowledge becomes specific to the 'new' common inter-organizational context, and different from what it used to be, in its previous intra-firm context. Therefore, once a firm deploys its knowledge to a partnership, it becomes substantially different from its original content. What renders this knowledge different is its joint use along with competing partners. Providing a partnership with firm-specific knowledge means transforming it into a partnership-specific resource, through its deployment to the two main activities noted above: knowledge sharing and knowledge creation. This joint use makes knowledge context-specific, and by means of this process partner-firms contribute to the creation of an inter-organizational routine. More precisely, both knowledge sharing and knowledge creation represent inter-organizational routines for competing partners.

Inter-organizational routines can also be conceived of as dynamic capabilities. Since routines are '*highly patterned and repetitious, or quasi-repetitious, founded in part in tacit knowledge* (Winter, 2003: 991), they are not easily modifiable in the short time, for they have a patterned life cycle in the context of the team where they have been developed, and this also applies to capabilities developed across firm boundaries (Helfat and Peteraf, 2003). Therefore an unbalanced distribution of knowledge by a partner-firm, either to knowledge sharing or to knowledge creation, given the hardly revisable nature of routines in the short time, may result in a negative outcome for the collaborative activity: '*the endowments present at founding set the stage for further capability development by preconditioning the emergence of a capability*' (Helfat and Peteraf, 2003: 1001).

The focal point is therefore how to cope with balance needs arising from partners' knowledge resource allocation to both knowledge sharing and creating activities. An excessive allocation to the former will result in a deeply reciprocal comprehension of partner's knowledge. Yet, given the difficulty of modifying routines, at least in the short term, this will also cause an ineffective knowledge creation process, because of the inappropriate amount of knowledge deployed at this stage of the partnership. Likewise, a higher allocation of knowledge resource to knowledge creation activities will result in a fruitful innovative effort, yet the actual effectiveness of these innovations could end up diminished by 'bugs' affecting new jointly developed products and processes stemming from an insufficient knowledge sharing activity.

Partner's Orientation and Behavioral Concerns

Partnerships having intangible outcomes as their goals, such as those aiming at knowledge development (Simonin, 1997), represent incomplete contracts (Jensen and Meckling, 1991), given the limited foresight of future knowledge outcomes, under different circumstances (Miller, 2002). Therefore providing a partnership with valuable knowledge causes a competing partner, on the one hand, to commit resources in a state characterized by high outcome uncertainty and on the other hand, to bear the risk of being expropriated of its rents and to commit to the partnership to a greater extent than the other partner does (Larsson *et al.*, 1998).

These concerns may arise from two different assumptions regarding a partner's behavior: opportunism (Williamson, 1979; Gulati and Singh, 1998) and myopia (Levinthal and March, 1993; Miller, 2002). Similarly to Gulati and Singh (1998: 791), who see trust as a distinctive means for addressing coordination costs and appropriation concerns, in this section, drawing upon Nahapiet and Ghoshal (1998), both future knowledge value uncertainty and appropriation concerns are addressed adopting a social capital perspective (Bourdieu, 1986; Coleman, 1990) on inter-organizational knowledge sharing and creation (Dyer and Singh, 1998; Nahapiet and Ghoshal, 1998).

Inter-organizational knowledge sharing and knowledge creation activities represent social and cognitive processes whose outcomes are embedded in inter-firm knowledge-developmental routines (Dyer and Singh, 1998). Social capital positively affects knowledge sharing and creation activities, for it facilitates the conditions for these processes to occur. Accordingly, a social capital perspective also helps partners to mitigate potentially hampering conditions, such as future knowledge value uncertainty and appropriation concerns (Ireland *et al.*, 2002). In particular, the structural, cognitive and relational dimensions of social capital affect the conditions that allow for knowledge sharing and creation processes. With respect to the first concern, future knowledge value uncertainty, the structural dimension highlights the importance of inter-firm ties, for, through these ties, partners access and exchange valuable pieces of information and know-how, while also having the chance to perform an appropriate information-screening and distribution activity. Besides, inter-firm ties help firms to acquire information and know-how sooner than companies not involved in such relationships. Thus the expected value of jointly developed knowledge may appear less uncertain, at least in the light of the faster and augmented information acquired by competing partners through such ties.

The cognitive dimension of social capital also helps future knowledge value to be assessed with less uncertainty, since shared codes and languages help partners to build categories and frames of reference for observing and interpreting the environment and, hence, for evaluating future benefits of knowledge sharing and creation processes. Accordingly, these may become less uncertain as to their outcomes, at least with respect to the shared 'meaning' and the definition of future joint activity results.

The third dimension of social capital, the relational dimension, also contributes to reduce the uncertainty related to the value of future jointly developed knowledge. Especially, trust and identification, by virtue of the effect on willingness to experiment, openness, and shared identity, reduce the uncertainty of knowledge development.

As regards the second issue, rent appropriation related to jointly developed knowledge exploitation, it is mainly the relational dimension of social capital that facilitates partners' reduction of this concern. In fact, trust, norms, expectations and obligations, and identification indicate, respectively, a willingness to be vulnerable to another party due to the belief in its reliability and perceived openness (or transparency – Dyer and Singh, 1998); a motivation to engage in knowledge development with a more collaborative, rather than a purely competitive, posture; and a commitment to behave correctly during and after the cooperative knowledge development process. This view is also supported by the procedural justice literature (Thibaut and Walker, 1975), and more precisely by the stream of research linking procedural justice to knowledge sharing and knowledge creation (Kim and Mauborgne, 1998).

KNOWLEDGE DEVELOPMENT, PARTNERS' GOALS, AND PARTNERSHIP PERFORMANCE

Knowledge Base Heterogeneity and Partners' Goals

The concept of knowledge base heterogeneity refers to the differences in partners' knowledge endowment composition, namely differences between the basic and specialized components of this endowment (Lane and Lubaktin, 1998). Basic knowledge refers to a general understanding of techniques and traditions upon which a discipline is based, while specialized knowledge regards the tacit competencies and capabilities which each partner holds and upon which the new and shared know-how should be developed during the collaboration. Therefore partners experience low heterogeneity to the extent to which they similarly hold either basic (explicit) or specialized (tacit) knowledge. Conversely , they will face high heterogeneity when coping with different compositions of their knowledge bases, one partner being mainly endowed with basic knowledge and the other one with specialized knowledge.

For example, in the biotechnology industry, the most critical input – scientific/explicit knowledge – is exchanged through publications and conference presentations (Powell, 1990) and sourced by means of tacit competencies drawing upon individual skills and social networks (Liebeskind *et al.*, 1996). In terms of co-opetition opportunity, potential allies of a biotech firm are both other biotech firms and pharmaceutical firms. In this case, a biotech firm is characterized by low heterogeneity compared with another biotech firm, since their basic knowledge bases largely overlap and high heterogeneity compared with a pharmaceutical firm, since the latter is more endowed with product testing and marketing competencies (Doz and Hamel, 1998; Liebeskind *et al.*, 1996).

Heterogeneity in partners' knowledge bases affects inter-organizational knowledge sharing and creation activities. In particular, high heterogeneity brings about a greater concern with the sharing phase, for partners do realize that, without effective exchange and combination activities of the components of their intellectual capital, the subsequent knowledge developmental process (that is, knowledge creation) may either be hampered or, in worse cases, fail. Thus

P_1: *In order to get to a better understanding of each other's knowledge base, highly heterogeneous partners shall be more concerned with the knowledge sharing process.*

Often competing partners characterized by similar knowledge endowments experience a learning race (Lane and Lubaktin, 1998), in order to get to the market first (Khanna *et al.*, 1998), and gain a first-mover advantage (Lieberman and Montgomery, 1988). This may happen because those partners facing a similarity in their knowledge bases have lower difficulties in sharing their own basic and specialized knowledge, thus concentrating their effort on knowledge creation. Yet this similarity in knowledge endowment, while lowering difficulties in knowledge exchange, will put emphasis on new jointly-created knowledge exploitation as a means to gain competitive advantage. Therefore

P_2: *In order to achieve a better competitive position compared to the partner, lowly heterogeneous partners shall be more concerned with the knowledge creation process.*

Allocative Balance and Partnership Performance

Before the partnership's activity unfolds, it is crucial for partners to know how knowledge can be shared on an inter-firm basis, and how new knowledge creation can effectively take place, the creation process (either of a new technology or of a new product) being the ultimate goal of the partnership. Dussauge *et al.* (2000) have argued that collaboration is an imperfect learning process where difficulties may lead partners to lose more than they gain; and Ariño and de la Torre (1998) have empirically demonstrated that partnership initial conditions inconsistent with partners' learning goals lead to the partnership's failure. Therefore, it is important to ascertain whether a firm entering a collaborative effort with a competing partner is aware of two aspects: (a) the amount of knowledge (mainly made up of know-how and human resources) it can deploy to that partnership at that given moment; (b) the balance between knowledge sharing and creating activities that this amount of knowledge brings about.

As noted above, knowledge sharing and knowledge creation activities represent inter-organizational routines. Thus, for co-opeting firms it is important to ascertain whether they are effectively sharing the know-how of the processes they are going to set up together. Yet the short-term 'constraint' (the amount of knowledge committed to the given relationship) brings about a need for a balance between knowledge sharing and knowledge creation activities. This implies that partner firms have to learn how to integrate their complementary knowledge endowment, beginning with an efficient and effective allocation to both the sharing and the creation activities.

In particular, knowledge sharing requires the integration of competencies, which in turn, needs a huge commitment of resources, mainly of human capital. As a result, an insufficient effort in this respect may render the subsequent joint knowledge creation activity either less valuable or, in the worst case, useless. Thus

> *P₃: In order to avoid a negative outcome (or a failure) from collaborative effort, highly heterogeneous partners shall commit higher resources to knowledge sharing activities.*

In addition, the knowledge creation activity is affected by the absorption capacity of each partner. This implies that partners owning similar knowledge bases will have easier access to each other's competencies. Yet co-opetitive partners may experience negative outcomes from collaborative efforts when they continue the partnerships after their learning goals have been achieved. Hence, those partners owning similar knowledge bases will have to concentrate on knowledge creation, the risk being that of performing poorly in innovative activities. Therefore

> P_4: *In order to avoid a negative outcome (or a failure) from collaborative effort, lowly heterogeneous partners shall commit higher resources to knowledge creation activities.*

Behavioral Assumptions, Technology Future Value and Appropriation Concerns

Gulati and Singh (1998) argue that, in alliances encompassing technology, allies have to cope with rent appropriation concerns as well as coordination costs. Scholars recognize the risk of a learning race between competing partners. That is, under certain circumstances a partner–firm may seek to outlearn its co-opetitor and exit the relationship (Khanna *et al.*, 1998). According to Gulati *et al.* (2000: 211) this may happen when the private benefit accruing to a partner after the learning race outweighs the common benefit of the alliance. These authors also argue that partners avoid starting a learning race only when they lack other collaborative opportunities, since if a partner has a number of other different partnerships, present or potential, the lesson learned in the extant partnership may create an incentive for this partner to defect. Yet such an opportunistic approach to knowledge-based partnerships is not always undertaken. Competing firms involved in a knowledge-based cooperative effort do recognize that an opportunistic posture may result in a negative outcome, since this kind of effort requires fair and long-lasting commitment. In this perspective, social capital dimensions (structural, relational and cognitive) impel partners to cooperate not merely for altruism or fairness. The main reason is that this is an effective way to reduce future technology uncertainty and opportunism in appropriation of rents stemming from jointly developed knowledge. Once a firm has acquired the reputation of *learning runner*, it is likely that its opportunities for collaboration will decrease over time, together with the potential for gaining rents accruing to new joint innovative efforts (Dyer and Singh, 1998), thus rendering vain its race.

Yet cooperation between competitors also depends on how much partners' heterogeneity does affect their competitive behavior. Those partners owning heterogeneous knowledge bases, before being preoccupied with rent appropriation, willl have to concentrate on effective knowledge sharing activities, in order to lower uncertainty of future technology value. That is, they will have to focus on the effective integration of each other's knowledge base, rather than on starting a learning race aimed at rent appropriation. Those partners whose knowledge bases are largely similar should recognize that their knowledge integration efforts are characterized by a lower uncertainty, and consequently the value of their jointly developed outcomes will be less uncertain. As a result they may aim at the exploitation of the output of their collaborative effort, being concerned that their co-opetitors may do the same thing. Therefore

> *P₅: Highly heterogeneous partners shall experience lower concerns for rent appropriation, and higher concerns for future value of jointly developed knowledge, compared to lowly heterogeneous partners.*

CONCLUSION

Firms agree to invest in competitive and cooperative relationships, even if there is no enforcement of idiosyncratic knowledge, in order to maintain the innovation pace required to match competitive pressure.

Although there are no enforcement mechanisms to protect inter-organizational knowledge creation, the effective management of the heterogeneity of partners' knowledge bases, the identification of allocation balance, and the facilitation of partners' commitment to the relationship can help to make inter-firm new knowledge development a less risky process. Managing heterogeneity effectively helps partner-firms to be more effective with respect to their expected outcomes, whilst lowering inappropriate concerns. Identification of balance facilitates allocation to either knowledge sharing or knowledge creation, thus increasing the efficiency and effectiveness of new knowledge developmental processes. These issues can also help identify appropriate inter-organizational mechanisms, not only for the enforcement of the investment partner-firms undertake, but also for the cooperation they have to maintain in order to simultaneously pursue innovation and competitive advantage. Getting late to the marketplace with an innovative product or offering an innovative technological solution after the main competitors, or offering a solution that is rejected by consumers because it is radically different from the existing *dominant designs*, may constitute even greater risks than those associated with idiosyncratic cooperative investments with competing firms.

REFERENCES

Anand, B.N. and T. Khanna (2000), 'Do firms learn to create value? The case of alliances', *Strategic Management Journal* (Special Issue) **21**, 295–315.

Ariño, A. and J. de la Torre (1998), 'Learning from failure: towards an evolutionary model of collaborative ventures', *Organization Science*, **9**, 306–25.

Arora, A. and A. Gambardella (1990), 'Complementary and external linkages: strategies of the large firm in biotechnology', *Journal of Industrial Economics*, **38**, 361–79.

Arora, A. and A. Gambardella (1994), 'The changing technology of technological change: technological innovation and division of labour', *Research Policy*, **23**, 523–32.

Barney, J.B. (1991), 'Firms' resources and sustained competitive advantage', *Journal of Management*, **17**, 99–120.

Bourdieu, P. (1986), 'The forms of capital', in J.G. Richardson, *Handbook of Theory and Research for the Sociology of Education*, New York: Greenwood, pp. 241–58.

Brandenburger A.M. and H.W. Stuart (1996), 'Value-based business strategy', *Journal of Economics & Management Strategy*, **5** (1), 5–24.

Burgelman, R. and R. Rosenbloom (1989), 'Technology strategy: an evolutionary perspective', in R. Burgelman, and R. Rosenbloom (eds), *Research on Technological Innovation, Management and Policy*, Vol. 4, Greenwich, CT: JAI Press, pp. 1–23.

Cohen, W.M. and D.A. Levinthal (1990), 'Absorptive capacity: a new perspective on learning and innovation', *Administrative Science Quarterly*, **35**, 128–52.

Coleman, J.S. (1990), *Foundations of Social Theory*, Cambridge, MA: Belknap Press of Harvard University Press.

Conner, K.R. and C.K. Prahalad (1996), 'A resource-based theory of the firm: knowledge versus opportunism', *Organization Science*, **7**, 477–501.

D'Aveni, R. (1994), *Hypercompetition*, New York: Free Press.

Dierickx, I. and K. Cool (1989), 'Resource stock accumulation and sustainability of competitive advantage', *Management Science*, **35**, 1504–11.

Doz, Y.L. (1996), 'The evolution of cooperation in strategic alliances: initial conditions or learning process', *Strategic Management Journal*, **17** (Summer Special Issue), 55–83.

Doz, Y. and G. Hamel (1998), *Alliance Advantage*, Boston, MA: Harvard Business School Press.

Dussauge, P., B. Garrette and W. Mitchell (2000), 'Learning from competing partners: outcome and duration of scale and link alliances in Europe, North America and Asia', *Strategic Management Journal*, **21**, 99–126.

Dyer, J.H. and K. Nobeoka (2000), 'Creating and managing a high-performance knowledge-sharing network: the Toyota case', *Strategic Management Journal*, **21**, 345–69.

Dyer, J.H. and H. Singh (1998), 'The relational view: cooperative strategy and sources of inter-organizational competitive advantage', *Academy of Management Review*, **23**, 660–79.

Gulati, R. and H. Singh (1998), 'The architecture of cooperation: managing coordination costs and appropriation concerns in strategic alliances', *Administrative Science Quarterly*, **43**, 781–814.

Gulati, R., N. Nohria and A. Zaheer,. (2000), 'Strategic networks', *Strategic Management Journal*, (Special Issue) **21**, 203–15.

Hamel, G. (1991), 'Competition for competence and interpartner learning within international strategic alliances', *Strategic Management Journal*, **12** (Summer Special Issue), 83–103.

Hamel G., Y Doz and C.K. Prahalad (1989), 'Collaborate with your competitors and win', *Harvard Business Review*, **67** (1), 133–9.

Helfat, C.E. and M.A. Peteraf (2003), 'The dynamic resource-based view: capability lifecycle', *Strategic Management Journal*, **24**, 997–1010.

Ireland, R.D., M.A. Hitt and D. Vaidyanath (2002), 'Alliance management as a source of competitive advantage', *Journal of Management*, **28**, 413–46.

Jensen, M.C. and W.H. Meckling (1991), 'Specific and general knowledge, and organizational structure', in L Werin and H. Wijkander, *Main Currents in Contract Economics*, Oxford: Blackwell.

Kale, P. and H. Singh (1999), 'Building alliance capabilities: a knowledge-based approach', *Academy of Management Best Paper Proceedings*, Chicago, Il.

Khanna, T. (1998), 'The scope of alliances', *Organization Science*, **9**, 340–55.

Khanna, T., R. Gulati and N. Nohria (1998), 'The dynamics of learning alliances: competition, cooperation and relative scope', *Strategic Management Journal*, **19**, 193–210.

Kim, W.C. and R. Mauborgne (1998), 'Procedural justice, strategic decision making, and the knowledge economy', *Strategic Management Journal*, **19**, 323–38.

Kogut, B. and U. Zander (1992), 'Knowledge of the firm, combinative capablities and the replication of technology', *Organization Science*, 383–97.

Lado, A.A., N.G. Boyd and S.C. Hanlon (1997), 'Competition, cooperation and the search for economic rents: a syncretic model', *Academy of Management Review*, **22**, 110–41.

Lane, P.J. and M. Lubaktin (1998), 'Relative absorptive capacity and inteorganizational learning', *Strategic Management Journal*, **17**, 461–77.

Larsson, R., L. Bengtsson, K. Henriksson and J. Sparks (1998), 'The interorganizational learning dilemma: collective knowledge development in strategic alliances', *Organization Science*, **9**, 285–305.

Levinthal, D.A. and J.G. March (1993), 'The myopia of learning', *Strategic Management Journal*, **14** (Winter Special Issue), 95–112.

Lieberman, M. and D. Montgomery (1988), 'First-mover advantages', *Strategic Management Journal*, **9** (Special Issue), 41–58.

Liebeskind, J.P., A.L. Oliver, L. Zucker and M. Brewer (1996), 'Social networks, learning and flexibility: sourcing scientific knowledge in new biotechnology firms', *Organization Science*, **7**, 428–43.

Makhija, M.V and U. Ganesh (1997), 'The relationship between control and partner learning in learning-related joint-ventures', *Organization Science*, **8**, 508–27.

Miller, K.D. (2002), 'Knowledge inventories and managerial myopia', *Strategic Management Journal*, **23**, 689–706.

Mody, A. (1993), 'Learning through alliances', *Journal of Economic Behavior and Organization*, **20**, 151–170 .

Mowery, D.C., J.E. Oxley and B.S. Silverman (1996), 'Strategic alliances and inter-firm knowledge transfer', *Strategic Management Journal*, **17** (Winter Special Issue), 77–91.

Nagarajan, A. and W. Mitchell (1998), 'Evolutionary diffusion: internal and external methods used to acquire encompassing, complementary and incremental technological changes in the lithotripsy industry', *Strategic Management Journal*, **19**, 1063–77.

Nahapiet, J. and S. Ghoshal (1998), 'Social capital, intellectual capital, and the organizational advantage', *Academy of Management Review*, **23**, 242–66.

Nelson, R.R. and S.G. Winter (1982), *An Evolutionary Theory of Economic Change*, Cambridge, MA: Harvard University Press.

Nicholls-Nixon, C.L. and C.Y. Woo (2003), 'Technology sourcing and output of established firms in a regime of encompassing technological change', *Strategic Management Journal*, **24**, 651–66.

Nohria, N. and R.G. Eccles (eds) (1992a), *Networks and Organization*, Boston, MA Harvard Business School Press.

Nohria, and R.G. Eccles (1992b), 'Face-to-face: making network organizations work', in N. Nohria and R.G. Eccles (eds), pp. 288–307.

Nonaka, I. (1994), 'A dynamic theory of organizational knowledge creation', *Organization Science*, **5**, 14–37.

Peteraf, M.A. and M.E. Bergen (2003), 'Scanning dynamic competitive landscape: a market-based and resource-based framework', *Strategic Management Journal*, **24**, 1027–41.

Polanyi, M. (1967), *The Tacit Dimension*, London: Routledge.

Porter, M.E. (1980), *Competitive Strategy: Techniques for Analyzing Industries and Competitors*, New York: Free Press.

Powell, W.W. (1990), 'Neither markets nor hierarchies: networks forms of organization', in B.M Staw and L.L. Cummings (eds), *Research in Organizational Behavior*, **12**, pp. 295–336.

Reed, R. and R. DeFillippi (1990), 'Casual ambiguity, barriers to imitation and sustainable competitive advantage', *Academy of Management Review*, **15**, 88–102.

Ryle, G. (1949), *The Concept of Mind*, London: Hutchison.

Simon, H.A. (1991), 'Bounded rationality and organizational learning', *Organization Science*, **2**, 125–34.

Simonin, B.L. (1997), 'The importance of collaborative know-how: an empirical test of the learning organization', *Academy of Management Review*, **40**, 1150–74.

Spender, J.-C. (1996), 'Making knowledge the basis of a dynamic theory of the firm', *Strategic Management Journal*, **17** (S2), 45–62.

Strategic Management Journal (2000), 'Strategic networks' (Special Issue), **21**,199–425.

Stuart, T.E. (1998), 'Networks' positions and propensities to collaborate: an investigation of strategic alliance formation in a high-technology industry', *Administrative Science Quarterly*, **43**, 668–98.

Thibaut, J. and L. Walker (1975), *Procedural Justice: A Psychological Analysis*. Hillsdale, NJ: Erlbaum.

Wernerfelt, B. (1984), 'A resource-based view of the firm', *Strategic Management Journal*, **5** (2), 171–80.

Williamson, O.E. (1979), 'Transaction cost economics: the governance of contractual relations', *Journal of Law and Economics*, **12** (1), 75–94.

Winter, S.G. (1987), 'Knowledge and competence as strategic resources', in D.J. Teece (ed.), *The Competitive Challenge*, Cambridge, MA: Ballinger, pp.159–84.

Winter, S.G. (1995), 'Four Rs of profitability: rents, resources, routines, and replication', in C.A Montgomery (ed.), *Resource-based and Evolutionary Theory of the Firm.*, London: Kluwer, pp. 147–78.

Winter, S.G. (2003), 'Understanding dynamic capabilities', *Strategic Management Journal*, **24**, 991–5.

3. Digital economy and sustained competitive advantage in the tourism industry

Jay B. Barney, Valentina Della Corte and Mauro Sciarelli

INTRODUCTION

Sustaining competitive advantage has long been the 'holy grail' of strategic management. Managers who can create sustained competitive advantages are promoted, consultants who can help create these advantages are hired, and academics who can explain how such advantages can be created are widely read. It seems that everyone wants to know how to create a sustained competitive advantage, or at least to know someone who knows how to create a sustained competitive advantage.

The data do suggest that firms that can sustain their competitive advantages are able to outperform the market, and outperform their competitors, in the long run.[1] At least this is what some observers would have you think. In this matter there are two aspects to take into account: whether it is possible to gain sustained competitive advantage in the new economy, and whether digital economy itself can be a source of competitive advantage. Supposedly, in the new economy, things are changing so rapidly that it is no longer possible to talk about 'sustained' competitive advantages. In this new economy, competitive advantages, if they exist at all, are supposed to be very short-lived, almost ethereal in nature. Some would have managers give up the search for sustained competitive advantages in the face of what one noted scholar (Schumpeter) called '*the gale of creative destruction*'. Others assert that information and communication technology can itself be a source of competitive advantage (Werthner, 2001a).[2]

Of course, digital economy has undoubtedly favored rapid changes: speed of competition, widespread knowledge and information, huge amounts of information both for suppliers and customers, and highly competitive global markets are factors that can influence contexts and firms' performances very much. This process has also increased inter-firm agreements and even alliances based on information and knowledge sharing.

However the question is whether digital economy is the key to companies' success. The answer is no for a simple reason: on one hand, high technological ventures lacking specific strategic resources have proved to be unsuccessful; on the other hand, in many successful cases sustained competitive advantage is achieved thanks to the whole range of strategic resources and competences, connected or not with new technologies.

And yet sustained competitive advantage is still possible in the new economy. Of course, not all firms in the new economy will gain such advantages. This was true before the new economy became all the rage; it will be true after the new economy becomes the old economy. It is also the case that some of the specific actions that firms can take to create sustained competitive advantages in the new economy are different from the actions they would have taken to create such advantages before the new economy.

Before going on with the analysis, it is necessary to clarify the definition of strategy we adopt in this chapter. Following Drucker (1994), we conceive strategy as 'a firm's theory of how it can gain superior performance in the markets within which it operates'. This definition includes both emergent and intended strategies, can be applied both at corporate and business levels, and introduces firm performance[3] implicitly into the discussion. It is important to point out the sources of superior performance and how permanent the consequent advantage can be. Taken together, these concepts – resources, strategy, superior performance, temporary and sustained economic rents, temporary and sustained competitive advantages – are fundamental in the resource-based logic. According to this approach, it is necessary to determine two basic factors: the critical attributes of a firm's capabilities and the competitive implications of different capabilities and different mixes of them.

But the fundamental economic logic that firms can use to identify the sources of sustained competitive advantage that they control apply just as well in the new economy as they did in the old economy. What is this logic? While different authors label it differently, they all agree on its core tenets.[4] These tenants include the following:

- Sustained competitive advantage[5] does not depend on the attributes of the industries within which a firm is operating, but rather on the capabilities a firm brings to those industries.
- Rare and costly to imitate capabilities are more likely to be sources of sustained competitive advantage than other types of capabilities.

- Firms that are organized, by themselves or in networks, to exploit these kinds of capabilities in their strategies can gain sustained competitive advantages.

In this chapter, our aim is to describe each of these core tenets, and to apply them to understand sources of sustained competitive advantage in the new economy. In order to reach this objective, we try to answer these questions:

1. Can e-commerce and digital economy be a source of competitive advantage?
2. Can this logic be applied in the tourism industry?

THE IMPACT OF THE NEW ECONOMY ON THE TOURISM INDUSTRY

We decided to examine firms operating in the tourism industry for several reasons. Tourism is regarded as a very attractive industry, whose economic trends show its importance in the general economy. Several companies try to enter and are extremely interested in this sector, even in the logic of conglomerate diversification.

Rather than an industry, tourism can be defined as a system: competitive advantage often refers to destinations as a whole and depends both on the typical resources of the site (natural, historical, etc.), on the capacities and skills of single firms (organizational skills and culture, customer satisfaction, specific routines and skills) and on network competences as well (common language and information flows, competences in managing relations among groups of firms, destination strategic planning and marketing) (Della Corte, 2000).

This is a very peculiar sector, made up of different types of firms, whose services are complementary: transport (airline companies, railways, etc.), hospitality (hotels, country houses, B&B, according to market segments), restaurants and attractions, tour operators, which assemble the products, and travel agents, just to cite the main ones. This configuration makes the sector very difficult to examine, since it contains other industries (airline industry, food industry, etc.). It is therefore very difficult to critically analyze the whole without taking into account the peculiarities of each of the industries that are mainly involved in or at least connected with tourism. At the same time, it is clear that in the tourism industry inter-firm and network relations are particularly important, just because of the complementarity of the services offered: vertical relations are necessary to create and sell packages; this makes inter-firm agreements and relations fundamental.

The tourism sector has always been technology-based both in business-to-business and in business-to-consumer relations. In business-to-business relations, there have always been specific systems (for example, CRS, converted into GDS[6]), Internet–based, that connect travel agents with airline companies, railways, and some hotel chains. In business-to-consumer relations, the traditional role of local travel agents has known the Internet channel as an additional channel.

In order to analyze the impact of ICT on the industry, it is however important to take into account that it is made up of different businesses: the main distinction is between leisure tourism and business tourism. In the former, it is important to distinguish *groups and organizations* from *individuals*, since these types of tourists have totally different habits, choose different destinations and tourism products and often use different channels to buy them (the former more traditional, the latter more Internet-oriented).

According to Forrester research valuations and forecasts, a hypergrowth of Internet and digital economy will take place all over the world, even if at different levels and times according to the country (see Table 3.1).

Table 3.1   Digital economy evolution process

Country	Take-off of on-line activities	Hypergrowth
USA	1998	2001
Canada	mid-1999	end of 2002
UK	2000	2003
Germany	mid-2000	mid-2003
Japan	end of 2001	2005
France	2002	beginning of 2005
Italy	mid-2002	mid-2005

The growth in Europe is considered to be mainly based on the deregulation process in the telecommunications industry, which will have a significant impact on tourism industry performance, on the amounts of investment in information highways and on citizens' culture and approach towards the new technologies (Martini, 2001). Italy, in this regard, seems to be one of the most traditional countries: in 2000 only 28.7 per cent of the total population had access to the Internet and only 2.9 per cent bought through e-commerce (Proactive International). If we consider that the corresponding percentages in England are 45.6 per cent and 13.1 per cent and in Germany 39.7 per cent and 8.1 per cent, that the average percentages in Europe are 34 per cent and 8 per cent, and that Italy has now reached 38 per cent and 5 per cent (Proactive International), it is clear that Italy remains far below other western countries.

And yet even in these more traditional countries, McKinsey's (1999) research (Figure 3.1) shows clearly that the potential for digital economy and e-commerce development in travel and tourism is higher than in other industries. It is clear that the net economy's importance and impact are higher in those industries where inter-firm systemic relations and networks are relevant to firms' strategies and competitive success. This is very true in the tourism industry, whose success is based mainly on the efficacy of established, institutional networks', as well as on the possibility of creating and promoting tourism destination management systems.

	High	News	Software	Insurance	Travel
			Interactive games	Music	Services
Fit with interactive media				Books	
			Sporting goods	Toys Cars	Medical services
		Convenience stores			
	Low				

Low   **Potential for relationships building**   High

Source: The McKinsey Quarterly, 1999, Number 2.

Figure 3.1   Potential for digital economy and e-commerce development in several industries

Another particular aspect of the tourism industry is that competition is global but the competitiveness is based on local factors and inter-firms relations. Strategic agreements and inter-firm alliances (Contractor and Lorange, 2002; Harrigan, 1988) are widespread in this sector, both *horizontally* at an international level (for example, between airline companies), arriving at a stage of 'quasi-oligopoly' market structure, and *vertically*, among different companies operating at the destination level (for example, hotels, transport, restaurants and travel agents specialized in incoming), in order to promote the destination itself (Della Corte, 2000). This is very true in the European context, where there are many small and medium enterprises that someway coexist with big multinational companies.

Besides, market structure differs greatly according to the area of the globe. Competition in this industry is made up of global competitors, at different levels. At an international level, there is a significant difference between

Europe and other continents. In Europe there are a few powerful tour operators and hotel chains, and many small and medium enterprises that are niche players. In other continents, multinational hotel chains and resorts are the main players in the industry, there are no significant tour operators, and small and medium enterprises are a very marginal phenomenon. In general, however, competition is made up of global players, niche players, 'high–quality' companies and portal and application providers (see Figure 3.2; Sabourin, 2001).

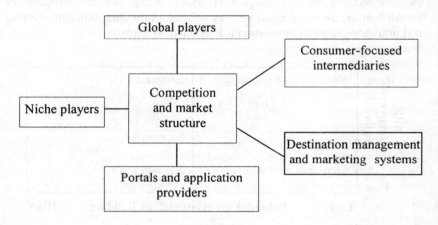

Figure 3.2

Big global companies tend to acquire firms in different companies and use the Internet and digital economy for price competition as well as a promotion channel for the company website, in order to gain some lock-in effects. Examples are multinational hotel chains such as Marriott, airline companies, and tour operators such as Thomson and Neckermann. Niche companies usually specialize in one specific market segment. They try to use the Internet mainly as a lock-in tool and to develop virtual communities for customers in order to increase customer retention. High–quality companies offer very high–quality service, with a consequent high customer satisfaction and retention rate: for these firms the Internet is nothing but an additional means of communication and interaction with customers.

In the last two categories it is possible to find local small and medium enterprises, offering complementary services as previously noted, and developing significant inter-firm alliances and networks in order to improve incoming (that is, tourist flows towards a specific destination). In these cases, destination management and marketing systems are created and developed: they are portals through which all information and offers are promoted. Some of them, such as Tiscover (initially applied to Austria's tourism industry) and Gulliver (Ireland), have proved to be very successful, owing to the networks and networking capabilities existing behind them. They offer all possible information on the destination as a whole, as well as the products provided by the companies involved in the network. In these cases, ICT is a very important instrument for destination competitiveness, which, however, is anyway bound to companies' skills and competences, coordination and destination management competences and, above all, trust and interaction capabilities among firms.

Application providers often refer to organizations operating in computer and software industries, whether connected (Trip.com and Travelocity.com, formed by CRS and GDS, such as Sabre and Galileo) or not (Expedia.com, formed by Microsoft) with the tourism industry, or simply portals of general on-line intermediaries (priceline.com, lastminute.com or, in Italy, ibazar.com).[7]

As shown in Figure 3.2, competition is varied and made up of different kinds of firm, sometimes operating in close but different industries, as well as destinations themselves, through the inter-firm networks products and offers. Many authors (Buhalis, 1998, 1999; Sabourin, 2001; Marcussen 2001; Carter, 2001; Missikoff, 2001) have studied the impact of ITC on the different kinds of company operating in the industry, underlining that digital economy can even change their roles, strategies and functions. However, our aim is to focus attention on what really makes firms' performances different, even those kinds of firm that seem to be totally overwhelmed by the new technology.

Finally, tourism has been facing deep and important changes recently: last year's events confirmed that the 'speed economy' can be dangerous and that we are gradually moving towards a 'safety economy', as it can be described observing companies' strategies and performances. This process has made competition much harder: tourism demand expectations are very high as far as product and service quality is concerned, and regarding the relationship between price and quality. So, many companies that try to keep low costs without caring about service standards have been having serious problems recently. This will lead to a more restricter selection of good competing firms, at different levels in tourism industries. The point is, however, whether we need new theories of competitive advantage in this new economy. According to the received theory (resource-based approach[8]), competitive advantage depends on exploiting valuable, rare, costly to imitate and non-substitutable resources and capabilities (Barney, 1991, 2001). The question is whether this theory applies in 'the new economy' and in particular in the tourism industry, which has always been a high technology-based sector. Our answer is yes and we'll explain why.

INDUSTRY VERSUS CAPABILITIES AS A SOURCE OF SUSTAINED COMPETITIVE ADVANTAGE IN THE NEW ECONOMY

For some time now, strategic management thinking has been dominated by a perspective that suggests that the industries within which a firm operates determine whether or not it can gain sustained competitive advantages. This perspective suggests that the critical issue facing managers is to discover 'attractive industries', that is, industries that are characterized by low levels of rivalry and other forms of competition and are protected from competitive entry by barriers to entry. Firms that operate in these attractive industries will enjoy sustained competitive advantages. Firms that operate in less attractive industries will not enjoy sustained competitive advantages (Porter, 1980, 1985).

Applying this 'industry attractiveness' perspective to competition in the new economy does, we think, generate – on average – a bleak prediction about the ability of firms to gain sustained competitive advantages in that economy. After all, what the new economy is all about is reducing barriers to information flow, thereby increasing the amount of information that is available to suppliers and customers and creating highly competitive worldwide markets. None of this increases the attractiveness of industries, at least in the way that attractiveness has traditionally been defined. And thus, according to this perspective, it should be the case that sustained competitive advantage should be *more difficult* – if not impossible – to attain in the new economy.

As mentioned before, the tourism sector is made up of different industries, although connected with each other. Let's think about a very unattractive industry – the worldwide airline industry: margins in this business are narrow, fixed costs are very high, and there is the risk of unsold capacity, while rivalry and the threat of clients, chartering processes and tour operators' direct investments in airplanes are all significant constraints on the ability of airline companies to gain sustained competitive advantages. Many of these companies are Internet-oriented and have been very influenced by the new economy. The situation, however, has even got worse: many companies have had to dismiss people, some have closed. The new economy seems to contribute to the industry's unattractiveness. But this 'industry attractiveness' perspective fails to recognize one very important point: the attractiveness of an industry cannot be evaluated independently of the capabilities that a firm brings to that industry. Consider an example. South West Airlines continues to sustain its competitive advantage, thanks to its rare and costly to imitate capabilities, which are anyway not due to the new economy: instead of considering the 'hub and spoke' or the revenue management systems as the possible solution to rivalry, South West has been finding different routes, constantly reinventing itself and the airline business, and improving service quality and human resources, being able to out-compete, in its niche market, its US competitors.

There are other interesting cases in the airline industry, such as Ryan Air, Go, Virgin and Volare Web (for whom e-commerce is one of the main, or the unique, distribution channels), that answer clients' need for cheap, frequent flights, which could even be compared to other means of transport (trains, buses, and so on). These companies, whose service on board is scant, of course, have chosen special destinations and secondary airports and invested in important competences in order to be more efficient than their competitors.

Thinking of another case, the hotel industry is conceived of as an attractive industry. And yet some companies outperform others. Marriott is an international hotel chain, among the leaders in the meetings and events business, that has recently developed its website for e-commerce as well, with an average increase, in the last three years, in on-line sales, of more than 200 per cent. Marriott, however, has very professional organizational competences, huge financial resources, high-tech competences inside the company, strategic intangible assets, such as the company image and, most of all, its brand, strong relationships with its clients and the possibility of high returns on investments on intangible assets. These are the main reasons for Marriott's success in the new economy.

There are some examples, also in the hotel industry, of small and medium enterprises (even bed and breakfasts), located in very attractive and famous destinations, that promote themselves and sell rooms by e-commerce. In these cases, however, it is very important for a certain number of firms, especially when they are not in the luxury or at least upper class, to have a common website, associated with the destination itself, through which to promote and commercialize their products/services. But in order to get the clients' trust and loyalty, it is necessary for these companies to invest in quality management, hospitality culture, and pointing out every typical and genuine feature in the destination; so specific capabilities and competences are required as well.

In the traditional intermediation industry (travel agents), which seems to be very unattractive (narrow margins, high price competition, many small and medium enterprises, low brand awareness, and low contractual power with suppliers), there are some international multiple chains, such as Thomas Cook, that outperform their competitors. Thomas Cook's main strategic resources are a well–known brand, high organizational competences, and strong relations with suppliers and customers. It's now one of the most important groups in Europe that have invested in connected activities (tour operators, and so on).

On the other hand, e-intermediation was considered to be attractive, but many cases have proved not to be successful. Just a few portals and companies are able to create an adequate brand awareness, to be trustworthy to clients and to select suppliers' offers. These aspects require both high-tech and tourism–specific competences that just a few e-companies have.

Apart from industry attractiveness, it is important to understand the sources and contents of a company's sustained competitive advantage.

RARE AND COSTLY TO IMITATE CAPABILITIES AND SUSTAINED COMPETITIVE ADVANTAGE IN THE NEW ECONOMY

If gaining sustained competitive advantage is not about 'picking' and operating in attractive industries, how can a firm gain and sustain a competitive advantage? The answer is: a firm gains and sustains competitive advantages by implementing strategies that meet customer demands through the exploitation of rare and costly to imitate capabilities. Examples of these are:

- capabilities that a firm possesses because of its unique history or unique resources (such as archeological sites, spas)
- capabilities that a firm possesses because of its close relationships with suppliers
- capabilities that a firm possesses because of its close relationships with its customers
- relationships a firm develops with its employees.

History and Resources

A firm's unique history can be extremely important for competing in the new economy. No one understands this better than Thomas Cook. Thomas Cook, with a tradition of more than 160 years, is the longest serving and one of the internationally best–known names in the tourism industry. It started as a single travel agency, then evolved into a chain and today represents the third largest travel group in the world, which works across all levels of the travel value chain – airlines, hotels, tour operators, travel and incoming agencies – thus providing its customers with the right product in all market segments across the globe, offering 'The Whole World of Travel'. The group encompasses 33 tour operators, about 3,600 travel agencies, a portfolio of

76,000 controlled hotel beds, a fleet of 87 aircraft and a workforce numbering some 28,000. The company is represented in the sales markets of Germany, Great Britain, Ireland, France, Belgium, Luxembourg, the Netherlands, Austria, Hungary, Poland, Slovakia, Slovenia, Egypt, India and Canada. What has always characterized Thomas Cook is the 'travel culture' that permeates the whole group at the different levels of the value chain and has helped in the successful process of selection of the target companies to acquire.

Relationships with Suppliers

Close and competitive relationships with suppliers and/or clients can also be a source of sustained competitive advantage in the new economy. Thomson and Neckermann are two important international tour operators whose main key to success has been the capability of developing lasting and intense relations both with suppliers and with customers. As regards their relations with suppliers, they have been establishing agreements with hotels and incoming agencies in different countries, buying huge numbers of rooms in different periods of the year. In Italy, for example, they control about 90 per cent of the flows towards some very attractive destinations, such as Ischia and Sorrento (very nice places in Campania, Southern Italy), with a very high contractual power. They also control or at least have long and established relations with a large number of travel agencies in many countries in Europe and in particular in their own countries (England and Germany, respectively). They mainly work in the 'groups' market, based on a deep organization rather than on individuals. Therefore they have been using the Internet and other new tools just to improve their efficiency in organization. Moreover, the 'groups' market is mainly based on very strong relationships with travel agencies. These relationships are also strategic because they help in the planning and budgeting process: some objectives are proposed to the clients (travel agents), with special commissions according to the results. Such a process cannot be applied in a context where digital economy is used even in the business-to-customer relation.

Some important groups, such as Cendant, have invested in different kinds of company within the tourism industry, starting with the real estate industry. In a few years, Cendant started acquiring hotel chains, airline companies, global distribution systems (Galileo, which is one of the three most widespread systems in the world), car rental companies, and so on. The advantage has consisted in creating important synergies among the different activities, with a widespread control of all main services typical of the tourism product.

Another interesting example is the Accor group, which is trying to expand in the sector and, meanwhile, to establish important alliances with other companies that are actually clients. An istance is the recent agreement with the tour operator TUI for reciprocal advantages: Accor's hotel rooms have been offered to TUI (German tour operator), which has guaranteed tourist flows from Germany; Accor's travel agents, on the other hand, promote TUI's destinations through their chains.

Relationships with Customers

Customer loyalty still exists in the new economy. This loyalty can be built by new economy firms fulfilling their promises in a timely and efficient manner. An example is Costa Crociere, the first Italian company and the first European one in the Mediterranean, which owns offices in 19 cities and 11 countries; it has 5,050 employees from different nations and is today almost totally controlled by Carnival Corporation (99.3 per cent of share capital). The market is made up of potential new customers who are constantly 'caught' and especially of habitual customers who decide to choose other cruises with the same company. In particular the latter are a very important measure of cruise companies' success.

Costa is developing digital economy, referring both to b2c and to b2b, in order to improve customer retention and its relations with travel agents. Of course these investments are very useful to the company to get information on different targets all over the world, to give virtual deep information on the ships and their facilities, and to develop a CRM (customer relation management) system, able to personalize the information and answer through an efficient e-mail process as well as to build a database on customers. However, what enables a firm like Costa to gain and sustain competitive advantages in the new economy is not the look of its website. Nor is it the data it collects about the preferences and buying patterns of its customers. These are attributes of its strategy that are rapidly being imitated by all the firms competing in this area. Rather, Costa's source of sustained competitive advantage stems from its brand, from the high quality of the ships and their facilities, and from the Italian-style services provided both on board and on land. In other words, the ability of Costa to gain and sustain competitive advantages depends on its ability to execute the mundane, non-technical, non-new economy aspects of its business day in and day out. That kind of performance can lead to customer loyalty, and to the willingness of customers to pay a little bit more to receive reliable quality service.

Even branding is possible in the new economy. In the US websites such as Travelocity.com and Expedia.com compete in very crowded segments of the e-commerce space. And yet these firms have been able to gain and sustain modest competitive advantages in these segments of the industry because of the brand awareness that they have created among customers. And, in the end, a brand is nothing more than a relationship between a firm and its customers – a relationship that competitors often find costly to imitate. Besides, the most renowned e-companies are those with high competences and commercial power with regard to the availability of tourism information, the selection of products and packages to insert, and the direct construction of products comprising elementary services (for example, a flight plus some nights in a hotel). In other words, these websites require a very efficient organizational structure able to monitor the market and transfer competitive and reliable offers to the system. Moreover, Travelocity.com has been formed by Sabre, one of the most important CRS in the world, and Expedia.com has been formed by Microsoft, acquiring the Worldspan database.

Relationships with Employees

In the turbulent world of the new economy, firms that are able to attract and retain competent employees may gain and sustain important competitive advantages. Stable employment enables employees to develop close relationships and innovative teams. Employees of this kind can be a source of real value in even the most rapidly changing competitive environment, because the teams within which they operate can be fast acting and flexible. Certainly, designing compensation schemes that create incentives for employees to remain with a firm – compensation schemes such as stock and stock options – can help create these teams. But most new economy firms have these compensation schemes, so they cannot, by themselves, be a source of sustained competitive advantage. In addition to these forms of compensation, firms that have a supportive and enabling culture, firms that encourage and reward risk taking, firms that stand for more than just making some quick money are often able to attract and retain employees who, in turn, can form flexible and valuable teams. And, to the extent that these teams are rare and costly to imitate, they can be a source of sustained competitive advantage.

It is still possible to gain and sustain competitive advantages in the new economy. Indeed, the kinds of capability that have always been the source of sustained competitive advantage in the old economy – capabilities that are rare and costly to imitate – can create sustained competitive advantages in the new economy. If anything, these kinds of capability are even more important in the new economy, since so many other potential sources of advantage are destroyed in the costless-information and worldwide competitiveness of the new economy.

Gaining and sustaining competitive advantage in the new economy

1. Exploit your firm's unique history:
   - establish unique relationships with numerous other firms, some of which may give you advantages that others will find costly to imitate;
   - exploit your competitive strengths in the old economy by linking your old economy and new economy operations.
2. Exploit your firm's relationships with its suppliers:
   - use new economy technology to gain access to low–cost supplies;
   - identify key suppliers with whom you will build long-term relationships.
3. Exploit your firm's relationships with its customers:
   - execute the non-new economy parts of your business;
   - develop brand awareness in the new economy.
4. Exploit your firm's relationships with its employees:
   - develop stable employment relationships with your crucial employees;
   - organize to emphasize flexibility over ownership and control;
   - rely on strategic alliances with partners to execute many business activities.

The tourism industry, in fact, has always been high–technology–based, as well as being a high–touch sector (which means that a strategic role is played by human resources, relationships and trust, not only in the promotion phase but also and mainly in the services provision phase).

ORGANIZING TO REALIZE COMPETITIVE ADVANTAGE IN THE NEW ECONOMY

While the sources of sustained competitive advantage are the same in the new and the old economies, the way firms are organized to exploit those sources of advantage may have to change dramatically. In the old economy, long product life cycles, slowly evolving technology, and predictable shifts in customer tastes made it possible for firms to vertically integrate into a wide range of value chain activities. Competition in this old economy was generally sufficiently stable for the costs of operating in all the value chain activities to be covered and a firm to still gain all the advantages of controlling the full vertical chain of production.

But the new economy is about short and then shorter product life cycles, rapid technological change, and unpredictable shifts in customer tastes. The stability and predictability of vertical integration may simply be impossible to realize in the new economy. Instead, unprecedented levels of organizational flexibility are required. This suggests that vertical integration, as a form of organization, will be largely replaced by the use of a variety of strategic alliances in the new economy. The quintessential new economy firm controls a few critical business functions within its boundaries, and manages the rest of its business activities through joint ventures, equity strategic alliances, and non-equity strategic alliances. Finding and learning to work with partners is the critical organizational skill in the new economy.

Many new economy firms have already figured this out. Most of the successful 'dot com' companies in the USA and in Europe – including Travelocity.com and Expedia.com – have hundreds of alliances that give them access to the resources they need to compete successfully, but enable them to retain the flexibility they need in a rapidly changing competitive environment (Eviaggi.com derives itself from a joint venture between GDS Amadeus and the Italian portal Kataweb).

That's also true for small and medium enterprises. For example, in the tourism industry, some destination management systems and organizations have proved to be successful. Let's think about Tiscover in Austria and Gulliver in Ireland, whose strategic resources are the networks behind them. DMS are portals of countries, regions or destinations, where you can find tourist information on the area, descriptions of sites and main attractions, as well as packages and products sold by local companies. These work in a network and usually offer products both for individuals and for groups, as a niche market compared with the global tour operators previously analyzed. And yet this market seems to be very interesting, in terms of both numbers of flows and profits for local firms. In this case, the single company success is strictly bound to the whole network success, based on the capabilities developed by each member of the network in working together, reciprocal trust, and the capacity of planning and emphasizing local resources. In these contexts net economy can be very useful to improve common languages, organizational efficiency and flows of information: the strategic network competences mentioned above, favored by new technology, generate themselves further synergies and economies as well as capabilities and competences, through a sort of 'virtuous cycle'.

For some old economy firms, the challenge of gaining and sustaining competitive advantages using the kinds of capabilities that have always been important, but gaining access to those capabilities through various forms of strategic alliances, may be very uncomfortable. But in the new economy, to gain access to the rare and costly to imitate capabilities that hold the promise for sustained competitive advantage, in a way that recognizes the reality of rapid changes in technology and customer demand, may force managers to abandon control for flexibility and vertical integration for strategic alliances. ICT, in fact, seems to generate a complex process, pushing, on one hand, towards disintermediation, through more direct relations both in business to business and in business to consumer; on the other hand, strategic networks and alliances seem to be the right way to keep up with innovation, and gaining and sustaining competitive advantage.

Moreover, taking into account the importance, in the tourism industry as well as in many other service industries, of the quality of the services provided in order to favor tourist satisfaction and retention, special skills and specific knowledge are extremely important; and continuous flows of communication and information among firms, the approach to customers and customer satisfaction, capabilities in problem solving, and starting and developing inter-firm relations are necessary features in order to promote and sell the destination as a whole, that is, as a system where companies can make even local, external resources extremely attractive and more enjoyable (Della Corte, 2000). It's interesting to notice that some areas that are not particularly attractive for their unique natural and/or historical resources are nevertheless visited by substantial tourist flows. This is due to the network capabilities of companies whose organizational and strategic resources make the destination itself attractive.

Network competences and capabilities, however, are important at a condition but are further developed by the network itself: new economies of scope, network economies and switching costs, transaction cost compression (Sabourin, 2001), rapid learning curves. This is more true for the innovation process, both for old economy and new economy firms. In that respect, for firms it becomes necessary to take into account the effects and changes brought by the new economy, but this is necessary just to keep up with innovation and progress, which can bring competitive parity, not to gain sustained competitive advantage. Besides, the new economy also requires new competences and capabilities. It can't be, however, a source of competitive advantage by itself.

CONCLUSION

So, is sustained competitive advantage possible in the new economy? This question is particularly relevant in the tourism industry, where information and communication technology is widespread, both in business-to-business and in business-to-consumer relations. We think the answer is clearly yes. To find these sources of sustained competitive advantage, firms need to seek to exploit the kinds of capabilities that have always been sources of sustained competitive advantage. These capabilities are rare and costly to imitate, and usually reflect a firm's unique history and its relationships with its suppliers, customers, and employees. However, the rapid and unpredictable pace of change in the new economy may mean that firms will have to be less vertically integrated and control–oriented than they were in the old economy. Instead, they will have to rely more heavily on strategic alliances and focus more on retaining their flexibility in the uncertain world of the new economy. Firms that can build traditional bases of sustained competitive advantage, and realize them through a more flexible organizational structure, in particular 'local systems of tourism offer' (tourism business districts), will prosper in the 'brave new world' of the new economy.

NOTES

1. Collis and Porras (1997). In one study, ten firms with sustained competitive advantages were identified, along with some of their close competitors. The long–term value creation of each of these firms was calculated by subtracting the total investment in them since their inception from their current market value, as reported in Ross (1999).
2. Werthner (2001a) emphasizes the role of ICT in the convergence and crossover processes, the information economy (as a radical part of economic activities) and the network economy (interdependences among firms).
3. The concept of superior performance refers to economic rents, when firms generate more value with resources they have acquired or developed than was expected by the owners of those resources, or to strategic advantages, when a firm is implementing value-creating strategies not currently being implemented by competing firms.
4. These labels include 'the resource-based view of the firm', 'the knowledge-based view of the firm', 'the capabilities perspective', and 'the competences perspective'. This view has much in common with the concept of core competences as developed by Hamel, Prahalad, Heene and others.
5. There are at least two ways to define *sustained competitive advantage* at firm level. A firm can be said to reach competitive advantage when it is engaging in activities that increase its efficiency or effectiveness in ways that competing firms are not (Barney, 1991). In the second definition, a firm creates a sustained economic rent, which means that it is able to consistently exceed the performance expectations of the stockholders. Even if some authors argue that firms that continue to use valuable resources to choose and implement strategies

in ways others cannot anticipate can gain sustained economic rents (Peteraf, 1993), whether this competitive advantage is a source of economic rents depends on the cost of acquiring or developing valuable, rare, costly to imitate, and nonsubstitutable resources. If this cost equals the value created no economic rent is generated (Barney, 1986a; Barney, 2001).

6. Global distribution systems are the information and booking systems generally adopted by travel agents to connect with airline companies, hotels, car rentals and other firms of the industry. They derive from the traditional computerized reservation systems, originally created by airline companies for the distribution of their services. See Poon (1988).

7. All of the firms shown in Figure 3.2 can adopt different business models: information providers (simple information tools), electronic booking services that offer the chance of on-line booking, electronic travel agents, electronic marketplaces (which offer many personalized services and post-sale assistance), and flexible comparison shopping services that are real intelligence agents (Jarvela, 1999).

8. Dierickx and Cool (1989); Barney (1991); Mahoney and Pandian (1992); Peteraf (1993); Wernefelt (1984); Aeker (1989); Conner (1991); Grant (1991); Hall (1992); Amit and Schoemaker (1993); Penrose (1959).

REFERENCES

Aeker, D.A. (1989), 'Managing assets and skills: the key to a sustainable competitive advantage', *California Management Review*.

Amit, R. and P.J.H. Schoemaker (1993), 'Strategic assets and organizational rent', *Strategic Management Journal*, **14**.

Andreu, A. and C. Ciborra (1996), 'Organisational learning and core capabilities development: the role of IT', *Journal of Strategic Information Systems*, **5**.

Baker, M., C. Hayzelden and S. Sussmann (1996), 'Can destination management system provide competitive advantage? Discussion of the factors affecting the survival and success of DMS', *Progress in Tourism and Hospitality Research* (2).

Barney, J.B. (1986a), 'Strategic factors markets: expectations, luck and business strategy', *Management Science* (32).

Barney, J.B. (1986b), 'Organizational culture: can it be a source of sustained competitive advantage?', *Academy of Management Review* (11).

Barney, J.B. (1991), 'Firm resources and sustained competitive advantage', *Journal of Management*, **17**.

Barney, J.B. (1996), *Gaining and Sustaining Competitive Advantage*, Addison-Wesley Publishing.

Barney, J.B (2001), 'Is the resource-based view a useful perspective for strategic management research? Yes', *Academy of Management Review*, **26**.

Barney, J.B. and W.G. Ouchi (1994), 'Information cost and organizational governance', *Management Science* (10).

Barney, J.B. and B. Tyler (1990), 'The attributes of top management teams and sustained competitive advantage', in M. Lawless and Gomez-Maja (eds), *Managing in High Technology Firm*, Greenwich, CT: JAI Press.

Bing, P. and D.R. Fesenmaier (2001), *A typology of tourism related web sites: its theoretical background and implications*, Working Paper 6 January.

Buhalis, D. (1998), 'Strategic use of information technologies in the tourism industry', *Tourism Management*, **19** (5).

Buhalis, D. (1999), 'Information technology for small and medium sized tourism enterprises: adaptations and benefits', *Information Technology and Tourism*, **2** (2).

Buhalis, D. and A. Spada (2000), 'Destination management system: criteria for success: an exploratory research', Enter Conference Proceedings, Vienna.

Buhalis, D., A.M. Tjoa and J. Jafari (1998), 'Information and communication technologies in tourism', Enter Conference Proceedings, Vienna.

Checkland, P. and J. Scholes (1990), *Soft Systems Methodology in Action*, Chichester: John Wiley & Sons.

Collis, J. and J. Porras (1997), *Built to Last*, New York: Harpers Business.

Contractor, F.J. and P. Lorange (eds) (2002), *Cooperative Strategies and Alliances*, Amsterdam: Pergamon Press.

Della Corte, V. (2000), *La Gestione dei Sistemi Locali di Offerta Turistica* [The management of tourism local systems], Padua: CEDAM.

Dierickx, I. and K. Cool (1989), 'Asset stock accumulation and sustainability of competitive advantage', *Management Science* (35), 1504–11.

Dwyer, L., P. Forsyth and P. Rao (2001), 'PPS and the price competitiveness of international tourism destination', Joint World Bank–OECD Seminar on Purchasing Power Parities, Washington, January 30–February 2.

Frew, A. and P. O'Connor (1999), 'Destination marketing system strategies in Scotland and Ireland: an approach to assessment', *Information Technology and Tourism*, **2** (1).

Gamble, P.R. (1990), 'Developing an information technology strategy for hospitality organizations', *International Journal of Contemporary Hospitality Management*, **1**.

Grant, R.M. (1991), 'The resource-based theory of competitive advantage: implications for strategy formulation', *California Management Review*, Spring.

Hamel, G. and A. Heene (eds) (1994), *Competence-based Competition*, London: Wiley.

Hamel, G. and C.K. Prahalad (1989), 'Strategic intent', *Harvard Business Review*, May–June.

Hannes, W. (2001), 'Internet/turismo', *La scommessa dell'ECTRL* (1) March.

Harrigan, K.R. (1988), 'Joint ventures and competitive strategies', *Strategic Management Journal* (9).

Hax, C. and N.S. Majluf (1991), *The Strategy Concept and Process: A Pragmatic Approach*, New York: Prentice Hall.

Hodgson, G.M. (1996), 'Evolutionary and competence-based theories of the firm', Working Paper 26, Cambridge University, February.

Holloway, J.K. (1994), *The Business of Tourism*, 4th edn., Longman.

Holloway, J.K. and C. Robinson (1995), *Marketing for Tourism*, 3rd edn., London: Blackwell.

Jensen, O. (1995), 'Development of competitive advantages of small firms within a local tourism industry, *Economica* (37).

Kosel, M. (2001), Open Standards Workshop, Open Travel Alliance, Montreal, April 27.

Lepape, B. (2001), Head Tourism sector European Commission – DG INFSO/B5. Enter Conference.

Lewis, C.C. and R.E. Chambers (1989), *Marketing Leadership in Hospitality*, New York: Van Nostrand Reinhold.

Mahoney, J.T. and J.R. Pandian (1992), The resource-based view within the conversation of strategic management', *Strategic Management Journal*.

Marcussen, C.H. (2000), 'Quantifyng trends in European internet distribution of travel and tourism services', Paper presented at the seminar on *Information Technology & Strategic Tourism Management*, Westminster University, London, 9–10 March.

Marcussen, C.H. (2001), 'Trends in European Internet distribution of travel and tourism services', Working Paper of Bornholm Research Centre, Denmark, 27 March.

Martini, U. (2001), 'Internet e le imprese turistiche: un'analisi dell'impatto della rete sul funzionamento del mercato turistico leisure', *Micro & Macro Marketing*, **X** (2), August.

Mintzberg, H. (1994), *The Rise and Fall of Strategic Planning*, Prentice Hall.

Missikoff, M. (2001), 'Turismo ed innovazione tecnologica verso il Web semantico' (Tourism and technological innovation towards the semantic web), *Proceedings of the Italian Conference on Innovation and Information Technologies for Tourism*, ITIT, Trento, 22–23 November.

Penrose, E. (1959), *The Theory of the Growth of the Firm*, Oxford: Basil Blackwell.

Peteraf, M.A. (1993), 'The cornerstones of competitive advantage: a resource-based view', *Strategic Management Journal* (14), 179–191.

Poon, A. (1988), 'Tourism and information technologies', *Annals of Tourism Research* (15).

Porter, M.E. (1980), *Competitive Strategy*, New York: Free Press.

Porter, M.E. (1985), *Competitive Advantage*, New York: Free Press.

Reichheld, F. and K. Aspinall (1993–94), 'Building high loyalty business systems', *Journal of Retail Banking*, Winter.

Ross (1999), 'The Stern Stewart Performance 1000', *Journal of Applied Corporate Finance*, **11**, 122–134.

Scharl, A., C. Bauer, A. Taudes, M. Natter and K. Wober (2001), 'Content analysis and tourism: competitiveness and success factors of European tourism web sites', European Forum Alphabach: E-business/benchmarking Europe.

Smeral, E. (1998), 'The impact of globalization on small and medium enterprises: new challenges for tourism policies in European countries', *Tourism Management*, **19** (4), 371–80.

Wagner, L.M. (2001), 'The sustainable development imperative and the travel and tourism industry', case study for the UN Vision Project on Global Public Policy Networks.

Wernefelt, B. (1984), 'A resource-based view of the firm', *Strategic Management Journal*.

Werthener, H. (2001a), 'E-Commerce and travel/tourism issues and challenges', EC3 – E-Commerce Competence Center, Vienna, IFIT.

Werthener, H. (2001b), 'Why is the information society technology relevant for tourism?', EC3 – E-Commerce Competence Center, Vienna, IFIT.

Website

www.mira.net, Dossier of the Research Center Mira on E-commerce, 'Capire l'E-Commerce e formulazione del progetto'.

4. Transferring organizational capabilities across transient organizations: evidence from Hollywood filmmaking

Simone Ferriani, Raffaele Corrado and Carlo Boschetti

INTRODUCTION

Since 1990 the organizational field has been deeply concerned with unlocking the processes that link firm-specific resources, knowledge and capabilities with the organizational functioning of the firm. Project-based organizations are fascinating and original sites for the study of these processes. Whether these forms of design are called temporary systems (Meyerson *et al.*, 1996; Goodman and Goodman, 1972), adhocracies (Mintzberg, 1979), project networks (Jones, 1996), synthetic organizations (Thompson, 1967) or single-project organizations (Faulkner and Anderson, 1987; Baker and Faulkner, 1991), project-based forms of organizing are typically to be found where complex, prototypal tasks require the temporary employment and collaboration of diversely skilled specialists. In order to cope with highly dynamic environments, wherein product demand shifts rapidly and unpredictably, these organizations bring together outsourced individuals to provide their expertise at a critical time or in a critical combination, without having to incur costly and long-lasting overheads (Jones *et al.*, 1997). Examples of industries in which project-based organizing has long been established include construction (Eccles, 1981), semiconductors (Saxenian, 1996), music (Lorenzen and Frederiksen, 2002), film production (Faulkner and Anderson, 1987; Robins, 1993; Baker and Faulkner, 1991; Jones, 1996; DeFillippi and Arthur, 1998), and knowledge-intensive professional service firms such as law, management consulting, and architecture (Starbuck, 1992).

Some features of project-based organizations appear at odds with capability- and routine-centered perspectives on firm functioning. In fact, while a key assumption of these approaches is that firms develop path-dependent organizational processes that shape and drive the organizational performance (Dosi *et al.*, 2000; Teece *et al.*, 1997; Grant, 1996; Nelson and Winter, 1982), project-based organizations exhibit no ostensible history-based path to build upon and drive their organizational behavior. A project-based organization is a temporary form of organization that ceases to exist as soon as its single target is achieved. This apparent paradox triggers some intriguing questions as to the organizational mechanisms that allow these systems to retain their best practices, combine their knowledge assets and consistently integrate them into valuable organizational capabilities.

Using the Hollywood motion picture industry as empirical grounding for our reasoning, in this chapter we show that in a project-based environment firm disbanding does not necessarily imply the termination of the collaborative interactions established during the project. We test our theoretical arguments with blockmodels and other network analysis techniques on collaborations that took place in 783 movies distributed in America between 1995 and 1999. Results demonstrate that project participants with complementary tasks tend to consolidate their collaboration over time, establishing teams that survive the disruptive pressures of the industry. While supporting the consistency of a knowledge-oriented focus in project environments, our findings highlight the role of teams as carriers of capabilities and ultimate repositories of the industry organizational memory.

The chapter is structured as follows. In the first section we illustrate the idea of project-based organizations as temporary firms. Using modern filmmaking as the empirical setting for our arguments we highlight the conceptual issues that arise when contrasting some key tenets from the modern organizational thinking with the peculiar features of these firms. In the second section these ideas are formalized within the framework of the knowledge-based theory. Building on anecdotal evidence from the industry, film projects are conceptualized as knowledge-based organizations striving to integrate ideas and competencies under conditions of extreme uncertainty. This discussion serves as the background for the empirical hypothesis formulated in the following section. Next we describe the data sample and methodology which we used to test the hypothesis. After discussing the results, we conclude by drawing some implications for the way our findings may help increase our understanding of project-based functioning and how they may relate to similar contexts.

PROJECT-BASED ORGANIZATIONS AS TEMPORARY FIRMS: THE CASE OF MODERN FILMMAKING

Project-based organizations have been described as temporary ventures in which 'diversely skilled people work together on a complex task over a limited period of time' (Goodman and Goodman, 1976: 474); they are typified by their interdependence of task accomplishment as well as the continuous interrelating of their members. Temporary systems tend to provide flexibility in environments that are highly uncertain by allowing for easier movement of specialized personnel (Faulkner and Anderson, 1987). In order to face turbulent environments, these organizational entities bring together outsourced professionals to provide their expertise at a critical time or in a critical combination, without having to incur costly and long-lasting overheads (Jones *et al.*, 1997). While industries such as theater and construction have a long-standing history of organizing on a project and temporary basis (Goodman and Goodman, 1972, 1976; Eccles, 1981), comparable characteristics are nowadays prevalent in several fields, salient examples including music, film production (Faulkner and Anderson, 1987; Robins, 1993; Baker and Faulkner, 1991; Jones, 1996; DeFillippi and Arthur, 1998), fashion (Mariotti and Cainarca, 1986), management consulting and architecture (Starbuck, 1992).

DeFillippi and Arthur (1998) illustrated some conceptual problems that seem to surface when we try to look at these organizations through the lenses provided by well–consolidated tenets in contemporary organizational thinking, whereby a key concern is represented by the processes that take place, develop and consolidate over time within the boundaries of the firm. Project-based organizations represent a model of a firm that is inherently transitory; they get established with their future dissolution in mind (upon project completion), regardless of the quality and/or success of the final accomplishment. This characteristic is hard to reconcile with a firm-centric, long-range perspective on organizational functioning, where the accumulation of knowledge and the development of organizational capabilities are typically assumed to be the outcome of organizational processes evolving with time and experience (Dosi *et al.*, 2000; Amit and Schoemaker, 1993; Grant a, 1996; Teece *et al.*, 1997). But what if survival and organizational continuity are not issues of concern for the organization under observation? What if the firm is the temporary manifestation of a 'one shot' production effort? If very little is known about the organizational functioning and behavior of these increasingly pervasive organizational forms, the extent to which prevailing tenets in the field may help to fill this gap is an open issue.

The American motion picture industry represents an ideal context for trying to address these problems. First, in the course of several decades, the American film industry, and Hollywood in particular, has undergone a gradual transformation that has led it to take on organizational traits and features that are typical of project-based business settings. Starting in the early 1950s and following a phase characterized by steady demand and a heavily integrated organizational structure (which had reached its climax with the 'Studio System' phenomenon) the American film industry began to experience some radical changes (Conant, 1960; Balio, 1985). A host of concurrent factors, most notably the 'Paramount Decision'[1] and the advent of television, triggered a transformation process that ultimately redefined the whole system-wide strategic, structural and organizational setting. Downsizing, deverticalization, an increasingly unpredictable demand and the subsequent tendency to turn to outsourcing practices were among the primary consequences of this process (Balio, 1985). As a result, by the end of the 1970s the organization of filmmaking hinged upon individual *film projects* and personal and informal networks rather than traditional hierarchies and in-house human resource departments. In this system, 'Firms and subcontractors combine for a specific project, disband when the project is finished, and then combine for new projects Self-employed subcontractors move from project to project, while the role of the company is to finance and distribute the finished product' (Jones, 1996: 58). In a continuous process of organizational formation and dissolution, the modern American feature film industry revolves around *single-project organizations* that are deliberately created for a limited purpose and disbanded upon project completion (Baker and Faulkner, 1991).

Second, the American film industry provides extremely detailed and updated data collections, including the composition and characteristics of the professional community that project firms draw their resources from. In particular, team membership is easily tracked since credits are available for key roles on each film. These features make the modern American film industry an appropriate ground for analyzing project-based dynamics. In addition, as Faulkner and Anderson (1987) point out, it is a well–observable industry because it is constantly in movement and draws attention to its movement.

Third, our choice of the empirical testing ground follows the lead of several researchers who have brought strategic and organizational lenses into the realm of filmmaking to draw useful implications for a broad range of organizations (Morley and Silver, 1977; Faulkner and Anderson, 1987; Baker and Faulkner, 1991; Eliashberg and Sawhney, 1994; Miller and Shamsie, 1996; DeFillippi and Arthur; 1998; Jones, 2001; Alvarez and Svejenova,

2002a). The use of movie industry data offers many advantages for testing organizational theories and much can be learned from this setting.

In order to disentangle and provide a more formal understanding of the organizational issues introduced earlier, in the next section we endeavor to situate the film project within the arena of modern organizational thinking. We do so by drawing on some key tenets from the knowledge-based view of the firm: film units are portrayed as bundles of knowledge resources to be combined into team level organizational capabilities. This knowledge-based conceptualization of the film project paves the way for an empirical examination of organizational dynamics within the milieu of the Hollywood film industry.

THEORETICAL FRAMEWORK

Key Tenets from the Knowledge-based View of the Firm

In the last decade the increasing emphasis of managerial disciplines on firm resources and competencies has inspired the development of several parallel streams of literature concerned with the internal organizational processes and dynamics driving firm behavior and functioning. Notable examples are the resource-based view (Rumelt, 1984; Barney, 1991), the dynamic capability approach (Teece *et al.*, 1997; Eisenhardt and Martin, 2000) and, most recently, the knowledge-based theory of the firm (Nonaka, 1991; Kogut and Zander, 1992; Grant, 1996a, 1996b; Eisenhardt and Santos, 2001). Sometimes depicted as an 'outgrowth' of the resource-based view, the knowledge-based approach is grounded in three key principles (Grant, 1996a, 1996b):

- the recognition of knowledge as the primary organizational asset,
- the role of the firm as knowledge integrator,
- the concept of organizational capabilities as sources of competitive advantage and drivers of firm performance.

Knowledge as primary asset

In an environmental context increasingly characterized by volatile markets, growing competition and a markedly dynamic demand, knowledge is a paramount resource for nurturing and sustaining organizational performance (Grant, 1996a, 1996b). As Nonaka (1991: 96) puts it, 'In an economy where the only certainty is uncertainty, the one sure source of lasting competitive advantage is knowledge'. Given that the knowledge stock accumulated within the firm represents the primary ground for competitive confrontation, the firm's capability of organizing, managing and operationalizing this asset (especially knowledge that is inherently tacit in nature) is a crucial requirement for developing a sustainable strategy.

Firm as knowledge integrator

'If knowledge is a critical input into all production processes, if efficiency requires that it is created and stored by individuals in specialized form, and if production requires the application of many types of specialized knowledge, then the primary role of the firm is the integration of knowledge' (Grant, 1996b: 377). Firms exist because they create ideal conditions for the integration process to take place, wherein markets (for usage costs associated with the existence of knowledge forms which are hardly transferable) and single individuals (for cognitive bounds) do not provide equally efficient alternatives. The organizational manifestation of this distinctive function is an organizational capability, that is, an ability to perform a productive task which relates either directly or indirectly to a firm's capacity for creating value through effecting the transformation of inputs into outputs.

According to Grant (1996b) the process of knowledge integration is sustained by at least two key conditions: the first relates to the presence of a base of *common knowledge* shared by the firm members; the second pertains to the *organizational structure of the firm*. The concept of common knowledge refers to the experience, vocabulary, behavioral rules and coding schemes shared by the various members of the organization. Common knowledge facilitates communication among organizational members and provides a platform of shared understanding that helps to prompt information and knowledge exchange among different specialists (Demsetz, 1991; Kogut and Zender, 1992). The organizational structure, in turn, may affect the likelihood of effective knowledge integration by conditioning the intensity of communication among the organizational members. Thus, while a hierarchical structure based upon rules and directives is more likely to fail wherever integration calls for the deployment of tacit knowledge, a team-based organizational model represents a viable solution for optimizing knowledge integration effectiveness (Argote, 1999). Because they facilitate close and continuous interaction among their members, teams establish an ideal ground for favoring the emergence of routines and enabling the deployment of tacit knowledge embodied within single actors.

Organizational capabilities

The integration of specialist knowledge is the essence of organizational capabilities, a concept that summarizes a fairly obvious reality of firm functioning: turning knowledge into goods and services production requires the blending of many areas of experience. While the salience of the knowledge integration function is in itself straightforward, the mechanisms that regulate this process are not at all outright. The routine metaphor, grounded in Nelson and Winter's evolutionary theory (1982), represents probably the most convincing conceptualization of such mechanisms: specialized individual skills gets integrated into the organization via interaction, social understanding and sequences of coordinated behavior that take shape along paths of shared experiences. Such experiences establish the communication system that underlies routine performance and sustain the capabilities of the organization. Routines allow the firm to deploy its tacit assets, based on knowledge that can hardly be articulated by its members and is, for that very reason, all the more valuable.

A Knowledge-based Analysis of Film Projects

Building on the above discussion, in this section the film project is likened to a knowledge-based organization striving to access a highly diversified knowledge base, and is translated into the mutual and harmonious commitment of a complex task. By intertwining secondary sources and archival interviews in the film industry with theoretical arguments, we try to establish a theoretical grounding for the issues of interest. These ideas are then translated into a testable hypothesis.

Film projects and knowledge resources
Each film may ultimately be viewed as the result of the joint effort of a plurality of individuals providing their skills, knowledge and expertise for the venture. As a result of the growing uncertainty that has shaped the motion picture industry from the mid 1950s, knowledge, in the form of technical skills and creative talent, has acquired absolute prominence for the success of the filmmaking venture (Miller and Shamsie, 1996). As pointed out by the world acclaimed director Peter Weir, 'behind movies shown worldwide there are just men and their talent'.[2] In contributing a wealth of specific knowledge and experience to the project, many specialists may prove critical to the quality of the final accomplishment: 'their various creative and mechanical abilities contribute to the final effect of the film' (movie director Sydney Pollack, in Squire, 1983: 24–25). Their skills are embodied within specific roles that serve as bundles of tasks and norms as well as repositories of the specialized knowledge that is used to enact positions (Baker and Faulkner, 1991).

Film projects and knowledge integration
Film projects are occasions of intense interaction over a short time span. During this period film professionals participate in a collaborative

environment where the exchange and sharing of knowledge and ideas are not only encouraged but also considered crucial for both the initiation and completion of the project (Morley and Silver, 1977; Daskalaki and Blair, 2002). In order to counterbalance the fragmentation of knowledge among many specialists, project members are challenged to establish proper patterns of collaboration and socialization (Alvarez and Svejenova, 2002a). Because the industry is based almost completely on temporary systems, and because the success of the film depends as much on interpersonal compatibility as on technical performance, the emphasis on collaborative skills is taken for granted by everyone. Collaborative skills are required for conveying implicit ideas (tacit knowledge) and interpenetrate one's vision of the film (Morley and Silver, 1977).

This process is reinforced by two enabling conditions: (a) a 'thick' industry culture that shapes behaviors and consolidates working practices in a way akin to the 'common knowledge' idea *à la* Grant (1996b); (b) an established habit to organize tasks and duties around teams. Concerning the first point, from their very entrance into the production network industry professionals are involved in an intense process of socialization that allows a quick absorption of the culture, conventions and values that regulate the industry (Jones, 1996). As a result of this process, whenever they are thired to start a new production, most of the project participants already share a common bulk of knowledge, which allows basic work principles and collaboration rules to operate without the need to renegotiate and rearrange them at any subsequent project (Baker and Faulkner, 1991). As to the second point, teams represent the key relational building blocks of film projects. Tasks as diverse as set decoration, sound recording and stage lighting are accomplished by functional multidisciplinary teams, usually led by a team leader who is ultimately responsible to the movie director (Morley and Silver, 1977; Chion, 1999). Teams help to establish feedback coordination, encouraging leeway and discretion, while coordination through the formal structure of rules and performance audit is relaxed (Faulkner and Anderson, 1987). This organizational structure results in high levels of mutual interdependencies that help to counteract the difficulties in dealing with a high degree of intangibility, an uncertain task environment and complexity of inputs and outputs (Jones, 1996; Faulkner and Anderson, 1987).

Film projects and organizational capabilities
We have previously highlighted the role of routines as basic mechanisms for the genesis of organizational capabilities. Time and shared experience are critical requirements for the development of organizational routines. The temporal dimension is crucial since the organizational dynamics that lead to the integration of specialized knowledge assets are the results of path-

dependent evolutionary processes. As noted by Teece *et al.* (1997: 528), 'Distinctive competences and capabilities generally cannot be acquired; they must be built. This sometimes takes years'. Despite this reasoning, while the integration of knowledge resources is clearly an essential condition for the smooth functioning of film projects, the transient nature of these organizations appears hardly reconcilable with an evolutionary, path-dependent perspective on the development of organizational capabilities. In contrast to permanent organizations that exist to carry out a relatively repetitive manufacturing or service task for which there is a continuing need, project teams exist to develop and realize an idea (usually embodied in a script). When project participants have completed their task they disband, dissolving the relational ties and arrangements they had been developing throughout the duration of the project. In other words, survival is not a critical issue, at least not in the long-term, evolutionary sense of the word, while there is neither an ostensible stable structure nor a permanent work environment in which to store the memory of the organization. In highly creative and prototypical transient organizations distinguished by a pronounced interorganizational mobility of their human assets, such as film projects, the existence of knowledge retention practices lying at the foundation of a learning process appears counterintuitive. What organizational mechanisms, if any, are responsible for the routinization of practices and behaviors that allows for the deployment of the skills tacitly held by the highly specialized professionals involved in the realization of the projects? Where do the organizational capabilities of the film project reside? How do they emerge and evolve over time?

Envisioning the organizational mechanisms that may enable this process is a matter of empirical assessment. It is a matter of establishing if and how some form of organizational continuity may exist in a context shaped by transient systems. The analysis that follows, by moving out attention from the organization to the interpersonal collaborative ties forged by team members over a series of projects, constitutes an attempt to surmount this apparent paradox.

HYPOTHESIS

We derived our hypothesis from two interlinked arguments that serve as a red thread across our reasoning:

(a) Industry organizational memory   For more than twenty years, while nurturing an uninterrupted process of creation/dissolution, temporary enterprises have sustained a relatively durable and resilient independent film

industry. Despite an environmental context characterized by a high degree of turbulence and dynamism, as is the case with creative industries by and large (Caves, 2000), the Hollywood film industry has maintained a position of indisputable worldwide leadership for several decades (Acheson and Maule, 1994; Kerrigan and Culkin, 1999). While there appear to be no enabling conditions for a single film project to develop its own organizational memory, the American film industry has been able to continuously foster and retain a memory of good practices (DeFillippi and Arthur, 1998). In discussing this issue, DeFillippi and Arthur's analysis hints at the existence of an organizational legacy process: 'From its inception the film-making enterprise is distinct from the continuing entity which much strategic management thinking is targeted at. The project-based enterprise *inherits* its strategic vision, rather than shapes its own' (1998: 129). DeFillippi and Arthur's reasoning builds on the consideration that in many instances these projects are profoundly shaped by ideas, collaborative relations, and shared experiences that crew members keep growing over successive projects. Because their organizational vision is largely in place before the formal filmmaking organization is formed, they contend, film projects are somewhat akin to biological entities that inherit their genetic traits. It is not clear, however, what allows for this genetic endowment to 'resist' the disruptive power of the organizational disbanding.

(b) Team capability As we pointed out earlier, the high interdependence that characterizes the activity of the movie professionals results in an organizational structure highly centered on teamwork. Teams provide a social context for establishing trusted complementarities and counteracting the risks, pressure and complexities associated with the realization of the project. When such complementarities prove to be effective they become valuable, turning the contribution of the team members into a system of practices that is by far superior to the sum of its individual parts (Jones and DeFillippi, 1996). The knowledge required to perform this complex task is diffused among several individuals, each of whom has a different responsibility, and it has a relevant interpretative component. The effectiveness with which individuals perform their tasks is contingent upon the interpretation of how others are simultaneously performing their tasks while adjusting to challenging environmental contingencies. For this collective task to be executed with precision a constant process of mutual adjustment and synchronization is required, to the point that 'when you find people you can work with you never want to give them up' (director Sydney Pollack quoted in Jones *et al.*, 1997: 12). Project participants are thus motivated to establish repeated ties with selected alters, which in turn foster the development of

relationship-specific learning and routines, such as cognitive schemata, patterns or gestalts, wich may deepen with multiple projects.

As the enactment of this shared knowledge requires a relatively stable collection of interacting members within the group, the disbanding of the film project organization, we submit, will not result in a high level of variation in the composition of teams over time. A high turnover would in fact disrupt the ability of members to draw upon experientially constructed schemata in order to operate in a synchronous fashion.

These ideas are grounds for believing that teams are the ultimate sources and carriers of the 'genetic legacy' that shape the genesis of film project organizations. We consolidated the above arguments as follows:

Hypothesis: *Project participants with complementary skills tend to establish mutual relational ties that will be reiterated across subsequent projects.*

The idea of complementariness purported here is akin to the concept of 'bilateral dependence' (Teece, 1986); that is, a critical *interdependence* among resources, and such that the single parts cannot stand out without the others, for only their joint contribution can lead to the successful achievement of the desired end.

DATA

In order to test our proposition we collected data from a sample of 783 movies produced and distributed in America by the seven Majors[3] and by the two largest independent producers (Miramax and New Line) over the five-year period 1995–1999.[4] Although the American feature film industry includes over 350 production companies (as accounted for by the Motion Picture Almanac), the seven historical Majors overwhelmingly dominate the industry, either directly, through their financial might, or indirectly, through distribution control. Miramax and New Line were included in order to reflect the increasingly significant market share gained by these two Independents (constantly above 6.7 per cent and 6.2 per cent respectively in the last seven years). Over the entire period these nine companies consistently captured a market share of approximately 95 per cent of the entire American box-office. Table 4.1 provides the five-year distribution of the 783 movies[5] by company.

For each movie of the sample we then identified a group of relevant project participants and we kept track of their pattern of collaborations for the five-year period. Project participants were identified through the Internet Movie Database (IMDB, 2001), which is an online source owned by

Amazon.com and largely supported by advertising. Most of the data provided by the Internet Movie Database are submitted on a voluntary basis and validated by an in-house staff of 70 members.

Table 4.1 Distribution of sampled movies by company

	1995	1996	1997	1998	1999	Total
20th Century Fox	15	16	17	13	4	**65**
Touchstone Pictures	4	8	6	13	14	**45**
Walt Disney Productions	3	4	10	11	11	**39**
Hollywood Pictures	14	9	6	6	5	**40**
Buena Vista Pictures	9	0	0	0	0	**9**
MGM	15	13	12	5	5	**50**
Paramount Pictures	17	15	20	15	10	**77**
TriStar Pictures	7	7	6	15	5	**40**
Columbia Pictures	24	21	18	5	13	**81**
Warner Bros.	25	22	26	15	10	**98**
New Line Cinema	20	15	14	11	8	**68**
Fine Line	1	3	8	0	0	**12**
Miramax Films	20	25	14	14	11	**84**
Universal Pictures	18	17	13	10	17	**75**
Total	192	175	171	133	113	**783**

In consideration of the great variety of professional figures that operate within the FPBE, the analysis was restricted to the following group of roles: director, cinematographer, editor, production designer and composer. This group includes some members of the so-called 'core team' (Goldman, 1983). This team represents the organizational heart of the film project during its shooting phase, as it includes all the key representatives from each of the departments into which the production crew is divided (Ascher and Pincus, 1999: 210). Although producers are undoubtedly a critical component of the core group too, and may sometimes have a part in decisions and choices made during the shooting phase, we decided to exclude them from the analysis since most of the sampled films had multiple producers, leading to complex attributive problems.

Overall, the 783 films reviewed involved a total of 1807 participants: 586 directors, 371 cinematographers, 477 editors, and 373 production designers. Only animation films were excluded from the sample because of the high specificity of tasks and roles.

Core Team Task Complementarities

The core team is a group of professionals to whom all the project members are ultimately responsible, and it revolves around the director. 'The director is the center, the person who coagulates the ideas and determines the final result' (director Philip Kaufman, quoted in Paul, 1979: 107). Like a complex resource, the director is the repository of an overarching combinative capability, and orchestrates all the crucial interaction processes within the core team (Boschetti, 1999). Not surprisingly it is the director who often chooses the main components of the troupe. Let us look at the nature of these relations.

Director–editor   The editor, in consultation with the director, articulates film timing and pauses, defining its most appropriate cinematographic rhythm (Ascher and Pincus, 1999). Almost every director has a preference for one editor who, as he/she does, understands their style and gives them what they want (Chion, 1999). Editors know the technique and have an excellent perception of film timing and visual pace, yet only the director has an all-round vision of the work and a clear sense of the rhythm that would serve it best. Free and open communication is necessary, as well as a personal relationship that is fine-tuned on the same wavelength (Alvarez and Svejenova, 2002b).

Director–cinematographer   The cinematographer's task is to provide the movie with a visual nuance suitable to the director's sensitivity and visual aspirations. Director Jerry Schatzberg emphasizes the need to dialog often and reach a common point of view with the cinematographer (Paul, 1979). 'The fact that the director is using the camera to tell his story demands absolute team work between the cinematographer and the director if anything worthwhile is to be accomplished'.

Director–production designer   The production designer is the head of a film's art department. He/she is responsible for providing 'shape and soul' to the physical setting wherein the characters are to move. Together with the director and the cinematographer, he/she works out the creative vision of the film. He/she must fully understand the intentions of the director to help to give the film its own style (Chiarini, 1965).

Director–composer   The composer discusses and defines with the director themes and narration passages to be underscored in order to translate the film musically. 'Collaboration with the director is indispensable... the work with the director, discussions regarding the style of the music and the development of ideas proceed step by step with the shooting of the film' (composer Roman Vlad, quoted in Manvell and Huntley, 1969: 199–201); and similarly composer Dag Wiren notes, 'the director says when he wants music and what he wants it to express. ... The worst sort of collaboration is when the director leaves everything to the composer'.

Given the tight complementarities that exist between the activity of the film director and each of these project participants, we postulate that these individuals will tend to establish stable trajectories of collaboration across multiple projects over time. We translated this idea into the following empirical sub-hypothesis:

Sub-hypothesis: *The director tends to establish stable patterns of interaction with each of the core members over subsequent projects. (Figure 4.1 illustrates this idea.)*

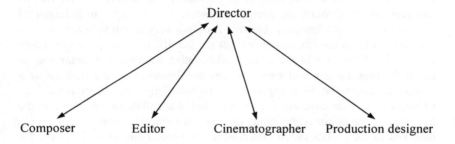

Figure 4.1 Sub-hypothesis

METHOD AND MEASURES

In order to test our hypotheses we measured project participants' collaborative stability building on Blau's (1977) index of heterogeneity. We then tested whether this stability was higher among those pairs of positions (directors–editors, directors–cinematographers, editors–cinematographers, and so on) that our hypotheses indicate.

In this study we observe collaboration ties between persons, as defined by their joint participation in the making of movies. A tie exists between two individuals if they jointly participated in the making of one or more movies in the period of observation. These ties connect persons; however we are interested in assessing patterns of collaborations across positions. We must then establish a correspondence between persons and positions. An ambiguity is raised by the fact that an individual could be observed in different positions in the making of different movies, or even in the same movie. We dealt with this ambiguity by coding the collaboration ties separately; for instance, of person X as a director and of person X as a production designer, as if they were different persons. For any pair of persons observed in the period (for instance, person X as director and person Y as editor) we measured the relation of collaboration implied by their joint participation in the making of one or more movies.

Measuring Collaboration

We coded as null the collaborative relation between two of the observed individuals if they never participated together in the making of a movie. In all other cases, we measured the strength of their collaboration throughout the period of observation. The number of movies in which both the individuals had participated through the period of observation could be an indicator of their collaboration's intensity, but this is only a very rough measure. It does not account for some circumstances that are specific to a single movie. There is indeed a difference in the actual collaboration between a director and an editor if three editors and two directors are involved in the making of a movie, as compared to a movie that involves only one director and one editor. In the first case we can expect that the collaboration between the director and the editor is somewhat diluted; consequently more weight should be given to the collaboration observed in the second situation. To allow for this, we coded the strength of collaboration relations by taking into account the total number of persons who occupied each type of position in the making of any single movie. The coding proceeded as follows:

1. The measure of one person's participation in the making of a movie was coded as the reciprocal of the number of individuals who occupied the same position. Thus, for instance, in the case of a movie with two directors and three editors each director's participation would be coded as $1/2$ and that of each editor $1/3$.
2. The collaboration between two individuals, implied by their joint participation in the making of a single movie, was measured as the product of their individual participations in that movie. Thus the amount of collaboration within any director–editor pair in the example above would have been coded as $1/6$.
3. This is not yet the total collaboration between i and j in the observed period, but only the measure of their collaboration in one movie. We

measured the total collaboration between individuals i and j as the sum of their collaborations across all the movies in which they both participated

We summarized these total collaborations in a square matrix $(897 \times 897)^6$ whose ij-th cell represents the cumulative strength of the collaborations between i and j in the observed period; the matrix is symmetric. We grouped the rows and columns according to the (unique) position each individual occupied, and obtained a partitioned matrix where all the values of the collaboration relations among, for instance, all the directors and all the editors were grouped in the same matrix sector.

Measuring Collaborative Stability

We measured how dispersed the collaborations of each individual with other individuals in a given position were; we computed separate measures for an individual's collaborations with others in each type of position; for example, for any director in the core member's matrix, we computed a dispersion index for his collaborations with production designers, another one for his collaborations with cinematographers, and so on. The lower the dispersion is, the more concentrated over a few individuals are the collaborations of the director through the period of observation, which in turn means that the collaborative stability of the director with those specific individuals in a given position is high in the observed period.

We used Blau's index of heterogeneity (1977). This measures how evenly a quantity is distributed across a number of categories. In our case the quantity is the sum of the individual collaborations over the people observed in a given position, while the potential collaborators among whom the total collaboration of the individual can be distributed take up the role of the categories; let c be their number. Blau's index of heterogeneity is a positive number whose maximum value depends on c and varies across different individuals who participated in different movies. To account for this we standardized the index by dividing for its maximum value. We took c as the number of positions of a given type observed across all movies in which the individual participated. In the case of a director's collaborations with editors, c was the total number of editor positions available across all movies in which the director participated.

We summarized the standardized heterogeneities in a matrix sized 897×5, which is partitioned in the same way as described above for the collaborations intensity matrix. Now, however, each matrix sector includes only one column because the collaborations of each individual with all the others in a given position are summarized in a single heterogeneity index.

Our hypotheses translate in the expectation that these heterogeneities are lower on average (that is, collaborations are more concentrated, and collaborative stability is higher) with regard to certain pairs of positions; that is, within certain sectors of the partitioned matrices.

The analysis proceeded as follows:

- For exploratory purposes, we computed the average heterogeneities in any pair of positions and compared the resulting pattern with that implied by our hypotheses.
- We then tested our hypotheses by grouping the heterogeneities in two sets, those expected to be relatively high and those expected to be lower according to the hypotheses, and tested the mean difference across the two sets.

RESULTS

In order to simplify the comparison between the hypothesis and the empirical evidence we translated our hypothesis into an equivalent *hypothesis matrix*. Shaded cells within the hypothesis matrix represent our theoretical expectations (a higher concentration of collaborations between individuals; that is, lower values of heterogeneity indexes). Hypothesis and results matrixes, together with the corresponding t-test, are reported below.

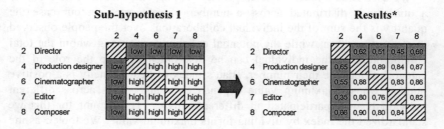

Figure 4.2   Core members: sub-hypothesis 1 and matrix of results

As illustrated in Figure 4.2, the results are fully coherent with our theoretical expectations. Collaborations among core members tend to concentrate along clearly defined relational trajectories. As predicted, the higher concentration measures correspond to the relation between the director and each of the other core members.

Table 4.2   Core members: t-test

	N	Mean	Std. deviation	Difference (low–high) Mean	Difference (low–high) Std. error[1]
Low	946	0,5484	0,4469		
				-0,2896*	0,0160
High	1798	0,8380	0,2815		

Notes:
*p<0,01 with equal variances not assumed.
[1]Equal variances not assumed.

The t-test is significant at the 0.01 (Table 4.2), suggesting that interactions tend to be more recurrent between project participants with critically complementary roles.

DISCUSSION AND IMPLICATIONS

Our research, we believe, stimulates a variety of reflection cues for the organizational field and contributes some original insights into the functioning of project-based organizations.

While in a project-based environment firms are akin to transient entities nurturing a continuous process of formation and dissolution, our results suggest that complementary resources, namely project participants performing complementary tasks within film projects, tend to develop recurrent combinatorial paths which, in turn, may counterbalance the absence of a permanent organizational structure. This process acts as a bridge between the transient nature of the project and the accumulation of organizational capabilities over time. The dissolution of the firm is then only part of the story. A better story is maybe to think of the project-based organization as a 'community of practice' (Brown and Duguid, 1991) or as an 'ecology' (Grabher, 2002) resulting from the coalescence of smaller communities that carry the organizational skills of the industry.

Second, while our analysis only allowed us to sketch a suggestive overview of the complex organizational processes – arrangements and decisions that shape the functioning of film projects – the results clearly support the necessity to shift the analysis from the level of the organization to the meso- and micro-levels of team and social interaction. By focusing on the collaborative patterns established by team members over time we provided evidence of a process of organizational persistence otherwise hardly detectable. Thus, while these firms exhibit no ostensible history-based path to build upon and drive their future behavior, team members working repeatedly together may trigger patterned sequences of learned behavior. These, in turn, may allow the redeployment of past experience in new situations. On the basis of these ideas, project-based organizations in the film industry were envisioned as an ephemeral medium whose functioning is molded by the continuous re-enactment of knowledge and skills that, like an *organizational legacy*, are transmitted and evolve via teams of professionals from project to project. This legacy, we submit, contributes to the dissemination of practices, routines and knowledge throughout the industry and represents a distinctive trait of the organizational dynamics that shape this context.

Third, because project participants in the film industry are embedded within a socially dense and well-localized professional community (Jones, 1996), projects represent as many occasions of learning for the community they belong to as for the participants. Thus, patterns of collaboration that survive the disruptive pressures of the environment and endure (in somewhat stable formats) through multiple ventures may act as repositories of experience that, project after project, to generate and underpin the collective memory of the community. Aldrich, lamenting a still too scarce understanding of the analytical levels involved in the selective mechanisms shaping the inception, evolution and death of organizations, noted (1999: 337–8):

we have only limited empirical evidence with which to evaluate the various claims regarding the most important unit of selection [...] Are organizations inseparable bundles of routines and competencies on which selection forces operate, selecting entire entities? Such a view would largely negate the notion of population level knowledge, for how could surviving organizations contribute anything to it? Or are organizations merely carriers of population level routines and competencies, and thus temporary repositories of the real stuff of organizational evolution?

Although our study delved into a somewhat peculiar segment of our modern economy and a still relatively emergent reality – the project-based organization – we believe it offered at least some hints for addressing these issues. Our findings seem to suggest that the Hollywood film industry is the object of selective forces acting upon group level routines, which then become the real units of environmental selection. In this context, routines, practices and capabilities flow through organizations, yet do not fully define them (Aldrich, 1999).

Limitations and Futre Directions

Noting the limitations of our study may provide ideas for extension and improvement. Because we only focused on the pattern of collaborations across firms no inference was drawn as to the impact of these dynamics on the performance of projects. While the establishment of stable trajectories of interaction seems to be a widespread practice of the industry, it may well be the case that enduring excessively tight and close cliques of collaboration would translate into diminishing returns for the team and, hence, for the organization. As Berman *et al.* (2002) have illustrated in the context of NBA basketball, while the stock of tacit knowledge is likely to accumulate as the members of a team learn to interact with each other, after a period of time the value of this stock of knowledge may begin to decay, owing to a process of knowledge ossification. Skills become routinized around a taken-for-granted way of interacting and internal variation is hindered. This idea is mirrored by director Peter Weir's observation[7] that when you stick to the same people for a certain period you may run out of what he calls 'creative frictions', that is, interactions that may trigger ideas and spark creativity. Thus you have to be ready to change. On the other hand, it takes a while to track the career credits of such an acclaimed director as Steven Spielberg, to discover that in the last ten years he has consistently and constantly collaborated with a stable nucleus of key members.[8] It would then be interesting to understand what circumstances may lead someone to prefer one strategy to the other, and how the outcome of this choice might be affected by internal as well as external contingencies. For example, one important internal factor with clear impact on this choice is the level of team cohesion. Cohesion refers to the desire that individual members have to remain part of the team (Cartwright, 1968). One avenue for future inquiry would be to assess the level of team cohesiveness and investigate how this may translate in terms of team capability and team persistence over time. This and similar internal processes merit closer qualitative and longitudinal examination. On the external side, the degree of uncertainty that surrounds the project appears equally critical in affecting the viability of one strategy versus the other. For example, projects in which the desired level of experimentation is high might be better off when a high degree of variation is allowed. In such an instance, having highly experienced teams involved in the production process might result in myopia or mindlessness towards promising variations (Levinthal and March, 1993; Levinthal and Rerup, 2003), whereas a more loose system of interactions could lead to a greater openness to ideas and change (Katz, 1982). This and related areas deserve further attention.

CONCLUSION

Using knowledge-based arguments as the conceptual scaffolding for our theoretical reasoning, we provided some original insights as to the organizational dynamics shaping a project-based environment, such as the American motion picture industry. Film projects were equated to knowledge-based organizations striving to manage highly specialized and heterogeneous knowledge assets in order to achieve a 'one shot' creative outcome. Venturing into a landscape ruffled by continuous waves of organizational formation and dissolution and hindered by uncertainties of all kinds (Faulkner and Anderson, 1987), these organizations have no choice but to be quick and effective in integrating the knowledge at hand into the complex process that leads from concept to screen. But even with the most careful design, the route of this journey remains partially obscure, often to be unveiled by trial and error (Weick, 1976), sometimes enlightened by the occurrence of serendipitous discoveries. Unfortunately, in coping with these difficulties, project members cannot draw on the organizational memory of the firm, simply because the firm in itself is an episodic event and as such it has no history, no past experiences to encode into an enduring set of routines that may prompt choices and guide behavior. Like boats designed for sailing the sea one time only, film projects cease to exist when this one-way journey is over. Crew members, however, do remain, and journey by journey they establish ties, develop patterns of collaboration and set up working teams. In each of these teams individuals are assigned to specific roles and responsibilities, while no single individual has the full knowledge required to undertake the role of others on the boat. Yet this knowledge has a strong mutual dimension. The effectiveness with which individuals perform their prescribed tasks is contingent upon their understanding of how other crew members are simultaneously acting to perform their tasks. Thus the knowledge is diffused, and because the task is complex and must be accomplished quickly, and implies a high degree of mutual adjustment, it is also experiential. It can only be built over time, via team members practicing repeatedly with each other. Such teams, we have contended, serve as the carriers of practices and capabilities necessary to execute the task and 'lead the boat' to its destination.

This research represents progress toward unlocking the organizational dynamics that shape the functioning of a project-based environment. Because film projects are temporary creative systems, they have much in common with scientific projects, consulting teams, task forces, and other short-term groups (Morley and Silver, 1977). Thus our findings should be of interest to managers of such groups. Clearly, generalizations from the film industry to the business world should be made with care. Replicating our analysis in other project-based settings will be crucial in fully exploring the power of our arguments. There is more work to be done.

NOTES

1. Based on this decision, in 1948 the American Supreme Court banned studios' collusive practices and forward integration strategies. As a result, the value of some of the main strategic assets of those firms was suddenly wiped out (Boschetti, 1999).
2. Personal communication with one of the authors (December, 1999).
3. Universal, Paramount, Warner Bros. Columbia-TriStar, Disney, 20th Century Fox and Metro-Goldwyn-Mayer (MGM).
4. 783 roughly corresponds to 85 per cent of the totality of feature films distributed by these nine companies over the five-year period.
5. Under the 'Buena Vista' brand are distributed all films from Walt Disney Pictures, which, in turn, comprises several 'divisions': Walt Disney Pictures; Touchstone Pictures; Hollywood Pictures, Miramax Films (Schatz, 1997). The Sony Group distributes movies via Columbia Pictures and TriStar Pictures. These two Majors, in fact, have been part of the Japanese giant since 1989. New Line is an Independent branch of the Time Warner Group. The 'New Line' brand includes New Line Cinema and Fine Line. The latter was indeed created in 1991 as a division of New Line.
6. Since we were interested in examining how professionals interact over subsequent projects, we only focused on professionals who had contributed to multiple movies. Thus 897 is the number of core members who took part in at least two projects over the five-year period. The number was obtained by subtracting 910, which is the number of individuals who contributed only one movie, from 1807 (the total number of core members, as described on page 15).
7. Personal communication with one of the authors.
8. Namely, Janusz Kaminski (cinematographer); John Williams (composer), Michael Kahn (editor).

REFERENCES

Acheson, K. and C. Maule (1994), 'Understanding Hollywood's organization and continuing success', *Journal of Cultural Economics*, **18**, 271–300.
Aldrich, H.E. (1999), *Organizations Evolving*, London: Sage Publications.
Alvarez, J.L. and S. Svejenova (2002a), 'Symbiotic careers in movie making: Pedro and Agustin Almodovar', in M. Peiperl, M. Arthur and N. Anand

(eds), *Career Creativity: Explorations in the Remaking of Work*, Oxford: Oxford University Press.

Alvarez, J.L. and S. Svejenova (2002b) 'Imprints of creative styles on project network governance', Working Paper presented at the 2002 Academy of Management Meeting.

Amit, R. and P.J.H. Schoemaker (1993), 'Strategic assets and organizational rent', *Strategic Management Journal*, **14**, 33–46.

Argote, L. (1999), *Organizational Learning: Creating, Retaining and Transferring Knowledge*, Boston, Kluwer Academic Publishers.

Ascher, S. and E. Pincus (1999), *The Filmmaker's Handbook: A Comprehensive Guide for the Digital Age*, New York, Plume.

Baker, W.E. and R.R. Faulkner (1991), 'Role as resource in the Hollywood film industry', *American Journal of Sociology*, **97** (2), September, 279–309.

Balio, T. (1985), *The American Film Industry*, Madison: The University of Wisconsin Press.

Barney, J.B. (1991), 'Firm resources and sustained competitive advantage', *Journal of Management*, **17** (1), 99–120.

Berman, S., J. Down and C. Hill (2002), 'Tacit knowledge as a source of competitive advantage in the National Basketball Association', *Academy of Management Journal*, **45** (1), 13–31.

Blau, P. (1977), *Inequality and Heterogeneity*, New York: Free Press.

Boschetti, C. (1999), *Risorse e strategia d'impresa – il caso delle imprese cinematografiche*, Bologna: Società editrice Il Mulino.

Brown J.S. and P. Duguid (1991), 'Organizational learning and communities of practice: toward a unified view of working, learning and innovation' , *Organization Science*, **1** (1), 40–47.

Cartwright, D. (1968), 'The nature of group cohesiveness', in D. Cartwright and A. Zander (eds), *Group Dynamics: Research and Theory* 3rd Edn., London: Tavistock Publications.

Caves, R. (2000), *Creative Industries: Contracts between Art and Commerce*, Cambridge: Harvard University, Press: section III, IV.

Chiarini L. (1965), *Arte e tecnica del film*, Universale Laterza.

Chion M. (1999*), I mestieri del cinema* Santhià: Grafica Santhiatese.

Conant, M. (1960), *Antitrust in the Motion Picture Industry: Economic and Legal Analysis*, Berkeley and Los Angeles: University of California Press.

DeFillippi, R.J. and M.B. Arthur (1998), 'Paradox in project-based Enterprise: the case of film making', *California Management Review*, **40** (2), 125–139.

Demsetz, H. (1991), 'The theory of the firm revisited', in O.E. Williamson and S.G. Winter (eds), *The Nature of The Firm*, Oxford: Oxford University Press.

Dosi, G., R. Nelson and S. Winter (2000) (eds), *The Nature and Dynamics of Organizational Capabilities*, Oxford and New York: Oxford University Press.

Eccles, R. (1981), 'The quasi-firm in the construction industry', *Journal of Economic Behavior and Organization*, 2, 335–57.

Eisenhardt, K.M. and J.A. Martin (2000), 'Dynamic capabilities: what are they?', *Strategic Management Journal*, 21, 1105–21.

Eliashberg, J. and M.S. Sawhney (1994), 'Modeling goes to Hollywood: predicting individual differences in movie enjoyment', *Management Science* (40), 1151–73.

Faulkner, R.R. and A.B. Anderson (1987), 'Short-term projects and emergent careers: evidence from Hollywood', *American Journal of Sociology*, 92, 879–909.

Goldman, W. (1983), *Adventures in the Screen Trade*, New York: Scribner.

Goodman, P.L. and P.L. Goodman (1972), 'Theater as a temporary system', *California Management Review*, 15, 103–8.

Goodman, R.A. and P.L. Goodman (1976), 'Some management issues in temporary systems: a study of the professional development and manpower in the theater case', *Administrative Science Quarterly*, 21, 494–500.

Grabher, G. (2002), 'Cool projects, boring institutions: temporary collaboration in social context', *Regional Studies*, 36 (3), 205–14.

Grant, R.M. (1996a), 'Toward a knowledge-based theory of the firm', *Strategic Management Journal*, 17 (Winter Special Issue), 109–22.

Grant, R.M. (1996b), 'Prospering in dynamically-competitive environments: organizational capability as knowledge integration', *Organization Science*, 7 (4), July–August, 375–87.

IMDB (2001), www.imdb.com.

Jones, C. (1996), 'Careers project-networks: the case of film industry', in M.B. Arthur and D.M. Russeau (eds), *The Boundaryless Career*, Oxford University Press.

Jones, C. (2001), 'Coevolution of entrepreneurial careers, institutional rules and competitive dynamics in American film', 1895–1920', *Organization Studies*, 22, 911–44.

Jones, C. and R.J. DeFillippi (1996), 'Back to the future in film: combining industry and self-knowledge to meet career challenges of the 21st century', *Academy of Management Executive*, 10 (4), 89–104.

Jones, C., W.S. Hesterly, B. Lichtenstein, S.P. Borgatti and S.P. Tallman (1997), 'Intangible assets of teams: how human, social and team capital influence project performance in the film industry', Working Paper, FilmTeam v7, 24 June.

Katz, R. (1982), 'The effects of group longevity on project communication and performance', *Administrative Science Quarterly*, **27**, 81–104.

Kerrigan F. and N. Culkin (1999), 'A reflection on the American domination of the film industry: an historical and industrial perspective', *Working Paper, Film Industry Research Group, University of Hertfordshire – Business School* (http://www.herts.ac.uk/business/groups/firg/research%20at%20FiRG.htm).

Kogut, B. and U. Zander (1992), 'Knowledge of the firm, combinative capabilities, and the replication of technology', *Organization Science*, **3**, 383–97.

Levinthal, D.A. and J.G. March (1993), 'The myopia of learning', *Strategic Management Journal*, **14**, 95–112.

Levinthal, D.A and C. Rerup (2003), 'Crossing an apparent chasm: mindful and less mindful organizational learning', Working Paper of the Wharton School, The University of Pennsylvania.

Lorenzen, M. and L. Frederiksen (2003), 'Experimental music: product innovation, project networks and dynamic capabilities in the pop music industry', *Industry and Innovation*.

Mariotti, S. and G.C. Cainarca (1986), 'The evolution of transaction governance in the textile-clothing industry', *Journal of Economic Behavior and Organization* (I), 351–74.

Meyerson, D., K.E. Weick and R.M. Kramer (1996), 'Swift trust and temporary groups', in R.M. Kramer and T.R. Tyler (eds), *Trust in Organizations: Frontiers of Theory and Research*, Thousand Oaks, CA: Sage Publications, pp. 166–95.

Miller, D. and J. Shamsie (1996), 'The resource-based view of the firm in two environments: the Hollywood film studios from 1936 to 1965', *Academy of Management Journal*, **39** (3), 519–43.

Mintzberg, H. (1979), *The Structuring of Organizations*, Englewood Cliffs, NJ: Prentice Hall.

Morley, E. and A. Silver (1977), 'A film director's approach to managing creativity', *Harvard Business Review*, Mar/Apr, **55** (2).

Nelson, R.R. and S.G. Winter (1982), *An Evolutionary Theory of Economic Change*, Boston: Belknap Press of Harvard University Press.

Nonaka, I. (1991), 'The knowledge-creating company', *Harvard Business Review*, November–December, 96–104.

Paul, W. (1979), 'Hollywood harakiri', in A. Aprà (ed.), *Hollywood 1969–1979 Industria, Autori, Film*, Venezia: Marsilio.

Robins, J.A. (1993), 'Organization as strategy: restructuring production in the film industry', *Strategic Management Journal*, **14**, 103–18.

Rumelt, R. (1984), 'Towards a strategic theory of the firm', in R. Lamb (ed.), *Competitive Strategic Management*, Englewood Cliffs, NJ: Prentice Hall, pp. 556–70

Saxenian. A. (1996), 'Beyond boundaries: open labor markets and learning in Silicon Valley', in M.B. Arthur and D.M. Russeau (eds), *The Boundaryless Career*, New York: Oxford University Press.

Squire, J.E. (1983), *The Movie Business Book*, New York: Fireside Books.

Starbuck, W.H. (1992), 'Learning by knowledge intensive firms', *Journal of Management Studies*, **29** (6), 713–40.

Teece, D. (1986), 'Profiting from technological innovation', *Research Policy*, **15**, 286–305.

Teece, D., G. Pisano, and A. Shuen (1997), 'Dynamic capabilities and strategic management', *Strategic Management Journal*, **18**, 509–33.

Thompson, J.D. (1967), *Organizations in Action*, New York: McGraw-Hill.

Weick, K.E. (1976), 'Educational organizations as loosely coupled systems', *Administrative Science Quarterly*, **21**, Jg., S. 1–19.

5. Knowledge transfer as a key process for firm learning: the role of local institutions in industrial districts

F. Xavier Molina-Morales and M. Teresa Martìnez-Fernàndez

INTRODUCTION

Social networks are an important part of the learning process by which firms not only discover new opportunities and obtain new knowledge, but also improve their already existing knowledge by interacting with one another. In fact, research on the knowledge-based view of the firm has suggested that social networks facilitate the creation of knowledge within organizations (for example, Kogut and Zander, 1992; Tsai, 2000).

However, a review of the social literature reveals contradictory perspectives about the optimal structure and content of the ties involved in social networks. Thus the closure or cohesive view (Coleman, 1988, 1990; Uzzi, 1996, 1997) stresses the benefits of a dense structure and strong ties in providing common norms and values, and the transmission of tacit knowledge and high-quality information. In contrast, the structural holes and weak ties view (Burt, 1992, 1997; Granovetter, 1973) emphasizes the benefits of a dispersed structure and weak ties in providing new and unique knowledge and opportunities through the brokerage position held by actors – a position that cannot be attained by unconnected actors.

Other authors have recently suggested that, rather than being contradictory perspectives, both views are in fact useful in explaining benefits for different strategic purposes. In other words, the cohesive characterization is suitable for *exploiting* existing knowledge and technologies while the dispersed characterization is much better for *exploring* new knowledge and technologies (Rowley *et al.*, 2000).

In this context, geographical proximity between firms (that is, being located within an industrial district) influences and shapes resources embedded in firms' social networks (Becattini, 1990; Porter, 1990). Proximity implies frequency and redundancy in relations, which are primary factors determining the structural and relational dimensions of social networks. In short, it can be suggested that geographical proximity is associated with social networks consisting of dense and strong ties that are suitable for pursuing exploitation strategies.

Following this line of thinking, the characterization of industrial district networks may evidence the existence of disadvantages in exploring strategies. In fact, the literature provides several examples of the limited capacity of industrial district firms to face radical external technological changes (Glasmeier, 1991). To deal with this challenge, we propose that local institutions, such as academic and research institutions, trade associations, industrial policy agents and so forth, can play a role as intermediary agents and therefore facilitate firms' access to new and exclusive knowledge. As a result of this division of labor in the districts, firms may build an optimal mix of ties, where connection with local institutions provides advantages as regards exploring, and intense relationships with the rest of the district firms enable existing knowledge and technologies to be exploited in an efficient manner.

We draw on the above theoretical foundations to analyze the causal relation between the use of local institutions by district firms and their innovation outcomes. A sample of 220 Spanish industrial firms was used to determine the differences between district and non-district firms in terms of participation by local institutions and in terms of innovation outcomes.

This chapter is structured as follows. First, we describe the theoretical foundations of social network perspectives and we go on to characterize the industrial district as a social network. Second, we describe the method employed, and finally we comment on the results and the implications that can be drawn from them.

THEORETICAL BACKGROUND

The Industrial District and the Social Capital Perspective

Social capital can be defined as the 'sum of resources that accrue to a firm by virtue of possessing a durable network of interfirm relationships' (Bourdieu and Wacquant, 1992: 119). As indicated by the definition, the focus here is on access to and flow of resources; that is, knowledge, information and other forms of capital.

Since its introduction, social capital has received considerable attention and researchers have extended the logic of social capital to the firm level (Burt, 1992; Tsai and Ghoshal, 1998). In effect, firms can be seen as social actors and in carrying out their business they establish a variety of interfirm ties. Such ties include relationships with customers, suppliers, trade and professional associations, and advisors, and enable a variety of information, knowledge and other forms of capital to be exchanged among firms. These external relationships thus represent social capital in different ways. They are channels of information that create opportunities for firms and, additionally, interactions among firms establish obligations and expectations that are based on norms of reciprocity and equity. Social capital is important because it enables us to explain differences in performance among firms.

Social theorists have presented and discussed different mechanisms and outcomes associated with social capital. The traditional perspective of social capital (Coleman, 1988, 1990) stresses the positive effect of the cohesive or dense structure of the networks on the production of social norms and sanctions that facilitate trust and cooperative exchanges. In the same vein and with regard to the relational dimension of social capital (Nahapiet and Ghoshal, 1998), the strong tie argument suggests that it provides organizations with two primary advantages: it enables exchanges of high–quality information and tacit knowledge to take place while also serving as a social control mechanism that regulates the interdependencies in partnerships (Uzzi, 1996, 1997). On the other hand, the structural holes approach (Burt, 1992, 1997) proposes an alternative perspective by advocating the benefits that are to be derived from access to diverse information and from brokerage opportunities linked to having non-redundant relationships. Likewise, Granovetter (1973) argues for the strength of the weak tie, and emphasizes how weak ties allow an actor to access new and exclusive information.

More recently, a number of authors have attempted to harmonize these perspectives. Rowley *et al.* (2000) stated that both perspectives are useful in explaining benefits for different strategic purposes. According to these authors, it is possible to establish a number of conditions under which firms are better connected in each type of network. One of the primary elements that defines the advantages firms can gain from each type of network is the extent to which their strategies are aimed at *exploring* emerging innovations and other significant changes in the environment or, on the contrary, are aimed at *exploiting* existing technologies, capabilities and information. Dyer and Nobeoka (2000) studied the evolution of Toyota's network of suppliers and came to the conclusion that this network was designed for exploiting purposes since it is built as a cohesive structure with strong ties. Another example can be found in Gargiulo and Benassi (2000). These authors suggested that cohesive social bonds could jeopardize the flexibility of firms, and therefore establish the need for a tradeoff between flexibility and safety in the network. In similar terms, Koka and Prescott (2002) used the three dimensions of social capital – volume, diversity and richness of ties – to argue that their effect on firms' performance depends on the variability or stability of the environment.

What kind of social network is generated within an industrial district? Since dispersion prevents or hinders the generation of the routines and redundancies of the interactions that are produced in face-to-face interactions, proximity between actors can be expected to induce frequency and redundancy of the ties (McEvily and Zaheer, 1999). In fact, the outcomes of this characterization of social capital have often been discussed in the industrial district literature. Consequently, proximity shapes social networks by producing a dense structure and strong ties, and firms therefore benefit from efficiency in *exploiting* existing opportunities by sharing high-quality information, tacit knowledge and cooperative exchanges.

Frost (2001) established a link between exploitation/exploration and the location of firms' external knowledge sources. This idea fits into what may be described as the strategic perspective of external sources of innovation (Powell *et al.,* 1996). Although in the same vein, a somewhat different line of thinking emphasizes the emerging properties of such networks and their embeddedness (Granovetter, 1985) in the social relations of technological innovation. Saxenian (1994), for example, notes that school, career and friendship ties are important mechanisms through which external technical knowledge is located, accessed and assimilated. Bianchi and Bellini (1991: 488) argued that innovation networks are to an important extent underpinned by 'social solidarity', which is best sustained through constant interaction and geographic proximity. Finally, Schrader (1991) and Von Hippel (1988) suggested that the norm of reciprocity is a governing feature of knowledge-sharing activity between actors in technological communities.

How can firms that are redundantly connected with other participants in an industrial district gain access to new and external information and opportunities at the same time? Social capital authors have suggested that firms may design a portfolio of ties (Uzzi, 1997) in order to combine properties from both characterizations of social networks, that is, dense and strong ties and disperse and weak ties. In the context of territorial networks we suggest that, rather than creating this portfolio internally, firms can use external parties (which are nevertheless still within the network) to connect themselves with disperse and weak tie networks. What we are suggesting is that individual firms may intensify internal relationships with district firms and maintain a single connection with other district actors so as to be able to use them to contact external disperse networks. Among these third parties we focus on local institutions and more particularly those which carry out activities related to research and innovation.

The Role of Local Institutions in Industrial Districts

The existence of local institutions in industrial districts has been widely discussed in the literature. Indeed the industrial district has also been viewed as a field of political action. Although a wide variety of arrangements exists, in general, there is a set of both private and public institutions within the industrial district that carry out supporting activities. For the purposes of this research, we define local institutions as locally oriented organizations that provide firms in the region with a host of collective support services. Examples of local institutions are technical assistance centers, universities, vocational training centers, local research institutes, and trade and professional associations.

Local institutions having links with external networks may provide the industrial district with new ideas and concepts that are continually being refined because of internal redundancy, proximity and transactional intensity. Consequently, firms can take advantage of having networks of ties with local institutions that provide a feasible source of information on the options available to enhance the firms' capabilities. This implies, on the one hand, a high propensity for experimentation, monitoring, information-processing and knowledge extraction and requires, on the other hand, network management of the kind described in Cooke and Morgan (1998).

As intermediaries, local institutions facilitate net value for firms by compiling and disseminating knowledge, as well as by reducing search costs. Besides providing specific support services and other resource benefits to local firms, local institutions act as repositories for knowledge and opportunities about innovations. Because these institutions interact with a large number of firms within the geographical cluster, they are exposed to a wide variety of solutions to organizational challenges. Local institutions use their broad experience gained from observing others who have dealt with similar problems to compile and disseminate summaries about capabilities and routines (Suchman, 1994). Indeed, local institutions facilitate managerial innovation by providing access to information and resources, which in turn enable firms to acquire new, and to extend existing, innovation capabilities (McEvily and Zaheer, 1999). Local institutions also reduce the search costs that arise from locating external sources of the knowledge and specialized know-how that is critical for the district firms. By maintaining an extensive network of ties, intermediaries (local institutions) generate search economies.

Individual firms in the industrial district can spend a substantial part of their time on developing other activities (Galaskiewicz, 1985). Therefore, rather than having many contacts with different external networks, a firm can maintain a single connection with the intermediary that specializes in providing access to information and resources. It can be said that local institutions serve as go-betweens for potential exchange partners that have complementary interests and transfer information but are otherwise unconnected. Rather than all firms being linked to one another, each of them can maintain a single connection with the local institution that specializes in providing access to information about potential exchange partners.

As can be seen in Figure 5.1, local institutions fulfill a role as network intermediaries for participating firms by serving as repositories of knowledge and by reducing search costs. Hence local institutions benefit firms by facilitating the exchange and combination, or the acquisition, of knowledge resources and consequently by creating net value for firms. We can express the proposition as follows:

Proposition: In the context of one particular regional/national economy, local institutions may act as intermediary agents, thus benefiting firms in their exploring activities.

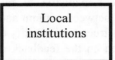

Benefits for clustered firms
- repository of knowledge
- search costs
- intensive exchange and combination of resources

Figure 5.1   The role of local institutions in industrial districts

RESEARCH METHODOLOGY

The empirical research drew upon a sample of Spanish industrial firms located along the east coast of the country (in the Valencia region). Although there are some significant exceptions, SMEs are clearly the predominant components in the industrial structure of the Valencia region. Moreover the industrial district *model* can be considered to be a key factor in the development of the region. In fact, Ybarra (1991) identified as many as 11 different industrial districts using a quantitative criterion. These Valencian industrial districts are chiefly to be found in mature or traditional sectors. The similarities with respect to the Italian model are frequently mentioned – even as regards the goods they produce (textiles, footwear, toys, furniture, ceramic tiles and so on). Although there are certain differences between one Valencian industrial district and another (Benton, 1992), overall and in contrast to other Spanish regions they are relatively successful and have an important projection in the international markets.

The firms selected for our empirical research were intended to be representative examples of the manufacturing firms in the Valencian region. Using a public database (ARDAN)[1] enabled us to identify the address and four-digit Standard Industrial Classification (SIC) of the companies included in the study. Firms from 18 different industrial segments or SIC epigraphs were used and, in order to define the sample, a random stratified process was employed to select firms with an assignation that was proportional to their size and product segments.

Data were collected using questionnaires distributed among firms. These were face-to-face questionnaires and were addressed to the general manager of each firm or, if this was not possible, the person to whom the manager had delegated his powers and duties. We collected complete data for 220 firms, the basic characteristics of which are shown in Tables 5.1 and 5.2.

With regard to the bias owing to non-respondent firms, there were no significant differences in terms of size and product and technological attributes. Since few empirical precedents were available to guide the development of indicators, fieldwork carried out between autumn and winter of 2001 was used to help refine the choice of constructs and identify the most relevant items. Selection of items was also based on the feedback obtained from a pilot questionnaire.

Once firms had been classified as belonging to one of two clusters according to their industrial district affiliation, they were checked for significant differences with respect to size and product segments. However, none was found.

RESEARCH DESIGN

Variables

Industrial district affiliation

When we collected data from managers they were given a list of industrial districts and were asked directly whether or not their firms belonged to one of the industrial districts on that list. On that point, we followed Becattini (2002), who suggested that scholar classifications must take into account classifications made by the actors concerned. Affiliation to the Valencian districts was represented by a dummy variable, which had previously been used to identify membership in similar studies, such as those by Hundley and Jacobson (1998) and Geringer et al. (2000).

Participation of the local institutions

To operationalize this variable we used McEvily and Zaheer's (1999) definition as a basis and adapted the items to our specific case: (1) You received support for R&D activities from local institutions; (2) You or your employees received specific training by local academic institutions; (3) Your firm received benefits from research activities carried out by academic institutions; (4) You consider that you cannot receive support from external firms directly instead of from local institutions; and (5) You consider the role played by the trade associations in the local area strategically important. A 5-point Likert scale, where 1 = fully disagree and 5 = fully agree, was used and the variable was measured by obtaining an average of all the items for each firm. We ran Cronbach's alpha to validate the aggregation of items.

Net value creation

As pointed out by Hitt *et al.* (1997), innovation in the firm is important for the creation of value and we therefore decided to assess product and process innovation. Previous research focused on theoretical and empirical developments of collective learning, and the concept of innovative milieux (Maillat, 1998) has already described the territorial organization in which innovation processes originate. As a consequence of a constant and direct exchange of knowledge among diverse actors, we can expect incremental innovations to take place more often than radical ones. In fact, it is the face-to-face interactions between incrementally innovating actors that allow implicit knowledge to be exchanged and this process can be expected to accelerate as an industry becomes mature (Malmberg and Maskell, 1997; Steinle and Schiele, 2002).

In order to assess innovation, one indicator was included in the questionnaire that asked respondents to report the number of innovations that had been developed in their field of activity over the previous three years. This measurement of innovation is based on Tsai and Ghoshal (1998). We used the following items as an indicator of product and process innovation: (1) Number of developments or introductions of new materials; (2) Number of developments or introductions of new intermediate products; (3) Number of developments or introductions of new components; (4) Number of developments or introductions of new product attributes; (5) Number of developments or introductions of new equipment; (6) Improvements in the level of automation; (7) Number of new organizational methods of the productive activities; and (8) Use of new energy sources. To measure the variable, we added up the number of innovations reported for each item over the period of time under consideration. Cronbach's alpha was run to validate the aggregation of items.

Size (control variable)

Following Grant *et al.* (1988), we also controlled for other variables, such as firm size, that are likely to affect dependent variables. We considered that it may be easier for larger firms to acquire innovation capacities. In fact, the use of size as a control variable is strongly supported by previous studies (for example, Hitt *et al.*, 1997). The number of employees per firm was utilized to operationalize this control variable.

Analysis Techniques

First, descriptive statistics (mean and standard deviation) were calculated for all multiple-item variables and, in order to find the validity of the aggregation, the value of Cronbach's alpha was also determined for the same variables. Secondly, using Pearson's correlation matrix we analyzed the correlation existing in all pairs of variables. Finally, in order to test the hypothesis, ANOVA variance analysis was employed to compare means between district firms and non-district firms. Two different analyses were run: first we compared indicators of local institution participation and then we compared indicators of net value creation between both groups of firms. F-tests showed whether these mean values were significantly different or not.

Results

Table 5.1   Descriptive statistics, mean, standard deviation, Cronbach's alpha and bivariate correlation for all pairs of variables (district firms)

Variables	Mean	S. D.	α	1	2	3
(1) Innovation (product and process)	3.87	1.99	0.64	1.000		
(2) Local institutions	3.22	0.89	0.85	0.101*	1.000	
(3) Size	1.26	0.47	–	0.067	0.083	1.000

Notes:

N = 129.

Pearson's correlation is significant at the levels: *$p<0.10$; **$p<0.05$; ***$p<0.01$; ****$p<0.001$.

α = Cronbach's alpha for all multiple-item variables

Table 5.2   Descriptive statistics, mean, standard deviation, Cronbach's alpha and bivariate correlation for all pairs of variables (non-district firms)

Variables	Mean	S. D.	α	1	2	3
(1) Innovation (product and process)	3.34	2.01	0.67	1.000		
(2) Local institutions	2.89	0.96	0.85	−0.127	1.000	
(3) Size	1.25	0.51	–	0.034	0.073	1.000

Notes:
N = 91.
Pearson's correlation is significant at the levels: $*p<0.10$; $**p<0.05$; $***p<0.01$; $****p<0.001$.
α = Cronbach's alpha for all multiple-item variables.

Tables 5.1 and 5.2 show descriptive statistics; Cronbach's alpha for the multiple-item variables and Pearson's correlation for all combinations of variables. For district firms (Table 5.1), the least favorable Cronbach's alpha value corresponded to the multiple-item scale measuring innovation, with a score of 0.64. With respect to Table 5.2, the least favorable value of Cronbach's alpha for non-district firms also corresponded to the multiple-item scale measuring innovation, which scored 0.67. Bearing in mind that the scale had not been used before, the values of the alpha were within the limits of tolerance suggested in the literature (Malhotra, 1997). We thus considered the feasibility and coherency of the scales to be valid.

As regards Pearson's correlation matrix, we will only comment on the most notable relations among different groups of variables. In Table 5.1, for district firms, there is a significant correlation between the local institutions' variable and innovation. With respect to Table 5.2, for non-district firms, as expected no relation between the local institutions and innovation was found to be significant. More specifically, in both groups of firms there is no correlation between size and the remaining variables.

Overall, the results shown in Table 5.3 favor our proposition. Differences in means were statistically significant for the variable local institutions and for all items used, since the least favorable was significant at $p<0.05$. The proposition can be considered to have been confirmed, since local institutions participate to a significantly higher extent in the activities carried out by the members of the industrial district than external firms do for all items used. Findings confirm the association between district location and the participation of local institutions in some strategically relevant firm activities, as suggested by McEvily and Zaheer (1999), among others.

Table 5.3   Descriptive statistics, means, standard deviation and comparison of means

	ID members (N = 129)		non-ID members (N = 91)		
	Mean	**S.D.**	**Mean**	**S.D.**	**F**
LOCAL INSTITUTIONS	***3.35***	***0.76***	***2.89***	***0.96***	***15.259*******
(1) You received support for R&D activities from local institutions	3.35	1.07	3.01	1.33	4.335**
(2) You or your employees received specific training by local academic institutions	3.45	0.98	3.00	1.19	9.334***
(3) Your firm received benefits from academic institution research activities	3.31	1.17	2.87	1.22	7.329***
(4) You consider that you cannot receive support from external firms directly instead of from local institutions.	3.30	1.13	2.74	1.14	13.270****
(5) You consider the role played by the trade associations in the local area strategically important	3.34	1.03	2.86	1.20	10.314***

Notes:
** Difference between district members and non-members significant at p<0.05.
*** Difference between district members and non-members significant at p<0.01.
**** Difference between district members and non-members significant at p<0.001.

The results in Table 5.4 also lend support to the proposition and, as predicted, there is an association between the existence of local institutions in the industrial district and the creation of net value in the firm, as measured in terms of the number of innovations. The results of the comparison between members of the industrial district and external firms indicated statistically significant differences between them. Consequently, findings suggested that district firms benefit from the existence of this common factor and present a higher rate of creation of value. Findings supporting the competitive superiority of district firms are in line with previous studies (for example, Decarolis and Deeds, 1999).

Table 5.4 Descriptive statistics, means, standard deviation and comparison of means

	ID members (N = 129)		non-ID members (N = 91)		
	Mean	**S.D.**	**Mean**	**S.D.**	**F**
INNOVATION (PRODUCT and PROCESS)	*3.87*	*1.99*	*3.34*	*2.01*	*4.925***
(1) Number of developments or introductions of new materials	0.50	0.50	0.37	0.49	4.193**
(2) Number of developments or introductions of new intermediate products	0.52	0.50	0.49	0.50	0.197(n)
(3) Number of developments or introductions of new components	0.45	0.50	0.35	0.48	2.775*
(4) Number of developments or introductions of new attributes of the products	0.44	0.50	0.33	0.47	3.346*
(5) Number of developments or introductions of new equipment	0.71	0.49	0.58	0.50	5.151**
(6) Improvements in the level of automation	0.76	0.43	0.71	0.45	0.799(n)
(7) Number of new organizational methods of the productive activities	0.52	0.50	0.46	0.50	0.888(n)
(8) Use of new energy sources	0.08	0.28	0.03	0.18	2.743*

Notes:
* Difference between district members and non-members significant at $p<0.1$.
** Difference between district members and non-members significant at $p<0.05$.
Accompanied by (n) indicates non-significance.

DISCUSSION AND CONCLUSION

This research has attempted to contribute to a better understanding of the role of social networks in the development of firms' competitive capabilities. In particular, territorial-based networks provide firms with a dense structure and strong ties, thus benefiting them by helping them to exploit existing knowledge and technologies. The existence of local institutions may make it easier for firms to explore new knowledge and technologies since they are connected to external disperse and weak tie networks. Consequently, firms inside an industrial district may combine diverse types of ties and links in order to establish connections and thus enhance their innovative capacity.

Our results show a number of coincidences, but also some significant discrepancies, with previous research findings. In McEvily and Zaheer (1999) a positive association between involvement in regional institutions and the assimilation of competitive capabilities by clustered firms is largely supported. Moreover, Decarolis and Deeds's (1999) research offered evidence of a causal relationship between localization and firm performance. To calculate the localization variable the authors used the address of the head office as well as a variable consisting of eight indicators representing the number of research institutions located in each cluster. Findings are in line with previous research focused on theoretical and empirical developments of collective learning (Capello, 1999; Lawson and Lorenz, 1999) and the concept of innovative milieux (Maillat, 1998), which described the territorial organization in which innovation processes originate. Findings also favor an approach that can be viewed as an extension of the knowledge and innovation theories of the firm at the territorial level (Foss, 1996; Keeble and Wilkinson, 1999). In emphasizing the role played by local institutions, this study is in line with those which warn against overembeddedness in relationships (Yli-Renko *et al.*, 2001) and encourage autonomous relationships (Woolcock, 1998). This combination of ties prevents us from considering the industrial district as a limited model, in contrast to the arguments of some authors (Bianchi, 1994; Harrison, 1994), and offers the possibility of avoiding certain risks, such as external technological shocks (Glasmeier, 1991). In the same way, findings may be in disagreement with others that emphasize generic problems of the existence of the internal homogeneity of the districts (for example, Lazerson and Lorenzoni, 1999).

In our opinion the main contribution of this paper may lie in its integrating two different theoretical perspectives – social capital and territorial externalities – and contrasting the implications of this integration empirically. By following on from the work of authors such as Rowley *et al.* (2000) and Burt (1998), our study also contributes to the social capital perspective. These researchers agree that dense and structural holes are not contradictory perspectives but instead serve to reach different goals. Thus both perspectives are useful to explain different strategic objectives which consider the need for the organization to be a mix or portfolio of ties, where strong ties are combined with unconnected external networks.

Our proposition supported a number of prescriptions for firms' strategies. We argue that firms should interact with local institutions and other cluster participants in order to improve environmental conditions. Dynamics between the formation of tacit and codified knowledge and other elements of the innovation processes call for a reassessment of institutional arrangements.

Firms may pursue diverse strategies for knowledge and skills resourcing, including strategic partnerships with key institutions so as to be able to influence the education and training of future researchers; research collaboration with individual academics or departments in universities in order to gain early access to research; and the creation of hybrid research organizations between firms and institutions in order to develop common research programs.

Mention must be made of some of the limitations of our research. Because of the use of district affiliation as a control variable, we are cautious about inferring any degree of causality among the key constructs. Another question may be raised as to the diversity of the local institutions. Since local institutions may be predominately from the same industry, the information accessed by local firms may be less diverse. Thus a deeper analysis is needed of how local institutions vary in terms of the scope of the activities they carry out. A final challenge we dealt with was that of operationalizing the local institutions within the territorial context. To a certain degree, this scale can be considered to be made up of exploratory or pilot studies. Any definition we come up with for it must, therefore, be tentative and future research will be needed to provide confirmation. In the same way, the choice of small manufacturing firms as the focus of this study limits the extent to which the findings can be generalized.

Our research has raised a number of further questions. The fine-grained process through which the network structure is created or modified is an interesting and important area for future research, which is also needed to elaborate the relationship between the different elements of the model and to confirm the definitions and scales used in the constructs. Another fruitful area of inquiry is that regarding the dynamics of how firms' networks evolve and change in response to external challenges and opportunities. In other words, to what extent does inertia constrain a firm's ability to reconfigure its pattern of network ties? Finally, the processes of cooperative competition in geographical clusters could greatly benefit from a more detailed analysis of the mixture of cooperation and competition inside networks. The balance between inter-firm cooperation and competition, while a popular idea, warrants greater research attention, particularly in the network context.

NOTE

1. The ARDAN database provides productive and financial information about all manufacturing firms except those with an annual revenue of less than 240 000 Euros (40 million pesetas).

REFERENCES

Becattini, G. (1990), 'The Marshallian industrial district as a socio-economic notion', in F. Pyke, G. Becattini and W. Sengenberger (eds), *Industrial Districts and Local Economic Regeneration*, Geneva: International Institute for Labor Studies, pp. 37–51.

Becattini, G. (2002), 'Industrial sectors and industrial districts: tools for industrial analysis', *European Planning Studies*, 10, 483–93.

Becattini and W. Sengenberger (eds), *Industrial Districts and Local Economic Regeneration*, Geneva: International Institute for Labour Studies, pp. 81–128.

Benton, L. (1992), 'The emergence of the industrial district in Spain', in F. Pyke, G.

Bianchi, G. (1994), 'Requiem for the Third Italy?', *34th European Regional Science Congress*, Groningen.

Bianchi, P. and N. Bellini (1991), 'Public policies for local networks of innovators', *Research Policy*, 20 (5), 487–97.

Bourdieu, P. and L. Wacquant (1992), *An Invitation to Reflexive Sociology*, Chicago, IL: University of Chicago Press.

Burt, R. S. (1992), 'Social structure of competition', in N. Nohria and R.G. Eccles (eds), *Networks and Organizations: Structure, Form and Action*, Boston, MA: Harvard Business School Press.

Burt, R.S. (1997), 'Contingent value of the social capital', *Administrative Science Quarterly*, 42, 339–364.

Burt, R.S. (1998), 'the network structure of social capital', *Social Capital Conference*, Durham, NC: Duke University.

Capello, R. (1999), 'Spatial transfer of knowledge in high-technology mileux: learning versus collective learning processes', *Regional Studies*, 33 (4), 353–68.

Coleman, J.S. (1988), 'Social capital in the creation of human capital', *American Journal of Sociology*, 94, 95–120.

Coleman, James S. (1990), *Foundation of Social Theory*, Cambridge, MA: Harvard University Press.

Cooke, P. and Morgan, K. (1998), *The Associational Economy: Firms, Regions and Innovation*, Oxford: Oxford University Press.

Decarolis, D.M. and D.L. Deeds (1999), 'The impact of stocks and flows of organizational knowledge on firm performance: an empirical investigation of the biotechnology industry', *Strategic Management Journal*, 20, 953–68.

Dyer, J.H. and K. Nobeoka (2000), 'Creating and managing a high-performance knowledge-sharing network: the Toyota case', *Strategic Management Journal*, 21, 345–67.

Foss, N.J. (1996), 'Higher-order industrial capabilities and competitive advantage', *Journal of Industry Studies*, 3, 1–20.

Frost, T.S. (2001), 'The geographic sources of foreign subsidiaries' innovations', *Strategic Management Journal*, 22, 101–23.

Galaskiewicz, J. (1985), *Social Organization of an Urban Grants Economy*, Orlando, FL: Academic Press.

Gargiulo, M. and M. Benassi (2000), 'Trapped in your own net? Network cohesion, structural holes, and the adaptation of social capital', *Organization Science*, 11 (2), 183–96.

Geringer, J.M., S. Tallman and D.M. Olsen (2000), 'Product and international diversification among Japanese multinational firms', *Strategic Management Journal*, 21, 51–80.

Glasmeier, A. (1991), 'Technological discontinuities and flexible production networks: the case of Switzerland and the world watch industry', *Research Policy*, 20, 469–85.

Granovetter, M. (1973), 'The strength of weak ties', *American Journal of Sociology*, 78, 1360–80.

Granovetter, M. (1985), 'Economic action and social structure: the problem of embeddedness', *American Journal of Sociology*, 91, 481–510.

Grant, R.M., A.P. Jammine and H. Thomas (1988), 'Diversity, diversification, and profitability among British manufacturing companies, 1972–1984', *Academy of Management Journal*, 31, 771–801.

Harrison, B. (1994), *Lean and Mean*, New York: Basic Books.

Hitt, M.A., R.E. Hoskisson and H. Kim (1997), 'International diversification: effects on innovation and firm performance in product-diversified firms', *Academy of Management Journal*, 40, 767–98.

Hundley, G. and C.K. Jacobson (1998), 'The effects of keiretsu on export performance of Japanese Companies: help or hindrance?', *Strategic Management Journal*, 19, 927–37.

Keeble, D. and F. Wilkinson (1999), 'Collective learning and knowledge development in the evolution of regional clusters of high technology SMEs in Europe', *Regional Studies*, 33, 295–303.

Kogut, B. and U. Zander (1992), 'Knowledge of the firm, combinative capabilities and the replication of technology', *Organization Science*, 3 (3), 383–97.

Koka, B.R. and J.E. Prescott (2002), 'Strategic alliances as social capital: a multidimensional view', *Strategic Management Journal*, 23, 795–816.

Lawson, C. and E. Lorenz (1999), 'Collective learning, tacit knowledge and regional innovative capacity', *Regional Studies*, 33, 305–17.

Lazerson, M.H. and G. Lorenzoni (1999), 'The firms that feed industrial districts: a return to the Italian source', *Industrial and Corporate Change*, 8 (2), 235–66.

Maillat, D. (1998), 'Innovative milieux and new generations of regional policies', *Entrepreneurship & Regional Development*, 10, 1–16.

Malhotra, Naresh K. (1997), *Marketing Research: An Applied Orientation*, New York: Prentice Hall.

Malmberg, A. and P. Maskell (1997), 'Towards an explanation of regional specialisation and of industry agglomeration', *European Planning Studies*, 5, 25–41.

McEvily, B. and A. Zaheer (1999), 'Bridging ties: a source of firm heterogeneity in competitive capabilities', *Strategic Management Journal*, 20, 1133–56.

Nahapiet, J. and S. Ghoshal (1998), 'Social capital, intellectual capital, and the organizational advantage', *Academy of Management Review*, 23 (2), 242–66.

Porter, Michael (1990), *The Competitive Advantage of the Nations*, New York: Free Press.

Powell, WW., K. Koput and L. Smith-Doer (1996), 'Interorganizational collaboration and the locus of innovation: networks of learning in biotechnology', *Administrative Science Quarterly*, 41 (1), 116–45.

Rowley, T., D. Behrens and D. Krackhardt (2000), 'Redundant governance structures: an analysis of structural and relational embeddedness in the steel and semiconductor industries', *Strategic Management Journal*, 21, 369–86.

Saxenian, A. (1994), *Regional Advantage: Culture and Competition in Silicon Valley and Route 128*, Cambridge, MA: Harvard University Press.

Schrader, S. (1991), 'Informal technology transfer between firms: cooperation through information trading', *Research Policy*, 20 (2), 153–70.

Steinle, C. and H. Schiele (2002), 'When do industries cluster? A proposal on how to assess an industry's propensity to concentrate at a single region or nation', *Research Policy*, 31, 849–58.

Suchman, Mark C. (1994), *On Advice of Counsel: Law Firms and Venture Capital Funds as Information Intermediaries in the Structuration of Silicon Valley*, Doctoral Dissertation, Stanford University.

Tsai, W. (2000), 'Social capital, strategic relatedness and the formation interorganizational linkages', *Strategic Management Journal*, 21, 925–39.

Tsai, W. and S. Ghoshal (1998), 'Social capital and value creation: the role of intrafirm networks', *Academy of Management Journal*, 41 (4), 464–78.

Uzzi, B. (1996), 'The sources and consequences of embeddedness for the economic performance of organizations', *American Sociological Review*, 61, 674–98.

Uzzi, B. (1997), 'Social structure and competition in interfirm networks: the paradox of embeddedness', *Administrative Science Quarterly*, 42, 35–67.

Von Hippel, E. (1988), *Sources of Innovation*, New York: Oxford University Press.

Woolcock, M. (1998), 'Social capital and economic development: towards a theoretical synthesis and policy framework', *Theory and Society*, 27, 151–208.

Yli-Renko, H., E. Autio and H.J. Sapienza (2001), 'Social capital, knowledge acquisition, and knowledge exploitation in young technology-based firms', *Strategic Management Journal*, 22, 587–613.

PART TWO

Strategic Capabilities and Knowledge Transfer:
Perspectives from Evolution, Learning and
Networks

6. Coupling combinative and relational capabilities in interorganizational best practice transfer: an evolutionary perspective[*]

Giovanni Battista Dagnino

INTRODUCTION

Strategic management practice and thinking have, in the last decade, devoted increasing attention to issues broadly gathered under the label of 'best practice management'. As it allows innovation and replication in firm strategy, products and capabilities, the identification and transfer of best practices has emerged as one of the most important and popular issues of the beginning of the new millennium. Guided by this emphasis, strategic literature on best practice has recently grown cumulatively in both its span and scope beyond the initial writings for practitioners (Hiebeler et al., 1998). More precisely, the study of best practice transfer has shown a critical interest in the identification and transfer of internal best practices in a single firm (Cool et al., 1997; O'Dell and Grayson, 1998), the transnational transfer of strategic best practices within multinational firms (Kostova, 1999; Lipparini and Fratocchi, 1999), the role of weak ties in sharing knowledge across a divisional firm's subunits (Hansen, 1999, 2002), the ability to replicate core manufacturing technologies quickly and efficiently between different facilities (Galbraith, 1996), and the impediments to the transfer of best practices within the firm (Szulanski, 1996, 1999).

Whereas the management and transfer of best practices has received considerable interest as regards the relations that are organized in the context of the large multinational or multidivisional corporation, to date much less consideration has been given to firm networks and systems. While institutional theorists predict that firms will share best practices as a means of improving legitimacy, network scholars have detailed the ways in which knowledge and resources can be shared across firms for the benefit of all parties involved. Given that strategic networks (Gulati *et al.*, 2000) and knowledge networks (Kogut, 2000) have assumed a foremost status in the business world and there is growing concern of scholarly inquiry with these issues, we argue that the time has come to focus on 'interorganizational best practice transfer'. More precisely, we shall focus on systems of firms. Shifting the emphasis from the firms to their resources and capabilities; by systems of firms we mean a way of organizing strategic resources in a complex and dynamic network of resources and capabilities (Dagnino, 1999). In our understanding, the system of firms has the ability to transfer best practices more rapidly, smoothly and effectively than an individual firm, through the action of two idiosyncratic strategic capabilities. While the system of firms' 'interorganizational combinative capabilities' combine in a single knowledge-ware the different kinds of knowledge that are scattered in various firms, its relational capabilities coordinate and connect several firms in a unique coherent system. The ability to couple these two capabilities in order to manage and recombine its value chain and to achieve superior performance represents the system of firms' unique metacapability.

The aim of this chapter is thus to show 'why' and 'how' systems of firms are more efficient in nurturing, managing and transferring the best business practices inside (and outside) their borders. To put it differently, we present a discussion on why and how firms *purposefully* and *resourcefully* transfer best practices with other firms with which they have connections. The purpose of the study is actually threefold. First, by introducing and discussing the concept of 'interorganizational best practice transfer' in relation to the systems of firms, we contribute to the advancement of the emerging strategic literature of best practice transfer. Second, by assembling in a coherent whole an interorganizational approach to the transfer of best practices which stems from the system of firms' ability to match idiosyncratically combinative with relational capabilities, we contribute to capability-based investigation in strategy. Third, by rooting our argument on the above premises, we finally search for relevance to managers and entrepreneurs operating in systems of organizations. In the tradition of sound strategy analysis which, starting from a positive orientation, is also able to make a normative and prescriptive contribution, we gather some suggestions valuable to managers and entrepreneurs in order for them to transfer the best practices in daily business operations so that systems of firms can create superior economic value.

The remainder of this chapter is organized as follows. Sections two and three are essentially definitional parts. Section two discusses the concept of best practice and disentangles the possibility of best practice transfer. Section three establishes the basic theoretical ground of the study. Drawing on earlier work (Dagnino, 1999) in the tradition of strategic capabilities and strategic networks, we define the system of firms as a complex and dynamic network of resources and capabilities and outline what resources and capabilities are critical, and why, in the transfer of best practices. In section four, by considering the system of firms as a way of reassembling and managing the ongoing business disintegration processes into bits and pieces of their value chains, we focus on the system of firms' 'combinative capability' (Kogut and Zander, 1992). Section five introduces the concept of 'relational capabilities' (Lorenzoni and Lipparini, 1999) and shows how it is related to the system of firms' interorganizational advantage. Section six emphasizes how systems of firms idiosyncratically couple these capabilities to manage and transfer business practices in order to produce superior value with the other side of the conundrum; that is, the relational capabilities (this coupling will be described as the 'double helix effect'). Section seven is devoted to presenting the major implications of the study of the best practice transfer process in systems of firms for strategy theory and managers' action. In this section, we finally marshal a set of conclusions, acknowledge the limitations of this study and open avenues for future research.

KEY DEFINITIONS IN BEST PRACTICE TRANSFER

Since the idea of best practice is far from being an unambiguous and undisputed one, we consider it worthwhile to start with a discussion of the problems related to the existing gulf between received managerial wisdom and the academic viewpoint, and to provide some basic definitions of the transfer of best practices.

Best Practice

The concept of best practice has received different responses from strategy thinkers and managers, opening up an intellectual gulf between the academics' standpoint and the practitioners' view and thus uncovering an underlying divide between the two communities. In strategic management thinking, the concept of best practice has been questioned and disputed quite a lot. On one side, some scholars argue that it is neither a viable nor a useful concept but, at best, a misleading and short-sighted one. It is not viable because it is very difficult to identify a practice that is 'really' the best one among others. Therefore no practice can guarantee a firm the acquisition of superior rents and competitive advantage. And it is useless because, once you have identified the supposed 'best' practice, it cannot easily be transferred among differing firms and dissimilar contexts. It is a misleading concept for operational efficacy, as best practices lead a firm to do better than what the other firms normally do; therefore they are (easily) *imitable*. The relative unproblematic imitability drives customers to consider a given product a commodity and forces firms to compete on price, thereby eroding rents and margins needed to sustain a superior performance (Porter, 2001). Put briefly, this conception of best practices denies any justification to a simple and highly normative concept that has been coined in industry almost exclusively for the purposes of getting legitimacy and/or consulting pretty well–paid work.

On the other side, to managers and consultants, the transfer of best practices appears to have a plainly unambiguous meaning. It indicates the firm's replication of an internal practice that is performed in a superior way in some part of the organization and is deemed superior to alternative internal practices or known alternatives outside the firm (Szulanski, 1996: 29). A *practice* is defined as a particular way of conducting organizational functions that has evolved over time under the influence of a firm's history, people, interests and actions, and that has become institutionalized in the system of firms (Kostova, 1999: 309).[1] In a nutshell, practices reflect the path-dependent shared knowledge and competence of the system firms. Examples of best practices could be: the sharing and implementing of ideas to reduce company-wide energy costs (power and fuel expenses) in the oil industry, and a continuous inventory measurement system in the computer industry.

Though we acknowledge that for both sides, academic researchers and managers, it is often difficult or even impossible to certify that, among the comparable ones existing throughout the world, the one identified is the 'absolute very best practice'; nonetheless we maintain that the concept of best practice remains interesting, useful and straightforward. It is interesting because, even if we cannot identify 'the absolute best practice of all', most of the time it is possible to identify a 'second' or a 'third' best practice; that is, a 'first best' practice with a limited validation and relevance to a specific time and context (or, in other words, we can say a 'better' or a 'good' practice). Since it may be rent-generating, although not indefinitely in time and space, a second best or bounded first best practice can also be important from a theoretical standpoint. Interestingly, though it has traditionally been deeply influenced by them, management theory does not address and apply to only the few 'first best firms in the world' (for example, GE and GM), but dynamically needs to consider all firms striving to compete effectively. The concept of best practice is useful and straightforward because often a bounded best practice (or a system of coordinated practices better organized and managed) is a sufficient means to capture and secure a competitive advantage for a firm (though it is restricted in time and space) and to create or protect value.

Best Practice Transfer

Since it may prove both unsuccessful and unproductive, it is worth noting that for a number of culturally oriented authors it is essential to reflect critically on the utility of a best practice transfer. Whereas we recognize that what is efficient and effective in a given space/temporal context may be inefficient and ineffective in a different context, in our opinion a successful intercontextual best practice transfer may be useful in the presence of a few relevant conditions such as follows: (a) there must be a pre-conceptualization and a clear *codification* of the practice (or systems of practices) to transfer; (b) the proposed goals in terms of target performance, transfer time, and what practice or system of practices or *ibridization* among practices to transfer must be well defined *ex ante* (that is, the search–transfer problem); (c) there must be a strong and stable commitment to practice transfer between the two managerial actors: the source and the recipient (that is, the commitment problem); (d) there must be a *pre-commitment* among all the individuals (and firms) involved in the transfer so that it is possible to establish cooperative behavior and mutual trust (that is, the so-called pre-commitment problem).

In the footsteps of Kostova (1999: 311), we hence stress that the transfer of the best practice is a pretty complex *non-linear process* that does not end with the adoption of the formal rules or routine which describe the practice, but continues until these rules become internalized at the recipient unit/firm. That is, the employees at the recipient unit/firm have to metabolize the practice and attach to it the same symbolic meaning and value that as the employees at the source unit do. Briefly, the success of the transfer is determined by the *degree of institutionalization* of the practice at the recipient unit (that is, the process by which a practice achieves a taken-for-granted status). [2]

Attached to the issue of institutionalization is the fact that knowledge management tends to focus on specific practices and practice transfer processes, overlooking *de facto* the importance of the philosophy and value-infused concepts underlying these practices (Pfeffer and Sutton, 2000). Whereas in the context of the single firm this process of institutionalization may be endogenously driven, coercive, difficult to implement and laborious to internalize, we argue that, since it possesses the strategic capabilities of institutionalization and tends to quasi-isomorphism, in the context of the system of firms' best practice institutionalization usually evolves more 'naturally' in securing economic and social exchange.

THEORETICAL SETTING

We start this section by discussing the theoretical premises of the work in the light of the system of firms and then we define the system of firms. To pursue this intention, we draw liberally from and build on two companion strategic perspectives that inform the research on best practice transfer in systems of firms: strategic capabilities and strategic networks (see Table 6.1).

Strategic Capabilities and the System of Firms

First, we consider the strategic or dynamic capabilities perspective (Teece et al., 1997; Eisenhardt and Martin, 2000; Dosi et al., 2000) which, generally taking an evolutionary standpoint in the vein of knowledge- and technology-related studies, relies on a set of needed-to-win firm dynamic capabilities. Capabilities building and continuous renewal are, in this view, at the very basis of the firm competitive advantage and value creation (Grant, 1996). According to Teece et al. (1997), within the dynamic capability framework the term 'dynamic' refers to the capacity to renew competencies so as to achieve *congruence* with the changing business environment, while the term 'capabilities' emphasizes the role of the firm's ability to appropriately adapt, integrate, and reconfigure internal and external organizational skills, resources, and functional competencies to achieve new and innovative forms of competitive advantage (*ibid.*: 514–16). In relation to the individual firm capability approach, the systems of firms' capabilities present some differences. First, whereas the dynamic capabilities approach is concerned with the levels of firm and industry (that is, internal and external capabilities), here it is the system of firms (that is, the network of resources and competencies) which is the originator and exploiter of its basic strategic capabilities. Second, there is a twofold nexus between resource, competence and capability. On one hand, past accumulated and networked resources and capabilities are the drivers of present and new capabilities of the system of firms. On the other hand, new capabilities massed together in a superadditive way through interfirm cumulative learning shape the system of firms' overall economic and organizational competence (see Carlsson and Eliasson, 1994). In this perspective, in the following section of the chapter we explain how systems of firms are able to integrate idiosyncratically their 'combinative' capabilities with their 'relational' capabilities.

Table 6.1　An integrative perspective on the investigation of
interorganizational best practice transfer

Analytical perspective	Strategic capabilities	Strategic networks	Systems of firms
CONCEPTUAL ROOTS	Resource-based theory Evolutionary economics Behavioral economics	Social networks Resource-based theory	Complex systems Resource-based and strategic capabilities Strategic networks
UNIT OF ANALYSIS	Resources Capabilities Competencies Innovation generation	External resources and capabilities	Complex dynamic networks of resources and capabilities
LEVEL OF ANALYSIS	Firm (Industry)	Firm network	(Firm) Intra-system Relations System
RELEVANT AUTHORS	Nelson and Winter (1982) Teece et al. (1997) Eisenhardt and Martin (2000)	Gulati (1999) Gulati et al. (2000)	

Source: Author's own elaboration.

Strategic Networks and the System of Firms

Now, we consider the approach that addresses interfirm enduring relationships and networks (Gulati, 1998; Lorenzoni and Lipparini, 1999) and, particularly, strategic networks (Gulati, 1999; Gulati et al., 2000). The latter perspective has recently met with success because, in order to achieve efficiency and to have access to needed-to-play capabilities, firms have dramatically increased their interest and action in forming and governing partnerships and alliances with external actors and generally cooperating with other firms (Kogut, 2000). Gulati et al.'s concept of 'strategic networks' is germane to the SBE in that (a) they are networks where stable interorganizational ties are strategically important to participating firms, and (b) there is a link between network configuration and value creation. In our view, this implies, on one hand, that the different firms (each) play a well-defined role sharing common superior objectives. And, on the other hand, that the locus of value creation is the interfirm network rather than the individual firm level. In this perspective, the network structure defines and limits the relationships between the units. The thrust of the argument is that firms enter a network of embedded ties in order to pursue mutual trust and valuable information exchange across organizational boundaries. A network of embedded ties accumulated over time may form the basis of a rich information and learning network (Gulati, 1999). But a strategic network is different from the system of firms in that (a) it is based primarily on structural and control factors (that is, it relies much more on 'static' structures than on 'dynamic' processes); (b) it is not related to a complex resource network, but to the 'distinctive capability' of single firms in the network; (c) it is rooted in an idiosyncratic concept of 'industry synergy' (that is, the symmetry between the characteristics and operations of the strategic network and the features and behavior of the firms within an industry); and (d) despite the authors' claims, as it considers that 'a firm's networks allows it to access key resources from its environment' (Gulati et al., 2000: 207), its focus really rests more on the firm level than on the network level taken as a whole.

The System of Firms as a Complex Network of Resources and Capabilities

We now discuss the concept of the system of firms and lay down the premises of its ability to recombine knowledge and favor multiple interactions among firms in the system. First, we consider the system of firms as a peculiar organizational form of reassembling and managing the ongoing business disintegration processes into bits and pieces of their value chains, which has the strategic capabilities of handling two or more value chains intertwined at a time. In our understanding, the system of firms provides a *coevolution environment* where the two kinds of capabilities above noted (that is, combinative and relational) are highly interrelated and tightly coupled.

Second, we argue that this may occur because the system of firms is an aggregate of firms that is to be viewed as a *complex dynamic network of resources and capabilities* (Dagnino, 1999). This is formed from two main evolving network levels. Starting from a sole resource/competence, the first level shapes a simple or elementary network of resources and capabilities. This includes a minimum of two firms and is capable of generating externalities of aggregation and agglomeration on the first level. A second level masses together all the resources, competencies and capabilities extant in the system of firms (and therefore all the firms) in a superadditive way so that a complex and dynamic network of resources and capabilities takes shape. This second moment plays a crucial role in the development of the system because it enacts a 'synergistic pool of variety' generating second-level economies of agglomeration. By 'synergistic pool of variety', we mean a collection of different firms (that is, the 'pool of variety') which performs in a superadditive way when it is pooled together via the resource and competence network

Table 6.2   The system of firms two-level configuration

	Embryonic system of firms (first level)	Developed system of firms (second level)	Example: prato industrial district
NUMBER OF FIRMS	Two or more	More than two	11,500
			First–network level
NETWORK OF RESOURCES AND CAPABILITIES	First-level Simple Some resources and capabilities	Second-level Complex All the existing resources and capabilities	Elasticity in textile manufacturing Support and synergies from the mechanic-textile sector
PROPERTIES	Adaptive Additivity	Superadditivity	
			Second-network level
ECONOMIES OF AGGLOMERATION	First-level Simple	Second-level Complex	Synergies obtained by concentration of highly specialized
SYSTEM'S CHARACTERS	(Embryonic development)	Shared values and identity Sense of belonging System's atmosphere Coevolution environment	firms Innovations in products, processes and the organization of work Establish an all firms consortium in advertising and distribution
TYPES OF STRATEGIC RENTS	Ricardian	Coleman	

Source: Author's own elaboration.

Third, it is worth noting that the system of firms' second level indicates the presence of a coevolution environment and a 'sense of belonging' allowed by the system's 'collective identity', through the commitment of the actors involved and an elevated sense of professionalization. Frequent personal and in-group interchanges, talks and meetings, and multiple fluxes of communication create a specific 'system-environment' which fosters collaborative practice and, in turn, nurtures trust, coordination and cooperation (or what Kogut (2000) has termed 'Coleman rents').

In Table 6.2 we visualize the fundamental characteristics and properties of the system of firms' two-level configuration and provide an illustration taken from the real world that regards the Prato industrial district, an aggregation of firms located in the northern part of Italy.

INTERORGANIZATIONAL COMBINATIVE CAPABILITIES IN SYSTEMS OF FIRMS

Moving from the premises of the section above, we show what resources and competencies are the critical ones in systems of firms, and why, and identify the capability to combine knowledge and to favor multiple interactions among firms in the system as the main drivers of best practice transfer in systems of firms. As regards the system's resources, we point out that the human or managerial resource is the crucial one to establish the necessary preconditions for a process of best practice transfer within a system of firms. This means that appropriate training and strong motivation of personnel (that is, professionalism) constitutes the basis for the success of a best practice transfer process within a system of firms. Beside the managerial resource, financial means are needed to establish benchmarking projects and to guarantee the proper and continuous support to transfer best practices. In this respect, though we agree with Szulanski (1996) that cost *per se* could be a poor descriptor of the difficulty of transfer, we nonetheless stress that the *cost of transfer* is not meant to be merely the cost of transfer of a single practice, but the cost of involving in a transfer process of extended time-periods a certain number or a complex/system of practices (that is, the whole per year estimated cost of transfer).

As regards the competence set needed to transfer best practices, much in the vein of evolutionary investigation (Nelson and Winter, 1982; 2002) we take into account:

1. the competence to replicate knowledge, routines, practices (*replication capacity*);[3]
2. the competence to identify and to select the best practices either inside

or outside the border of the system of firms (*search capacity*);[4]

3. the competence to absorb knowledge, routines, practices (that is, the *absorptive capacity*) by the recipient firm in the context of the system of firms;[5]

4. the competence to retain and to institutionalize knowledge, routines, practices (that is, *retentive capacity*) by the recipient organization in the context of the system of firms.

Guided by these specific resources and competencies, two basic capabilities emerge and help to transfer best practices in a system of firms: (a) the capability to *combine* in a single knowledge-ware the different kinds of knowledge which are traditionally scattered in various firms (that is, interorganizational combinative capability); and (b) the capability to *coordinate* and *connect* a certain number of firms in a unique system of firms (that is, relational capability). The system's integration *metacapability* refers to the ability to couple these two strategic capabilities in order to manage and recombine the value chain and to achieve superior performance. The compound outcome of these abilities is to initiate, transfer and distribute knowledge practice in the whole system of firms in a way that is as consistent and efficient as possible while improving its overall quality and quantity.

Following our previous contention, in this section we consider the system of firms as a particular organizational mode of breaking down, reassembling and managing into bits and pieces of their value chains the ongoing business disintegration processes. We thus focus on the first of the two kinds of key capabilities: the system of firms' combinative capability. In the line traced by Van den Bosch *et al.* (1999: 566), we establish and discuss the concept of 'interorganizational combinative capabilities' in the framework of the systems of firms' best practice transfer.

As we have previously anticipated, the systems of firms are considered organizational forms capable of reassembling and managing the ongoing business disintegration processes into bits and pieces of the value chains. As it is able to handle two or more (parts of) value chains intertwined at a time, the disintegration of a firm's value chain and its reintegration in a combination of different firms' value chains is a relevant system of firms' knowledge-based capability, which stands at the very basis of its organizational advantage. Extending Kogut and Zander's (1992) concept of combinative capability, we focus on the systems of firms' combinative capabilities. According to Kogut and Zander (1992: 391), combinative capabilities are 'the intersection of the firm capability to exploit its knowledge and the unexplored potential of the technology' (that is, *technological opportunity*). A firm's combinative capabilities synthesize and apply current and acquired knowledge. In the context of the system of firms, we advance the notion of *interorganizational combinative capabilities* which represent its capabilities of combining and recombining the elements of the value chains *uniquely* and *relentlessly*, in a way which concurrently is difficult to reproduce and may allow the transfer of best practices more rapidly and effectively. We thus articulate our first proposition as follows:

Proposition 1
Given that interorganizational combinative capabilities reside in the system of firms' ability to combine and recombine the elements of its value chains uniquely and continuously, and given that these value chain (re)combinations are difficult to imitate and replicate, they are expected to allow a more rapid and effective intersystem practice transfer. Thus, the stronger the degree of interorganizational combinative capabilities existing in a given system of firms in a particular time/place context, the easier and the more intense the best practice transfer will be.

In more detail, the system of firms may have the capability of breaking down and recombining two or more value chains (see Porter, 1985) that initially belonged to the individual firms in the system (Lorenzoni, 2000). This interorganizational combinative capability is displayed variously by:

1. the combination of two value chains intertwined ('dyadic combination');
2. the combination of *multiple asymmetric* value chains intertwined ('simple multiparty combination');
3. the combination of *multiple symmetric and asymmetric* value chains intertwined (complex multiparty combination).

As it identifies the most basic form of a system of firms, the combination of two value chains of two firms is the simplest mode of combination. Through systematic cooperation and repeated interfirm relationships, it results in a significant gain in the system efficiency that is mainly related to production and logistics costs and associated with a relative advantage toward competition. If the system of firms is at the very beginning of its evolutionary cycle and the complex dynamic network of resources and competencies is not yet formed, the transfer of best practice is generally enhanced between the source and the recipient and this casts the roots for a more advanced and articulated system of firms.

The combination of multiple asymmetric value chains implies multiple and repeated interfirm linkages, a system of firms affirmed in its basic components, and the possibility of intertwining different upward and downward symmetric value chains. Note that the characteristic feature of such a model is the combination of a number of *asymmetric* value chains; that is, the economic combination of a big firm with multiple small firms. Since the large firm typically possesses a notable contractual and relationship power influence over the small ones, this generally means an easier and smoother governance system. The best practice transfer process is driven by the big firm ('lead' or 'focal' firm), which usually plays the role of the source unit and decides what practices have to be transferred, when, in which direction and where.

Since it includes multiple value chains (and thus multiple firms) with different dimensions and contractual powers, the combination of multiple symmetric and asymmetric value chains is ultimately the most difficult-to-govern value chain combination model of system of firms. For this reason, on one hand it may favor the processes of concentration and vertical development and, on the other hand, it is characterized by the highest degree of uniqueness and systems specificity. While this situation is as difficult to govern as it is difficult to imitate, it may generate superior efficiency at all levels of the recombined value chain (that is, the so-called 'honeycomb value chain'). This appreciative framework may allow the identification of the best practices and propel their transfer among all the firms involved in the system in a way that is usually as speedy as it is successful.

RELATIONAL CAPABILITIES: THE SYSTEMS OF FIRMS' INTERORGANIZATIONAL ADVANTAGE

In this section, we advance the argument that the system of firms is the locus where firms interact and share knowledge with other firms. This ability to interact and share significant knowledge is driven by *relational capabilities* (Lorenzoni and Lipparini, 1999) and is a distinctive organizational capability of the system of firms *per se*. We outline how this ability is such an effective driver of the identification and transfer of best practices in the system of firms.

In strategy literature, relational capabilities are viewed as capabilities to *continuously* interact with other firms (Lorenzoni and Lipparini, 1999). The unfolding of relational capabilities occurs because they are profoundly associated with a key underlying concept, namely, the concept of organizational routines as 'grammars of action' (Pentland and Reuter, 1994). In this view, organizational routines are models of action which continuously guide firm interaction in a semi-automatic fashion; they are functionally similar, but incompletely fixed and subject to a limited variation in time and space (also named 'liberty degree') as they are cyclically applied and reapplied within and between organizations.[6]

Such routine-driven firm interactions allow knowledge sharing and the creation of new knowledge. The ability to develop, integrate and transfer knowledge residing both inside and outside the single firm boundaries emerges thus as a distinctive organizational capability of the system of firms. The system of firms may provide an environment appropriate for organizing knowledge access and transfer across different actors in a network. This means that, in contexts where complex knowledge is fragmented among different firms and actors, the system of firms emerges as an *equilibrating interorganizational configuration* able to guarantee knowledge access and sharing as well as to reconstruct and renew knowledge innovatively (that is, the effect caused by the 'synergistic pool of variety').

From an economic standpoint, relational capabilities may convey to a system of firms' relevant relational economies; that is, a significant reduction in relational costs of firm interactions. Specifically we refer to (a) a reduction in the costs of establishing and maintaining interfirm relationships and (b) a reduction in the costs related to the identification of possible partners or allied firms. *Vis-à-vis* the context of the individual firm, these cost reductions lie at the very basis of the system of firms' interorganizational advantage. Additionally, today interfirm relationships are yielded by contemporary developments in technology that allow rapid information links and network flows among different firms. Thus we articulate our second proposition as follows:

Proposition 2
Given that relational capabilities represent the system of firms' ability to make the interaction among firms (more) continuous and intense, they are expected to allow a significant reduction in the relational costs of firm interaction and knowledge sharing within the system. Thus the stronger the relational capabilities existing in a given system of firms in a particular time/place context, the less the relational costs associated with firm interaction and the more intense the sharing of knowledge will be.

Extending previous work (Lorenzoni and Lipparini, 1999), relational capabilities are here conceptualized at two distinct levels: *coopetitive* and *institutional*. We define 'coopetitive relational capabilities' as the capabilities to conduct economic exchanges among a number of firms by competing and cooperating simultaneously. Since it allows the combination of competitive and cooperative behaviors, coopetition is a median strategy concept referring to interfirm relationships halfway between competition and cooperation (Brandenburger and Nalebuff, 1996; Lado et al., 1997). Since institutionalization is the process by which an interfirm relationship achieves a taken-for-granted status within a system of firms, 'institutional relational capabilities' are in turn the capabilities to institutionalize some particular kinds of interfirm relationships in the system of firms. Additionally, institutionalization is the process by which the interfirm relationship may gain symbolic meaning at the system level.

Albeit theoretically distinct, both coopetitive and institutional relational capabilities are likely to be interrelated and *coevolutionary* in nature. Higher levels of coopetitive relational capabilities are likely to be associated with higher levels of institutional relational capabilities. The linear causality of this relationship can be advanced because coopetition and institutionalization are both evolutionary processes in the system of firms that allow it (via its reproduction and the accumulation of its knowledge base) to achieve a significant interorganizational advantage (Dagnino, 1999).

As regards the transfer of best practice in systems of firms, relational capabilities may allow firms to overcome two conventional barriers to best practice transfer: (a) the lack of relationships between the source and the recipient of the transfer process; (b) the ignorance of particular circumstances of time and place (Hayek, 1945). The latter is the ignorance related to the possible existence of a particularly useful practice in some part of the system of firms. This ignorance is usually associated with a particular language or communication gap.

First, accumulated relational capabilities as defined above may be able, by definition, to pre-empt the obstacle to a practice transfer created by the absence of ties (weak or strong, formal or informal) between the source and the recipient of a transfer. Second, relational capabilities are usually able to contrast the possible unawareness of the location of the best practices in some parts of the system of firms. Phrases such as 'if we only knew what we know' (O'Dell and Grayson, 1998) and the 'knowing/doing gap' (Pfeffer and Sutton, 2000) have become representative of frequent business situations in which managers realize that inside their firms lies, unknown and untapped, a vast treasure house of knowledge and best practices which (if properly diffused) could enhance operational efficiency and overall performance. We state our third propositions as follows:

Proposition 3a
Coopetitive relational capabilities, defined as the ability to conduct economic exchanges in the context of multiple firms that are competing and cooperating simultaneously, and institutional relational capabilities, defined as the system of firms' ability to institutionalize some particular kinds of interfirm relationships, are likely to be

positively related to each other. Higher levels of coopetitive relational capabilities are expected to be associated with higher levels of institutional relational capabilities.

Proposition 3b
Accumulated relational capabilities are likely to pre-empt obstacles to practice transfer between the source and the recipient caused by the absence of ex ante ties between the source and the recipient. The existence of strong relational capabilities in a given system of firms is likely to be positively related to the awareness of the location of the best practices in any parts of the system. Higher levels of relational capabilities are expected to be associated with more intense relationships among the firms in the system and with a higher knowledge about the exact location of the practices residing in the system.

COUPLING COMBINATIVE AND RELATIONAL CAPABILITIES IN SYSTEMS OF FIRMS: THE STRATEGIC MANAGEMENT OF THE 'DOUBLE HELIX' IN BEST PRACTICE TRANSFER

As argued in the preceding sections, since it coevolves and self-reinforces with time, the system of firms is able to provide a *coevolution environment* (Van den Bosch et al., 1999) where the two kinds of capabilities (combinative and relational) are highly interrelated and tightly coupled. Somewhat recalling the human DNA, we label this *integration metacapability* as the 'double helix effect'[7] and explain the strategic role it usually plays in best practice transfer (see Figure 6.1). The interorganizational relationships between and among human beings are central in the definition of this metacapability which, though it has to do with history and chance in its evolutionary course, is in essence a human-guided method for capability governance and control. Accordingly our reasoning leads us to talk of systems 'metacapability' because we believe that the system of firms presents a higher-level idiosyncratic capability of coupling and integrating different lower-level capabilities which transcends a mere simultaneous but disjoint possession of two or more capabilities (combinative and relational) and is one of its fundamental evolutionary weapons.

First, by coupling combinative and relational capabilities the system of firms integrates combinational rents with relational rents. This twofold integration is realized, on one hand, because interorganizational combinative capabilities synthesize and apply current and acquired knowledge, generating distinctive knowledge (re)combinational rents; and, on the other hand, because relational capabilities enable the interaction and sharing of significant knowledge among firms and produce economic valuable relational rents.

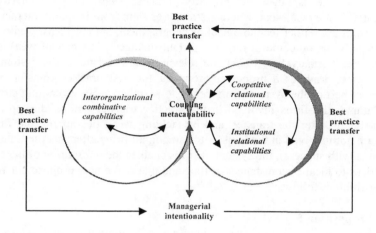

Source: Author's own elaboration.

Figure 6.1   The 'double helix effect' in systems of firms best practice transfer

The production and application of current and acquired knowledge is, in this way, performed at the interfirm level where (as in the DNA's double helix) the two capabilities are connected in a single entity. We are thus able to articulate our fourth proposition as follows:

Proposition 4
Given that interorganizational combinative capabilities synthesize and apply current and acquired knowledge, they are likely to generate combinational rents. Given that relational capabilities enable the interaction and sharing of significant knowledge among firms, they are likely to produce relational rents. By coupling combinative capabilities and relational capabilities, systems of firms are likely to generate combinational rents and relational rents, and to integrate the latter with the former:

Second, in order to create variance and to profit from modicums of diversity in systems of firms, these capabilities establish the basis for an environment where weak and strong ties are coupled and mutually consistent (Lorenzoni and Lipparini, 1999: 333). That is what would provide firms with a better balance of exploration and exploitation (March, 1991). And just such a mix is what is actually found in investigations of social networks and is known as the 'small-world property' (Watts, 1999) or 'dual network property' [8] We recall that, whereas strong ties stem from frequent interaction and proximity, either technological or geographical, among firms, weak ties are usually the outcome of rare and distant linkages. This mix of weak and strong ties (Granovetter, 1973) is a relevant characteristic of the system of firms as it provides a proper environment for best practice transfer in a different part of the system (from center to periphery). By leveraging strong ties among the firms involved in the practice transfer before, during, and immediately after the transfer, and by tackling weak ties among the firms that are not involved in the transfer (or among all firms after that the transfer has met with success), the system of firms enables the *adaptation* of the best practices to local circumstances of time and place. We now propose our fifth proposition as follows:

Proposition 5
Since the system of firms' coupling of combinative and relational capabilities establishes the bases for an environment where weak and strong ties are coupled and mutually consistent, and this mix is a characteristic of the so-called 'small world', the system of firms may display the 'small-world property'. Since the mix of weak and strong ties is a relevant characteristic of a system of firms, it is likely to provide a proper environment for best practice transfer in its different parts. The higher the system of firms' capability to provide a good mix of weak and strong ties, the more rapid the best practice transfer inside the system is going to be.

Third, this capabilities meta-connection permits the system of firms to overcome the limits to best practices transfer at three levels: (a) it enhances the system's *absorptive capacity* at the recipient's level (Cohen and Levinthal, 1990; Zahra and George, 2002); (b) it enhances the system's *retentive capacity* at both the source's and the recipient's levels (Szulanski, 1996); (c) stretching and mitigating the ignorance barriers by means of interfirm intense communication and extensive connection, it speeds up the process of interfirm knowledge and practice transfer. By the combination of a number of bits and pieces of best practices, absorptive and retentive capacities drive, in turn, virtuous processes of practice *contamination* and *assimilation*. This process is executed as follows: (a) by identifying knowledge complexity of best practices and dividing each single practice into independent pieces or units; (b) by recombining these bits and pieces of practice either (1) into the same practice already applied elsewhere or (2) with other pieces of other practices in a new practice (see Schumpeter, 1934, for innovations spreading out from new combinations). We now articulate our sixth propositions:

Proposition 6a
Coupling combinative and relational capabilities allows the system of firms to overcome the limits to best practices transfer in that: (a) they are likely to enhance the system's absorptive capacity at the recipient's level; (b) they are likely to enhance the system's retentive capacity at the source and the recipient levels; (c) they are expected to speed up the process of interfirm practice transfer, stretching and mitigating the ignorance barrier by means of interfirm intense communication and connection.

Proposition 6b
Thus, the higher the system of firms' metacapability, the higher (a) its absorptive capacity at the recipient level, (b) its retentive capacity at source and recipient levels, (c) its interfirm ability to communicate and stay connected.

Dell Computer's understanding of virtual integration (Dell, 1998; Narayandas and Randan, 1996; Randan and Bell, 1999) shows how combinative and relational capabilities are developed in the company as quickly as the metacapability to integrate the first two capabilities. Whereas combinative capabilities allow Dell to combine every familiar single piece of its direct strategy (that is, customer focus, supplier partnerships, mass customization, just-in-time manufacturing) in a highly innovative and distinctive manner, relational capabilities are the bedrock of Dell's stable interfirm relationship with its suppliers and customers. Technology, and specifically network and web-based information technologies, is in turn Dell's driving metacapability that enables coordination and relational capabilities across company boundaries to achieve higher levels of efficiency and productivity.

Sun Microsystems' open system integration (Farlow et al., 1996; Coetteler and Austin, 1998; Nolan et al., 1999; Rosenberg and Silverman, 2001) provides a helpful illustration of how combinative and relational capabilities are cultivated in the company as the metacapability to integrate the first two. Whereas combinative capabilities allow Sun to combine in an innovative and idiosyncratic way every single bit of its open systems strategy (N-tier architecture, network computing, performance control, division of cognitive labor), relational capabilities lie at the very basis of Sun's long-term interorganizational relationships with its partners. Commitment to the open systems strategy and technology strategy (network computing and Internet technologies) represents Sun's metacapability that enables combination and relational capabilities to blur interfirm borders to gain superior performance.

Southwest Airlines' commitment to 'relational coordination' (Hoffer Gittel, 2003) presents us with the metacapability of constructing and maintaining an integrated and highly effective system in which information and know-how are shared inside and across firm boundaries. Since it shows the capability to combine and utilize different types of knowledge, traditionally scattered around firms (for example, by developing a set of practices such as hiring and training for relational competence, investing in frontline leadership and building relationships with key suppliers), Southwest shows a high level of interorganizational combinative capabilities. Since it displays the capability to coordinate and connect in its daily flight operations a plurality of strategic partners (airports, air traffic control and airplane manufacturers) in a single unique system of firms, Southwest exhibits considerable relational capabilities.

Fourth, since creating an environment for transfer may not be sufficient *per se* for an effective best practice transfer, coupling combinative and relational capabilities also provides the proper business *atmosphere* and a favorable *organizational context* to overcome the practice transfer problem. Through enduring commitment, frequent interchanges and meetings, and multiple fluxes of communication, a 'collective identity' and 'sense of belonging' are both infused into the system and enable shared organizational values and a specific 'system atmosphere' that feeds trust and cooperation among the actors involved in the best practice transfer. This 'system atmosphere' provides the system of firms with a number of related best practice transfer-oriented conditions: (a) a context appropriate to develop and transfer the (very) best practices; (b) a context appropriate to circulate and upgrade the best practice in the frame of a shared system of values and rent division; (c) a context suitable to exploit and render the best practices synergic in relation to complementary resources and competencies available in the other networked actors; and (d) a context appropriate to organize a production system able to be strategically competitive, value-creating and value-enhancing. We now formulate our seventh proposition:

Proposition 7

Coupling combinative and relational capabilities may provide the appropriate business 'atmosphere' and a favorable 'interorganizational context' to overcome the various transfer problems. Thus, the higher the system of firms' metacapabilities the higher (and more rapid) the best practice transfer, the higher the circulation and upgrading of best practice in the context of a shared value system and rent division and the higher the capability to organize a production system able to be strategically competitive, value creating and value-enhancing.

Fifth, in order to make processes of best practice transfer successful, on the operational side we introduce and discuss some interorganizational capability-driven arrangements designed to select, juxtapose, replicate and enhance knowledge and best practices in the context of the systems of firms. These interorganizational arrangements of interaction are 'benchmarking teams', 'best practices teams' and 'knowledge and best practice networks or communities' (O'Dell and Grayson, 1998; Hansen, 2002). In a system of firms, all three may be coexistent and mutually interactive. While our definition of the three arrangements is virtually consistent with the definition supplied by extant best practice literature and in particular by O'Dell and Grayson (1998), on the operational side the system of firms presents some specific interfirm features.[9] In more detail, there are three organizational forms of interaction among the three arrangements. In a dyadic combination of two value chains, the stable best practice team is generally located at the level of the leading firm, while the benchmarking teams are structurally located in both firms.

In a simple combination of multiple asymmetric value chains, whereas the numerous benchmarking teams are localized in the firms of the system, the single best practice team refers to the leading firm. As it is formed by different individuals coming from the firms that are most interested in the process of best practice transfer (either as practice recipients or practice sources), the more 'stable' best practice team is nevertheless interorganizational. Knowledge and best practice networks or communities began to spread out, in part spontaneously, throughout the system in order to assure a knowledge and communicational equilibrium within the system of firms.

In the complex combination of multiple symmetric and asymmetric value chains, there are typically several interorganizational benchmarking teams and several interorganizational best practice teams located at different organizational levels and firms in the system. Whereas the interorganizational benchmarking teams are scattered throughout firms and value chains in the system of firms, the interorganizational best practice teams are led by the focal firms, which (alternatively or collectively) contribute to the system governance and knowledge transfer. A complex network of knowledge and best practice communities providing an interorganizational best practice database is also a basic characteristic of this formula. Benchmarking teams, best practice teams and knowledge and best practice communities and networks are all interorganizational, since they are workgroups formed by gathering a number of individual persons. In particular, as firms within the system possess different competencies, they usually provide different levels of knowledge utility to these groups, stemming from the individuals who are assigned to interorganizational teams and come to buttress the dynamic and heterogeneous outgrowth of interfirm relationships over time.

Finally, complex benchmarking and best practice teamwork, coupled with information technology, allow the system of firms to support the use of the 'interorganizational best practice database' that facilitates knowledge and best practice sharing and transfer. New information technology tools, such as on-line technology networks and internal directories, groupware and high-definition imaging, support employees seeking interorganizational best practices and cooperation (O'Dell and Grayson, 1998).

DISCUSSION AND CONCLUSION

The transfer of best practice has emerged as an evolutionary, dynamic, process-related and people-oriented process that currently drives organizational and interorganizational performance. Strategic management has recently been considerably concerned with the transfer of best practices in relation to the context of the individual firm (Hansen, 1999; Kostova, 1999; O'Dell and Grayson, 1998; Szulanski, 1996). Yet there has been a lack of systematic attention paid to strategic aggregations and networks of firms, which have started to have an important role in the current business landscape. This chapter started with the aim of filling this gap, especially as regards the level of the system of firms. The study began with the objective of explaining 'why' and 'how' systems of firms may provide a favorable environment for the transfer of best practices. As observed in the course of the chapter, through its intertwined value chains the system of firms builds a sort of architecture of strategic capabilities (Grant, 1996) for best practice transfer to produce a superior economic and knowledge value. Learning commitment, mutual trust and a desire to share on the part of the people involved in it are understandably the natural accompaniments of every evolutionary process of knowledge transfer in a system of firms. Since the other guiding purpose of this study, which we closely link to the theoretical analysis, was to provide some relevant implications for managers, in this concluding section we summarize our theoretical results and supply business managers and entrepreneurs with some suggestions (about the selection, replication, and improvement of best routines and practices) to enhance the transfer process of best practices in systems of firms' daily operations.

Implications for Strategy Theory

Since it has tried to bridge three strands of present strategy literature in the analysis of interorganizational best practice transfer – strategic capabilities, strategic networks and the mainly practitioner-oriented literature on the transfer of best practices – this chapter contributes to research and theory development towards a more holistic view of strategy. We argue that this approach is pretty much in the tradition of recent evolutionary theorizing (Nelson and Winter, 2002); an open framework which definitionally lays the groundwork to accommodate multiple views and approaches even across multidisciplinary and multifield investigation.

First, with the aim of bridging the intellectual chasm between business practitioners and academicians by explaining how the concept of best practice is interesting, useful and straightforward, the study has helped to disentangle the theoretical and definitional problems in relation to best practice and best practice transfer.

Second, by taking the system of firms as its basic level of analysis and by defining some of its vital characteristics, abilities and functions, this chapter has contributed to the work on interfirm relationships and networks. Systems of firms have been observed as complex and idiosyncratic nexuses of interaction among qualities of interfirm relationships which combine resources and capabilities difficult or impossible to possess by an individual firm in a single external space for resources and competencies and best practice interactions.

Third, by extending, applying and coupling the two concepts of combinative and relational capabilities in the context of the system of firms, this chapter helps to encourage a greater emphasis on theory building in the strategic capabilities literature. We have shown that it is not only possible but also theoretically desirable to look for an integration of different kinds of strategic capabilities, especially in the presence of firm systems which, with regard to the individual firm, are usually able to allow much easier capability interaction, (re)combinations and development.

Fourth, by emphasizing the systems of firms' knowledge-oriented attitude and knowledge-based advantage, this study complements the emerging knowledge-based theory (KBT) of the firm, especially as regards interfirm networks, with some new insights. The KBT of the firm argues that a firm's ability to integrate the knowledge efforts of different actors is an essential precondition for achieving superior performance. KBT generally strives both to deconstruct the black box of the firm's production function into its more basic components and interactions and to reconstruct the resource-based theory by providing a platform for a new view of the firm as a dynamic, developing, quasi-autonomous system of knowledge generation, diffusion and application (Nonaka, 1994). According to this idea, the firm's knowledge repository and its ability to generate or replicate knowledge lie at the core of a more sound strategic theory of the firm (Porter Liebeskind, 1996; Teece, 1998).[10] In this understanding, a growing body of literature has focused on the processes of knowledge sharing and knowledge transfer within the firm (Zander and Kogut, 1995; Hansen, 1999, 2002) and, more recently, between firms or firm networks (Grant and Baden-Fuller, 1995; Dyer and Nobeoka, 2000). Although firms are generally superior to markets and strategic alliances in integrating knowledge to produce goods and services, networks and systems of firms can overcome the limits of firms by encompassing highly differentiated knowledge processes while offering efficiency in knowledge utilization. This is significantly important for such knowledge as tacit knowledge, typically embodied in strategic best practices and believed to be critical for the establishment of systems of firms' competitive advantages.

Fifth, this chapter sheds additional light on the idea of investing in 'systems atmosphere' and on building and maintaining 'social capital' in systems of firms. Although strategy literature on business atmosphere and social capital has greatly developed in recent times, progressively gaining considerable strength and advancing in both speculative sophistication and methodology (Nahapiet and Ghoshal, 1998), it remains nonetheless in its adolescence and requires much more cumulative research to consolidate, especially in relation to interorganizational networks and systems of firms. Our conceptualization of a system of firms is, in particular, the ideal cradle for starting and developing social capital in an appropriate interorganizational context that generally strives to support a shared and effective systems atmosphere.

Implications for Managerial Practice

As regards managerial implications, this chapter suggests that best practice transfer in a system of firms can possibly be the subject of managerial purposive design. Best practice interorganizational identification and transfer could be enhanced by structuring and managing a number of valuable interorganizational arrangements: interorganizational benchmarking teams, interorganizational best practices teams and knowledge and best practices networks and/or communities. As noted earlier, if cleverly planned and mutually implemented, these elements of interorganizational design may help to guarantee the selection, replication, and enhancement of best practices throughout the system of firms. Ultimately, in our opinion, the coupling and integration of combinative and relational capabilities across firm boundaries, by which it becomes possible to accelerate the process of best practice transfer and interaction, is destined to be an increasingly important part of system of firms' management action.

Second, we consider the crucial role played by new technologies, and particularly network- and web- or Internet-based technologies. As we may observe in a number of cases such as Dell (Dell, 1998; Magretta, 1998) and Sun (Southwick, 1999; Lanza; 2000), commitment to strategy and technology is viewed as a driving metacapability that enables the coupling of combinative and relational capabilities across company boundaries to achieve higher levels of efficiency and productivity. The acceleration in the pace of innovation contributes to the rapid aging of strategic best practices. In order to survive the present multiple intertwined innovation processes, it is necessary for firms to forge, identify and introduce new (technology-driven) best practices continually and to select and transfer them most rapidly inside their organizations. This is exactly what Dell recognized early on, envisioning the computer industry future before its competitors and revolutionizing its course and Sun envisaged introducing and strongly committing itself to its vision of an open systems strategy. Put briefly, developing practices to forecast demand earlier and better than competitors is now of the utmost importance for the system of firms to capture and sustain economic advantages.

Limitations and Further Research

Like any other study, this chapter shows some intriguing limitations that in turn leave avenues open for further investigation. First, like any explorative work in a nearly untouched subfield of strategy inquiry, this study suffers from underdetermination in that, pursuing an initial integration of different strategy research streams in systems of firms (strategic capabilities, strategic networks and best practices), it has focused attention on only a part of the whole best practice transfer process. Whereas it is centered especially on the *transfer* of best practice in the context of the system of firms, little attention has been accorded to interorganizational best practice structuring, implementation, maintenance and revision, or to the continuous execution of the best practice throughout the system. We thus leave an avenue open for further inquiry in this important research direction.

Second, there are a number of questions related to the genesis, evolution and diffusion prediction of particular practices to transfer and to how systems of firms' strategic capabilities of transferring may significantly influence (or even *mutate*) the process of best practice identification and transfer (that is, the processes of circular causation and feedforward). In particular, we acknowledge that, because of the current acceleration in the pace of innovation and the related quicker aging of strategic best practices, systems of firms confront a new critical challenge: to forge, identify and introduce new best practices continually and to select and transfer them rapidly. So firm systems always need to be preparing the next generation of best practices. Hence we leave further research on best practice genesis, continuous evolution and effective diffusion prediction to forthcoming additional investigation.

A third limitation is related to the fact that, since it lacks original empirical analysis (see the Appendix for case study support), this chapter is essentially theoretical and definitional in nature. Observed from a different viewpoint, this may be considered a fruitful opportunity for further study and exploration, as the study provides a sound initial foundation for further empirical research that can be carried out, applying the theoretical concepts proposed and discussed herein to a number of systems of firms, whose environments may enhance knowledge flow and best practice transfer or making comparative studies over time of a series of longitudinal cases (Yin, 1984; Eisenhardt, 1989) of systems of firms and interorganizational arrangements.

NOTES

*   I wish to thank the participants in the seminars and sessions at the Academy of Management Meetings (Seattle), EURAM Conferences (Milan, St. Andrews), and EGOS Colloquium (Helsinki), Mark Ebers, Paddy McEvoy, Peter Ring and Maurizio Sobrero for helpful discussions, Antonio Capaldo, Rosario Faraci, Anna Grandori, Emanuela Todeva for detailed comments. This study has been partly conducted during a research period at the Wharton School, University of Pennsylvania. Financial help from the University of Catania is gratefully acknowledged.

1.   According to Szulanski (1996), organizational practices are the routine use of organizational knowledge that often presents a tacit component, embedded partly in individual skills and partly in collaborative social arrangements. According to the Chevron Corporation, a best practice is 'any practice, knowledge, know-how, or experience that has proven to be valuable or effective within one organization that may have applicability to other organizations' (O'Dell and Grayson, 1998: 167).

2. According to Kostova (1999: 311), institutionalization is also a process by which the practice may achieve *symbolic* meaning for the employees at the recipient unit or firm.

3. Replication involves transferring or redeploying competencies from one concrete economic setting to another. Since productive knowledge is embodied, this cannot be accomplished by simply transmitting information. Only in those instances where all the relevant knowledge is fully codified and understood can replication be collapsed into a simple problem of information transfer. Often the contextual dependence of original performance is poorly appreciated, so, unless firms have replicated their systems of productive knowledge on many prior occasions, the act of replication is likely to be difficult. Indeed replication and transfer are often impossible without the transfer of people, though this can be minimized if investments are made to convert tacit knowledge into codified knowledge (Teece et al., 1997).

4. I thank my colleague Rosario Faraci for having kindly noticed that, since the system of firms is a network of resources, competencies and capabilities, the fact that the system is endowed with competencies may seem tautological. Actually, in this account of the system of firms our concern is to stress *what* specific kinds of systems competencies are strategic for making a best practice transfer process as 'smooth' as possible.

5. As regards the concept of absorptive capacity, see Cohen and Levinthal (1990), Lane and Lubatkin (1998), and Zahra and George (2002).

6. As Pentland and Reuter (1994: 484) put it: 'Because organizational routines are complex interactional products that usually require the participation of multiple individuals, they are unlikely to unfold the same way every time'.

7. As it is the bulb of the system reproduction and achieves superior performance, a visual representation of the integration process of these two kinds of strategic capabilities (combinative and relational) roughly resembles, in the context of the system of firms, the helix of human DNA and allows us to suggest this intriguing biological metaphor. To make this analogy more clear, we acknowledge that, as occurs in human DNA, there are sorts of 'chemical attractors' in a system of firms; since they may ease the best practice replication process, these are represented by interfirm network ties among the firms within the system.

8. According to Watts (1999: 495), a network displays small-world properties when 'almost every element of the network is somewhat "close" to almost every other element, even those that are perceived as likely to be far away. This property portrays the complex coincidence of high local clustering and short global separation as shown to be a general feature of sparse, decentralized networks that are neither completely ordered nor completely random'. Though we acknowledge

that the small-world phenomenon is originally a basic attribute of personal networks, we contend that the concept may be extended and applied both fruitfully and effectively to systems of firms.

9. Benchmarking teams are formed to assess the current state of a firm on a particular process, identify gaps and problems, and search for best practices outside the firm or even locally within the firm. They have usually a definite (interim) life span, with clear-cut kick-off and end dates for their work. Best practice teams tend instead to be an ongoing part of the networking infrastructure of a firm with a charter supporting the identification, transfer and implementation of the best practices. Knowledge and practice communities and networks eventually emerge as a grass-roots response to the breakup of former networks due, for instance, to downsizing, re-engineering or restructuring (O'Dell and Grayson, 1998).

10. Guided by both the universal attention to knowledge-related phenomena (that is, the knowledge economy and the knowledge society) and its emphasis on the process of knowledge accumulation, deployment and transfer within a firm, knowledge management has become one of the most popular and researched subjects in strategic management in the early 2000s.

REFERENCES

Brandenburger, A.M. and B.J. Nalebuff (1996), *Co-opetition*, New York: Doubleday.

Carlsson, B. and G. Eliasson (1994), 'The nature and importance of economic competence', *Industrial and Corporate Change*, 3 (3): 687–711.

Coettelee, M., and R.D. Austin (1998), Sun microsystems: realizing the potential of web technologies, Discussion Case 9–198–007, Harvard Business School.

Cohen, W.M. and D.A. Levinthal (1990), 'Absorptive capacity: a new perspective on learning and innovation', *Administrative Science Quarterly*, 35: 128–152.

Cool, K.O, I. Dierickx and G. Szulanski (1997), 'Diffusion of innovations within organizations: electronic switching in the Bell system', 1971/1982, *Organization Science*, 8 (5): 543–559.

Dagnino, G.B. (1999), 'The system of business enterprises as a complex dynamic network of resources and competencies', Academy of Management Best Papers Proceedings, 59th Annual Meeting, Chicago.

Dell, M. (1998), *Direct from Dell: Strategies that revolutionized an industry*, New York: Harper Business.

Dosi, G., R.R. Nelson and S.G. Winter (eds.) (2000), *The Nature and Dynamics of Organizational Capabilities*, New York: Oxford University Press.

Doz, Y. (1996), 'The evolution of cooperation in strategic alliances: Initial conditions or learning processes?', *Strategic Management Journal*, Summer Special Issue, 17: 55–83.

Dyer, J.H. and K. Nobeoka (2000), 'Creating and managing a high performance knowledge-sharing network: the Toyota case', *Strategic Management Journal*, Special Issue, 21: 345–367.

Eisenhardt, K.M. (1989), 'Building theories from case study research', *Academy of Management Review*, 14 (4): 532–550.

Eisenhardt, K.M. and J.A. Martin (2000), 'Dynamic capabilities: What are they?', *Strategic Management Journal*, Special Issue, 21 (10-11): 1105–1121.

Farlow, D., G. Schmidt and A. Tsay (1996), *Supplier Management at Sun Mycrosystems (A)*, Discussion Case OIT-16 A, Stanford University Graduate School of Business.

Galbraith, C.S. (1996), 'Transferring core manufacturing technologies in high-technology firms', *California Management Review*,

Glaser, B. and A. Strauss (1967), *The Discovery of Grounded Theory: Strategies of Qualitative Research*, London: Weidenfeld & Nicolson.

Grant, R.M. (1996), 'Prospering in dynamically-competitive environments: organizational capability as knowledge integration', *Organization Science*, 7 (4): 375–387.

Grant, R.M. and C. Baden-Fuller (1995), 'A knowledge-based theory of interfirm collaboration', *Academy of Management Best Papers Proceedings*, 55th Annual Meeting.

Gulati, R. (1998), 'Alliances and networks', *Strategic Management Journal*, Special Issue, 19 (4): 293-317.

Gulati, R. (1999), 'Network location and learning: the influence of network resources and firm capabilities on alliance formation', *Strategic Management Journal*, 20 (5): 397–420.

Gulati, R., N. Nohria and A. Zaheer (2000), 'Strategic networks, *Strategic Management Journal*, Special Issue, 21: 203–15.

Hansen, M. (1999), 'The search-transfer problem: the role of weak ties in sharing knowledge across organization subunits', *Administrative Science Quarterly*, 44: 82–111.

Hansen, M. (2002), 'Knowledge networks: explaining effective knowledge sharing in multiunit companies', *Organization Science*, 13: 232–248.

Hayek, F.A. (1945), 'The use of knowledge in society', *American Economic Review*, 35 (4): 519–530.

Hiebeler, R., T. Kelly and C. Ketteman (1998), *Best Practices: Building Your Business with Customer-focused Solutions*, New York: Simon & Schuster.

Hoffer Gittel, J. (2003), *The Southwest Airlines Way: Using the Power of Relationships to Achieve High Performance*, New York: McGrawHill.

Johnston, R. and P.R. Lawrence (1988), 'Beyond vertical integration: the rise of the value-adding partnership', *Harvard Business Review*, July August: 94–101.

Kogut, B. (2000), 'The network as knowledge: generative rules and the emergence of structure', *Strategic Management Journal*, Special Issue, 21: 405–425.

Kogut, B. and U. Zander (1992), 'Knowledge of the firm, combinative capabilities, and the replication of technology', *Organization Science*, 3 (3): 383–397.

Kostova, T. (1999), 'Transnational transfer of strategic organizational practices: a contextual perspective', *Academy of Management Review*, 24 (2): 308–324.

Lado A.A., N. Boyd and S.C. Hanlon (1997), 'Competition, cooperation, and the search for economic rents: a syncretic model', *Academy of Management Review*, 22 (1): 110–141.

Lane, P.J. and M. Lubatkin (1998), 'Relative absorptive capacity and interorganizational learning', *Strategic Management Journal*, 19: 461–477.

Lanza, A. (2000), *Knowledge Governance: Dinamiche Competitive e Cooperative Nell'economia della Conoscenza* (Knowledge Governance: Competitive and Cooperative Dynamics in the Knowledge Economy), Milan: EGEA.

Lorenzoni, G. (2000), 'Reti di imprese ed imprenditorialità diffusa', in G. Lorenzoni and A. Lipparini (eds), *Imprenditori e Imprese*, Bologna: Il Mulino 171–197.

Lorenzoni, G. and A. Lipparini (1999), 'The leveraging of interfirm relationships as a distinctive organizational capability: A longitudinal study', *Strategic Management Journal*, 20: 317–338.

Lipparini, A. and L. Fratocchi (1999), 'The capabilities of the transnational firm: Accessing knowledge and leveraging inter-firm relationships', *European Management Journal*, 17 (6): 655–667.

Magretta, J. (1998), 'The power of virtual integration: an interview with Dell Computer's Michael Dell', *Harvard Business Review* (March April): 73–84.

March, J.G. (1991), 'Exploration and exploitation in organization learning', *Organization Science*, 2: 71–87.

Mason, J. (1996), *Qualitative Reasoning*, London: Sage.

Nahapiet, J. and S. Ghoshal (1998), 'Social capital, intellectual capital and the organizational advantage', *Academy of Management Review*,

Narayandas, D. and V.K. Randan (1996), 'Dell Computer Corporation' Discussion Case 9–596–058, Harvard Business School.

Nelson, R.R. and S.G. Winter (1982), *An Evolutionary Theory of Economic Change*, Cambridge, MA: Belknap Press.

Nelson, R.R. and S.G. Winter (2002), 'Evolutionary theorizing in economics', *Journal of Economic Perspectives*, 16 (2): 23–46.

Nolan, R.L., W.B. Harding and K.A. Porter (1999), 'Sun Microsystems and the N-tier architecture', Discussion Case 9–399–037, Harvard Business School.

Nonaka, I. (1994), 'A dynamic theory of organizational knowledge creation', *Organization Science*, 5 (1): 14–37.

O'Dell, C. and C.J. Grayson (1998), 'If we only knew what we know: identification and transfer of internal best practices', *California Management Review*, 40 (3): 154–174.

Pentland, B.T. and H.H. Reuter (1994), 'Organizational routines as grammar of action', *Administrative Science Quarterly*, 39 (3): 484.

Pfeffer, J. and R.I. Sutton (2000), 'The Knowing Doing Gap', Boston: Harvard Business School Press.

Porter, M.E. (1985), *Competitive Advantage*, New York: Free Press.

Porter, M.E. (2001), 'Uniqueness worth more than best practices', Excerpt from a talk given at Bocconi University, Milan, December 4.

Porter Liebeskind, J. (1996), 'Knowledge, strategy, and the theory of the firm', *Strategic Management Journal*, Winter Special Issue, 17: 93–107.

Randan, V.K. and M. Bell (1999), 'Dell Online', Discussion Case 9–598–116, Harvard Business School.

Rosenberg, M. and B. Silverman (2001), 'Sun Microsystems Inc.: Solaris Strategy' Discussion Case 9–701–058 Harvard Business School.

Schumpeter, J.A. (1934), *The Theory of Economic Development*, Boston: Harvard Business School Press.

Southwick, K. (1999), *High Noon: The Inside Story of Scott McNealy and the Rise of Sun Microsystems*, New York: John Wiley.

Szulanski, G. (1996), 'Exploring internal stickiness: impediments to the transfer of best practice within the firm', *Strategic Management Journal*, Winter Special Issue, 17: 27–43.

Szulanski, G. (1999). 'The process of knowledge transfer: a diachronic analysis of stickiness', *Organizational Behavior and Human Decision Processes*.

Teece, D.J., G. Pisano and A. Shuen (1997), 'Dynamic capabilities and strategic management', *Strategic Management Journal*, 18 (7): 509–533.

Teece, D.J. (1998), Research directions for knowledge management, *California Management Review*, 40 (3): 289–292.

Van den Bosch, F.A.J., H.W. Volberda and M. de Boher (1999), 'Coevolution of firm absorptive capacity and knowledge environment: Organizational forms and combinative capabilities', *Organization Science*, 10 (5): 551–568.

Watts, D.J. (1999), Networks, dynamics and the small-world phenomenon, *American Journal of Sociology*, 105 (2): 493–527.

Yin (1984), *Case Study Research*, London: Sage.

Zahra, S.A. and G. George (2002), 'Absorptive capacity: a review, reconceptualization, and extension', *Academy of Management Review*, 27 (2): 185–203.

Zander, U. and B. Kogut (1995), 'Knowledge and the speed of transfer and imitation of organizational capabilities: an empirical test', *Organization Science*, 6 (1): 76–92.

APPENDIX

Context and Method of the Case Studies

As an explanatory complement to the explorative investigation of the relations between strategic capabilities and interorganizational best practice transfer, we examined three distinguished US-based firms operating respectively in the computer, software and airline industries. Though we acknowledge that the three case studies extracted from two technology- and network-based industries and one kinship-based industry may not lay down sufficient initial ground to proceed to a number of inductive generalizations that the process of theory building commonly requires, we contend that our choice may yet be contributional and straightforward as it conveys a significant descriptive backdrop and is methodologically supported. A theoretical sampling approach was adopted to select the sample cases (Glaser and Strauss, 1967; Mason, 1996). According to Mason (1996: 93–4), 'theoretical sampling means selecting groups or categories to study on the basis of their relevance to your research questions, your theoretical position and analytical framework, your analytical experience, and most importantly the explanation or account which you are developing'. This thinking has guided the selection of appropriate sample cases. In this research context, the main theoretical issues were related to the investigation of how the three selected firms which, together with their partners, are viewed as systems of firms, have been able to show efficiency in adopting and transferring interorganizational best practices within their range by coupling combinative and relational capabilities idiosyncratically. The best practice sets selected as specific analytical units in each of the cases reported are referable to what Doz (1996) has mindfully defined as 'cases within the case'. The longitudinal case studies of these firms are represented below as illustrative examples. Within these firms, multiple sources of evidence were used: internal documents and public sources were studied primarily to create an introductory longitudinal picture of how the process of practice adoption and transfer has evolved and changed through the use of a mix of combinative and relational capabilities roughly from the mid-1980s to the end of 2002. We recognize that further inquiry may imply the administration of semistructured interviews to managers, additional informal discussions directly conducted and the careful comparative scrutiny of the three ensuing cases.

Case Study 1: Dell Computer

First of all, we present and discuss the Dell Computer case as a representative example of the successful, rapid and pervasive transfer of best practices in a widely known system of firms. On the basis of his long-term vision and a highly innovative direct strategy, in just 15 years (1985–2000) Michael Dell and his staff have succeeded in establishing and growing an $18.2 billion company operating in the computer industry. Dell has also revolutionized the computer industry by pursuing business velocity (the Dell's 1995–2000 five-year average sales growth was 45.3 per cent), coordination and focus at the same time.

First, we consider the Dell tightly related 'direct model' (Narayandas and Randan, 1996; Randan and Bell, 1999; Dell, 1998) as a characteristic system of firms. This occurs as Dell stitches together a business with many partners, both customers and suppliers, that are treated as intimately as if they were inside the company (Magretta, 1998; Dell, 1998). The Dell system is, in this view, a complex network of resources and competencies. Since it represents a system of firms, Dell has developed its direct system in a way that is practically opposite to vertical integration. As it blurs the traditional boundaries of the value chain(s) among suppliers, manufacturers and end users, and uses interorganizational combinative capabilities as a glue to coordinate and combine in a single knowledge-ware the different kinds of knowledge which are scattered in various firms, it is usually called 'vertical disintegration'. In addition to the large number of long-lasting relationships with proximate suppliers, another of Dell's network ties lies in the abandonment of the conventional arm's length model of transactional governance, and the progressive investment in the relational side of the exchange (that is, relational capabilities). As Michael Dell put it:

Suppliers

With our service providers, we're working to set quality measures and, more important, to build data linkages that let us see in real time how we're doing— when parts are dispatched, for instance, or how long it takes to respond to a request of service ... *The supplier effectively becomes our partner*. They assign their engineers to our design team, and we start to treat them as if they were part of the company. (Magretta, 1998: 75)

Customers

Boeing for example has 100,000 Dell PCs, and we have 30 people that live at Boeing, and if you look at the things we're doing for them or for other customers, we don't look like a supplier, *we look more like Boeing's PC department. We become intimately involved in planning their PC needs and the configuration of their network. (ibid.: 79)*

Second, in pursuing this twofold supplier-and-customer connection, 'virtual integration' harnesses the economic and strategic benefits of two different business models: *coordination* and *focus*. It offers the advantages of a tightly coordinated supply chain that have traditionally come through vertical integration, while, at the same time, it benefits from the focus and specialization that drive actual virtual companies. In a nutshell, virtual integration allows firms at the same time to be efficient and responsive to change.

Third, Dell's understanding of virtual integration shows how both combinative and relational capabilities are developed in the company as quickly as the metacapability to integrate the first two. Whereas combinative capabilities allow Dell to combine every familiar single piece of its direct strategy (customer focus, supplier partnerships, mass customization, just-in-time manufacturing) in a highly innovative and distinctive manner, relational capabilities are the bedrock of Dell's stable interfirm relationship with its suppliers and customers. Technology, and specifically network and web-based information technologies, is then Dell's driving metacapability that enables coordination and relational capabilities across company boundaries to achieve higher levels of efficiency and productivity.

Fourth, in this Appendix we describe and summarize four of Dell's most meaningful organizational practices that (by working in closely related daily operations with both suppliers and customers) have been successfully transferred within the Dell system and institutionalized inside the company's 'virtual value chain': demand forecast, customer strategy, inventory management and in-factory load of customer's software.

Demand forecast

We see forecasting as a critical sales skill. We teach our sales-account managers to lead customers through a discussion of their future PC needs. We'll *walk a customer through every department of his company, asking him to designate which needs are certain and which are contingent.* (Magretta, 1998: 79; emphasis added)

Customer strategy

Our customer strategy is one area where our model has evolved. We've become good at developing what we call 'scalable' businesses—that is, those in which we can grow revenues faster than expenses. We really look closely at financial measures like gross margins by customer segment—and we focus on segments we can serve profitably as we achieve scale. People are sometimes surprised to learn that 90% of our sales go to institutions–business or government–and 70% to very large customers that buy at least $1 million in PCs per year. So, over time you cut the market into finer and finer segments? Yes, for a lot of reasons. One is to identify unique opportunities and economics. The other is purely a managerial issue: you can't possibly manage something well if it's too big. Segmentation gives us better attention and focus. (*ibid.*: 77)

Inventory management
In our industry there's a lot of what I call bad hygiene. Companies stuff the channel to get rid of old inventory and to meet short-term financial objectives. We think our approach is better. *We substitute information for inventory and ship only when we have real demand* from real end customers. (*ibid.*: 77; emphasis added)

In-factory load of customer's software
Our solution was to create a massive network in our factory with high-speed, 100-megabite Ethernet. We'll load Eastman Chemical's software onto a huge Dell server. Then, when a machine comes down the assembly line and says, 'I'm Eastman Chemical analyst workstation, configuration number 14', all of a sudden a few hundred megabites of data come rushing through the network and onto the workstation's hard disk, just as part of the progressive built through our factory. If the customer wants, we can put an asset tag with the company's logo on the machine, and we can keep an electronic register of the customer's asset. (*ibid.*: 79)

The wide adoption throughout the Dell system of the best practices outlined heretofore corroborates the existence of a value-impregnated model in a tightly coordinated value chain. This model shapes both an environment favorable to change and a 'system atmosphere' that feeds trusts and interfirm cooperation and fosters Coleman rents. Accordingly, as suggested, best practice adoption and transfer at Dell has been so far as comprehensive as possible.

Case Study 2: Sun Microsystems

We now introduce and discuss the Sun Microsystems case. For its early commitment to an 'open systems strategy', this is to be considered a captivating case representative of a system of firms where the interorganizational transfer of best practices has been managed quite unexpectedly in a sufficiently smooth and efficient way. Three Stanford classmates and one UC Berkeley student founded Sun, which stood for Stanford University Network, in 1982. Growing vigorously and rapidly since then, Sun Microsystems has become (in 2001) an $18.2 billion global firm operating in the network computing solutions business. Sun was founded with one driving vision: the *open systems strategy*: a vision of computers that talk to each other no matter who built them. While other firms sought to protect proprietary, stand-alone architectures, Sun focused on taking companies into the network age, providing systems and software with the scalability and reliability needed to drive the electronic marketplace (Sun Mission Statement, 2001).

First, Sun Microsystems is organized as a loosely coupled, highly aligned set of companies building their core technologies (Farlow et al., 1996). Consequently Sun operates the network as the work environment, not as an adjunct to it – get everybody living on the network: customers, suppliers, employees at home, employees traveling (Nolan et al., 1999).

Suppliers
Sun, its *customers and partners collaborate to create and deliver proven solutions* that reduce your risk and time-to-market–without locking you into a single-vendor solution. ... That's why we've established *long-standing relationships* with leading companies worldwide.

Customers
Customer flexibility to select best-of-breed vendors and swap out components as their business needs change–a benefit derived from Sun's open standards-based solutions, a one-stop, end-to-end *customer relationship management (CRM) solution* that delivers multi-channel integration and a consistently superior customer experience. (Sun Website, 2001)

Second, the Sun system, like the Dell system, is a complex network of resources and competencies. Since it represents a system of firms, Sun has developed its complex system by deploying and developing loosely coupled systems at different levels that are compatible with the latency of the Internet, versus tightly coupled systems that are characteristics of dedicated private networks. These loosely coupled systems have been shown to provide great stimuli to knowledge flows and have succeeded in organizing an environment which is most favorable to transfer of knowledge and organizational practices. In addition to pinpointing some of Sun's best practices, we comment on Sun's open systems strategy in relation to network computing and its *multilevel relational network*, which together explain the key role combinative and relation capabilities play inside this firm. Then, in order to show how and to what extent Sun has developed interorganizational (meta)capabilities appropriate to transfer best practices, we shall recapitulate this argument.

Open systems strategy and network computing

Before Sun, computer vendors traditionally sold systems based exclusively on proprietary architectures. By contrast, from its inception Sun embraced open systems, publishing specifications and interface protocols.[11] Following its commitment to an open systems strategy, Sun decided in 1996 to move to a network computing paradigm. It thus established three design principles: (a) support an expanded view of the user; (b) do not depend on a specific desktop; (c) develop reusable services (Nolan et al., 1999). This policy has fueled the company's fast growth and rapid knowledge exchange between all its preferred partners, and particularly customers and suppliers.

N-tier Architecture

The N-tier architecture is a sort of by-product of Sun's relational strategy. Sun selects a limited number of its most innovative and dynamic partners for every relational product (semiconductors, memories, integrated circuits). Each partner is part of a more or less exclusive relation proportionate to the commitment needed on a given product in a definite time-period. Sun called its architecture 'N-tier architecture', referring to the fact that at any given time any application could call upon other application services, which resided on other servers, or tiers, so the number of tiers for an actual application could vary to a number greater than four. In general, the more complex an application the greater and stronger the number of tiers.

Performance control

Sun's performance measurement and control follows a set of practices and routines that are atypical for US industrial relations, resembling more the Japanese approach: a few strategic partners with a long-term relationship. *The management of the relational network implies regular assessment of partner commitment and measurement of its contribution.* Sun has developed appropriate procedures termed 'look and assess' and 'total cost of ownership' or TCO (Lanza, 2000; Nolan et al., 1999).

Division of cognitive labor

The rapid obsolescence of computer solutions business forces Sun to activate partnerships in the context of which operates a division of cognitive labor. This division of cognitive labor occurs as a rule through concurrent engineering in new product development; the strategic partners are involved in competence-oriented tasks according to their aptitudes (Lanza, 2000: 163). *The division of cognitive labor is generally managed through quasi-permanent and quasi-structured teams.* In Sun's relational network, these teams are connected virtually and commonly assigned to different phases of product development.

By way of summary, Sun's open system integration shows how combinative and relational capabilities are developed in the company as the metacapability to integrate the first two. Whereas combinative capabilities allow Sun to combine in an innovative and idiosyncratic way every single bit of its open systems strategy (N-tier architecture, network computing, performance control and division of cognitive labor), relational capabilities are the very basis of Sun's long-term interorganizational relationship with its relevant partners. Commitment to both open systems strategy and technology strategy (network computing and Internet technologies) is Sun's metacapability that enables combination and relational capabilities blurring interfirm borders to gain sustainable superior performance.

Case Study 3: Southwest Airlines

Third, we present and discuss the Southwest Airlines case. Southwest Airlines is a remarkable US company with a consistent record of profitability and performance in a rather turbulent and cyclic industry. In more detail, Southwest Airlines has an unsurpassed track record, as it has been profitable every year for 32 years. Additionally, for most of 2002 the total market value of Southwest (about $9 billion) was larger than that of all other major US airlines combined. In view of these reports, *Fortune* magazine has termed Southwest 'the most successful airline in history'. Contrary to what is generally thought, Southwest's low costs are not based on low wages; more of its employees are unionized than in any other major US airline and they are paid around the industry average. Rather, Southwest is able to offer low prices owing in large part to the highly productive use of its major assets: its aircraft (Boeing 737) and its people.

Given that it takes a fully *holistic* collective perspective on work and is able to integrate and coordinate the knowledge of multiple parties in their daily operations, similarly to what we have observed in the preceding cases of Dell and Sun, in our view Southwest's system is to be seen as a complex network of resources and competencies. To implement this kind of strategy, a strategy based on leanness, speed and reliability, requires highly effective working relationships among all parties involved. The so-called 'secret ingredient' that makes Southwest so distinctive is, in a nutshell, its ability to build and sustain *high performance relationships* among managers, employees, unions and suppliers (Hoffer Gittel, 2003: xi). These relationships are characterized by a process of 'collective identity shaping', which is implemented by means of shared goals, shared knowledge and mutual respect.

Over time Southwest has carefully developed a set of interorganizational practices that build and sustain strong relationships among those actors who are crucial to the firm's success. Southwest has developed its complex capability system by deploying and developing strong *relational coordination*; that is, a well–integrated supply chains in which information and know-how are readily shared across firm boundaries. As is well recognized, effective coordination requires frequent, timely, problem-solving communication carried out through relationships of shared goals, shared knowledge, and mutual respect. With strong and intense relationships, the parties involved embrace rather than reject their connections with one another, enabling them to coordinate more effectively with one another. Shared goals motivate parties to move beyond what is best for their own narrow area of responsibility and act with regard for the overall work process (Hoffer Gittel, 2003: 35). Shared knowledge among parties provides greater stimuli to knowledge flows and supports the administration of an environment which is favorable to the condivision of knowledge and facilitates the transfer of best practices. More specifically, Southwest is committed to continuously building and sustaining relationships with strategic suppliers, to hiring and training strategy and to cooperative supervision management.

Relationships with strategic suppliers

We acknowledge that Southwest has invested substantial time and effort in developing effective partnerships with the three 'outside' parties on which it is most dependent: airports, air traffic control, and aircraft manufacturers. Each of these parties provides a critical resource to Southwest: Southwest can fly the airplanes, while the airports manage the ground facilities, the US government monitors air traffic control, and Boeing makes the airplanes. This multiparty relationship system has been set up in order to start a strategic process that we may call the process of 'cooperative exploration of ambiguity', and thus to exploit the benefits potentially stemming from interorganizational learning.[12] By treating its *suppliers as partners*, Southwest successfully extends its sphere of influence beyond its employees to encompass its entire value chain (Hoffer Gittel, 2003: 192-3).

Hiring and training strategy

Southwest places a great deal of importance on the hiring process to identify people with *relational competence* and *teamwork ability* (that is, the Southwest way). At Southwest relational competence is considered a critical ingredient of organizational success, as it refers to the ability to relate effectively with others. According to a ramp manager, 'Something we look at is people who are very team oriented from prior work experiences'. Yet even people who perform highly skilled jobs, such as engineers, doctors and pilots, need relational competence to integrate their work effectively with the work of their fellow employees. In the same way, training at Southwest is geared toward building functional expertise and relational competence. Each newly hired employee receives both classroom training (from 1 to 2 weeks, depending on the job) and on-the-job-training (from 2 to 3 weeks, depending on the job). In the course of being trained for a specific job, the employee learns about the jobs of each other functional group that interfaces with the job for which he or she is training. The training is therefore geared toward fostering relational competence. By learning about the overall work process, the employees understand where they fit and how their jobs relate to and support those of their colleagues (Hoffer Gittel, 2003: 85-8).

Cooperative supervision and frontline leadership

At Southwest, each supervisor is responsible for 10 to 12 frontline workers, the highest supervisor-to-employee ratio in the industry. The job of the supervisor goes far beyond a focus on measuring performance and disciplining the 'bad apples'. Southwest supervisors are 'player coaches' having managerial authority but also performing the work of the frontline workers. Supervisors take part cooperatively in the frontline work on a regular basis, even highly *physical* work such as baggage handling (Hoffer Gittel, 2003: 74). This management practice is something that would be considered simply incredible by most of the comparable major US airlines, where strict functional assignment is the rule and the supervisor role is commonly detached from physical and manual operations.

Flight departure process

As an outcome of the Southwest system and its strong commitment to job flexibility, partner relationships and intense communication, the Southwest flight departure process shows a strategic 'quick-turnaround-at the-gate practice'. This practice has outperformed (in terms of time and cost) the practices of all the other airlines in the industry and has become the 'key benchmark' for both incumbents and low-cost newcomers. A statistical analysis of supervising, hiring and training practices suggested that hiring for relational competence contributes to higher levels of relational coordination. It also contributes to improved flight departure performance, particularly faster turnaround times, greater staffing productivity, fewer customer complaints, fewer lost bags, and better on-time performance (Hoffer Gittel, 2003: 91-2).

Concerning its relational competence system, Southwest has been able to both develop and foster it in its internal relationships and to leverage and extend it to the relationships with outside parties. To sum up in our own terms, Southwest possesses the fundamental metacapability of idiosyncratically coupling combinative and relational capabilities. This has been mindfully called 'relational coordination': that is, the construction and maintainance of an integrated operational system in which information and know-how are readily shared inside and across firm boundaries. In that it shows the capability to (re)combine and utilize different types of knowledge, traditionally scattered around (by developing a set of practices such as creating boundary spanners, hiring and training for relational competence, investing in frontline leadership, making unions its partners and building relationships with key suppliers), Southwest shows a high level of interorganizational combinative capability. In that it displays the capability to coordinate and connect in its daily flight operations a plurality of parties (airports, air traffic control and airplane manufacturers) in a single unique system of firms, Southwest displays mature relational capability.

NOTES

1. For its open-ended character facilitating compatibility, interfaceability, testing and standards setting, the open systems strategy has proved to be very profitable for both Sun and its customers.
2. Johnston and Lawrence (1988) have called these kinds of partnerships 'value-adding partnerships', arguing that such models have advantages over independent firms trying to negotiate with each other in the absence of partnership, and advantages over vertically integrated companies that bring all activities in-house. Value-adding partnerships are in this view 'a set of (relatively) independent companies that work closely together to manage the flow of goods and services along the entire value-added chain'. Value-adding partnerships allow each partner to focus on what they do best.

7. Heuristics and network position: a cognitive and structural framework on innovation

Armando Cirrincione and Stefano Pace

INTRODUCTION

What the drivers of innovation are and why one firm is more innovative than others are fundamental questions for both literature and practice. We can draw a basic distinction between an approach that bases innovation on internal capabilities and another one that puts the emphasis on the network to which the firm belongs. In the first approach, innovation is seen as originating within the firm thanks to its capabilities, primarily cognitive ones, since innovation is linked to new knowledge.[1] Teece et al. (1997) develop the concept of the dynamic capabilities of the firm, meaning the capabilities that enable it to constantly innovate. Andriopoulos (2001) provides a comprehensive review of the various contributions that strive to list the internal determinants of a firm's creativity: organizational climate, leadership style, organizational culture, resources and skills (human resources), structure and systems. Cohen and Levinthal (1990), with their concept of absorptive capacity, mediate between an internal perspective and the openness of the organization to external knowledge.

At the other end of the spectrum, and dating from Hayek's work (1945), innovation is considered a network-based phenomenon: new knowledge is created through exchanges among partners of a network (distributed innovation). Knowledge does not reside in a single subject or organization but is network-based (Romano and Rullani, 1998). More recently, a third stream of research supports the community-based structure as an alternative arrangement to foster new knowledge and innovation (Sawhney and Prandelli, 2001; Wenger, 1999).

The aim of this chapter is to pair together the network and the cognitive arguments. The hypothesis suggested is that a broker firm – the firm that holds a structural hole position (Burt, 1992) within a network – has the advantage of being exposed to different cognitive heuristics (above all when the network is formed by nodes belonging to different industries). Combining these heuristics, the structural hole firm expresses a bigger innovativeness. Some authors have shown the innovativeness of structural hole firms employing a cognitive concept such as memory (Hargadon and Sutton, 1997), but they do not address the specific content of that cognitive process, focusing more on the structural position. While this chapter acknowledges the relevance of structural position in a network, it adds the heuristics concept to explain the innovative process: the broker firm is more innovative since it can share many heuristics, thanks to its structural hole occupation. In this view the structural and the cognitive arguments are deeply intertwined.

In the following section we review the recent literature on network, knowledge and innovation. Then we explain a cognitive approach to innovation seen as stemming from the utilization of heuristic by the firm during the searching activity of its problem-solving process. We associate the network and the cognitive facets, arguing that the innovation should be explained by both of them. Finally an empirical case is described and conclusions are drawn.

NETWORK, KNOWLEDGE AND INNOVATION: A THEORETICAL BACKGROUND

Burt (1992) studies the different structures that a network may assume. He focuses on structural holes, which are gaps 'in the flow of information between subgroups in a larger network' (Hargadon and Sutton, 1997: 717). A firm that occupies a structural hole can exploit the different streams of knowledge coming from different sub-groups, combining them into new knowledge, producing innovation. The path dependence that occurs inside the sub-groups creates some redundancy of knowledge, hampering innovation and refining what is already known. The broker can integrate and innovate these streams of knowledge.

The literature has dealt with the issues of network arrangements and innovation. A seminal work is that of Powell et al. (1996). The authors find a positive relationship between central position, the development of interactive capabilities and learning. But, owing to the data they accessed, they did not distinguish between alternative structures of network or different types of relationship. Ahuja (2002) poses the question of which is the best network arrangement for innovation, either dense or with structural holes. He argues that the answer is industry-contingent: 'when speedy access to diverse information is essential, structural holes are likely to be advantageous; when developing a collaborative milieu and overcoming opportunism are essential, closed networks are likely to be more beneficial' (Ahuja, 2000: 451). The work by Bonaccorsi and Giuri (2001) shows that for innovation along a specific technological trajectory a hierarchical network is more effective than a dispersed one.

While the previously cited works deal with the structure of the network, Granovetter (1973) focuses attention on the type of ties. His contribution, even though not specifically focused on innovation and not at the organization level, is relevant to understanding networks and it has been used by innovation theory scholars too. Weak ties (the ties with low levels of frequency, depth and intimacy compared to strong ties) allow for a broader span of connections and a richer exposure to different knowledge by the node. Hansen (1999) shows that complex knowledge requires strong ties to be transferred, while weak ties better suit less complex knowledge. Rowley et al. (2000) discover that in interconnected strategic alliance networks strong ties can impact negatively on the firm's performance. Coleman (1988) would prefer strong ties for knowledge circulation, owing to the higher trust among the subjects. A dense network, in Coleman's view, would be preferable for innovation, rather than a network with structural holes.

Hargadon and Sutton (1997) integrate the macro- and the micro-perspective on a firm's innovation, analyzing both position in the network and internal routines. They argue that the innovativeness of a company depends 'on both its network position as a broker and on organizational memory that allows it to acquire, retain, and retrieve new combinations of information obtained through such a position' (ibid.: 717).[2] The case analyzed by the two authors is that of the largest product design consulting firm in the USA: IDEO, based in Chicago. This company deals with business customers belonging to different industries. Working for them, IDEO makes itself familiar with their particular knowledge and expertise. Therefore IDEO is able to recombine the knowledge received from them, developing new ideas viable for other industries.[3] The contribution of the two authors validly mixes structure and capabilities explanations for the innovation process, but the relationship between these two drivers seems not to be fully addressed. IDEO is a case of excellence, but another firm might have, for instance, a good brokering position inside the network and a bad organizational memory, or vice versa. In their contribution it seems that the mere fact of being in a structural hole allows for such an accumulation of information that the recombination is just the final and natural act. But covering a structural hole should not necessarily imply the possession of the organizational memory described by the two authors. Furthermore Hargadon and Sutton use the concept of memory to explain the capability of IDEO to achieve innovation. Memory is a concept derived from the cognitive sciences and then applied to organization. The firm described by the two authors is able to store information and then retrieve the pieces that are more relevant for a new product design. But it is the memory itself that can impede creativity. It is not clear why more information leads to creation and more innovation. It is plausible the exact opposite effect: having too much information creates a path dependence that impedes creation. Memory is a cognitive function that categorizes information in order to keep it for future utilization. This categorization may hamper the creative process, not foster it. One can challenge the notion that information leads directly to new knowledge creation. The link between information and new knowledge may be not so direct and consequential. More than information, what is relevant for innovation is the processing scheme used by the organization, its heuristic and cognitive routines.

In this chapter we would like to show that the position within a network and the internal capabilities of the firm are intertwined in a different way: the structural hole position leads to a creativity understood as the combination of different heuristics, not as the combination of information or knowledge.

STRUCTURAL CREATIVITY: INNOVATION AS HEURISTICS COMBINATION

Innovation is an outcome of knowledge, but knowledge is not sufficient. Knowledge is the fuel for the problem-solving process that leads to new ideas and their application, thus to innovation.

Knowledge grows through searching activities or through experience (Gavetti and Levinthal, 2000). Searching activity consists in looking forward for solutions to current problems. Experience is looking backward to the firm's past accomplishments that may be applied again (learning by doing) or it is the observation of other firms' behaviour (learning by interacting). Yet knowledge accumulation in itself does not necessarily lead to creative solutions. Pico della Mirandola with his legendary memory was less creative than Leonardo da Vinci with his heterogeneous knowledge from arts to medicine, from engineering to physics. There is something at work inside knowledge that grants innovation, switching the issue from quantity to quality of knowledge.

The cognitive psychologist Johnson-Laird (1988) suggests a two-stage theory of the searching activities conducted by the mind: 1) generation of new ideas; and 2) evaluation of the generated ideas, in order to retain only the viable ones. During both stages the solver employs criteria so embedded and implicit that they are called 'constraints'. Constraints are the beliefs, the core assumptions, the boundaries of the subject's problem-solving. Creativity is the relaxation of those constraints in order to get a new vision of the problem and then its solutions. With the same quantity of knowledge we can get several innovative solutions depending on the constraints relaxed.

An example devised by Duncker (1945) can help to illustrate the aforementioned concepts. Duncker poses the following puzzle. A person has a candle and a box of thumb tacks. The task is to fix the candle to a wall. Usually people are stumped until a sudden insight prompts them to empty the box, fix the box to the wall with some thumb tacks and then put the candle inside the box. People who do not solve the puzzle are stopped by the constraint that the box is a container just for the thumb tacks. The creative solvers relax that constraint and they consider the box as a container for anything, including a candle. From that relaxation of constraints the solution is achieved. The difference between the creative solver and the failing person does not lie in the level of knowledge, since both of them have the same knowledge (candle, box and thumb tacks), but in the different use of knowledge.

A set of constraints is a heuristic. In cognitive psychology a heuristic is a strategy of discovery that is followed, more or less consciously, by a person or a group in a problem–solving activity. It contains the cardinal points of the searching activity and so it represents the structure of the group's knowledge (Johnson-Laird, 2002; Legrenzi, 2002; Legrenzi and Girotto, 1998). The heuristic used to explore possible solutions largely remains at a level that Polanyi (1966) would define as 'tacit knowledge'. This means that one is not conscious of the knowledge needed to discover something (Legrenzi, 2002); one simply uses it. When we try to solve a problem we unconsciously describe and frame it in our mind using our tacit heuristic. Then we evaluate possible solving ideas by referring to explicit constraints, such as a set of rules, dominant taste, or just our understanding of possible and impossible. We try, we assess the outcomes, and then we use them as feedback to enhance the process of searching. To enhance the process means to relax constraints in a new way; relaxing could lead to a new representation of the problem and to the final answer. Relaxing constraints is not an attribute of a heuristic, but it can spring from the application of a heuristic that does not look at the problem with the same set of constraints.

This heuristic approach can be applied to the firm seen as knowledge processor. The high level of density within a network's sub-group allows for the development of a well–refined stream of knowledge linked to a single heuristic. But this same density impinges on the capability to innovate, owing to the path dependency of knowledge (Nelson and Winter, 1982). Past knowledge may act as an obstacle to innovation, funnelling the group towards refinement of what is already known, rather than to a newly created knowledge. By contrast, the broker, occupying a structural hole, shares the different heuristics of the various sub-groups. It has the potential of innovative solutions derived from the use of different heuristics, thus a different set of constraints, that it acquires by interacting with firms in different sub-networks. This elaboration is coherent with recent literature on network and innovation, but our contribution tries to go beyond the relationship of 'the more knowledge, the more innovation'. Innovation does not necessarily spring from a recombination of information as in Hargadon and Sutton's (1997) theory, but may arise from a combination of different heuristics by the structural hole firm. What is considered a constraint for an industry may be relaxed thanks to a different perspective, gained from another industry's frameset. Elaborating different heuristics would push the brokering firm towards innovative solutions. A case study can help in illustrating this approach.

THE BENETTON CASE

The Italian textile and clothing industry shows a very interesting application for our framework: the Benetton group, one of the most successful corporations in the world. Benetton started its activity in the 1970s, within the main industrial district in the north-east of Italy, where several small firms were located operating in the textile and clothing industry. Within that cluster of firms, Benetton was a manufacturing company connected with other firms through commercial and interpersonal relations, being part of a whole, dense network of clothing manufacturers.

The network of manufacturers was driven by a specific heuristic, made of constraints and priorities. The priorities concerned efficiency in production and economies of scale (getting high volume of production). The ideal situation would have been to massively produce only one type of standard garment (one design and one colour, as in a Tayloristic chain). The constraints for manufacturers were to produce *the right collection* of clothes and garments for the next season, in terms of design and colours. 'Right collection' means a certain combination of styles and colours that the market will require. Mismatching this requirement would determine the failure of the season for the manufacturer; to make garments using dyed fibre: this is a constraint that requires knowing the colour at the beginning of the manufacturing process, well before sales.

These priorities and constraints (efficiency, market match and use of dyed fibres) implied the necessity of collecting orders from stores six to nine months in advance, in order to timely manufacture the right number of items in the right colours. Getting orders well before the actual sales allowed for both matching market requirements and achieving production efficiency. The problem of choosing the right clothing collection was shifted from the producer to the stores, at the distribution level, since stores had to sense the market and place the corresponding orders a long time in advance. The stores took the risk of mistakes in forecasting customers' needs.

Stores were entrepreneurial firms that followed specific heuristics according to the nature of their retailing business. Retailing had specific priorities and constraints, different from the manufacturers'. In retailing the priority concerned stocking just the right clothes (design and colours that consumers ask for); the constraint concerned placing orders with the manufacturers a long time in advance, taking the risk of mistakes in forecasting. (See Figure 7.1.) During the 1970s Benetton chose a strategy of integration, becoming a franchiser and building a network of several franchisee shops in Italy with its own brand, '012 Benetton'. Consequently Benetton was also deeply involved in a different network of firms: the stores. From the cognitive psychology point of view this means that Benetton shared two different heuristics, the manufacturers' and the retailers', each with its own set of priorities and constraints.

When Benetton entered the network of retailers, it had to become aware of their different priorities and constraints. Manufacturers had constraints referring to efficiency, productivity, scale and dyed fibres; the orders placed well before the sales were a solution to these constraints. This solution was a constraint for retailers: placing the orders in advance caused the risk of mismatching the market's requirements. The ideal situation for the manufacturer was to make the same type of garment without variations, while the ideal for the retailer was to order in real time the colour and design combination actually required by the customer.

Bridging the gap between the network of manufacturers and the network of retailers, Benetton could be involved in the two different heuristics. That position led Benetton to create an important innovation in the process of manufacturing clothes: to colour the final product (the garment) at the end of the manufacturing process rather than colouring the fibres at the start of the process. (This innovation was called '*tinto in capo*': dye upon the garment). With that innovation it was possible for Benetton to produce large volumes of clothes in the same neutral colour; dyeing was just the last process before delivery to the stores. By doing this, Benetton could exploit economies of scale (efficiency), while eliminating the retailers' constraint (the need to place orders with manufacturers a long time in advance) and achieving their priorities. Benetton's idea of colouring garments eliminated the need for long–term planning for colours, while matching the season's requirements. Benetton relaxed the constraint of the dyed fibres, thus achieving the priorities of both manufacturers and retailers, and erasing their constraints too.

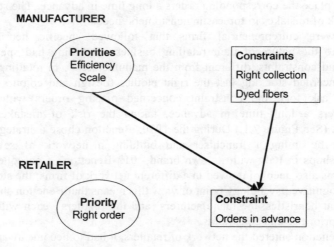

Figure 7.1   Heuristics in the garment industry

Why was Benetton the most likely subject to find this solution? The answer lies in the creative process of eliminating constraints and maintaining the traditional priorities, both for manufacturers and for retailers. The reason why Benetton devised the innovation concerns the two different heuristics it was involved in thanks to its position in the structural hole.

CONCLUSION

The network approach looks at the innovation process as a recombination of information gathered from different sub-networks, without explaining how that recombination actually occurs. Being a broker would imply being creative: the network and the position within that network seem to be dominant compared with the cognitive psychology approach to the innovation process. In the structuralistic view creativity is just a recombination of knowledge and this means that brokering knowledge leads to being creative. By contrast, cognitive psychology underlines that knowledge is just one component of creativity, necessary but not sufficient. In order to be creative we need to use knowledge obtained from different contexts, thus characterized by different heuristics. Benetton did not know more than its competitors; it knew 'differently' from them. Creativity is not only about how large our library is, but also about how different its books are.

The contribution that this chapter aims to provide is an integration of the structuralistic and cognitive psychology views, suggesting that the network position and the cognitive perspective are strictly related. A purely structural explanation or a purely cognitive theory seems to fail in explaining innovative processes, since they disconnect the 'black box' from the network. Moreover the cognitive side can be explained by leveraging on the modern cognitive studies on creativity, employing the heuristic concept, related to the rules of knowledge rather than its elements (information).

Future researches can examine the relationship more deeply, asking whether the structural hole position is the only way to have different heuristics or whether new heuristics can be developed somehow independently of the network position. Furthermore cases and examples of innovative processes previously studied may be reinterpreted according to the framework illustrated here in a search for confirmation or refutation.

NOTES

1. Companies such as 3M are among the best examples of that approach, since the main source of innovation is the creativity of the employees.
2. They cite the example of Edison, a firm whose incredibly high level of innovation can be explained by the fact that it covered a structural hole in the scientific network, combining scientific fields that otherwise would have been isolated.
3. Among the 3.000 or so products designed by IDEO, we can mention the Apple's computer mouse, AT&T telephones and the Crest toothpaste tube (Hargadon and Sutton 1997, 719).

REFERENCES

Ahuja, G. (2000), 'Collaboration networks, structural holes, and innovation: a longitudinal study', *Administrative Science Quarterly*, **45** (3): 425–455.
Andriopoulos, C. (2001), 'Determinants of organizational creativity: a literature review', *Management Decision*, **39** (10): 834–340.
Bonaccorsi, A. and P. Giuri (2001), 'Learning, technological competition and network structure in the aero-engine industry', *LEM Laboratory of*

Economics and Management, Sant'Anna School of Advanced Studies, Pisa (Italy), Working Paper Series, May, No. 11.

Burt, R.S. (1992), *Structural Holes: the Social Structure of Competition*, Cambridge, MA: Harvard University Press.

Cohen, W.M. and D.A. Levinthal (1990), 'Absorptive capacity: a new perspective on learning and innovation', *Administrative Science Quarterly*, **35** (1), Special Issue: Technology, Organizations, and Innovation: 128–152.

Coleman, J.S. (1988), 'Social capital in creation of human capital', *American Journal of Sociology*, **94**: 95–120.

Duncker, K. (1945), 'On problem solving', *Psychological Monographs*, **58** (5).

Gavetti, G. and D.A. Levinthal (2000), 'Looking forward and looking backward: cognitive and experiential search', *Administrative Science Quarterly*, **45**: 113–137.

Granovetter, M. (1973), 'The strength of weak ties', *American Journal of Sociology*, **78**: 1360–1380.

Hansen, M.T. (1999), 'The search-transfer problem: the role of weak ties in sharing knowledge across organization subunits', *Administrative Science Quarterly*, **44** (1): 82–111.

Hargadon, A. and R.I. Sutton (1997), 'Technology brokering and innovation in a product development firm', *Administrative Science Quarterly*, **42**: 716–749.

Hayek, F.A. (1945), 'The use of knowledge in society', *American Economic Review*, **4**: 519–530.

Johnson-Laird, P. (1988), *The Computer and the Mind*, Cambridge, MA: Harvard University Press.

Johnson-Laird, P. (2002), 'How jazz musicians improvise', *Music Perception*, **19**.

Legrenzi, P. (2002), *Prima Lezione di Scienze Cognitive*, Bari-Roma: Laterza.

Legrenzi, P. and V. Girotto (1998), 'Mental models in reasoning and decision making', in A. Garnham, and J. Oakhill (eds), *Mental models in cognitive science*, Erlbaum Hove, UK: Taylor and Francis, pp. 95–118.

Nelson, R. and S. Winter (1982), *An Evolutionary Theory of Economic Change*, Boston, Cambridge, MA: The Belknap Press of Harvard.

Polanyi, M. (1966), *The Tacit Dimension*, London: Routledge.

Powell, W.W., K. Koput and L. Smith-Doerr (1996), 'Interorganizational collaboration and the locus of innovation: networks of learning in biotechnology', *Administrative Science Quarterly:* **41**: 116–145.

Romano, L. and E. Rullani (1998), *Il Postfordismo: Idee per il Capitalismo Prossimo Venturo*, Milan: ETAS Libri.

Rowley, T., D. Behrens and D. Krackhardt (2000), 'Redundant governance structures: an analysis of structural and relational embeddedness in the steel and semiconductor industries', *Strategic Management Journal*, **21** (3): 369–386.

Sawhney, M and E. Prandelli (2001), 'Communities of creation: managing distributed innovation in turbulent markets', *California Management Review*, **42**: 24–54.

Teece, D.J., G. Pisano and A. Shuen (1997), 'Dynamic capabilities and strategic management', *Strategic Management Journal*, **18** (7): 509–533.

Wenger, E. (1999), *Communities of Practice: Learning, Meaning, and Identity*, Cambridge UK: Cambridge University Press.

8. Developing dynamic capabilities with IT

José A. Medina-Garrido, José Ruiz-Navarro and Sebastian Bruque-Camara

INTRODUCTION

A resource-based view of the firm understands that the heterogeneous resources and capabilities possessed by companies will explain both the existence of the firm and any difference in its results. The company is understood to be a specific set of resources. Amit and Schoemaker (1993) define resources as a stock of factors which are possessed or controlled by the company. Capabilities are the skills of resource coordination and mobilization. Capabilities (flow) are resources (stock) which work together (Grant, 1991) by means of well–established routines (Nelson and Winter, 1982). They have their own dynamism; they represent resources in movement.

Resources and capabilities are core when they are fundamental to the performance of a company and its strategy (Grant, 1991; Prahalad and Hamel, 1990). Growth, the opportunity to provide new products and enter new markets, does not depend so much upon demand as upon the resources and capabilities possessed by a company (Penrose, 1958). The combination, development, exploitation and protection of the company's specific resources provide the basis for its competitive advantages. Resources and capabilities are complementary when they lever the performance of other resources and capabilities (Milgrom and Roberts, 1995).

Dynamic capabilities are the ability of a company to integrate, build and reshape internal and external capabilities in order to provide a rapid response to any change in its environment (Teece et al., 1997). The dynamic capabilities of an organization reflect its ability to achieve innovative ways in which to compete in any given circumstances. The aforementioned dynamism relates to the capacity to change routines and even the resources which go to make up those routines. Creating dynamic capabilities in order to achieve new competitive advantages requires a knowledge of how to change core capabilities.

To develop the resource-based theory of the firm it is necessary to specify concepts (Wernerfelt, 1995) and the role to be played by complementary capabilities (Teece et al., 1994) in creating dynamic capabilities (Teece et al., 1997). This approach allows other capabilities to be taken into consideration when, although they may not yet be core capabilities, they may become so in the future. These dynamic capabilities will allow the company to anticipate or adapt to changing environments.

It must be pointed out that in highly complex circumstances company boundaries are blurred and environment and organization may be confused. In situations such as these greater emphasis should be placed on human assets, information systems, and knowledge management. Information technology (IT), supporting an information system, plays a decisive role in this context (Lowendahl and Revang, 1998; Davenport et al., 1998).

The resource-based view of the firm is useful for studying IT (Mata et al., 1995). On the one hand, previous literature defines IT as an infrastructure (ITI) of hardware, software and communications media, whereas this view considers IT as a resource. On the other hand, contributions about organization routines (Nelson and Winter, 1982) explaining ITI connectivity and its informative content (intangible assets) do not abound. The management of these routines and intangible assets turns ITI from a commodity into a valuable asset.

Mata *et al.* (1995) state that ITI provides no advantage in itself, although skills in the management of ITI could produce advantages if they enabled the firm to perceive and exploit other capabilities that could prove to be sources of competitive advantage (Barney, 1991). In this chapter these ITI management skills, or IT capabilities (ITC), refer to the aforementioned management of routines and intangible assets, assets that could support the creation of core capabilities.

ITC support the creation of new capabilities by providing a means of coordinating personnel, enhancing communication, storing, processing and transferring information to wherever it may be required. These ITC functions play a key role as catalysts in the creation of dynamic capabilities.

Literature relating IT to the resource-based view of the firm does not abound. This chapter proposes a dynamic capability creation process supported by ITC which addresses this gap.

The development of dynamic capabilities is relevant in complex contexts where ITC may play a key role. These complex contexts, originating from the internal complexity of the organization and the external complexity of the environment, make it necessary to assess the validity of current theories and, additionally, to discover new concepts leading to new theories. By studying the creation of dynamic capabilities, this chapter aims to proceed along the latter road, the one on which single, strategic and organizational theories may give way to equally valid eclectic solutions (Lowendahl and Revang, 1998). The added value of this chapter lies in its proposal of a dynamic capabilities creation model, and its study of the complementary role of ITC in this creation process.

A DYNAMIC CAPABILITIES CREATION MODEL

According to Lorenzo-Gomez and Ruiz-Navarro (1997) and Ruiz-Navarro (1998), dynamic capabilities are seen to possess two principal forms of generation (Baden-Fuller and Volberda, 1996, 1997; Baden-Fuller and Stopford, 1994; Burgelman, 1994; Garud and Nayyar, 1994). Dynamic capabilities come from either (1) dormant or latent capabilities, which are accumulated through collective experiences and reside in 'organizational memory', so they are not in use; or (2) peripheral capabilities, which are in use but are not considered core capabilities of the company. Although neither of the aforementioned capabilities forms part of current core capabilities, they may provide a source for future capabilities.

The search for new capabilities may be approached from two different angles. The first refers to the development or acquisition of new capabilities from external sources. This capacity has been identified by Garud and Nayyar (1994) as absorptive capacity. The second way to develop new capabilities is by taking advantage of capabilities that already exist in the company, dormant from the past (dormant capabilities), separate from core capabilities (peripheral capabilities), or current core capabilities. The capacity to transform existing capabilities into new ones is called transformative capacity (Garud and Nayyar, 1994). Figure 8.1 outlines the aforementioned sources of dynamic capabilities. The creation process will be explained in greater detail below, with special emphasis on the role played by ITC in transformative capacity.

The concept of transformative capacity contrasts with that of absorptive capacity, whereby a firm perceives and makes use of external capabilities. Absorptive capacity is insufficient if an accumulation of capabilities dependent upon paths followed in the past is required; if the moment when the capability is acquired is critical[1]; or if, in a changing environment, the company has no desire to react to external changes but rather intends to create some such changes itself.

Absorptive capacity, by definition, allows for imitable capabilities that are unlikely to provide any source of competitive advantage.

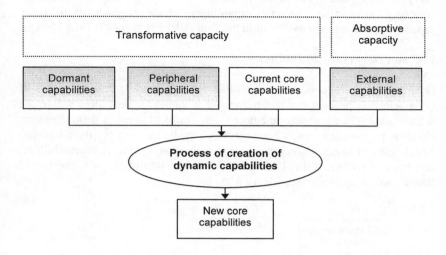

Figure 8.1 Sources of dynamic capabilities

To be a source of sustainable competitive advantage, a resource must be valuable, scarce and difficult to imitate or acquire (Barney, 1991). As this is unlikely with external capabilities, absorptive capacity only provides a sustainable competitive advantage if combined with complementary capabilities belonging to the company, and, if these are valuable (either in their own right or jointly with complementary capabilities), scarce and difficult to imitate or acquire.

Transformative capacity may generate company-specific and difficult to imitate capabilities of great strategic value for the company because internal capabilities are more likely to be company-specific, path-dependent, socially complex, and causally ambiguous. A capability creation process should not, however, neglect people. Human resources may sometimes become stumbling blocks, and at other times true instigators of new capabilities. People may therefore be regarded as complementary capabilities (Teece, 1987; Teece et al., 1994) that must be taken into account. If they do not support, understand and correctly perceive the process, the creation of new capabilities may well fail and lead to old capabilities re-emerging in the form of rigidities.

ITC have three different roles to play in the creation of dynamic capabilities: (1) to support the identification of the organization's historic (dormant) and peripheral capabilities; (2) to keep a catalogue of capabilities or a map of people who possess them (Davenport et al., 1998; Garud and

Nayyar, 1994); and (3) to act as transmitters, spreading them throughout the company, generating dynamic capabilities which originate from those capabilities that already exist within the firm (Ulrichet al.,1993; Doz, 1994).

ITC and Dormant Capabilities

Dormant capabilities may be transmitted over a period of time by means of (1) a selection process that determines what should be kept alive within the organization; (2) the development of skills aimed at keeping them dormant; (3) their reactivation, when necessary, and synthesis; and (4) their transfer. These tasks of selection, maintenance, reactivation, synthesis of capabilities, and transfer (Ulrich et al., 1993; Doz, 1994), are part of the aforementioned transformative capacity (see Figure 8.2).

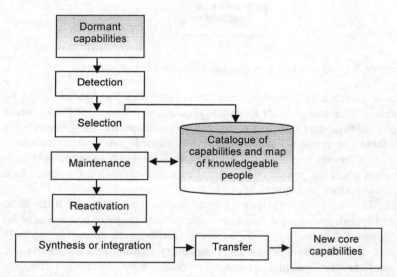

Figure 8.2   Dynamic capabilities creation process from dormant capabilities

But why should such knowledge remain dormant? It may seem to do little more than produce apparently unnecessary costs. The answer lies in the fact that delays exist in technological development, from the supply side, and in the development of the market, from the demand side. Demand for a product or service may arise in the future as a result of institutional changes, changes in customer requirements or, from the supplier's point of view, a convergence of asynchronous technological vectors (where some vectors were temporary bottlenecks for others) that make new services or products possible. Lost dormant capabilities could prove difficult or even impossible to rebuild or acquire when they are required by new conditions of supply and demand (Garud and Nayyar, 1994). It may also be observed that the different types of restructuring undergone by a firm may lead to a loss of key capabilities (dormant and peripheral, possessed by outsourced personnel) that might support future competitive advantages (Hamel and Prahalad, 1994).

The role played by ITC in the creation of dynamic capabilities derived from dormant capabilities is to help with the transmission of the latter. It does this because ITC may (1) satisfy the demand for information required for the selection of capabilities which are to remain dormant (instead of them being forgotten); (2) help to maintain them through the proper integration of ITC, complementary human resources and business capabilities (Powell and Dent-Micallef, 1997); (3) collaborate when necessary in their reactivation and synthesis (Garud and Nayyar, 1994) by integrating (Doz, 1994) simple skills in complex capabilities (by means of mechanisms such as rules, guidelines and organizational routines), both valuable and difficult to imitate; and (4) promote their transfer throughout the firm (also counting on the support of the previously mentioned complementary resources and capabilities).

The quantity of information to be managed by ITC during the selection, maintenance, reactivation and synthesis, and transfer of dormant capabilities (helped by the complementary capabilities required for this end) depends upon certain characteristics of the type of capability to be transferred through time. These characteristics are whether it is (1) tacit or explicit, that is, whether or not it can be described as a whole or coded; (2) simple or complex, the former requiring little information in its description and the latter requiring a great deal; and (3) systemic or independent, the former needing to be described in relation to other capabilities and the latter to be described in its own right.

Capabilities that are tacit, complex or systemic are more difficult to transmit over a period of time (dormant capabilities) (Garud and Nayyar, 1994) or through space (peripheral capabilities). If this were not the case (and they were explicit, simple, and independent), they would be more homogeneously spread throughout companies, easy to obtain from scratch, and thus of less strategic value. It is not worth maintaining easily transmitted dormant capabilities (explicit, simple and independent) unless the firm possesses the ability to prevent others from gaining access to them, or they gain value only when combined with complementary capabilities belonging exclusively to the firm and without which they are worthless.

ITC have three different roles to play in the process of selection, maintenance, reactivation, synthesis, and transfer: (1) to support decision making; (2) to facilitate communication; and (3) to act as a catalogue or map of capabilities. Firstly, ITC support the decision making that may take place in any of these tasks, by supplying necessary information, providing prospective and simulation tools, statistics, and so on. In this way, they will help at the selection stage to collect information of an internal or external character that allows for a decision to be made as to whether the assessed capability may be regarded as an option (in financial terms) for future competitive advantages. ITC also help to carry out simulations which reflect the impact that the decision to maintain will have on other units. During the maintenance stage, they allow for an ordered view of the catalogue of capabilities or the map of people who possess tacit capabilities (see Figure 8.2), facilitating inspection of their content and, if necessary, their update. In the process of reactivation, ITC facilitate the inspection of catalogued dormant (and peripheral) capabilities, collaborate in the normalization of the capabilities (if possible) to facilitate integration, and monitor market and technological variables which may trigger reactivation and synthesis. Finally, the information supplied by ITC will improve the transfer process of the synthesized capability, by supporting its articulation (making tacit capabilities explicit, wherever possible) and the internalization of capabilities (transforming explicit capabilities into know-how by performing the job) (Doz, 1994).

The second role of ITC is that of facilitating communication processes through the means that they provide for personnel to communicate with each other, by-passing functional, hierarchical, geographical and temporal boundaries. In this way the mechanisms of lateral coordination (liaison work, work groups and permanent committees, integrating managers and matrix structure, and so on) become enriched, thereby increasing the capacity of the organization for processing information. By playing this role in the selection process, ITC provide mechanisms for running and coordinating work groups, helping them to identify the capabilities to be catalogued or knowledgeable people to be mapped. At the maintenance stage, ITC help to develop means whereby researchers, technicians and engineers may share the information to be maintained and easily reach knowledgeable people, if necessary, using the aforementioned map. ITC facilitate reactivation and synthesis by encouraging researchers and workers to make their advances more widely available, providing a means for sharing information and transferring it in such a way that the convergence of capability vectors is rapidly detected. Both formal and informal communication, as well as improved lateral links, stimulate the process of transferring synthesized capabilities, making those that are explicit more widespread, and supporting learning by doing (Doz, 1994) from knowledgeable people, which is necessary in the case of capabilities that are difficult to structure.

Thirdly, in collaboration with human resources, ITC act as a repository for descriptions of capabilities and constitute the catalogue and the map (Davenport et al., 1998) alluded to earlier in connection with the maintenance task. This catalogue contains an inventory of capabilities and, wherever possible, standardizes and codes the information to make it more accessible to those who participate in the work of maintenance and reactivation at any given time, wherever they may be. Standardization aims to minimize the amount of information required for reactivation to be registered (in rapidly changing environments the amount will be greater), and to facilitate discovery of convergence between different capacities. Where normalization is not possible (when dealing with tacit capabilities), the support of the human resources that retain these dormant capabilities becomes fundamental. The catalogue must include a map of the worksites where these tacit capabilities are possessed, and details of how to contact those who possess them. As the firm looks ahead to further future synthesis, the standardization of catalogued capabilities should be extended to include the normalisation of recently synthesized developments.

It must not be forgotten that the quantity of information required for selecting, maintaining, reactivating and transferring capabilities, and their location (human resources or ITI) is influenced, as mentioned earlier, by the type of capabilities in question; thas is, whether they are explicit or tacit, simple or complex, independent or systemic.

ITC and Peripheral Capabilities

Capabilities are rarely found to be widespread throughout an organization; they are more likely to be found where they were produced, in individuals or small groups who possess the relevant know-how and in those who undergo the learning process. Sometimes they even spread to an organizational sub-unit or to a specific function. These are known as peripheral capabilities. If they are spread out and shared among different sub-units, functions or processes, the likelihood of discovering new opportunities increases. In addition, newly emerging opportunities may mean combining a number of capabilities cultivated in different parts of the organization (Doz, 1994).

ITC play a double role in the management of peripheral capabilities. In the first place, ITC may be peripheral capabilities upon which to construct dynamic capabilities; in addition, they may help to locate and manage other peripheral capabilities of a different nature.

Among the different types of peripheral capabilities that may be offered by ITC, we might first mention that of providing a source of creation for new products and services, by intervening in their information content. For example, the ITC of a specific business unit might lead to the creation of products with a greater informative content, or to an increase in services that are additional to the product, through access to electronic markets. Another possibility is that of ITC exerting influence on the processes involved in the firm's value production chain, by creating, modifying or destroying activities on either the physical or the informative side of the value chain. ITC also create, modify or destroy the chain's links, both external (with the value chains of clients and suppliers) and internal (Porter and Millar, 1985). Design work, for example, which is usually regarded as a manufacturing activity, could be undertaken by the sales department, thanks to computer-aided design systems (CAD) that would better adapt the product to the client's specific needs, thus producing the destruction and creation of different activities and links within the value chain. One outstanding feature of this process is the ability to integrate independent systems, thus generating such benefits as synergies and economies of scale (no redundant data or information, consistent information, minimum cost in updating information, savings on storage, data quality).

When ITC is used for locating and managing other peripheral capabilities, the concepts of detection, storage, synthesis and transfer, previously explained for dormant capabilities (see Figure 8.2), will also prove useful (unlike selection and maintenance, since peripheral capabilities are in use). The support function provided by ITC in decision making and fostering the communication and storage of information (all of which were described in depth in the previous section) are also applicable to the detection, inventory, synthesis and transfer of peripheral capabilities, all of which are useful in the creation of dynamic capabilities. Improvement of lateral links and communication with the organization as a whole makes it possible to cross the functional, hierarchical, temporary, geographic or external boundaries of the business unit, such as suppliers or clients. It is these boundaries that keep peripheral capabilities in their place of origin.

The facilities provided by ITC in improving communication within the company, encouraging both formal and informal lateral links, would be one way of detecting concealed peripheral capabilities. Other capabilities will require no search at all, since they are quite familiar to members of the organization. Detected capabilities enlarge the catalogue (or the map of knowledgeable people, if tacit capabilities), and they require no maintenance, since they are living capabilities. When necessary, catalogued capabilities, or even capabilities that are not yet catalogued, may be aggregated to other capabilities, thus forming dynamic capabilities. The transfer process is conducted in the same way as with dormant capabilities, with the advantage that there is no need to search either the organizational memory of individuals or that of the information system, since it is possible to rely on those who currently exercise these capabilities.

The process of creation of dynamic capabilities from peripheral capabilities is summarized in Figure 8.3.

The Final Model

Transformative and absorptive processes do not take place independently. On the contrary, the synthesis stage integrates dormant, peripheral, current core and external capabilities.

Nothing has been said about current core capabilities. These are strategic for the firm and a source of current competitive advantage. Some firms carry out a formal process of detecting and cataloguing them, in order to develop and avoid neglecting them. In other firms the emergent path prevails, as these capabilities are well known and present in people minds.

The dynamic capabilities creation process explained above reflects a programmatic perspective as opposed to one based on the emergent production of new capabilities. In the emergent path, the company naturally and regularly develops certain capabilities. Nevertheless, in complex contexts, companies feel obliged to programme the development of their capabilities with the aim of speeding them up, instead of simply relying on emergent processes (Garud and Nayyar, 1994). Furthermore formalization of the new capabilities creation process may encourage a more ambitious strategic proposal (Hamel and Prahalad, 1989) and increase both the skills of those involved and their desire to share and transfer capabilities.

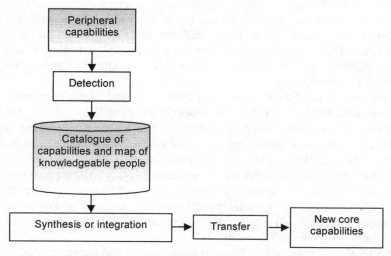

Figure 8.3 Dynamic capabilities creation process from peripheral capabilities

The final dynamic capabilities creation model considers both the programmatic and the emergent path, and all possible sources of dynamic capabilities, both internal and external (see Figure 8.4). The role of ITI will not simply be to supply information and transfer it through the formal capability creation processes (programmatic path). It will also be to intervene in informal processes (emergent path), by improving communications between members of the firm.

THE NEED FOR COMPLEMENTARY RESOURCES AND CAPABILITIES

In addition to what has been stated in previous sections, the stages involved in the development process of dynamic capabilities require complementary resources and capabilities (Teece, 1987; Teece *et al.*, 1994). Complementary resources and capabilities arise when a resource, or capability, produces greater results in the presence of other resources or capabilities than it does on its own (Wernerfelt, 1984; Teece, 1986; Amit and Schoemaker, 1993; Black and Boal, 1994; Milgrom and Roberts, 1995). This would occur, for example, with the introduction of an EDI system combined with pre-existing confidence in the supplier. This relationship with the supplier is a complementary business capability that would be essential for the EDI system to be successful.

If ITC are not integrated with complementary resources and capabilities, then they are not in themselves efficient, either in creating and maintaining competitive advantages, or in supporting the creation process of new capabilities. When complementary resources and ITC capabilities are working together, they are difficult to imitate, thus sustainable competitive advantages become more feasible.

Powell and Dent-Micallef (1997) ask why it is that some companies encounter difficulties and while others prosper when using the same ITI, and why ITI-based advantages dissipate so quickly. The answer they suggest is that ITI, complementary human resources and business capabilities must be integrated. Nevertheless, according to Mata et al. (1995), ITI are an improbable source of competitive advantage, unlike ITC. Thus the integrated management of ITC and complementary resources and capabilities could improve the creation of dynamic capabilities and become a source of sustainable competitive advantages. A list of these complementary resources and capabilities is given in Table 8.1.

The idea of a close relationship between technological and human resources is not new.

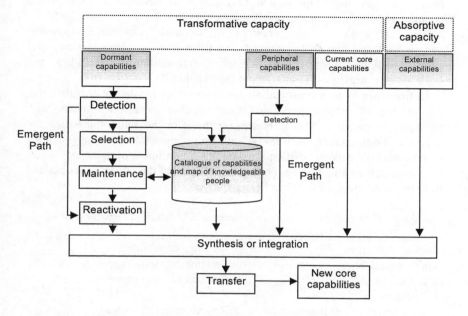

Figure 8.4 Process of creation of dynamic capability

The socio-technical approach (Trist and Bamforth, 1951; Rice, 1958; Emery and Trist, 1965; Miller and Rice, 1967) clearly expressed the notion that companies should consider both their human and technological dimensions. The human relations school (Roethlisberger and Dickson, 1939; McGregor, 1960) and contingency theory (Lawrence and Lorsch, 1967) also noted this relationship.

The capture and integration of capabilities residing in human resources will be necessary for the creation process of dynamic capabilities. '[It] suggests that an understanding of organisational knowledge means viewing the firm not as a container of competencies but as a complex social institution' (Scarbrough, 1998). An appropriate environment must be created to achieve this aim (Davenport et al., 1998). Most of the information that an organization contains does not lie in its computers, but rather in certain of its people who possess it and add value to this information by interpreting it and putting it into context (Davenport, 1994). In this sense, regardless of the aforementioned formal catalogue and programmatic path of creation of dynamic capabilities, most sources of new capabilities (dormant, peripheral and current core) are tacit in people's minds. Thus the informal and emergent path is a very important source of creation of new capabilities, which completes the programmatic model shown in Figure 8.4.

The ITC role in the creation of dynamic capabilities requires complementary human resources, such as open organization and communication, consensus, top management commitment, flexibility, and experience in strategic–ITI integration (see Table 8.1).

In firms where open organization and communication do not already exist, the sharing of information about tacit existing capabilities meets with managerial resistance. Managers sense a threat to the status quo when the need for middle management levels with information transmission functions is reduced. This makes it difficult to gain the commitment of managers. Their resistance acts as an isolating mechanism, protecting the advantages obtained from the combination of ITC and open cultures.

Table 8.1   Complementary human resources and business capabilities

Human resources	Business capabilities
Open organization	Relationship with suppliers
Open communication	Connect IT with suppliers
Consensus	IT training
Commitment of top management	Redesigning processes
Flexibility	Orientation towards teamwork
Strategic integration/ITI	Benchmarking
	ITI planning

Source: Adapted from Powell and Dent-Micallef (1997).

This new approach to dynamic capabilities management may involve an important process of change. The required flexibility, consensus and commitment are not easy to achieve, in the midst of widespread inertia and resistance to change (Rumelt, 1995).

Regarding the role played by human resources in the integration of the firm's global strategy (and particularly the strategic implications of a programmatic process of dynamic capabilities creation) with ITI strategy, it should be pointed out that the use of ITI in the firm's information system undergoes an evolution from its precarious beginnings in the organization to taking on a strategic role. This evolution is only made possible by accumulating experience provided by human resources through a learning process (Gibson and Nolan, 1974; Nolan, 1979). This accumulation process constitutes an ITC and requires long periods of time, otherwise temporal compression diseconomies may operate (Dierickx and Cool, 1989).

In addition, with regard to complementary business capabilities, the ITC role in the creation of dynamic capabilities requires a close relationship and IT connections with suppliers, suitable IT training and planning, redesigning processes, orientation towards teamwork, and benchmarking capabilities (see Table 8.1).

The capacity to maintain a relationship of trust with the supplier appears to require certain communication abilities and complex, tacit coordination which competitors may find difficult to imitate. ITI training may not be a strategic capability, as it is widely available on the market, but the use of specific technologies with specific training may produce idiosyncratic and causally ambiguous organizational capabilities (Mata et al., 1995). The tacit and specific nature of integration between ITI and business processes in a company may also act as an impediment to imitation.

Owing to the fact that one of the most important characteristics of ITC is that they enable people to work as a team, reducing spatial and temporal asynchrony, the capacity to manage teamwork becomes vital in obtaining advantages (that is, dynamic capabilities) from ITC.

Benchmarking is suspect as a source of sustainable competitive advantage, as it imitates the capabilities of others instead of developing them internally and specifically for the company. This capability supports the aforementioned absorptive capacity, and so it is an unlikely source of competitive advantage. It might be valuable only if used for increasing the innovative capabilities of the company (Powell and Dent-Micallef, 1997), or in combination with scarce and inimitable complementary resources or capabilities (Garud and Nayyar, 1994).

ITI planning capability, a particular kind of ITC, provides a source of advantage when oriented towards the planning of company-specific ITI. In addition, for Barney (1991), an ITI planning system may produce advantages if it enables the company to perceive and exploit other capabilities (amongst which peripheral and dormant capabilities may be of special interest), any of which may provide a source of dynamic capabilities.

Not only do ITC require the aforementioned complementary resources and capabilities, they also produce synergic effects, which is why such complementary resources and capabilities are fostered by ITC. Such was the case of BP Exploration, a subsidiary of British Petroleum, where the difficulty of storing tacit knowledge in computerized catalogues was recognized and led to the encouragement, thanks to ITC, of remote virtual team work (Davenport et al., 1998). This led, on the one hand, to the creation of dynamic capabilities, capturing dormant capabilities in an emergent path (it was the programmed path which relied on the catalogue) and, on the other hand, to locating peripheral capabilities in a simpler and more efficient manner.

DISCUSSION

The maintenance of dormant capabilities, the search for peripheral capabilities, the identification of current core capabilities and the possession of the necessary complementary resources and capabilities, when all of these (separately or jointly) are difficult to acquire and imitate, may constitute an internal source of dynamic capabilities. However other solutions do exist, such as the capacity to absorb external capabilities (see Figure 8.1), mergers with other organizations, the acquisition of a whole company which possesses the desired capabilities, or the establishment of some kind of temporary alliance or agreement with other companies. Nevertheless absorption of external capabilities is not free of drawbacks (as mentioned earlier), and acquisition may entail a financial problem. Moreover acquisition and merger involve the acquisition of other undesired resources and capabilities, the difficulty of integrating different business cultures, and the enormous investment in time needed to make the firms work as a single company.

Alliance or agreement would appear to be a more feasible option. This is illustrated by Baden-Fuller and Volberda (1997), for whom the limits of a company do not end with its legal standing but with the limits of its knowledge of the creation and exploitation of processes. In any event, alliances will lend resources and capabilities to the cause but will not transfer them to a company deficient in such resources and capabilities if they are inimitable. Difficulties in their imitation arise when they are obtained at a specific point of time, are developed over a long period, happen to be causally ambiguous or socially complex, or are specific to the company of origin.

The model developed in this chapter presents some limitations. In the first place, the existence of dormant capabilities is not possible in newly–created companies. These companies do, however, have the advantage of greater flexibility for change because they have less inertia or rigidity originating from the past. On the other hand, peripheral capabilities are more often found in large, complex and diversified companies than in smaller companies.

Furthermore although the role played by ITC in the management of dynamic capabilities has been highlighted in this chapter, the role of human resources must not be ignored. Capabilities reside in people, who are able to create dynamic capabilities. ITC have only a complementary role, although they are essential when firms are geographically dispersed. But it must be mentioned that existing ITC could produce elements of inertia or rigidity, deriving from routines that are outdated, undesirable, and difficult to eradicate, and could resist necessary change.

A third limitation is the absence of a methodology that indicates which dormant and peripheral capabilities are to be inventoried, thus constituting a promise of future dynamic capability. Although previous literature offers certain clues, it seems to have been left to the judgement of management. The options of whether or not to maintain dormant capabilities, and whether or not to inventory any detected peripheral capabilities, are usually studied a posteriori, after they have been successful in the creation of dynamic capabilities.

It is important to consider the negative impact that restructuring might have on the development of dynamic capabilities (Garud and Nayyar, 1994; Hamel and Prahalad, 1994). The loss of key personnel in whom organizational memory resides no doubt affects the existence of dormant capabilities. On the other hand, the outsourcing of activities and processes limits the possibilities of obtaining dynamic capabilities originating from the peripheral capabilities of the outsourced process (Hitt et al., 1998).

Finally the proposed model may appear similar to knowledge management models. Nevertheless this model underlines the role of ITC and goes beyond knowledge management, as it may include other intangible assets in addition to knowledge. Examples of these would be reputation, patents, contact networks, strategic databases (Hall, 1992, 1993) and organizational routines.

CONCLUSION

The theory of resources and capabilities must consider not only core capabilities but a whole range of capabilities, core and non-core. In addition, it must explain how core capabilities are created. The perspective of dynamic capabilities (Teece *et al.* 1997) takes other capabilities into account, thus possibly providing options for obtaining future core capabilities. These dynamic capabilities will allow the company to anticipate or adjust to changing environments. This chapter proposes a programmatic dynamic capabilities creation model.

According to Lorenzo-Gomez and Ruiz-Navarro (1997) and Ruiz-Navarro (1998), dynamic capabilities can be seen to possess two different non-exclusive generating paths, the first leading from latent or dormant capabilities (Baden-Fuller and Volberda, 1996, 1997; Baden-Fuller and Stopford, 1994; Burgelman, 1994; Garud and Nayyar 1994), and the second from peripheral capabilities (Lorenzo-Gomez and Ruiz-Navarro 1997, Ruiz-Navarro 1998).

Mata *et al.* (1995) state that ITI offers no advantage in itself, but skills in the management of ITI (ITC) may produce advantages if they enable the company to perceive and exploit other capabilities that may in turn provide future sources of competitive advantage (Barney, 1991). Consequently ITC are seen to fulfill three different functions in the creation of dynamic capabilities. Firstly, they support people in identifying the repository of capabilities, by collecting historical and peripheral data concerning these capabilities. Secondly, they keep a catalogue of capabilities, in collaboration with complementary human resources, and accumulate experience in their use by means of a learning process. Finally, they act as transmitters, generating dynamic capabilities from the company's existing capabilities.

This chapter proposes a framework that shows how ITC facilitate the creation of dynamic capabilities by supporting the tasks of detection, selection, cataloguing, maintenance, reactivation, synthesis (Garud and Nayyar, 1994), and transfer (Doz, 1994) of dormant capabilities on the one hand, and the detection, cataloguing, synthesis and transfer of peripheral capabilities on the other.

Nevertheless the development of dynamic capabilities requires certain complementary resources and capabilities. In fact, if ITC does not integrate with complementary resources and capabilities, it is not efficient on its own in supporting the creation process of new capabilities. Appropriate integration must occur between ITC, complementary human resources and business capabilities (Powell and Dent-Micallef, 1997).

NOTE

1. For instance, previous developments of a capability may make it easier to absorb, but this is not the case when the capability becomes specific for a company.

REFERENCES

Amit, R. and P. Schoemaker (1993), 'Strategic assets and organizational rent', *Strategic Management Journal*, **14**: 33–46.
Baden-Fuller, C. and J. Stopford (1994), *Rejuvenating the Mature Business*, London: Routledge.
Baden-Fuller, C. and H. Volberda (1996), 'Strategic renewal in large complex organisations: a competence based view', Working Paper, *16th Strategic Management Society Annual Conference*, Phoenix, AZ November.
Baden-Fuller, C. and H. Volberda (1997), 'Dormant capabilities, complex organizations and renewal', Working Paper, *American Academy of Management*, Boston, August.

Barney, J.B. (1991), 'Firm resources and sustained competitive advantage', *Journal of Management*, 17 (1): 99–120.

Black, J.A. and K.B. Boal (1994), 'Strategic resources: traits, configuration and paths to sustainable competitive advantage', *Strategic Management Journal*, 15: 131–148.

Burgelman, R.A. (1994), 'Fading memories: a process theory of strategic business exit in dynamic environments', *Administrative Science Quarterly*, 39: 24–56.

Davenport, T. (1994), 'Saving IT's soul: human-centered information management', *Harvard Business Review*, 72 (2): 119–131.

Davenport, T.H., D.W. De Long and M.C. Beers (1998), 'Successful knowledge management projects', *Sloan Management Review*, 39 (2): 43–58.

Dierickx, I. and K. Cool (1989), 'Assets stock accumulation and sustainability of competitive advantage', *Management Science*, 35 (12): 1504–1511.

Doz, Y. (1994), 'Managing core competency for corporate renewal: towards a managerial theory of core competencies', Working Paper, INSEAD.

Emery, F. and E. Trist (1965), 'The causal texture of organizational environments', *Human Relations*, 18: 21–32.

Garud, R. and P.R. Nayyar (1994), 'Transformative capacity: continual structuring by intertemporal technology transfer', *Strategic Management Journal*, 15: 365–385.

Gibson, C.F. and R.L. Nolan (1974) 'Managing the four stages of EDP growth', *Harvard Business Review*, 52 (1): 76.

Grant, R.M. (1991), 'The resource-based theory of competitive advantage: implications for strategy formulation', *California Management Review* (Spring), 114–135.

Hall, R. (1992), 'The strategic analysis of intangible resources', *Strategic Management Journal*, 13: 135–144.

Hall, R. (1993), 'A framework linking intangible resources and capabilities to sustainable competitive advantage', *Strategic Management Journal*, 14: 607–618.

Hamel, G. and C.K. Prahalad (1989), 'Strategic intent', *Harvard Business Review* (May–June), 63–77.

Hitt, M.A., B.W. Keats and S.M. Demarie (1998), 'Navigating in the new competitive landscape: building strategic flexibility and competitive advantage in the 21st century', *The Academy of Management Executive*, 12 (4): 22–42.

Lawrence, P. and J. Lorsch (1967), *Organization and Environment: Managing Differentiation and Integration*, Homewood, IL: Irwin.

Lorenzo-Gomez, J.D. and J. Ruiz-Navarro (1997), 'Reinventing core competencies in mature industries: strategic renewal in large complex organizations', Working Paper, *17th Strategic Management Society Annual Conference*, Barcelona, October.

Lowendahl, B. and O. Revang (1998), 'Challenges to existing strategy theory in a postindustrial society', *Strategic Management Journal*, **19**: 755-773.

Mata, F.J., W.L. Fuerst and J.B. Barney (1995), 'Information technology and sustained competitive advantage: a resource-based analysis', *MIS Quarterly*, **19** (4): 487–506.

McGregor, D. (1960), *The Human Side of Enterprise*, New York: McGraw-Hill.

Milgrom, P. and J. Roberts (1995), 'Complementarities and fit: strategy, structure and organizational change in manufacturing', *Journal of Accounting and Economics*, **19** (2–3): 179–208.

Miller, E. and A. Rice (1967), *Systems of Organization: The Control of Task and Sentient Boundaries*, London: Tavistock.

Nelson, R.R. and S. Winter (1982), *An Evolutionary Theory of Economic Change*, Cambridge, MA: Harvard University Press.

Nolan, R.L. (1979), 'Managing the crises in data processing', *Harvard Business Review*, **57** (2): 115.

Penrose, E.T. (1958), *The Theory of the Growth of the Firm*, New York: Oxford University Press.

Porter, M.E. and V.E. Millar (1985), 'How information gives you competitive advantage', *Harvard Business Review*, **63** (4): 149–161.

Powell, T.C. and A. Dent-Micallef (1997), 'Information technology as competitive advantage: the role of human, business, and technology resources', *Strategic Management Journal*, **18** (5): 375–405.

Prahalad, C.K. and G. Hamel (1990), 'The core competence of the corporation', *Harvard Business Review*, **68** (3), 79–91.

Rice, A. (1958), *Productivity and Social Organization: The Ahmedabad Experiment*, London: Tavistock.

Roethlisberger, F. and W. Dickson (1939), *Management and Worker*, Cambridge, MA: Harvard University Press.

Ruiz-Navarro, J. (1998), 'Turnaround and renewal in a Spanish shipyard', *Long Range Planning*, **31**: 51–59.

Rumelt, R.P. (1995), 'Inertia and transformation', in C.A. Montgomery, (ed.), *Resource-based and Evolutionary Theories of the Firm: Towards a Synthesis*, Utrecht: Kluwer Publishers, pp.101–132.

Scarbrough, H. (1998), 'Path(ological) dependency? Core competencies from an organizational perspective', *British Journal of Management*, **9**: 219–232.

Teece, D.J. (1986), 'Profiting from technological innovation: implications for integration, collaboration, licensing and public policy', *Research Policy*, **15**: 285–305.

Teece, D.J. (1987), *The Competitive Challenge: Strategies for Industrial Innovation and Renewal*, New York: Harper & Row.

Teece, D.J., G. Pisano and A. Shuen (1997), 'Dynamic capabilities and strategic management', *Strategic Management Journal*, **18** (7): 509-533.

Teece, D.J., R.P. Rumelt, G. Dosi and S. Winter (1994), 'Understanding corporate coherence: theory and evidence', *Journal of Economic Behavior and Organization*, *23*, 1–30.

Trist, E. and K. Bamforth (1951), 'Some social and psychological consequences of the longwall method of coal-getting', *Human Relations*, **4**: 3–38.

Ulrich, D., M.A. Von Glinow and T. Jick (1993), 'High-impact learning: building and diffusing learning capability', *Organizational Dynamics*, **22** (2): 52–66.

Wernerfelt, B. (1984), 'A resource-based view of the firm', *Strategic Management Journal*, **5**: 171–180.

Wernerfelt, B. (1995), 'The resource-based view of the firm: ten years after', *Strategic Management Journal*, **16**: 171–174.

9. On the relationship between knowledge, networks, and local context

Maria Chiara Di Guardo and Marco Galvagno

INTRODUCTION

In recent decades the sociological explanation of economic activities has received increasing academic attention. The point is clear: 'the anonymous market of neoclassical models is virtually nonexistent in economic life, and transactions of all kinds are rife with social connections' (Granovetter, 1985: 495). In this mood, a number of studies in management have recognized the long-term dynamics of 'continuous interaction among firms' (for example, Nohria and Eccles, 1992), and highlighted the necessity to refocus by shifting their attention from single-firm behaviors to a number of inter-firm relationships structures, which include networks of firms (Powell, 1990; Nohria and Eccles, 1992), keiretsu and keiretsu-like relationships (respectively in Japan and the USA) (Dyer, 1996a, 1996b), networks of learning (Powell et al., 1996), dyadic relations (Dyer and Singh, 1998), and strategic networks (Gulati et al., 2000; Gnyawali and Madhavan, 2001).

Three things come into view from these streams of research. They are: (1) the notion that firms' behaviors are embedded within a network of inter-firm relationships; (2) the concept of network resources that emerge from participation in a network of inter–firm relationships; (3) the recognition that network resources play a strategic role in determining firms' performance.

Drawing upon these results, but going beyond them, we want to investigate a different, although related, argument. The external environment confronted by individual firms within a network may be different in significant respects from the environment faced by similar firms outside that network. In particular, we want to explore how the environment shapes and influences the performance of an assembly of interacting firms.

To this end, we refer to the studies about local business networks and regional clusters. Presumably, clusters of related firms have been contributing to economic growth for quite a while, but the contemporary turn towards a knowledge-based economy in many parts of the world has certainly sharpened our interest in understanding the nature of this process.

A key result emerging from these studies is that a firm's immediate environment affects its competitive success over time (Porter, 1990). The increasing academic interest in these particular kinds of aggregate organizational forms is made clear by the following concepts: Marshallian local industrial districts (Becattini, 1987; Becattini, 1989; Brusco, 1982; Piore and Sabel, 1984; Pyke et al., 1990; Best, 1990; Grabher 1993; Saxenian, 1991; Saxenian, 1994), *milieux innovateurs* (Perrin and Maillat, 1989); networks of innovators (Freeman, 1991); industrial cluster (Porter, 1990, 1998; Feldman, 1994; Krugman, 1995; Pouder and St. John, 1996; Porter and Solvell, 1998; Enright, 2000); business networks (Staber et al, 1995).

Ultimately, although communication and transport technologies prevail over most of the geographical and historical barriers dividing regions, competitive advantage is still and increasingly to be found in localities where conditions are particularly favorable to growth. Porter defines these locations as a geographic concentration of interconnected firms and institutions in a particular field, and calls them clusters (Porter, 1990).

To date, several studies have shown that these kinds of agglomeration exhibit superior performance outcomes relative to the rest of the industry population. Some scholars explain the superior performance in terms of agglomeration benefits (Arthur, 1990) or external economies (Langlois, 1992); others in terms of access to, creation, and flow of knowledge (Maskell, 2001).

We believe that the question of how knowledge is created, utilized and transferred in a local business network still requires a better understanding (Tallman *et al.* 2004). These research streams provide useful insight into the superior performance of a local business network, and they can help researchers when they make comparative analysis regarding alternative organizational structures. However scholars have ignored the process by which superior performance is created. Although knowing the inputs, structure and desired outputs of an agglomeration of interrelated firms provides a useful context for studying this process, these factors do not tell us how the local context can improve firms' performance through a process of knowledge exchange and creation. More precisely, given that the superior performance of a local business network is related to knowledge, and that knowledge is a property of individuals and therefore embedded in relationships between those individuals (Boisot, 1998), what is the process by which knowledge flows from firm to firm in a local business network? Moreover, how does the local context play a part in the creation of new knowledge? And how do firms contribute to the improvement of the knowledge of the local business network?

In this chapter, we concentrate on the process of value creation within local business networks. We argue that in a local business network the locus of value creation is found within the local context and its ability to create a network of exchange knowledge relations among the various (local) agents. In order to build a model that explains the process of knowledge transfer among individuals and organizations in a local business network, we combine the knowledge based view (Kogut and Zander, 1992; Conner and Prahalad, 1996; Foss, 1996a, 1996b) and the network perspective (Thorelli, 1986; Jarrillo, 1988; Powell, 1990; Uzzi, 1997; Gulati, 1999; Gulati et al., 2000). The knowledge-based view (KBV) within the framework of the resource-based approach is concerned with firm-level analysis; the network approach literature is far more descriptive and seeks to understand how networks affect competition (Nielsen, 2000). It appears that these two approaches are diametrically opposed: the knowledge-based view is exclusively engaged with analysis of the individual firm's knowledge creation and accumulation, and has nothing to say about inter-firm relations; the primary research interest of the network perspective is, on the other hand, to identify, categorize and theorize relations between firms (networks). We argue that it is indeed feasible for knowledge researchers to draw in a fruitful way on network insights (and vice versa) (Foss, 1999; Dagnino, 1999; Nielsen, 2000). More specifically, the idea of the local business network provides one possible bridge between the two approaches.

We will first present a critical review of the knowledge-based theory, which provides an outline of the main theoretical perspectives within this field of research about knowledge transfer, and a review of the network theory approach, which analyzes the importance of the relations among different organizations by focusing on the process of sharing and transferring knowledge. A description of our conceptual model, which explains how local context influences the performance of firms belonging to a local business network, follows. Finally, the conclusions and implications for firms and research are discussed.

THEORETICAL BACKGROUND

From Resources and Competencies to Knowledge

In the context of the resource-based view, particular attention has been directed towards the notion of organizational capabilities or competencies (Barney, 1986, 1991; Prahalad and Hamel, 1990; Hamel, 1994). Resources are usually considered to be finite in supply and to diminish in value when shared with other parties (De Gregori, 1987); capabilities refer to the dynamic, non-finite firm-specific and path-dependent processes that are not obtainable in the market place, are difficult to copy, and are accumulated through long-term and continuous learning (Lado and Zhang, 1998, Kusunoki et al., 1998). More importantly, organizational capabilities are considered to constitute the fundamental source of sustained competitive advantage (Grant, 1996; Kusunoki et al., 1998). Firms are heterogeneous with respect to their resources and capabilities, since they are endowed with unique abilities to accumulate, develop and deploy those assets to formulate and implement value-creating strategies (Barney, 1991; Peteraf, 1993). As Teece et al. (1997) note, these assets are idiosyncratic, at least in the short run, and firms are to a greater or lesser extent stuck with the kind of strategic assets they possess.

A number of resource-based scholars have recently begun to explore the general processes by which organizational capabilities are developed. It is within this framework that the emerging knowledge-based view of the firm posits that the fundamental input and primary source of value in building organizational capabilities is knowledge (Grant, 1996). Knowledge is recognized as a principal source of economic rents, and the management of knowledge is mainly a strategic objective as companies seek to enhance their competencies, capabilities and processes in order to gain competitive advantage. The theoretical challenge is to interpret the knowledge of a firm as resulting from a set of capabilities that constitute its sources of competitive advantage; the creation of new knowledge does not occur in isolation from already existing capabilities. Instead, new learning (such as innovations) is the product of the firm's combinative capabilities to exploit its existing knowledge base and the unexplored potential of its technology in use (Kogut and Zander, 1992). In this process the organizing principles associated with the mechanisms by which the codification and transfer of personal and group knowledge is facilitated play a crucial role. Firms 'are repository of capabilities, as determined by the social knowledge embedded in enduring individual relationships, structured by organizing principles' (Kogut and Zander, 1992: 396).

Despite this, we see a weakness in the knowledge-based approach and it is the exclusion of the context within which, and the process whereby, knowledge is generated and enhanced. Knowledge, in this view, is seen as a firm-specific and cumulative competence or resource. The main point is that it is important to study how knowledge is generated, exchanged and combined in order to create new knowledge (Coombs and Hull, 1998; Dagnino, 1999; Nielsen, 2000).

A fresh contribution on the process of knowledge creation is that of

Nonaka (1991, 1994). He introduces two interesting concepts: (1) the dynamic conception and (2) the relational conception of knowledge and the process of transformation of personal knowledge into organizational knowledge. The basic assumption is that knowledge transfer is deeply affected by the difference between tacit and explicit knowledge (Nonaka, 1994). This distinction originated in the work of Polanyi (1962) and relates to the idea that certain cognitive processes and/or behaviors are underpinned by operations that are inaccessible to consciousness. The difference between tacit and explicit knowledge has sometimes been expressed in terms of know-how and information respectively, or in terms of the corresponding distinction between knowledge that is embodied and knowledge that is theoretical in nature. Embodied and tacit knowledge is characteristic, for example, of an expert who acts and makes judgments without explicit reflection; that is, without focused attention on the principles or rules involved in his actions. This kind of knowledge is 'vague, difficult to codify, and often only serendipitously recognized'. Conversely, information involves knowledge that is consciously accessible and that can be digitized or explicitly codified and transmitted without loss of integrity once the syntactical rules for deciphering it are known (Kogut and Zander, 1992).

Nonaka's model of knowledge transformation puts emphasis on the creation of new knowledge through transformation of given knowledge. He starts from the two basic types of knowledge, explicit and implicit knowledge, both conceptualized as individual knowledge, which is transformed into organizational knowledge through four processes: (1) socialization; (2) externalization; (3) combination; (4) internalization. Socialization refers to the primary knowledge transformation process by which the implicit knowledge of organizational members is transformed into the implicit knowledge of novices through experience; that is, observation, imitation and application of the observed behavior. In order for implicit knowledge to become explicit, externalization has to take place. The third process consists in reorganizing explicit knowledge with other types of explicit knowledge and is referred to as combination. Finally, internalization denotes the process by which explicit knowledge is internalized by organizational members to become implicit and results in routine action. Each of these processes leads to the creation of new knowledge, whereby explicit and implicit knowledge can be regarded as complementary. Moreover Nonaka (1994) underlines that the four processes of knowledge transformation dynamically relate to each other and ideally result in a knowledge spiral reinforcing itself. The knowledge is created, transferred and integrated among individuals in organizations, through a dynamic process of conversion of tacit to explicit knowledge (and vice versa). A basic 'tool' for this conversion to take place involves dynamic interaction, dialogue and experimentation among individuals within the context of self-organizing teams (Nonaka, 1994) or communities of practice (Brown and Duguid, 1991). The knowledge spiral starts on an individual level, proceeds on a social level, and ends up on an inter-organizational level (Dagnino, 2000).

On these premises, we believe it is promising to shift the focus from an internal perspective to an external one, and direct attention to the inter-organizational level of knowledge creation. As firms become increasingly heterogeneous internally and more interconnected with other organizations, it is important to challenge the assumptions on which the KBV is built, and consider whether the firm is actually the relevant level of analysis. Moreover we argue that some resources and capabilities, starting with knowledge, are built into the relationship with other firms.

From a Firm Perspective to a Network Perspective of Knowledge Creation

We argue that it is possible to apply the theory of knowledge creation developed for a single firm to a network of different interrelated organizations. Network theorists have already tried to do so (Jarillo, 1988; Grindley, 1991; Powell and Di Maggio, 1991). They view the firm as a network of relationships between sub-units, groups and individuals, which is in turn embedded in a wider network of relationships with customers, suppliers, competitors and other organizations. 'Firms in the network are defined as actors of dyadic (pair-wise) relations within the structure of the overall network of relations' (Granovetter, 1992). The network acts as an ensemble of learning in facilitating the creation and transfer of knowledge. Knowledge networking is defined as people, resources, organizations, and relationships among them, assembled in order to accumulate and use knowledge, primarily by means of knowledge creation and transfer processes, for the purpose of creating value (Powell, 1990; Nohria and Eccles, 1992; Gulati, 1999; Gulati et al., 2000). Powell et al. (1996: 121), examining inter-firm networks, noted that knowledge creation took place in the context of an evolving community of partners, where the sources of new knowledge creation were 'commonly found in the interstices between firms, universities, research labs, suppliers and customers'. In other words, knowledge creation is by definition a dynamic process of interaction, in which the vital acts of creation occur in spaces that are exogenous to partnered firms. Gulati (1999) articulates a concept of 'network resources' which he defines as resources that are available to a firm but which inhere within inter-firm networks. These resources become available to firms that are network members owing to the information advantages they obtain from participation in a network, because participation creates a conduit for highly tacit information flows which enable the identification of new options that expand a firm's opportunity set.

When a network perspective is adopted, the issue of knowledge creation becomes more related to the social structure of the context where the process takes place, which is the space external to individual firms. Porter (1998: 225) argues that 'many of the competitive advantages of clusters depend on the free flow of information, the discovery of value-adding exchanges or transactions, the willingness to align agendas and to work across organizations, and strong motivation for improvement. Porter (2000: 116) defines what he terms a cluster as 'a geographically proximate group of interconnected companies and associated institutions in a particular field, linked by commonalities and complementarities'. Relationships, networks, and a sense of common interest underline these circumstances. The social structure of clusters thus takes on central importance. Firms may build knowledge in two different ways: through the exploitation of their own experiences or through relationships with other organizations. The relative importance of each of the two is context-dependent but the latter is especially important in the case of firm aggregates and networks. The key in this process is shared experiences and perspectives and the development of a common language. More generally, the social context within which capabilities are embedded plays a crucial role in their functionality (Oliver, 1997).

A particular aspect of the social context is the local specificity. 'Only by being in the same local environment, and by meeting repeatedly in person, can and will such more subtle forms of information be exchanged' (Bathelt et al., 2002: 1). Since organizational capabilities are embedded in the local area, the local context within which organizational capabilities are realized affects their functionality. What is of maximum importance here is the ease with which knowledge is shared and created in the local context, where physical proximity helps to promote the rapid exchange of tacit knowledge. Codified knowledge may travel the world with gradually less friction thanks to relaxed trade regimes, emerging markets for intellectual property rights and improvements in information and communication technologies. One of the main distinguishing features of geographical agglomerations of similar economic activity or local business networks is that they provide opportunities for the transmission of sticky, non-articulated, tacit forms of knowledge between firms located there. The main argument regarding the spatial aspects of this has been that the more codified the knowledge involved, the less space-sensitive these processes should tend to be. If, on the other hand, the knowledge involved is diffuse and tacit, the argument is that such interaction and exchange is dependent on spatial proximity between the actors involved.

Owing to the implicit nature of the exchanged knowledge, spatial and cultural proximity represents an important precondition for the exchange of knowledge. In studying the networks located in Silicon Valley, Saxenian (1990) emphasizes that it is the relationship between individuals of different organizations that facilitates the transmission of knowledge across agents, firms and even industries. Knowledge transfer depends on how easily that knowledge can be transported, interpreted and absorbed. This depends on communication flows and relationships between organizations. Firms characterized by geographic proximity tend to create rules that promote cooperation between them. As these rules generate the structure of a network, the structure itself influences subsequent behavior.

The local context is defined as a complex system of tangible and intangible resources where different forces converge. It ceases to be an exogenous, predefined and static element to which firms have progressively to adapt in order to optimize its exploitation, and it is no longer envisioned as the limiting space that binds the maximizing behavior of the entrepreneur and in which it is only possible to act with an appropriate positioning strategy (Usai, 2000). On the contrary, the local context gradually evolves and becomes a complex and dense communication network, which ultimately envelops the operators, providing links to exchange knowledge. This interpretation of the local context enhances the values of the local knowledge, strongly connected to the reference site. It favors the unrepeatable way in which a network organizes itself in an area identified by a given cultural and economical environment.

THE CONCEPTUAL MODEL: LINKING KNOWLEDGE CREATION AND THE LOCAL BUSINESS NETWORK

Having set the stage by drawing on knowledge and business network concepts, we devote this section to filling the gap in the literature on the process of knowledge creation in a local business network. We present a model that explains how local context influences the performance of firms belonging to a local business network.

The literature refers to such agglomerations as knowledge clusters, regional innovation systems or technological districts (Braczyk et al., 1998; Malecki and Oinas, 1999; Lorenzen and Mahnke, 2003). These agglomerations denote groups of interconnected technology-leading firms (including suppliers, customers and competitors), highly skilled labor (often engineers), and private and public institutions (typically universities and research facilities, specialized service suppliers and employers' associations), specialized within a few and related economic activity areas and clustered together in particular regions or urban areas. Storper (2000) uses the term 'territorialization' to describe a local network including institutions, culture, industrial structure and the dominant internal organizations of firms. The strong correlation between the business spatial concentration and the dynamics of local spread of innovation has been clearly pointed out (Malecki, 1985; Markusen et al., 1986; Porter, 1990; Saxenian, 1994). It has been found that the qualitative and quantitative development of hi-tech areas is based on the connections between the knowledge production centers (universities, research centers, R&D divisions, local authorities, and so on) and the recipient local firms. This clearly means that the production of knowledge is primarily a local activity (Audretsch, 2000), and regions are very specialized in terms of what kinds of technologies their firms patent (Storper, 2000). Previous researches have shown that knowledge transfers are often geographically constrained (Jaffe et al., 1993; Audretsch and Feldman, 1996; Almeida and Kogut, 1999). When this mechanism operates through interaction among people, knowledge transfer is geographically limited.

We suggest that the knowledge-based perspective, and Nonaka's model of knowledge creation, may be profitably applied to the analysis of the process of knowledge creation and accumulation within a local business network. According to Nonaka's model (1994), the socialization among firms in the same local business network provides a fundamental means of converting tacit knowledge through dynamic interaction between individuals from different organizations. Firms and the local context are increasingly tied by a coevolving network in which they not only influence each other, but also converge toward a shared model of knowledge creation, which is, consequently, one of the fundamental and direct sources of strategic innovation and value creation. Given that (1) inter-relationships among organizations in a network consist of knowledge flows resulting in new knowledge accumulation and integration (Hamel, 1994; Nonaka, 1994; Galunic and Rodan, 1998), and that (2) tacit knowledge is not easily transferred and shared, the existence of multiple kinds of resources, competencies and knowledge, intertwined by manifold levels of local network relationships and interactions, opens the way to a model of co-production of value. This model is portrayed in Figure 9.1 as the double spiral process of interaction, intra-organizational/inter-organizational.

The rationale for the model as the follows. There is a knowledge spiral that begins and ends within the firm and another that interacts with the local context. We argue that firms motivated by a desire to generate new knowledge, in addition to recycling, recombining and exploiting their existing knowledge, will need to interact with the context, by exchanging knowledge. We are interested in three main issues. First, how shall firms increase the quantity of knowledge within the local context? Second, how shall firms improve the quality of knowledge within the local context? Third, how shall firms increase their capacity to absorb it?

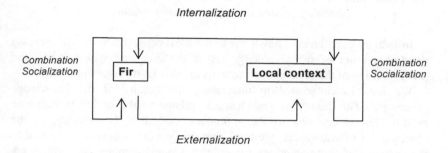

Figure 9.1   The double spiral process of interaction, intra–organizational/inter–organizational

The quantity of knowledge in the local context depends on the knowledge exchanged among firms. By focusing only on the external/local spiral, it is possible to claim that the more knowledge a focal firm puts into the local context, the greater is the pool of knowledge other firms may absorb from. Within this framework, the local context is defined as a complex system of tangible and intangible resources and competencies where different forces converge. The local context, as a relational link, acquires a leading role in the process of knowledge transfer among the firms. The speed with which the process of knowledge transfer is achieved can be explained by the receptive capacity of the local context. This interpretation of the context enhances the values of the local and idiosyncratic knowledge, strongly connected to the reference site. It favors the unrepeatable why in which a network organizes itself in an area identified by an embedded knowledge system, which can constitute for the firms a fundamental source of sustained competitive advantage (Dunning, 1998, 2000). Moreover the local context gradually evolves and becomes a complex and dense knowledge source. In fact, the dynamic externalities associated with the context become more important as the knowledge becomes more sophisticated, idiosyncratic, tacit, complex and context–dependent. Organizations benefit from being part of a knowledge-creating milieu in which private firms, universities, technical colleges, and government research institutions are all mixed up. The idea is that all firms receive benefits (in the form of new knowledge) proportional to the knowledge they put into the local context. The role of the local context is clear: it helps to remove obstacles to fair dealings, so that more opportunities are offered for the exchange of tacit knowledge, ideas and interactive learning (Ring and Van de Ven, 1994; Gulati, 1999).

Proposition 1: *The ability of a firm to externalize knowledge to the local context is positively related to its business performance.*

In fact, by transferring knowledge to the local context, a firm will increase the full amount of the knowledge set in the area and will improve the predisposition of the local context to transmit new knowledge to the firm.

We are also interested to understand the quality of the knowledge exchanged. The quality of knowledge is related to the ability to combine existing knowledge and to the aptitude to socialize. In referring to the combination of knowledge, we think that the process is positively related to the presence of complementary capabilities. Complementary capabilities are defined as the opposite of *similar* ones (Richardson, 1972). The technology management literature stresses how there is greater potential to learn from combinations of a complementary nature. Organizational learning allows a firm to acquire and develop cognitive and behavioral skills, which can lead to profound, lasting modifications to how the firm operates, and thus enhance the performance outcomes. Complementarities in firms' technological resources can create opportunities for synergies in organizational learning through economies of fitness (Larsson and Finkelstein, 1999). This is true inside the firm as well as among firms. Inside the organization, in addition to the well-known importance of economies of scope in R&D (Henderson and Cockburn, 1996), knowledge complementarities have a positive influence on dynamic knowledge accumulation in response to changing environment conditions (Helfat, 1997). Moreover Kodama (1992) notices that the combining of existing but diverse technologies into hybrid technologies has become increasingly important for innovation and performance. In organizational linkages, the knowledge and technology complementarity of participants has been shown to enhance learning and outcomes performance in the local context. Exceptional gains from the trade, exchange or combination of knowledge bases among firms thus stem from the existence of complementarity between the bases themselves.

Proposition 2: *The complementarity of knowledge in the local context is positively related to firms' performance.*

Last but not least, we assume that socialization in the local context is the basis for the process of fostering the spiral of knowledge creation. The primary element in socialization is trust. The level of trust between individuals and organizations and within the local context as a whole influences the nature of economic activity. Trust influences the level of risk and uncertainty arising from the transaction. Trust is highly important for the efficient operation of a knowledge-based exchange process, since the exchange of knowledge gives rise to a high level of risk and uncertainty. Risk and uncertainty are reduced by the presence of a high level of trust, in situations where the complexity of the relationship precludes having recourse to complete contracts. Clearly the exchange of knowledge, and particularly tacit knowledge, is not amenable to enforcement by contract. Hence the importance of trust in the exchange of knowledge (Roberts, 2000). Zaheer et al. (1998) distinguish between interpersonal and inter-organizational trust. The former is the trust placed by a person in his or her opposite member in the partner organization; the latter is the total amount of trust placed in the partner organization by the members of another organization. This distinction is important in the process of local knowledge exchange because it does not imply trust in all partners, but trust in a particular exchange partner based on the socialization process, influenced by experience and by living in the same local context. The knowledge production within the local business network takes place from both horizontal and vertical direct interactions among organizations. It has been shown (Zaheer et al., 1998) that inter-organizational trust improves exchange relations. The inter-organizational trust among firms can create a favorable 'economic environment' in which the circulation of knowledge and ideas, the exchange of information and the transfer of knowledge can improve firms' performance. Moreover, since relationships take place at various levels, between firms and between individuals, interpersonal trust is also essential to the process. Interpersonal trust refers also to the case where there are no business relations between firms, albeit shared 'third party' relations (such as common suppliers, service providers, or employees), or some social interaction of employees or managers (for example, in local clubs or associations). A high level of face-to-face contact in both professional and social life promotes the growth of interpersonal trust, which is required to develop the high level of inter-organizational trust that is essential for the successful transfer of tacit knowledge in that particular context.

Proposition 3: *The level of interpersonal and inter-organizational trust in a local context is positively related to the performance of the involved firms.*

DISCUSSION AND CONCLUSION

This chapter integrates knowledge-based theories of the firm with studies of local agglomerations to produce a model that helps to explain the competitive advantages enjoyed by proximate firms located in a geographical cluster. We tried to redirect research on to the local business network, using the concept of the local context defined as a complex system of tangible and intangible resources and a dense communication network, which ultimately envelops the operators, providing links to exchange knowledge. We believe that this model provides concepts useful in understanding the mechanisms behind the sustained competitive advantage of clusters described by Porter (1990) and in understanding the interaction of the cluster and firm with knowledge flow. The thesis is that the locus of value creation is found within the local context and its ability to create a network of exchange knowledge relations among the various (local) agents. A critical consideration in this framework is the transferability of knowledge: the flow of knowledge among firms within a local context. Transferability results both from the character of the knowledge itself and from the characteristics of the firms involved. We found that the characteristic of context-specific knowledge and its effect of increasing the absorptive capacity for firms embedded is not an industry-specific concept.

The view we offer extends the literature on the local business network in a number of ways. First, we tried to integrate the knowledge-based view and the network perspective. We have applied a conceptual category developed within the KBV, Nonaka's model of knowledge creation, to the analysis of the process of knowledge creation and accumulation within a local business network. According to that model, socialization among firms in the same local business network provides a fundamental means for converting tacit knowledge through dynamic interaction between firms and the local context. The model presented consists of a knowledge spiral that begins within the firm and ends in the local context and explains how the local context can improve firms' performance through a process of knowledge exchange and creation. The model shows that the more knowledge a focal firm puts into the local context, the greater is the knowledge that other firms may absorb in a mutual reinforcing cycle.

Second, we have proposed that the recombination of knowledge in a business network is fostered by the complementarity of the knowledge residing in the local context itself. We thus added a dimension to the process of knowledge creation. While the first proposition referred to the *quantity* of knowledge, we also make explicit reference to the *quality* of the present knowledge. We submit that the complementarity of knowledge elements, as opposed to their similarity, increases the richness of the recombination process.

Also, we have argued that interpersonal and inter-organizational trust play a fundamental role in promoting the process of the 'knowledge spirals'. Given the significant chances of opportunistic behavior, the extent to which firms can rely on trust makes transactions smoother and decreases reliance on contracts (which can hardly be complete) or makes their use more productive (Poppo and Zenger, 2002), it may foster the willingness to share resources and knowledge and avoid the fear of learning races, and it may complement incomplete measures of effort and performance.

For managers within a cluster, our model highlights the importance of firm-specific architectural knowledge for absorbing the cluster-specific and firm-specific (temporarily private) component knowledge to achieve competitive advantage. The cluster's members cannot count on private component knowledge for sustained advantage. Being located in an agglomeration rich in knowledge resources is more conducive to firm growth than being located in a region that is less endowed with knowledge resources.

We would also like to suggest some avenues for future research. As we have noticed, the economic value of location is a conduit for accessing external knowledge resources, which in turn manifests itself in higher rates of growth. However there is still little empirical evidence linking the performance of firms, measured in terms of growth, to geographic location. Furthermore it would be fruitful to know more about how the informal relationships between individuals within a cluster can improve the cluster-specific knowledge.

REFERENCES

Almeida, P. and B. Kogut (1999), 'Localization of knowledge and the mobility of engineers in regional networks'. *Management Science*, **45** (7), 905–17.

Arthur, W.B. (1990), 'Silicon Valley location clusters: when do increasing returns imply monopoly?', *Mathematical Social Sciences*, **19**.

Audretsch, D.B. and M.P. Feldman (1996), 'Innovative clusters and the industry life cycle', *Review of Industrial Organisation*, **11**, 253-73.

Audretsch, D.B. (2000), 'Knowledge, globalization, and regions: an economist's perspective', in J.H. Dunning, (ed.), *Regions, Globalization, and the Knowledge-based Economy*, New York: Oxford University Press.

Barney, J. (1986), 'Strategic factor markets: expectations, luck and business strategy', *Management Science*, **32**, 1231-41.

Barney, J.B. (1991), 'Firm resources and sustained competitive advantage', *Journal of Management*, **17** (1), 99-120.

Bathelt, H., A. Malmberg and P. Maskell (2002*)* 'Clusters and knowledge: local buzz, global pipelines and the process of knowledge creation' DRUID Working Paper, 2002-12, Copenhagen.

Becattini, G. (ed.) (1989), *Modelli Locali di Sviluppo*, Bologna: Il Mulino.

Becattini, G. (1987), *Mercato e Forze Locali: il Distretto Industriale*, Bologna: Il Mulino.

Best, M. (ed.) (1990*)*, *The New Competition: Institutions of Industrial Restructuring*, Cambridge, MA: Harvard University Press.

Boisot, M.H. (ed.) (1998), *Knowledge Assets: Securiting Competitive Advantage in the Information Economy*, New York: Oxford University Press.

Braczyk, H.-J., P. Cooke and M. Heidenreich (eds.) (1998), *Regional Innovation Systems*, London : UCL.

Brown, J.S. and P. Duguid (1991), 'Organizational learning and communities of practice: toward a unified view of working, learning and innovation'. *Organization Science*, **2** (1), 40-57.

Brusco, S. (1982), 'The Emilian model: productive decentralization and social integration', *Cambridge Journal of Economics*, **6**, 167-84.

Conner, K.R. and C.K. Prahalad, (1996), 'A resource-based theory of the firm: knowledge versus opportunism', *Organization Science*, **7**, 477-501.

Coombs, R. and R. Hull (1998), 'Knowledge management practices and path-dependency in innovation', *Research Policy*, **27** (3), 237-53.

Dagnino, G.B. (1999), 'The system of business enterprises as a complex dynamic network of resources and competencies', *Academy of Management Best Papers Proceedings*, Chicago, IL.

Dagnino, G.B. (2000), *Conoscenza, Complessità e Sistemi di Imprese*, Torino: G. Giappichelli.

De Gregori, T.R. (1987), 'Resources are not; they become: an institutional theory', *Journal of Economics Issues*, **21**, 1241-63.

Dunning, J.H (1998), 'Location and the multinational enterprise: a neglected factor?', *Journal of International Business Studies*, **1** (29).

Dunning, J.H. (2000). *Regions, Globalizations and the Knowledge-based Economy*, Oxford University Press.

Dyer, J.H. (1996a), 'How Chrysler created an American keiretsu', *Harvard Business Review*, **74** (4), 42-56.

Dyer, J.H. (1996b), 'Specialized supplier networks as a source of competitive advantage: evidence from the auto industry', *Strategic Management Journal*, **17**, 271-91.

Dyer, J.H. and H. Singh (1998), 'The relational view: cooperative strategy and sources of interorganizational competitive advantage', *Academy of Management Review*, **23**, 660-79.

Enright, M.J. (2000), 'Regional clusters and multinational enterprises', *International Studies of Management and Organization*, 2 (30), 114-38.

Feldman, M.P. (1994), 'The university and high-technology start-ups: the case of Johns Hopkins University and Baltimore', *The Economic Development Quarterly*, 8, 67-77.

Foss, N.J. (1996a), 'Knowledge-based approaches to the theory of the firm: some critical comments', *Organization Science*, 7, 470-76.

Foss, N.J (1996b), 'More critical comments on knowledge-based theories of the firm', *Organization Science*, 7, 519-23.

Foss, N.J. (1999), 'Networks, capabilities, and competitive advantage', *Scandinavian Journal of Management*, 15, 1-15.

Freeman, C. (1991), 'Networks of innovators : a synthesis of research issues', *Research Policy*, 20.

Galunic, D.C. and S. Rodan (1998), 'Resource recombination in the firm: knowledge structures and the potential for Schumpetarian innovation', *Strategic Management Journal*, 19.

Gnyawali, D.R. and R. Madhavan (2001), 'Cooperative networks and competitive dynamics: a structural embeddedness perspective', *Academy of Management Review*, 26 (3), 431-45.

Grabher, G. (1993), 'On the weakness of strong ties: the ambivalent role of interfirm cooperation in the decline and reorganization of the Ruhr', in G. Grabher (ed.), *The Embedded Firm: On the Socioeconomics of Industrial Networks*, London: Routledge, pp. 255-77.

Granovetter, M. (1985), 'Economic action and social structures: the problem of embeddedness', *American Journal of Sociology*, 91, 481-510.

Granovetter, M. (1992), 'Problems of explanation in economic exchange', in N. Nohria and R. Eccles (eds) (1992*)*, *Networks and Organizations: Structure, Form and Action*, Boston, MA: Harvard Business School Press.

Grant, R.M. (1996), 'Toward a knowledge-based theory of the firm', *Strategic Management Journal*, 17 (Winter Special Issue), 109-22.

Grindley, P. (1991), 'Turning technology into competitive advantage', *Business Strategy Review*, 2 (1), 35-48.

Gulati, R. (1999), 'Network location and learning: the influence of network resources and firm capabilities on alliance formation', *Strategic Management Journal*, 20 (5), 397-420.

Gulati, R., N. Nohria and A. Zaheer (2000), 'Strategic networks', *Strategic Management Journal*, 21 (Special Issue), 203-15.

Hamel, G. (1994), 'The concept of core competence', in G. Hamel and C.K. Prahalad (eds) (1994), *Competing for the Fu*ture, Boston, MA: Harvard Business School Press.

Helfat, C. (1997), 'Know-how and asset complementarity and dynamic capability accumulation: the case of R&D', *Strategic Management Journal*, 5 (18), 339-60.

Henderson, R.M. and I. Cockburn (1996), 'Scale, scope and spillovers: research strategy and research productivity in the pharmaceutical industry', *Rand Journal of Economics*, 27 (1), 32-59.

Jaffe, A.B., M. Trajtenberg and R. Henderson (1993), 'Geographic localization of knowledge spillovers as evidenced by patent citations', *Quarterly Journal of Economics*, 108 (3), 577-98.

Jarrillo, J.C. (1988), 'On strategic networks', *Strategic Management Journal*, 9, 31-41.

Kodama, F. (1992), 'Technology fusion and the new R&D', *Harvard Business Review*, 4 (70), 70-78.

Kogut, B. and U. Zander (1992), 'Knowledge of the firm, combinative capabilities and the replication of technology', *Organization Science*, 3, 383-97.

Krugman, P.R. (ed.) (1995), *Development, Geography and Economic Theory*, Cambridge, MA: The MIT Press.

Kusunoki, K., I. Nonaka and A. Nagata (1998), 'Organizational capabilities in product development of Japanese firms: a conceptual framework and empirical findings', *Organization Science*, 9, 699-718.

Lado, A.A. and M.J. Zhang (1998), 'Expert systems, knowledge development and utilization, and sustained competitive advantage: a resource-based model', *Journal of Management*, 24, 489-509.

Langlois, R.N. (1992), 'External economies and economic progress: the case of the microcomputer industry', *Business History Review*, 66 (1), 1-52.

Larsson, R. and S. Finkelstein (1999), 'Integrating strategic, organizational, and human resource perspectives on mergers and acquisitions: a case survey of synergy realization', *Organization Science*, 10 (1), 2-26.

Lorenzen, M. and V. Mahnke (2003), 'Governing MNC entry in regional knowledge clusters', in V. Mahnke, and T. Pedersen (eds) (2003), *Knowledge Flows, Governance and the Multinational Enterprise*, New York: Palgrave Macmillan.

Malecki, E. (1985), 'Industrial location and corporate organization in high-tech industries', *Economic Geography*, 61, 345-69.

Malecki, E. and P. Oinas (eds) (1999), *Making Connections: Technological Learning and Regional Economic Change*, Aldershot: Ashgate.

Markusen, A., P. Hall and A. Glasmeier (1986), *High-tech America: the What, How and Why of the Sunrise Industries*, Boston: Allen and Irwin.

Maskell, P. (2001), 'Knowledge creation and diffusion in geographic clusters', *International Journal of Innovation Management* (Special Issue), 5 (2), 213-38.

Nielsen, B.B. (2000*)*, *Strategic Knowledge Management: a Research Agenda*, Paper presented at the 60th Academy of Management, Toronto, Canada.

Nohria, N. and R.G. Eccles (eds) (1992), *Networks and Organizations: Structure, Form and Action*, Boston, MA: Harvard Business School Press.

Nonaka, I. (1991), 'The knowledge-creating company', *Harvard Business Review*, Nov-Dec, 96-104.

Nonaka, I. (1994), 'A dynamic theory of organizational knowledge creation', *Organization Science*, **5**, 14-36.

Oliver, C. (1997), 'Sustainable competitive advantage: combining institutional and resource-based views', *Strategic Management Journal*, **18**, 697-713.

Perrin, J.C. and D. Maillat (1989), *Milieux Innovateurs et Processus d'Innovation dans les Entreprises*, Paris: Economica.

Peteraf, M. (1993), 'The cornerstones of competitive advantage: a resource-based view', *Strategic Management Journal*, **14**, 179-91.

Piore, M. and C. Sabel (1984), *The Second Industrial Divide*, New York: Basic Books.

Polanyi, M. (1962), *Personal Knowledge: Towards a Post-critical Philosophy*, London: Routledge & Kegan Paul.

Poppo, L. and T. Zenger, (2002) 'Do formal contracts and relational governance function as substitutes or complements?', *Strategic Management Journal*, **23** (8), 707-25.

Porter, M.E. (ed.) (1990), *The Competitive Advantage of Nations*, New York: Free Press.

Porter, M.E. (1998), 'Clusters and the new economics of competition', *Harvard Business Review*, **76** (6), 77-90.

Porter, M.E. (2000), 'Location, competition and economic development: local cluster in a global economy', *Economic Development Quarterly*, **41**, 116-41.

Porter, M.E. and O. Solvell (1998), 'The role of geography in the process of innovation and the sustainable competitive advantage of the firm', in A.D. Chandler, P. Hagstrom and O. Solvell (eds) (1998), *The Dynamic Firm*, New York: Oxford University Press.

Pouder, R. and C.H. St. John (1996), 'Hot spots and blind spots: geographical cluster of firms and innovation', *Academy of Management Review*, **4** (21), 1192-225.

Powell, W.W. (1990), 'Neither market nor hierarchy: network forms of organization', in B.M. Staw and L.L. Cummings (eds), *Research in Organizational Behavior*, Greenwich, CT: Jai Press, **12**, pp. 295-336.

Powell, W.W. and P.J. Di Maggio (1991*)*, *The New Institutionalism in Organizational Analysis*, Chicago: The University of Chicago Press.

Powell, W.W., K. Koput and L. Smith-Doerr (1996), 'Interorganizational collaboration and the locus of innovation: networks of learning in biotechnology', *Administrative Science Quarterly*, **41**, 116-45.

Prahalad, C.K. and G. Hamel (1990), 'The core competence of the corporation', *Harvard Business Review*, **68**, 79-91.

Pyke, F., G. Becattini and W. Sengenberger (eds) (1990), *Industrial Districts and Inter-firm Cooperation in Italy*, Geneva: International Institute for Labor Studies.

Richardson, G.B. (1972), 'The organization of industry', *Economic Journal*, **82**, 883-96.

Ring, P.S. and A.H. Van de Ven (1994), 'Developmental processes of cooperative interorganizational relationships', *Academy of Management Review*, **19** (1), 90-118.

Roberts, J. (2000), 'From know-how to show-how?: Questioning the role of information and communication technologies in knowledge transfer', *Technology Analysis & Strategic Management*, **12** (4), 429.

Saxenian, A. (1990), 'Regional networks and the resurgence of Silicon Valley', *California Management Review*, Fall, 39-112.

Saxenian, A. (1991), 'The origin and dynamics of production networks in Silicon Valley', *Research Policy*, **20**.

Saxienan, A. (1994), *Regional Advantage*, Cambridge, MA: Harvard University Press.

Staber, U. H., N.V.Schaefer and B. Sharma, (eds) (1995), *Business Networks: Prospects for Regional Development,* Berlin: De Gruyter.

Storper, M. (2000), 'Globalization and knowledge flows: an industrial geographer's perspective', in J.H. Dunning (ed), *Regions, Globalization, and the Knowledge-based Economy*, New York: Oxford University Press.

Tallman S., M. Jenkins, N. Henry and S. Pinch (2004), 'Knowledge, clusters, and competitive advantage', *Academy of Management Review*, **29** (2), 258-71.

Teece, M., G. Pisano and A. Shuen (1997), 'Dynamic capabilities and strategic management', *Strategic Management Journal*, **18**, 509-33.

Thorelli, H.B. (1986), 'Networks: between markets and hierarchies', *Strategic Management Journal*, **7**, 37-51.

Usai, G. (2000), *L'Efficienza nelle Organizzazioni*, Torino: Utet.

Uzzi, B. (1997), 'Social structure and competition in interfirm networks: the paradox of embeddedness', *Administrative Science Quarterly*, **42**, 35-67.

Zaheer, A., B. McEvily and V. Perrone (1998), 'Does trust matter?: exploring the effects of interorganizational and interpersonal trust on performance', *Organization Science*, **9** (2), 141-59.

PART THREE

Strategic Capabilities and Knowledge Transfer:
Perspectives from Mergers, Acquisitions and
Alliances

10. Knowledge transfer in mergers and acquisitions: how frequent acquirers learn to manage the integration process

Arturo Capasso and Olimpia Meglio*

INTRODUCTION

This chapter focuses on knowledge transfer within those firms that are frequently engaged in merger and acquisition activities. Essentially we explore to what extent these firms develop a distinctive capability to manage the post-acquisition phase in order to unlock value from their deals. The hypothesis is that some firms, having been involved in several mergers or acquisitions, improved their capability in managing the acquisition process because they succeded in capitalizing on their previous experiences.

Since the mid-1980s a large theoretical literature on mergers and acquisitions has emerged, dealing with this interesting subject from different perspectives. For business policy scholars, acquisitions are an effective tool to implement deliberate corporate strategy or the unique occasion to shift towards an emergent one (Mintzberg and Waters, 1985). They can either allow a firm to adjust its products-markets portfolio, at a speed not achievable through internal development, or provide an opportunity to gain the benefits from pooling assets and sharing capabilities, in a way not obtainable through non-equity partnerships. From an organizational perspective, acquisitions can either bring into a company those resources the organization could not develop internally or leverage existing ones. Financial economists carried out extensive empirical researches on the performances of the acquiring firms, concluding that acquirers' abnormal returns are not distinguishable from zero.[1]

As a matter of fact, the debate on acquisition performance is still lively in the academic literature. Whatever the aggregate performance implication of acquisition activity, it is essential for scholars, as well as practitioners, to understand why some firms perform better than others in creating economic value from their acquisitions. In order to answer this question, several types of explanation, rooted in different research streams, have been proposed. Most academic research on acquisitions focuses on such topics as the financial impact of acquisitions, the recommendations for screening potential targets or the acquisition effects on the organizations involved. While these issues are fairly complicated, there is a widespread belief that, from an acquiring firm perspective, many acquisitions fail to achieve their goals. Even when the underlying economic rationale is sound, the expected synergies have to be exploited from combining two distinct organizations with their respective structures, systems and histories.[2]

According to Haspeslagh and Jemison (1991) there are two different ways for acquisitions to increase shareholder wealth. The first, value capture, involves shifting value from the target firm's shareholders, or other stakeholders, to the acquiring firm's shareholders; it is a one-time event, largely related to the transaction itself. The second, value creation, which is central to our research, is the result of managerial action and interaction between the firms. Although managers acknowledge the importance of this process, negotiators often tend to disregard its details because of its complexity, uncertainty and the over-commitment occurring during the due diligence phase (Haunschild, Davis-Blake and Fichman, 1994). Moreover no general rules exist for the integration process, since it depends on aspects such as the acquisition type (Chatterjee, 1986), the level of integration (Shrivastava, 1987), who gets involved and the capabilities to be transferred (Haspeslagh and Jemison, 1991). Sometimes operational integration of the firms is not essential in speculative acquisitions or when a holding company engages in a portfolio building strategy. Obviously, in our analysis, we focus on strategic deals, where operational integration is crucial to the value creation.

Our hypothesis suggests that some of the acquiring firms, and in particular those firms that can be described as frequent acquirers,[3] could achieve better than average performances in acquisition activity as a result of their capability to learn from previous experiences, transferring knowledge, within their organizations, from one deal to another.

After a brief literature review, we analyze the main issues of the post-acquisition integration process and propose a conceptual framework of the integration capability. Then we present an empirical investigation based on a comparison of case studies, and we end the chapter by suggesting some conclusions and a research agenda for future work in this field.

LITERATURE REVIEW: FRAGMENTATION IN M&A ACADEMIC STUDIES

Scientific literature on mergers and acquisitions is frequently referred to as 'fragmented': the M&A phenomenon has been analyzed with different paradigms (although the functionalist one prevails), schools of thought, methods and units of analysis. As a consequence, no general theory on acquisitions has emerged yet (Bower, 2004; Javidan, Pablo, Singh, Hitt and Jemison, 2004).

Cooper (2001) points out that academic literature is still in a pre-paradigmatic stage, which can help in understanding a complex phenomenon such as acquisitions, but only if similarities and differences of various approaches are correctly reviewed along various dimensions.

In this chapter, as shown in Figure 10.1, we will adopt a classification based on schools of thought, methods employed and issues of the acquisition process analyzed.

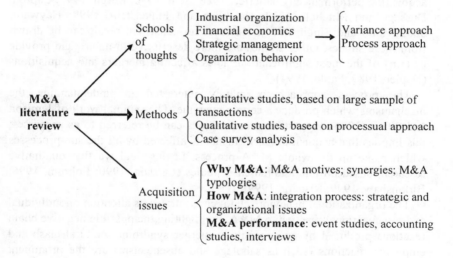

Figure 10.1   M&A literature fragmentation

The different schools of thought can be divided into two clusters:

- economics-related: industrial organization (IO) and financial economics (FE);

- management-related: strategic management (SM) and organizational behavior (OB).

Industrial organization and financial economics are mainly concerned with the effects of mergers and acquisitions: IO studies the impact of merger wave on the whole economic system (Scherer, 1980), while FE focuses on shareholders' value. Quantitative studies, generally using event study methodology, show that the target's shareholders earn abnormal returns, but no significant gain accrues to acquirer's ones (Jensen and Ruback, 1983; Franks, Harris and Titman, 1991; Loderer and Martin, 1992; Agrawal, *et al.*,1992).

Fragmentation strikingly emerges in the strategic management field, in which two different research approaches prevail (Tsoukas and Knudsen, 2002). The variance approach searches for variables explicative and predictive of the phenomenon investigated; we can cite several quantitative studies which aim at finding a relationship between a variable such as acquisition typology, resources redeployment or integration capability and acquisition performance (Chatterjee, 1986; Seth, 1990; Bergh, 1997, Capron, Dussage and Mitchell, 1998; Haleblian and Finkelstein, 1999; Hayward, 2002; Zollo and Singh, 2004). However no consistent result can be drawn from these studies. Other studies are more descriptive in nature and provide patterns of the most significant variables affecting mergers and acquisitions (Napier, 1989; Pablo, 1994).

The process approach is mainly interested in understanding the mechanisms which produce a certain outcome. The seminal work of Jemison and Sitkin (1986) suggests that acquisitions can be referred to as processes; this implies that acquisition performance is affected by all the sub-processes which make up the whole M&A process. In this field we find qualitative research, based on longitudinal case studies (Larsson, 1990; Lohrum, 1996; Birkinshaw, 1999; Risberg, 1999).

The organizational behavior school concentrates its attention on individual and organizational reaction to M&A, highlighting the possible negative chain reactions produced by an acquisition: merger syndrome, cultural clash and employee reactions (such as sabotage and absenteeism) are the prominent topics of this research stream (Marks and Mirvis, 1985; Nahavandi and Malekzadeh, 1988; Sinetar, 1981; Pritchett, 1985).

From this review some relevant conclusions emerge:

- empirical analyses of M&A activities reveal a great variance in terms of performance; attempts to find factors with explicative and predictive power fail to produce consistent results;

- acquisition performance is thus still a puzzle for academics and practitioners: event studies methodology is well suited to analyzing value-capturing deals but can offer a misleading performance measure of value-creating acquisitions, as in these deals performance is the outcome of the integration process, which is shaped by the interaction between task and human integration;
- the adoption of a process perspective implies a methodology which examines how the phenomenon evolves over time; in this regard, longitudinal analysis is a very suitable methodology (Pettigrew, 1990; Van de Ven, 1992).

LOOKING FOR AN ALTERNATIVE FRAMEWORK

The theoretical framework proposed here is multidimensional in nature: acquisition performance is the outcome of several processes, in which strategic, organizational, economic and financial factors play different roles and interact with each other. According to this framework, value creation stems from:

- the strategic planning process, synergy evaluation, negotiation and due diligence in the pre-acquisition phase
- post-acquisition phase integration processes.

The processual perspective implies describing actors, actions, and individual and organizational competencies which characterize each process and potentially affect acquisition performance. Focusing the analysis on actors and actions highlights how acquisition performance derives from social and economic factors (Larsson, 1990). Their interaction may produce either virtuous or vicious development of acquisition processes.

Figure10.2 shows all the processes which make up the whole acquisition process. It does not mean, however, that value is added in each stage of M&A process: what seems linear is actually circular, therefore it is misleading to split the whole process into a pre- and a post-acquisition phase. Synergies occur when resource sharing and capabilities transfer between firms during the integration process improve a firm's competitive position and, consequently, its performance (Sirower, 1997). In most studies, synergies are measured by the degree of relatedness, operationalized as the degree of similarity between acquirer and target, according to SIC codes. By using this measure, researchers equate synergies with similarity between the industries in which the acquirer and the target operate. While industry similarity might be a potential source of synergies, through the elimination of redundancies or the achievement of scale economies, it does not exhaust all the different sources of synergies. Synergistc benefits from resource combinations are more likely to be uniquely valuable when based on complementarity rather than similarity (Harrison, Hitt, Hoskisson and Ireland, 1991, 2001).

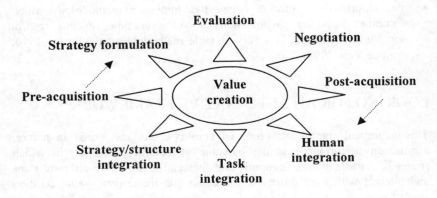

Figure 10. 2   The acquisition process

Moving from potential to actual synergies, the thorny issue is the integration process, which refers to the process of asset rationalization, activity integration and employee acculturation that normally takes place after the deal has been signed. Haspeslagh and Jemison (1991: 106) define integration as an 'interactive and gradual process in which individuals from two organizations learn to work together and cooperate in the transfer of strategic capabilities'. Defining integration as interaction reflects the prominent role the human factor plays; this is consistent with Birkinshaw's (1999) distinction between task and human integration. Task integration refers to how the value-adding activities of the two companies are put together to generate synergies. It involves capabilities transfer from one company to the other, and resource sharing between the two. Quite often task integration also includes rationalization of activities, through downsizing and asset sales. Human integration refers to the process of generating satisfaction and, ultimately, shared identity among employees of the merged company. In the period immediately following the acquisition decision, the human integration process has to alleviate all the negative attitudes that change and uncertainty bring. Afterwards, its objective switches toward the building of a unifying organizational culture.

The trade-off between economic and social aspects determines priority setting. If the integration team starts with rationalization (closing duplicate facilities, reducing overheads) it will make rapid progress on the cost side, but will face the prospect of an unenthusiastic and scared work force. If the team starts with acculturation (building relationships between employees from the two firms, fostering a common culture) it will end up with happy employees but very little cost savings. And doing both at the same time may not be the answer indeed, because of the apparent hypocrisy: telling employees their involvement in the integration process is vital to the success of the enterprise, and in the next breath announcing that there will be a significant staff reduction. Many managers involved in acquisitions face this basic dilemma. Task integration and human integration are often at cross-purposes. In the days following an acquisition announcement, for example, managers should meet one to one with every employee to allay understandable concerns. But the demand for rapid action and cost control typically makes such a move prohibitive. In contrast, closing one of the acquired firm's plants should help the task integration process, but will almost certainly hinder the human integration process, unless handled very carefully. Thus the ultimate goal of full task and human integration is clear, but the route chosen, and the trade-offs that route implies, are a source of continuous conflict for the individuals responsible for the integration process.

In order to shed light on the integration process we summarize in Table 10.1 the main integration issues: integration levels, integration phase and decision processes. The table highlights the complexities and the relationships among actions during the entire process. Reading it horizontally offers a diachronic picture of the M&A process, identifying the steps necessary for goals to be achieved. This underlines that good integration starts during negotiation and due diligence. Reading the table vertically makes us understand the multiple relationships among integration levels and the trade-offs between decisions and actions.

According to Table 10.1, integration planning should be based on goals which should be precise, that means relying on reliable data and information and interpreting them correctly, and consistent and well-timed, that implies identifying priorities and planning a critical path among integration tasks.

As for the actors in the integration process, we identify three levels:

- top management, responsible for defining the integration model, appointing the integration manager and approving his/her choices, such as the transition team leaders' appointments;
- the integration manager, responsible for running the integration process. The role resembles that of any other process-leadership position a company might create to drive any change-process

Table 10.1   The integration issues

	Pre-acquisition phase	Integration	Value creation
Strategy	Create a vision, identify goals and timing ensure consistency between goals and business Appoint team members	Fix priorities according to goals fix strategy to develop competencies and best practices	Shape strategy and structure develop new competencies
Organization	Identify resources to save Cultural analysis Define roles and responsibilities Communication plan	Implement integration plan	Strong leadership Define career plans for key people Align resources and competencies with strategic goals
Management	Governance model: relationship between corporate level and business level Appoint transition team leaders	Allocate resources to specific goals Align changes, processes and businesses	Strategic business unit empowerment
Processes	Plan integration in detail Identify best practices	Eliminate duplication and redundancies Re - engineer processes Fix goals, priorities and performance measures	Processes monitoring
Resources and technology	Resources, competencies and their architecture assessment	Rationalize assets Productivity assessment Outsourcing decisions Licensing evaluation	Technology check Outsourcing decisions Resources and competencies redeployment

implementation it undertakes (Sitkin and Pablo, 2004). It does involve project management: the integration manager helps to create integration teams, consolidate operations and transfer critical skills from one company to the other. Yet an effective integration manager does much more, not only reporting to top management but also helping to set the company's agenda. The integration manager should have an excellent decision-making instinct and distinctive skills to work cross-functionally. Critical is a strong trust relationship with the key executives, since the integration manager often acts as its proxy and confidant;

- transition team leaders, responsible for undertaking specific integration tasks, under the integration manager's supervision.

The attainment of single integration goals takes place thanks to integration mechanisms (Larsson, 1990), which are the tools available to the acquirer to foster the interaction between the joining firms, the coordination of this interaction, and the collective, interpersonal and individual levels of the human side of the combination (see Table 10.2).

Table 10.2 Integration mechanisms

Integration mechanisms	Description	Purpose
Restructuring	Accumulation/stabilization of similar activities Combination/timing of flows of related activities	Asset rationalization
Formal planning	Formal pre-adjustment of activities to one another by specifying the actions in advance	Goal timing Ambiguity and uncertainty reduction
Management information system	Budget and reporting systems standardization	Improve communication process
Transition teams	They are made up of members from both organizations to leverage on the coordinative integration efforts	Flexible way of structuring the transmission of new information
Socialization	Improve the coordination of the firm interaction by creating a common orientation	Reduce employee resistance by enhancing acculturation
Mutual consideration	It is directed toward a more favorable employee	Reduce resistance by decreasing conflicts of

	interpretation	interest
Human resource systems	Job design/reward systems/ personnel policies/career planning	Reduce individual employee resistance

Source: Capasso et al. (2002: 534).

INTEGRATION CAPABILITY

The resource-based view and knowledge-based view have conceptualized acquisition processes as an effective tool for resources and knowledge transfer (Capron, Dussage and Mitchell, 1998; Puranam, Singh and Zollo, 2003). More recently many scholars have attempted to conceptualize integration capability as a factor explaining why some acquirers perform acquisitions better than others. This goal is not new in the field of strategic and organization studies: dynamic capability (Teece, Pisano and Shuen, 1997) is one of the prominent concepts developed to explain the different degrees of firms' success.

The hypothesis assumed in this work is that integration capability arises from learning processes inside frequent acquirers. Despite the great variance in acquisition performance, we can in fact account for acquirers such as General Electric, Cooper Industries, Newell and Cisco, whose successes could be explained by a capability in managing acquisition processes.

The research questions are as follows:

- Is it possible for frequent acquirers to learn how to manage acquisition processes?
- If so, which are the learning mechanisms suited to this task?
- Which context factors act as facilitators of the learning process?

Answering these questions should help us to understand how to create an integration capability, which can be referred to as a dynamic capability (Teece, Pisano and Shuen, 1997). Our line of reasoning is based on some basic concepts: knowledge (as stock and as a learning process) and dynamic capabilities. As regards knowledge, academic literature agrees on the existence of two main kinds of knowledge:[4]

- codifiable (explicit) knowledge, embedded in the firm's routines;
- non-codifiable (tacit) knowledge, embedded in individuals.

From a dynamic point of view, the learning process has been described as unfolding through a variation–selection–retention cycle. It starts from variation, which takes place when individuals and/or groups come up with new solutions to old problems or new ones. Dynamic capabilities, according to Teece, Pisano and Shuen (1997), are the firm's ability to integrate, build and reconfigure internal and external competencies to address a rapidly changing environment. Yet this definition sounds tautological: capabilities are abilities. How capabilities come into being and evolve over time are topics generally overlooked in the academic literature. Zollo and Winter (2002) provide an alternative definition of dynamic capabilities, which are referred to as 'a learned pattern of collective activity through which the organization systematically generates and modifies its operational routines in pursuit of improved effectiveness'. All this implies a distinction between search/learning and operational routines,[5] modified by the former. A dynamic capability emerges only when search routines systematically modify operational ones, in response to external opportunities/threats and internal feedbacks.

A learning process is a recursive cycle, stemming from tacit experience accumulation, articulation and codification activities. These being the building blocks of our line of reasoning, the next step is to investigate how firms experiencing several acquistion processes develop an integration capability and which learning mechanisms are best suited to this end.

Academic studies are generally concerned with the learning processes of recurring events, which show a high degree of similarity. Yet acquisition processes are rare, heterogeneous and complex, with a high degree of causal ambiguity. Thus tacit learning mechanisms, such as learning by doing, are not suitable to keep up with them. Haleblian and Finkelstein (1999) found a U-shaped relationship between the number of acquisitions undertaken (a proxy of acquisition experience) and acquisition performance; empirical evidence suggests that seven acquisitions are the number of transactions necessary to avoid the risks of erroneous generalization in heterogeneous contexts. As a consequence, it is misleading to replicate an integration model only because it produced positive outcomes in a previous acquisition. In this regard, tacit experience does not prove to be a well-suited learning mechanism. Undertsanding similarities and differences between acquisitions derives from articulation and condification activities. Organizational competence improves as members of an organization become more aware of the overall performance implications of their actions, and is the direct consequence of a cognitive effort more or less explicitly directed at enhancing their awareness of these causal links (Zollo and Winter, 2002). Brainstorming sessions and post-mortem analysis, devoted to understanding action- performance links, are a case in point.

Codification activity consists of writing down the output of the articulation process; checklists and best practice manuals are typical examples. This task provides a significantly higher degree of understanding of what makes a certain process succeed or fail, compared to simply discussing it in a brainstorming session (Zollo and Winter, 2002). This is a core activity in business consulting firms to nurture their competencies through knowledge sharing. Yet the learning mechanisms discussed above are a necessary but not sufficient condition to create an integration capability; integration capability arises from a systematic learning process which is the result of the coevolution of a tacit experience accumulation process with explicit knowledge articulation and codification activities.

Turning back to acquisition trajectories (acquisition typology and past acquisition performance) and investigating the role played by organizational context, integration capability stems from learning mechanisms whose role and importance depend on:

- past acquisitions' features: degree of similarity, performance;
- experience in other corporate acitivities, such as alliances (experience spillover);
- organizational and cultural context.

Mergers and acquisitions are rare events in organizational life, so it is difficult for firms to learn from their past experience. Hayward (2002) argues that this failure relates to the quality rather than the quantity of a firm's experience. Acquisitions are rare and heterogeneous events; when prior acquisitions are highly dissimilar to one another, acquirers lack the specialist skills to extract gains from any one type of acquisition. Past acquisition performance affects the learning process: successful acquisitions satisfy managers and prevent them from searching for new solutions, while large failures prevent analysis because they raise questions about managers' competence. In contrast, small losses encourage managers to experience new ways to improve the effectivness of the acquisition process. From these premises, Hayward suggests that focal acquisition performance is inversely related to the degree of similarity of the businesses of prior acquisitions and depends on past acquisition performance (there is an inverted U-shaped relationship between prior acquisitions and focal acquisition performance).[6]

As for the role of other corporate activities on acquisition performance, we can cite Zollo and Reuer's work (2000), which investigates the role played by experience spillovers. Experience spillovers can be defined as the impact of the experience accumulated in the execution of activity j on the performance of activity i (*ibid.*, 2000). Alliances, in fact, are rare and heterogeneous events and like acquisitions, show a high degree of causal ambiguity. Zollo and Reuer compare acquisitions and alliances along two dimensions: integration levels and top management replacement. The higher the similarities between acquisitions and alliances, the more positive the effect of experience spillover: this means that acquisitions implying a low level of integration take advantage of firm's previous experience in managing alliances. If acquisition demands a high level of integration, the firm's previous experience in managing alliances may have a detrimental effect on acquisition performance.

Last but not least, organizational and cultural factors: organizational structure and culture facilitate internal knowledge transfer. Hargadon (1998) developed case studies of firms that act as knowledge brokers (such as business consulting or product design firms). Knowledge brokers are generally able to transfer solutions from one area to another, thus relying extensively on internal knowledge transfer to operate successfully. The main features of knowledge broker firms are fluid project teams and a culture based on sharing knowledge freely with other organizational members.

The model proposed in Figure 10.3 is complex in nature and implies a relevant learning investment in developing an integration capability. We can imagine a sort of *continuum* in which the learning investment increases as firms come to rely on articulation and codification rather than on the routinization process. An example is a brainstorming session organized to extract the lessons learned from managing an acquisition: it can be expensive in terms of both the direct cost (time devoted to this task) and the opportunity cost, measured as the sacrifice of time dedicated to active tasks. Our point of view is that firms undertake this investment only if they have been and will be frequent acquirers.

A fruitful insight is provided by Eisenhardt and Martin (2000) who ground their analyzes in resource-based-view literature with regard to dynamic capability. They assume that dynamic capabilities are processes (strategic and organizational ones) embedded in firms, such as product development, alliancing and strategic decision making whch create value for firms within dynamic markets by manipulating resources into new value-creating strategies. Eisenhardt and Martin's inquiry into the features of dynamic capabilities help us to understand how integration capability could work in post-acquisition integration processes. They argue that, although they are often characterized as unique and idiosyncratic, commonalities related to more effective routines for other dynamic capabilities emerge.

The acquisition process is a case in point: think of pre-acquisition routines that assess cultural similarity (Larsson and Finkelstein, 1999) or post-acquisition routines that redeploy resources between the merging firms (Capron and Mitchell, 1998). Commonalities across firms have an important corollary in equifinality, which means that firms develop an effective dynamic capability from different starting conditions and follow different paths, depending also on the market dynamism.[7]

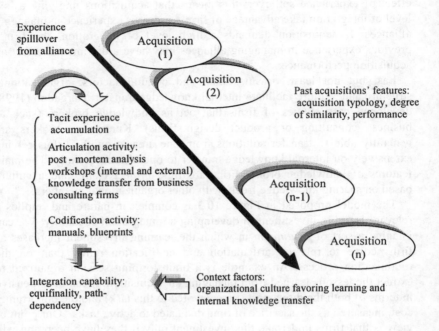

Experience spillover from alliance

Acquisition (1)

Acquisition (2)

Past acquisitions' features: acquisition typology, degree of similarity, performance

Tacit experience accumulation

Articulation activity: post - mortem analysis workshops (internal and external) knowledge transfer from business consulting firms

Acquisition (n-1)

Codification activity: manuals, blueprints

Acquisition (n)

Integration capability: equifinality, path-dependency

Context factors: organizational culture favoring learning and internal knowledge transfer

Figure 10.3   The integration capability development model

Zollo and Winter (2000) describe different approaches taken by Hewlett Packard and Corning in developing their competencies in managing strategic alliances. They are supposed to be experienced players in this arena; however their ways of building their competencies were quite the opposite. While Corning avoided any kind of codification, almost relying on experience and apprenticeship systems, HP developed a large variety of collective learning mechanisms to create best practices.[8]

EVIDENCE FROM CASE STUDIES

Consistent with the equifinality of integration capability, our analysis will now move on to describe the acquisition process developed by well-known systematic acquirers. The companies investigated are General Electric (Ashkenas, DeMonaco and Francis 1998; Ashkenas and Francis, 2000), Cisco (O'Reilly, 1998), Cooper Industries (Collis and Johnson, 1995; Collis and Stuart, 1995), Newell (Collis and Johnson, 1998; Fry, 2000; Montgomery and Gordon, 2001), IT Holding, Dada, Whirlpool, BuongiornoVitaminic and SanpaoloIMI (see Tables 10.3 and 10.4). The aim is to identify a pattern, if any, in their acquisitive behaviors. Even if our findings cannot allow us to generalize, they constitute an intermediate step toward a more extensive case survey analysis.[9] A case survey constitutes a relatively inexpensive and powerful method of identifying and testing patterns across studies, particularly when the area investigated is dominated by case studies, the organization is the unit of analysis, the researcher is interested in incorporating a broad range of conditions and experimental design is not critical.

Table 10.3   The analysis of the acquisitions

Company	Acquisition typology	Acquisition criteria	Negotiation and due diligence
Buongiorno Vitaminic	International expansion	1-2 players Cost driving sinergies Target firms in financial difficulties	Friendly acquisitions
Cooper Industries	Related diversification consistent with Cooper's philosophy Deliberate and sometimes emergent acquisitions	Broaden existing product lines Widespread brand name Broad customer base Enhance distribution system Strengthen a business unit's market position	The process is responsibilty of CEO Light acquisition staff Deals done quickly
Cisco	Related acquisitions	1-2 players in each segment Small technolog firms (60-100 employees)	Informal conversation Careful scrutiny of management style, organizational culture, cultural fit Employee agreements

Dada	Acquisition typology depending on business unit Reach extension; competencies Portfolio stretching	1-2 players in each market segment	Friendly acquisitions
General Electric	No acquisition typology is dominant Acquisitions differ in terms of shape and size	Strategic and organizational fit with GE	Cultural assessment Strengths and weaknesses Evaluation Appoint integration manager
IT Holding	Diversification: brand extension Total look concept	Brand leaders Significant synergy potential	Acquisition process planned in detail Acquisition generally follows either a jont venture or a licensing Friendly acquisitions
Newell	Horizontal acquisitions are dominant International expansion after 1990	Domestic small companies manufacturing staple products under brand names ranking 1-2 in market share	Gradual approach (equity stakes) Thorough knowledge of strengths and weaknesses of target company
Sanpaolo IMI	Geographic roll out	Target firms in financial difficulties	Friendly acquisitions
Whirlpool	International expansion	A single country of the geographic area is entered Significant synergy potential	Acquistion generally follows a joint venture Friendly acquisitions

Table 10.4   The analysis of the integration process

Company	Integration mechanisms	Integration model	Learning mechanisms
Buongiorno Vitaminic	Restructuring Top management replacement Transition teams (to implement acquirer's processes and best practices) Formal planning	Different models in each acquisition: assimilation and integration models are both adopted	Tacit experience accumulation No kind of articulation and codification of acquisition experience
Cooper Industries	Integration leader Formal planning Monitoring of financial goals (VP of finance)	Acquired company broken up and combined to minimize product transfer and resource sharing among business units. Duplication eliminated Best people from each acquisition retained. Extensive training of personnel 'Cooperization' (cultural assimilation)	Consistently with the centralization of corporate function and decentralization of operation, learning is mainly tacit. However the integration process is in a certain way 'routinized', so articulation and codification are supposed to be put in use
Cysco	Business development unit (finance and HR personnel supplemented by leaders and technology specialists) Integration processes monitored and	Engineering, marketing and sales units integrated into sponsoring business unit HR, service, manufacturing and distribution merged in Cisco infrastructure Cultural integration	Project management group involved in M&As acts as a source of institutional knowledge and learning Post-mortem analysis (articulation and

	controlled by project management (group made up of experienced employees)	fostered by integration teams	codification of learning)
Dada	Integration leader Formal planning, even if not very detailed No reward and benefit system harmonization No career plan harmonization	Different models in each acquisition: assimilation and integration models are both adopted	Tacit experience accumulation No kind of articulation and codification of acquisition experience
General Electric	Integration manager Formal planning (process mapping) Audit staff (integration audit) Communication plan	Extensive resource redeployment Corporate education center to train people Development of common tools, practices and language (assimilation of acquired entity into GE) Prominent role of integration leader	Team dedicated to learn and refine acquisition process Workshops on M&As with internal personnel and external consultants (articulation and codification of experience)
IT Holding	Formal planning restructuring Reward and benefit system harmonization One-to-one communication Socialization Business consulting firms act as advisors	Symbiotic approach Extensive bilateral resources and competencies redeployment Autonomy granted to designers	Tacit experience accumulation No kind of articulation and codification of acquisition experience Business consulting firms' integration competencies

Newell	Integration leader (president or a controller) Corporate business development responsible for the acquisition process	Newellization: • extensive top management replacement • centralization of key administrative functions • simplification of the acquired business's strategy • implementation of Newell's divisional operating control system	Not available
Sanpaolo IMI	Integration leaders Transition functional teams Integration committee	Assimilation model: SanPaolo procedures, MIS, career paths and product lines are adopted	Tacit experience accumulation Articulation and codification activities
Whirlpool	Transition teams Management information system Communication plan Reward and benefit systems, harmonization Career plan system harmonization	Whirlpoolization (cultural assimilation) Resource sharing and redeployment across each function	Tacit experience accumulation No kind of articulation and codification of acquisition experience Business consulting firm's integration competencies

Consistent with the processual view, well suited to the phenomenon under study, we will split the analysis into two phases: the pre-acquisition stage and the post-acquisition one.[10] The analysis will be supplemented by recognition of the main learning mechanisms adopted/developed to refine the acquisition process.

Despite the limited number of cases taken into account, it is possible to extract some common best practices which seem to be successfully adopted by the acquirers. In particular, they are the following:

- well - defined acquisition criteria: target companies are exactly identified (frequently top players in particular market segments) and suited to the acquirer's strategy. Acquisition typology seems not to influence the acquisition performance;
- clear vision at top management level, which implies rapidity of change process implementation and clear role identification and appointment of the right leaders;
- the integration process takes place without too much resistance either in terms of task integration or in terms of human integration;
- the acculturation process follows the pattern of assimilation, using the typologies developed by Nahavandy and Malekzadeh (1988); the absence of resistance recalls the idea that the quality of the acculturation process determines the quality and the speed of the integration between the merging firms;
- learning mechanisms and articulation of previous experiences play a crucial role in developing an integration capability; as for GE and Cisco, learning is a never-ending process which parallels the day-by-day management;
- Whirlpool, IT Holding, BuongiornoVitaminic and Dada made no investment in articulation and codification activity, as Sanpaolo-IMI did; however Whirlpool and IT Holding were supported by business consulting firms in developing and implementing integration processes; therefore, in a certain way, they bought the integration competence developed by business consulting firms. This corroborates the idea discussed before, that integration capability can be a discriminant factor affecting acquisiton performance;
- experience spillovers play a role in the Whirlpool and IT Holding cases.

As shown in the tables, all integration mechanisms are put into use, according to different acquisition goals. This demonstrates a significant consistency between goals and action undertaken. Evidence suggests that pervasive integration approaches, which are normally related to organizational turmoil, can be successful if correctly implemented. For instance, suitable integration mechanisms, such as face-to-face communication and human resources systems, can prevent reactions both at individual and organizational level. Dada is a negative case in point: integration failed because integration mechanisms did not actually work. Integration leader was just a formal role, without any responsibility or authority, since political factors, such as power and different visions, hindered a rational approach to integration problems.

CONCLUSION

Mergers and acquisitions are still a puzzle for academics and practitioners. Despite the considerable number of transactions carried out so far, the acquiring firms' performances are, on average, disappointing. However, some well-known acquirers, such as General Electric, Cooper Industries and Cisco, manage to take advantage of acquisitions as powerful strategic tools. This induces several scholars in strategic management to investigate the critical factors for success in the acquisition game, assuming, among other hypotheses, the existence of an integration capability.

This research stream is still in its infancy and the relation between integration capabilities and acquiring firm's performance has not yet been conceptualized. The first empirical tests have not reached conclusive results, and in some cases they seem to infer that no causal linkage exists between learning mechanisms, exploited both in previous acquisitions and in other corporate development activities, and the acquirer's performance (Haleblian and Finkelstein, 1999; Zollo and Reuer, 2002). For all these reasons further and deeper research in this field is highly recommended.

In this chapter, after developing a theoretical framework of how integration capability takes place, we have analyzed several cases of frequent acquirers. The case studies are too small a sample to generalize but in some of them, specifically Cisco and General Electric, it comes out clearly how accumulation, articulation and codification of previous acquisition experience helped the management teams in planning and implementing new acquisition integrations. For some other acquirers, notably Whirlpool and Ittierre, business consulting firms played an essential role in the integration process, testifying that an integration competence is evidently necessary for effectively exploiting synergy and capability transfers. Obviously more evidence is necessary to advance in this line of inquiry: this means extending empirical investigation to other frequent acquirers, in different industries and geographical areas.

In a methodological perspective, a processual analysis is a suitable way to reflect the dynamic nature of processes, which typically unfold over time. Entering the field at different points in time can allow the researcher to account for how different learning mechanisms interact and affect the firm's integration capability. Moreover this approach is consistent with the resource-based view and equifinality hypothesis developed by Eisenhardt and Martin (2000). Case survey analysis (Larsson, 1993) can supplement this research program. Dealing with individual situations or small numbers of cases of special interest can either stimulate new empirical and theoretical research or enrich professional knowledge, providing useful insights for practitioners involved in post-acquisition integrations.[11]

NOTES

* This chaper is the outcome of an intense collaboration between the authors; however, Arturo Capasso wrote the first and the last sections, while Olimpia Meglio wrote the rest.

1. This is the recurrent conclusion in the majority of empirical studies. In this regard there is a widespread consistency between academic literature findings and those reported in business consulting firms' surveys. For more details see Pautler (2003).
2. Conventionally the acquisition process is assumed to begin as soon as the first talks take place between the merging companies and the subsequent moves are carried on. It can be split into pre- and post-acquisition phases, the latter starting with the legal combination. Describing the acquisition process in different phases has been quite a common approach in the literature. Marks (1982) identified three different phases (pre-combination, legal combination and post-combination), while Haspeslagh and Jemison (1991) describe the acquisition process as containing four major phases (idea, acquisition justification, acquisition integration and results). Buono and Bowditch (1989) identified as many as seven different combination phases (precombination, combination planning, announced combination, initial combination, formal combination, combination aftermath and psychological combination). Risberg (1999) points out that it is difficult to identify when each phase ends and the next starts. Moreover they do not necessarily correspond with time: two events, occurring at the same time, can frequently be referred to as different phases. In addition, some parts of the organizations and some individuals experience different phases at the same time. Therefore it is difficult to talk in terms of the whole organization being in one phase or the other.
3. Epstein (2004) adopts the expression 'serial acquirer'. In our terminology serial acquirer refers to acquisitions of the same typology.
4. For an extensive review of the knowledge-based view see Eisenhardt and Santos (2002).
5. An organizational capability is a high-level routine (or collection of routines) that, together with implementing input flows, confers upon an

organization's management a set of decision options for producing significant outputs of a particular type (Winter, 2000).

6. In this regard, it is difficult for firms to learn from acquisition experience that is associated with success or great failure. Instead, small losses from prior acquisitions promote learning and superior performance on subsequent acquisitions. See Hayward (2001).

7. 'Eisenhardt and Sull (2000) discussed the use of simple routines in high-velocity markets. They described, for example, how Yahoo's very successful alliancing process is largely unstructured, consisting of a two-rule routine that sets the boundary conditions for managers wishing to forge alliances. The rules are: no exclusive alliance deals and the basic service provided by the deal must be free. There is little else to the routine. These rules set the boundary conditions within which Yahoo managers have wide latitude for making a variety of alliancing deals' (Eisenhardt and Martin, 2000: 1111 – 12).

8. Database with detailed post-mortem analyses, manuals and internal workshops/seminars.

9. 'The basic procedure is to (1) select a sample of case studies relevant to the chosen research question, (2) develop a coding scheme for systematic conversion of qualitative case descriptions into quantified variables, (3) use multiple raters to code the cases, measuring inter-rater reliability, and (4) statistically analyse the coded data: For an exhaustive description of case survey methodology see Larsson (1993); for an application of case survey methodology see Larsson and Finkelstein (1999).

10. Van de Ven (1992) offers an instructive formal definition of a process. He argues that process is used in three ways in the literature: (1) as a logic used to explain a causal relationship in a variance theory, (2) as a category of concepts that refer to activities of individuals or organizations and (3) as a sequence of events that describes how things change over time. Of these three approaches only the third explicitly and directly observes the process in action and thereby is able to describe and account for how some entity or issue develops and changes over time. For more details about how a processual analysis is carried out see Pettigrew (1990).

11. The role of clinical papers in the development of business economics was affirmed by Jensen (1989) in a well-known editorial of the *Journal of Financial Economics*.

REFERENCES

Agrawal, A., J.F. Jaffe and G.N. Mandelker (1992), 'The post-merger performance of acquiring firms: a re-examination of an anomaly', *Journal of Finance,* 47 (4) 1605–21.

Ashkenas, R.N. and S.C. Francis (2000), 'Integration managers: special leaders for special times', *Harvard Business Review,* Nov–Dec, 108–116.

Ashkenas, R.N., L.J. DeMonaco and S.C. Francis (1998), 'Making the deal real: how GE Capital integrates acquisitions', *Harvard Business Review,* Jan–Feb, 165–70.

Bergh, D.D. (1997), 'Predicting divestiture of unrelated acquisitions: an integrative model of *ex ante* conditions', *Strategic Management Journal,* 18 (9), 715–31.

Birkinshaw, J. (1999), 'Acquiring intellect: managing the integration of knowledge intensive acquisitions', *Business Horizons,* May-June, 33–40.

Bower, J.L. (2004), 'When we study M&A, what we are learning?', in Pablo, A.L. and M. Javidan (eds.), *Mergers and Acquisitions: Creating Integrative Knowledge,* Malden: Blackwell Publishing.

Buono, A.F. and J.L. Bowditch (1989), *The human side of mergers and acquisitions,* San Francisco, CA: Jossey-Bass.

Capasso, A., E. Imperiale and O. Meglio (2002), 'Quality management In post-acquisition integration processes', *Proceedings of the 7th World Congress for Total Quality Management,* Verona, 320–35.

Capron, L. and W. Mitchell (1998), 'Bilateral resource redeployment and capabilities improvement following horizontal acquisitions', *Industrial and Corporate Change,* 7 (3), 453–84.

Chatterjee, S. (1986), 'Types of synergy and economic value: the impact of acquisitions on rival firms', *Strategic Management Journal,* 7, 119–39.

Collis, D.J. and E.W. Johnson (1995), *Cooper Industries' Corporate Strategy (B),* Case 9–795–154, Harvard Business School.

Collis, D.J. and E.W Johnson (1998), *Newell Company: Acquisition Strategy,* Case 9-794–066, Harvard Business School.

Collis, D.J. and T. Stuart (1995), *Cooper Industries' Corporate Strategy (A),* Case 9-931-095, Harvard Business School.

Cooper, P. (2001), 'Fragmentation in strategic management', in Voledrba H.W. and T. Elfring (eds), *Rethinking Strategy,* London: Sage.

Eisenhardt, K.M. and J.A. Martin (2000), 'Dynamic capabilities: what are they?', *Strategic Management Journal,* 21, 1105–21.

Eisenhardt, K.M. and Santos F.M. (2002), Knowledge-based view: a new theory of strategy?, in Pettigrew A., H. Thomas and R. Whittington (eds), *Handbook of Strategy and Management,* London: Sage.

Epstein, M.J. 2004, 'The drivers of success in post-merger integration, *Organizational Dynamics*, 33 (2), 174–89

Franks, J., R. Harris and S. Titman (1991), 'The post-merger share price performance of acquiring firms', *Journal of Financial Economics*, 29, 81–96.

Fry, J.N. (2000), *Newell Company: the Rubbermaid Opportunity*, Case 9B00M010, Ivey School of Business.

Haleblian, J. and S. Finkelstein (1999), 'The influence of organizational acquisition experience on acquisition performance: a behavioural perspective', *Administrative Science Quarterly*, 44, 29–46.

Hargadon, A. (1998), *Knowledge Brokers: a Field Study of Organizational Learning and Innovation*, Chicago: Academy of Management Annual Meeting.

Harrison, J.S., M.A. Hitt, R.E. Hoskisson and R.D. Ireland (1991), 'Synergies and post-acquisition performance: differences versus similarities in resource allocation', *Journal of Management*, 17, 173–90.

Harrison, J.S., M.A. Hitt, R.E. Hoskisson and R.D. Ireland (2001), 'Resource complementarity in business combinations: extending the logic to organizational alliances', *Journal of Management*, 27, 679–90.

Haspeslagh, P.C. and D.B. Jemison (1991), *Managing Acquisitions*, NewYork: Free Press.

Haunschild, P.R., A. Davis-Blake and M. Fichman (1994), 'Managerial over-commitment in corporate acquisition process', *Organization Science*, 5, 528–40

Hayward, M.L. (2002), 'When do firms learn from their acquisition experience? Evidence from 1990-1995', *Strategic Management Journal*, 23, 21–39.

Javidan, M., A.L. Pablo, H. Singh, M.Hittand and D. Jemison (2004), 'Where we've been and where we are going', in Pablo, A.L. and M. Javidan (eds), *Mergers and Acquisitions: Creating Integrative Knowledge*, Malden: Blackwell Publishing.

Jemison, D.B. and S.B. Sitkin (1986), 'Corporate acquisitions: a process perspective', *Academy of Management Review*, 11, 145–63.

Jensen, M.C. (1989), 'Clinical papers and their role in the development of financial economics', *Journal of Financial Economics*, 24, pp. 3–6.

Jensen, M.C. and R.S. Ruback (1983), 'The market for corporate control: the scientific evidence', *Journal of Financial Economics*, 11, 5–50.

Larsson, R. (1990), *Coordination of Action in M&A: Interpretive and System Approach Toward Synergy*, Lund Studies in Economics and Management 10, Lund University Press.

Larsson, R. (1993), 'Case survey methodology: quantitative analysis of patterns across case studies', *Academy of Management Journal*, 36 (6), 1515–46.

Larsson, R. and S. Finkelstein (1999), 'Integrating strategic, organizational and human resource perspectives on mergers and acquisitions: a case survey of synergy realization', *Oragnization Science*, 1, 1–26.

Loderer, C. and K. Martin (1992), 'Post-acquisition performance of acquiring firms', *Financial Management*, Autumn, 69–79.

Lohrum, C. (1996), *Post-acquisition Integration: Towards an Understanding of Employee Reactions*, Doctoral dissertation, Research Report 65, Swedish School of Economics and Business Administration, Helsinki, Finland.

Marks, M.L. (1982), 'Merging human resources: a review of current research', *Mergers & Acquisitions,* 17, 38–44.

Marks, M.L. and P. Mirvis (1985), 'Merger syndrome: stress and uncertainty', *Mergers & Acquisitions*, Summer, 50–55.

Mintzberg, H. and J.A. Waters (1985), 'Of strategies, deliberate and emergent', *Strategic Management Journal*, 6 (3), 170–84.

Montgomery, C.A. and E.J. Gordon (2001), '*Newell Company: Corporate Strategy*, Case 9-799-139, Harvard Business School.

Nahavandi, A. and A.R. Malekzadeh (1988), 'Acculturation in mergers and acquisitions', *Academy of Management Review*, 13 (1), 79–90.

Napier, N.K. (1989), 'Mergers and acquisitions, human resources issues and outcomes: a review and a suggested typology', *Journal of Management Studies*, 26 (3), 271–89.

O'Reilly C. (1998), *Cisco Systems: the acquisition of technology is the acquisition of people*, Case No. HR-10, Graduate School of Business, Stanford University.

Pablo, A.L. (1994), 'Determinants of acquisition integration level: a decision-making perspective', *Academy of Management Journal*, 37 (4), 803–36.

Pautler, P.A. (2003), *The Effects of Mergers and Post-merger integration: a Review of Business Consulting Literature*, Washington DC: Bureau of Economics Federal Trade Commission (first draft).

Pettigrew, A.M. (1990), 'Longitudinal field research on change: theory and practice', *Organization Science*, 1 (3), 267–92.

Pritchett, P. (1985), *After the Merger: Managing the Shockwaves*, Homewood, Illinois: Dow Jones Irwin.

Puranam, P., H. Singh and M. Zollo (2003), 'A bird in the hand or two in the bush? Integration trade offs in technology-grafting acquisitions', *European Management Journal*, 21 (2), 179–84.

Risberg, A. (1999), *Ambiguities thereafter: An Interpretive Approach to Acquisitions*, Lund Studies in Economics and Management 46, Lund University Press.

Scherer, F.M (1980), *Industrial Market Structure and Economic Performance*, Chicago: Rand McNally.

Seth, A. (1990), Value creation in acquisitions: a reexamination of performance issues, *Strategic Management Journal*, 11, 99–115.

Shrivastava, P. (1987), 'Post-merger integration', *Journal of Business Strategy*, 7 (1), 65–76.

Sinetar, M. (1981), 'Mergers, morale and productivity', *Personnel Journal*, 60, 863–67.

Sirower, M.L. (1997), *The Synergy Trap*, New York: Free Press.

Sitkin, S.B. and A.L. Pablo (2004), 'Leadership and M&A process', in Pablo, A.L. and M. Javidan (eds.), *Mergers and Acquisitions: Creating Integrative Knowledge*, Malden: Blackwell Publishing.

Teece, D.J., G. Pisano and A. Shuen (1997), 'Dynamic capabilities and strategic management', *Strategic Management Journal*, 18 (7), 509–33.

Tsoukas, H. and C. Knudsen (2002), 'The conduct of strategy research', in Pettigrew A., H. Thomas and R. Whittington (eds), *Handbook of Strategy and Management*, London: Sage.

Van de Ven, A.H. (1992), 'Suggestions for studying strategy process: a research note', *Strategic Management Journal*, 21, 981–86 .

Winter, S.J. (2000), 'The satisficing principle in capability learning', *Strategic Management Journal*, Special Issue, 13, 169–88.

Zollo, M. and J.J. Reuer (2002), *Experience Spillover Across Corporate Development Activities*, Paper presented at 'Fusioni, acquisizioni e alleanze: un imperativo strategico per la Nuova Europa?' Conference, Milan: University 'L.Bocconi'.

Zollo, M. and Singh H. (2004), 'Deliberate learning in corporate acquisitions: post-acquisition strategies and integration capabilities in U.S. bank mergers', *Strategic Management Journal*, 25 (13), 1233–56.

Zollo, M. and S.J. Winter, (2002), 'Deliberate learning and the evolution of dynamic capabilities', *Organization Science*, 13, 339–51.

11. Merger and acquisition integration: the influence of resources[1]

Maria Iborra and Consuelo Dolz

INTRODUCTION[2]

The high percentage of failures in mergers and acquisitions makes them a risky strategy that needs to be improved. Evidence shows that these operations do not always create value: Jansen (2002), in a revision of the academic studies on this topic to date, found that the rate of failure oscillates between 56 per cent and 78.5 per cent, and that failures have negative consequences for employment and for the top management executives of the acquired companies.

In view of this, the acquisition literature of the 1980s and 1990s tried to understand the performance of these operations. The aim was to improve the formulation of these strategies. The strategic fit, the organizational fit and the cultural fit were the key issues for understanding acquisition performance (Kitching, 1967; Kusewitt, 1985; Chatterjee, 1986; Porter, 1987; Shelton, 1988; Fowler and Schmidt, 1989; Hunt, 1990; Seth, 1990; Datta, 1991; Chatterjee et al., 1992; Larsson and Finkelstein, 1999). Recently, however, the literature has proposed approximating the formulation of these strategies from a resource-based view. From this perspective, acquisitions are seen as a way of renewing the resource base of the firm (Vermeulen and Barkema, 2001) or as a way to reconfigurate its resource structure (Karim and Mitchell, 2000; Capron et al., 2001). This resource-based view provides a more dynamic interpretation of acquisitions as a means of buying resources (Capron, 1999; Ahuja and Katila, 2001) and also as an alternative means of changing the configuration of the resources of the firm (Karim and Mitchell, 2000; Capron et al., 2001). In addition, yet another change has emerged. In the second half of the 1990s, the growth of technological acquisitions resulted in academic research applying a knowledge-based view to these new recent acquisitions (Bresman et al., 1999; Ranft and Lord, 2002). These works also clearly show the relevance of the links between formulation and implementation in technological acquisitions.

While formulation issues have been widely analyzed, studies of the integration phase are scarce and, in general, they do not take integration into account fully. In this respect, the literature has dealt with the communication problems (Von Krogh, 1994), the levels and the reasons for top management turnover (Walsh, 1988; Hambrick and Cannella, 1993; Kesner and Dalton, 1994; Iborra, 2000; Ranft and Lord, 2000; Krug and Hegarty, 2001) and the acculturation process (Nahavandi and Malekzadeh, 1988; Buono and Bowditch, 1989; Larsson and Lubatkin, 2001) as specific challenges to be faced in the integration process of mergers and acquisitions. A more complete view of the integration process can be found in the work of Haspeslagh and Jemison (1991). They propose a typology of why and how integration process types differ. Absorption, preservation, symbiosis and holding are the basic integration types. More than ten years after Haspeslagh and Jemison's proposal, studies of different integration types remain scarce. Recent works highlight that integration type must be explained taking into account the resources and capabilities in terms of the knowledge type that is involved. The development in the multinational literature of the ways to improve knowledge transfer and creation inter- and intra-firm can be applied to the integration types in acquisitions (Goshal and Barlett, 1988; Kogut and Zander, 1992; Bresman et al., 1999; Birkinshaw et al., 2000). Symbiotic and absorption types can thus be studied in the light of the resource and knowledge type involved. Technological acquisitions have raised attention to the knowledge type involved in the integration phase (Hakanson, 1995; Bresman et al., 1999; Birkinshaw et al., 2000; Ranft and Lord, 2002).

Therefore, we propose that the types of resources that a company wants to buy hold the key in understanding the selection of the integration type. Building from the resource-based view and from the knowledge-based view, we will explain why different resources and different knowledge need different integration types.

So, the aim of this chapter is to analyze the integration process. Specifically, (1) it analyzes and describes two variables to define the integration process, integration level and integration approximation, (2) it explains what resources and capabilities are related to the selection of the integration type, and (3) it relates integration type, its level and approximation, to acquisition performance.

THE INTEGRATION PROCESS: INTEGRATION LEVEL AND INTEGRATION APPROXIMATION

The first task is to analyze how integration processes differ. The aim of the integration process is value creation, that is, to transform potential synergies into real synergies. Pablo (1994) defines integration as the realization of changes in functional activities, structures, organizational systems and cultures that allow the organization to consolidate as a whole.

Haspeslagh and Jemison (1991), using three different sources of cases studies, propose the four well-known integration types. Apart from this work, the literature has not empirically dealt with this issue. However there have been propositions that define integration types in a normative way. It is possible to find out from these normative types the variables in which the integration processes differ.

For some researchers the integration level defines the integration type (Pritchett, 1985; Pablo, 1994). Pablo (1994) claims that integration level accounts for the degree of post-acquisition change in the cultural, administrative and technical make-up of a firm. She focuses on integration as a means of coordinating and controlling objectives after acquisition.

On the other hand, the integration type can be defined by an approximation to the integration process that defines how integration is carried out and why it is done in that way (Haspeslagh and Jemison, 1991; Marks and Mirvis, 2001). The types defined by Haspeslagh and Jemison (1991) or McCann and Gilkey (1990) can be defined as follows:

- Preservation: the possibility of keeping each company operating separately. There are no changes in the companies. Marks and Mirvis (2001) define the same type.
- Symbiotic integration: the two firms change their way of doing things to form a collaborative action. As Haspeslagh and Jemison (1991) point out, in symbiotic acquisitions the firms first preserve and then gradually become interdependent. The symbiotic integration of Haspeslagh and Jemison seems similar to the 'best of both' and the 'transformation' types of Marks and Mirvis (2001).
- Absorption: one of the firms loses its autonomy and independence and is assimilated by the other firm. There is a complete consolidation of the firms, of the operations, the culture and the organization. We can fit the absorption type and the reverse absorption of Marks and Mirvis's typology here.

In the preservation case, there is no integration, so the approximation and level of integration are different from those in the other two types. However symbiotic integration and absorption need a high integration level, although the symbiotic process is an interaction process between the firms, while absorption is a one-way process, usually dominated by the acquirer. As Haspeslagh and Jemison (1991) point out, the question in absorption acquisitions is not how much companies are integrated, because the limits between both companies are going to disappear in a shorter or longer period.

In the same way, symbiotic acquisitions need a preservation of both companies at first but, after this, changes can be made, the firms finally becoming one. So the integration level in preservation is different from that in absorption or symbiotic approximation; but these last two approximations can be similar in their integration level in the long term.

Thus we propose that integration processes differ in terms of level and approximation. Integration level refers to the degree to which the functions of the acquiring and the acquired firms must interact. Approximation to integration refers to the perspective with which the firms are integrated; it defines how the interaction is done. So integration level implies how many or how few functional areas and systems are integrated, and integration approximation implies how these functions and systems are integrated.

This is a key question. Preservation is by definition an autonomous type; it gives independence to both the acquired and the acquiring firms. So in that sense we can't talk about integration, because there is no interaction between the firms in any function or system. But do symbiotic and absorption types differ in integration level? Can we say that absorption has a higher integration level than symbiotic integration? Haspeslagh and Jemison (1991) and McCann and Gilkey (1990) argue that the integration level is higher in absorption than in symbiosis in the first integration period but not necessarily in the long term.

On the other hand, recent studies are using a functional level, instead of a business level or a corporate level, to analyze integration type. These studies are usually focused on technological acquisitions and they explore how R&D units are integrated in those acquisitions. Such studies show that managers integrate firms in terms of specific functions, not firms as a whole, and that it is possible to find different integration levels and approximations in different functions (Hakanson, 1995; Bresman et al., 1999; Ranft and Lord, 2002). The work of Bresman et al. (1999) reports a symbiotic type for the R&D function, with absorption taking place in the rest of the firm. Ranft and Lord (2002), in their study using grounded theory, found that managers think of integration as a functional matter and that they make different choices about integration for different functions.

So we propose that the absorption and symbiosis integration types of Haspeslagh and Jemison (1991) require a high integration level towards the end of the process. The difference between them is not the number of functions being integrated but the method or the approximation used to do this. Absorption is a one-way integration type, where the acquiring firm dominates the process. All the functions that are integrated go in the same direction, that of the acquirer.[3] Symbiosis is a two-way interaction type, where both the acquiring and acquired firms look for different ways of integrating different functions; some functions can be dominated by the acquirer and some by the acquired firm, some remain autonomous and some interact in a new way.

DETERMINANTS OF INTEGRATION TYPE: THE INFLUENCE OF RESOURCES

The literature has proposed taking into account a great number of variables in order to explain integration type or to explain the level of integration and the perspective used. It has proposed variables such as the performance of the acquired firm, its size, the strategic fit between the firms, or the climate of the operation as determinants of integration type (Pritchett, 1985; Hunt et al, 1987; Hunt, 1990; Neira, 1992). Pablo (1994), one of the works that deals directly with this issue, points out that there are three types of characteristic that can explain integration level: entrepreneurial, cultural and political characteristics. Entrepreneurial factors include the strategic aim as well as the organizational aim. Cultural characteristics relate to the degree of multiculturalism that can explain the integration level of an acquisition. Lastly, political factors make reference to the power distribution between the acquirer and the acquired firm, and how they influence the integration level.

Haspeslagh and Jemison (1991), on the other hand, defend the idea that integration type must be chosen taking into account the need for strategic interdependence and the need for organizational autonomy. These two variables contain the entrepreneurial variables of Pablo (1994). They propose that other variables, such as the performance of the acquirer, the climate and others, can be taken into account for the choice of the integration type but that the two most relevant are the ones mentioned above. In Haspeslagh and Jemison's (1991) typology the determinants of each type, the need for strategic interdependence and the need for organizational autonomy, are born of the resources and capabilities that are involved in the acquisition. The types of resources and capabilities are the determinants of the selection of a symbiotic type, an absorption type or a preservation type (*ibid.*).

The literature shows, from an efficiency perspective on merger motives,[4] that resources are a key variable in understanding decision making for value creation in acquisitions (Capron et al., 1998, 2001; Capron, 1999; Karim and Mitchell, 2000; Ahuja and Katila, 2001). According to efficiency theory an acquisition can be used as a way of buying resources and capabilities that allows the acquiring and acquired firms to gain synergies by using, transferring, or creating resources and capabilities. We can consider that a firm buys different things: tangible or intangible resources that are not people-dependent and a group of intangible resources and capabilities that are people-dependent (Hall, 1992; 1993). This classification allows us to improve Haspeslagh and Jemison's view in line with recent findings. Coff (1997) highlights the hazards of creating value by means of human assets and shows why and how creating value with resources and capabilities that are people-dependent has specific challenges that are born of the human nature of those resources.

Buying tangible resources is an acquisition motive. Firms try to use the tangible resources that the other firm has instead of building their own resources. They are buying its facilities, looking for greater capacity, or they are buying its products and its market share to improve effectiveness or expand their own markets. Buying tangible resources, in a narrow sense, means that the acquirer does not need the human assets of the acquired firm to use the tangible resources. Normally the primary motive is to buy production capacity or market share but it may also need the means to make them work. Tangible resources can be physical resources or financial ones.

If the principal motive for buying a firm is to use, share or transfer physical assets we may expect firms to work together in a close way (Capron, 1999) and systems bringing information, planning and control in the same way. Task integration can be obtained quickly. There is no risk for managers in forgetting about human-integration processes. Physical assets do not cause the management dilemmas that human assets do; they do not present the threat of turnover and the same information dilemmas (Coff, 1997). There is no risk of losing the physical assets. We can expect that all the functions and systems of the firm will be highly integrated to make them work. So a high integration level can be expected in all the functions and systems.

Buying tangible resources-financial assets-is a well-known acquisition motive. They are part of the combination benefits type in Haspeslagh and Jemison (1991)'s typology. To use or to share financial assets does not need any functional change. It may require some change in managerial systems, but no more changes are needed. So we can expect no change in functional activities when buying financial assets but maybe some changes in planning and control and in information systems.

What can we expect from the transfer of intangible resources that are dependent on people? Coff (1997) highlights that some attributes of human assets are related to two management dilemmas: information problems and the threat of voluntary turnover. Both dilemmas are shown in Haspeslagh and Jemison's work on symbiotic acquisitions. The symbiotic type is seen as having to work with the trade-off between transferring capabilities and protecting them. High levels of integration will be needed for capability transfer but will increase the risk of losing capabilities. As Birkinshaw et al. (2000) have found, firms that bought intensive knowledge firms were more worried about the risk of losing capabilities than about the aim of improving task integration for transfer. Only when a first step of social interaction had been taken would they try to improve and reinforce the transfer between the firms. A similar finding is reported in Ranft and Lord (2002), but they highlight that in their cases the managers were trying to retain specific employees or groups-not top managers-at low levels of the firm, in specific areas of the firm. Losing a key employee was seen as losing the source of the acquired firm's technologies and capabilities.

So we can expect that when a firm is buying human assets-intangible resources that are people dependent-or knowledge that is tacit and socially complex-the level of integration will be as high as necessary, but as low as possible, and will be different for different activities or systems. So which functions would we expect to be changed for each type of transfer? In other words, how much integration would there be (integration level)?

The most well-known transfer type is the technological knowledge transfer. Neither Bresman et al. (1999) nor Hakanson (1995) look at the interaction between knowledge transfer and other activities of the firm. Capron (1999) and Capron et al. (1998, 2001) found that product innovation redeployment was related to manufacturing activities and marketing expertise. Product development capabilities will need interactions in the R&D function, but also at the manufacturing level and at the marketing level at least (Eisenhardt and Martin, 2000).

So from these different studies we can expect that know-how transfer will involve a high integration level and that this integration level is broader than only one function in this acquisition type. Thus we can expect that:

H1: The integration level is related to the sources of value creation.
H1a: Integration level is positively related to strategic motives. Integration level is positively related to creating value by means of buying tangible resources-physical assets or intangible resources which are non-people-dependent-as well as creating value through intangible resources which are people-dependent.
H1b: Integration level is negatively related to tactical motives. Integration level is negatively related to creating value by buying financial assets.

Buying tangible resources does not involve the risk of protecting capabilities or turnover risk (Haspeslagh and Jemison, 1991; Coff, 1997) so we can expect the acquirer to move quickly and in a dominant way (Bower, 2001), that is, to use a perspective imposed by the acquiring firm. We have in this case an absorption approximation for each activity of the firm but also for its systems. The tendency of firms to apply their own perspective in a win-lose mode has already been demonstrated in the literature. Works on relative standing have shown how the management of the acquirer tends to feel superior to the acquired firm (Hambrick and Cannella, 1993; Lubatkin et al., 1999).

What are the implications for the integration type when the acquirer firm is buying intangible resources that are people-dependent? Technological know-how transfer is positively related to the use of communication, visits and meetings (Bresman et al., 1999). So, in that sense, technological know-how transfer is related to an integration type in R&D units characterized by the need for time and the use of social integration mechanisms. As Birkinshaw et al. (2000) show, firms buying technological know-how seem to slow down the integration process to ensure that human integration is taken care of before task integration is initiated. In the same way, but in a broader context, Coff (1997) proposes that, in coping with the risk of turnover, firms can use an organizational design based on clan control and organic structures, as well as using participation or shared governance. Ranft and Lord (2000) found that knowledge transfer was positively related to the retention of key people. They found also that autonomy, status and commitment explain the retention of the key individuals of the acquired firm. Ranft and Lord (2002) also highlight some of those issues in their cases; they propose that retaining key people was one of the most important integration issues and that a high autonomy level is positively related to preserving capabilities but negatively related to knowledge transfer. They found also that incentives, communication and TMT composition played a key role in retaining key people. They found that TMT composition was used as a way of interacting. In three of their cases, the top management team included people from the acquired firm. In these cases the aim was not to retain executives of the acquired firm as a whole, but individuals of key functional areas. The promotion of key people was also seen in a symbolic way: the relative standing of the acquired firm was improved, signaling that their expertise and contribution mattered to the acquirer.[5]

The important point is that, in managing acquisitions of know-how, the trade-off between transferring capabilities and retaining key people must be balanced. Autonomy can be an option to retain key people (Lubatkin et al., 1999; Ranft and Lord, 2000). But for complex knowledge transfer strong ties are needed-frequency of interaction and closeness of interaction-(Hansen, 1999).

We can expect, then, that at the functional level key people's relative standing will be increased if the acquired ways of doing things are chosen as the way of doing things in the merged firm. In other words, retaining key people has been linked to relative standing. Autonomy can partially explain retention; improvement of key people of the target to top management team has also been seen as an explanation (Cannella and Hambrick, 1993; Ranft and Lord, 2000). We can expect that using the target way of doing things or at least creating a new way of doing things for both firms will also help to retain key people and at the same time make it easier to transfer capabilities that need interaction between firms.

So we can expect that:

H2: Integration approximation is related to the sources of value creation.
H2a: An absorption approximation is positively related to the acquirer buying tangible or intangible resources which are non-people-dependent.
H2b: A symbiotic approximation is positively related to the acquirer buying intangible resources that are dependent on people.
H2c: A preservation approximation is positively related to the acquirer buying resources for tactical motives.

The last part of our work explores the relationship between the integration processes and the value creation in acquisitions. As we have pointed out, a high level of integration will allow the transfer of intangible resources as well as tangible resources. As different case studies show the transfer of know-how needs close interactions between the firms, and the transfer of human assets as well as physical resources is not possible without close interaction between the firms (Hakanson, 1995; Bresman et al., 1999; Ranft and Lord, 2002). So we can expect that value creation will be positively related to the integration level: to the number of functions being integrated during the acquisition process.

On the other hand, symbiotic approximation means that the firm looks at the best way of integrating each of the functions and systems of the firm. It implies that the firms try to retain the best of each firm to improve the transfer and creation of different sources of resources. Symbiotic approximation allows firms to create value from the use of physical assets, looking for classical scale economies and scope economies, and to create value by the use, transfer or creation of know-how resources, allowing firms to deal with sustainable sources of value creation. Knowledge transfer as well as knowledge creation in technological acquisitions is related to close interaction between firms, high levels of communication and social mechanism of interaction, and ways of improving status between the firms; in other words, to the presence of a symbiotic approximation to integration. From this reasoning we can expect:

H3: Acquisition performance is positively related to the integration level and to the use of symbiotic integration.

METHODOLOGY

Our subjects of analysis were Spanish companies taking part in a merger or acquisition in the period 1992–1999. The database was built on the basis of companies that between 1992 and 1999 had registered an acquisition or a merger appearing in the Official Bulletin of the Company Registry.

The instrument used to gather data was interview by postal questionnaires, sent to the CEOs of the companies appearing in our database. The survey was pre-tested by two complementary methods. First, it was sent to two CEOs who had been involved in mergers and acquisitions in recent years, and then the different questions were discussed with them. Second, the survey was discussed with five researchers who were trained in mergers and acquisitions literature.

The survey has four parts. The first is linked to several classification variables. The second part deals with the buying decision and the negotiation process. It contains questions about the level of strategic, organizational and cultural analysis and the time spent on each of them; it also asks about the motives behind buying the acquired firm. The third part of the survey looks at the integration process. Lastly, the survey asks some questions related to the integration performance as well as the acquisition performance.

A total of 92 questionnaires were answered; the sample error was 10.14 per cent for a level of trust of 95 per cent. Twelve of the questionnaires were eliminated owing to a lack of information or because they did not fit the sample criteria. Tabulation and statistical treatment of the data were done using the SPSS computer package. Descriptive variables about the years of the acquisitions in the sample are given in Table 11.1.

Eighty-one per cent of the firms did not have experience in managing mergers and only 19 per cent did. Among these, only three firms had earlier international experience in mergers and acquisitions, the rest having national experience only.

Most of the companies (90.8 per cent of the acquirers, and 96.2 per cent of the target firms) operate in only one industry. The industries of the acquirers and the acquired firms are shown in Table 11.2; this table shows the type of acquisitions using CNAE codes.[6] This industrial distribution is similar to those in others studies of Spanish mergers and acquisitions. Martínez Serrano et al. (1995) found that service sector firms accounted for 42.7 per cent of the acquired cases and 50 per cent of the acquiring cases in Spain in the 1986–1991 period. The second industry for activity was the manufacturing sector (47 per cent of the acquired cases and 39.2 per cent of the acquiring cases), while primary industry only accounted for 10.3 per cent of the acquired cases and 10.8 per cent of the acquiring cases. Mascareñas and

Izquierdo (2000) found that acquirers belonged to the service sector in 53 per cent of the cases and to the manufacturing sector in 47 per cent of the cases.

Table 11.1   Acquisitions per year

Year	Frequency	Percentage
1992	4	5.0
1993	4	5.0
1994	7	8.8
1995	6	7.5
1996	13	16.3
1997	19	23.8
1998	17	21.3
1999	8	10.0
n.d.	2	2.5
Total	80	100.0

Table 11.2   Acquisitions per industry

Industry	Percentage of acquired	Percentage of acquirer
Agriculture, fishing	1.3	1.3
Manufacturing	42.6	44.3
Service	55.2	51.9
n.d	0.9	2.5
Total	100.0	100.0

With respect to the strategic fit shown in Table 11.3, acquisitions are only of a diversification type in 10 per cent of the cases using industry codes. Like Larsson and Finkelstein (1999), we also look to strategic fit, focusing on the similarities and complementarities in markets, products and technologies. Looking at the industry sameness or industry fitness has been a new proposal for measuring the combined potential (Larsson and Finkelstein, 1999). In this way we obtained a more fine-grained view of strategic fit, shown in Table 11.4. More than 74 per cent of the acquisitions were in highly identical markets, but only 44 per cent were highly identical in products and 54 per cent in technologies. In around 16.5 per cent of the firms markets were not the same, and in more than 31 per cent of the firms technologies were not identical. Complementary markets and complementary products are relevant in more than 40 per cent of the cases. Complementary technology was present in more than 27 per cent of the cases.

Table 11.3   Strategic fit

	Frequency	Percentage
Diversification	8	10
No diversification	72	90
Total	80	100

Table 11.4   Acquisition fitness at markets, products and technologies

	Identical markets	Identical products	Identical technologies	Complementary markets	Complementary products	Complementary technologies
Not at all	11.4	17.7	24.1	38.0	44.3	50.6
Less than some	5.1	3.8	7.6	7.6	6.3	8.9
Some	8.9	6.3	15.2	8.9	7.6	12.7
More than some	17.7	3.4	24.1	20.3	19.0	16.5
All	57.0	41.8	29.1	25.3	22.8	11.4
Total	100.0	100.0	100.0	100.0	100.0	100.0

Size is shown in Table 11.5. Relative size was widely different, from a minimum of 4.3 per cent to a maximum of 96.15 per cent, the mean size being 38.93 per cent. Earlier studies had found a high level of unsuccessful acquisitions in cases where the acquired firm size was less than 2 per cent of the acquiring firm size (Kitching, 1967). None of our cases represents that situation.

Table 11.5   Acquisition size

Sales (mill ∈)	Minimum	Maximum	Mean
Acquired sales	0.036	1110.21	48.95
Acquirer sales	0.054	5282.74	195.34

Definitions of Variables

Integration level

This is a scale of seven dichotomic items that measures whether, after the acquisition, the acquirer and the acquired firm are integrated or autonomous. The seven items represent the following functional areas and systems: human resources, production, marketing, logistics, information systems, planning and control systems. The α Chronbach of the scale is 0.9346. With this variable we are measuring the level of post-acquisition change in firm configuration (Pablo, 1994).

Integration type

This is defined as the approximation used for integration in the seven areas defining three different groups (Haspeslagh and Jemison, 1991). We first define the classification criteria and then two independent researchers classify each acquisition in one of the three following types:

- Absorption: an acquisition is classified as absorption if the policies of the acquirer are adopted in all the functional areas and systems that are integrated. Also, an acquisition is classified as this type if the policies of the acquired firm are adopted in all functional areas and systems that are integrated. This means that one single choice has been made for all functions and systems that have been integrated. It is a one-way integration approximation.
- Preservation: an acquisition is classified as preservation if the choice adopted for all the seven policies has been autonomy. In a narrow sense there is no integration process.
- Symbiosis: an acquisition is classified as symbiotic if different policies have been adopted for different areas of integration. In some functional areas and systems the choice has been to adopt the policies of the acquirer, sometimes the ones of the acquired firm, sometimes a new policy has been created and in others autonomy has been chosen. Each function can be treated differently, or some of them, but there is not a single choice for all the functions and systems of the acquired firm.

Partner selection motive

This is graded (1 to 5), where a motive has been important for the selection of the acquisition partner. We have taken into account the following motives: (1) to buy physical assets, (2) to buy intangible assets, but not human assets as the brands of the acquired firm, (3) to buy intangible assets that are people-dependent: this is measured by a six-item scale that considers the capability of the acquired firm in developing brands, the capability of the acquired firm in developing products, the capability of the acquired firm in improving processes, the knowledge of the acquired firm about distribution channels, the knowledge of the acquired firm about markets, and the technological knowledge of the acquired firm; the α Chronbach of the scale is 0.8342, (4) to buy the skills of general management of the acquired firm and (5) to buy a firm looking for financial assets: this was measured by a two-item scale that takes into account the tax situation of the acquiring firm and the tax situation of the acquired firm. The α Chronbach of the two-item scale is 0.8624.

Much of the literature on mergers has centered on efficiency theories and on the study of the different sources of value creation and on the possible synergies to be obtained during the process (Kitching, 1967; Kusewitt, 1985; Chaterjee, 1986; Hunt et al., 1987; Porter, 1987; Shelton, 1988; Fowler and Schmidt, 1989; Hunt, 1990; Seth, 1990; Haspeslagh and Jemison, 1991; Larsson and Finkelstein, 1999). We have seen how the motives that explain the reason for the mergers and acquisitions have been considered as potential benefits hoped to be achieved by the process. For this reason, the questionnaire reflects the various possible motives, including those of an eminently strategic nature, such as the obtaining of tangible or intangible resources, and those of a more tactical nature, such as the pursuit of tax improvements.

Acquisition performance
This is measured following recent studies that look at the real synergies that are obtained after acquisition. It is measured as the total synergies according to the Larsson and Filkenstein (1999) scale. Acquisition performance is defined as a scale of 11 items that measures the degree of synergy realization in a process of merger or acquisition, specifying the benefits achieved in purchases, production, marketing, market power, administration, vertical economies, access to new markets, cross-selling, transfer of know-how, and other sources of synergy. All these items reflect the main types of synergy associated with a merger using the proposal of Larsson and Finkelstein (1999), which is coherent with and integrates the previous studies in the literature. Each item was codified on a scale from 1 to 5 (Not at all, Very little, A little, A lot, Totally). In this way, we apply an overall measure of synergy realization reflecting all the possible synergies that may be obtained in a merger process. The α Chronbach of the scale was 0.85.

ANALYSIS OF THE RESULTS

The first aim of the study was to identify integration level and integration approximation as the main variables of the integration process in mergers and acquisitions.

Table 11.6 shows the level of integration that the firms choose: 34 per cent of the firms are given autonomy in either one functional area or one system or in more than one; 5 per cent are totally autonomous, not integrated at all. But in nearly 29 per cent of the cases total autonomy versus total integration is not the choice. This means that different integration autonomy choices are made for different functions and systems. The mean integration level is 5.43.

Table 11.6   Level of integration

	Frequency	Percentage
0	4	5.0
1	1	1.3
2	1	1.3
4	5	6.3
5	7	8.8
6	9	11.3
7	46	57.5
n.d.	7	8.8
Total	80	100.0

Table 11.7   Approximation to integration

	Frequency	Percentage
Preservation	8	10.0
Absortion	37	46.3
Symbiotic	32	40.0
n.d.	3	3.8
Total	80	100.0

Regarding the approximation to integration, as we can see in Table 11.7, only 10 per cent of the firms are a preservation type and the cases of absorption and symbiotic integration are similar to each other, though the absorption percentage is higher. The mean level of integration in absorption is 6.43 and in the case of symbiosis the mean integration level is 6.13, lower than in the absorption approximation.

From these results we can say that firms choose different integration levels and approximations for different functional areas and systems. The likelihood of integration is higher if the selection of the acquirer's way of doing things is predominant in all functions. But in 40 per cent of the cases the choice is not the same for all the functions and systems. In these cases the acquirer firm integrates at least some functions or some systems using the acquirer's way, creating a new way of doing things, or it does not integrate all the functions and systems of the acquired firm.

The second objective was to analyze the impact of the resources on the choice of the integration level and integration approximation. Some descriptive variables about acquisition motives are shown in Table 11.8. Tangible assets, financial as well as physical, seem to play a key role in buying the firms: 40.1 per cent of the firms think that buying the physical assets of the acquirer was an important reason; more than a quarter of the firms took the financial assets into account as an important issue. Brand assets appear as an important motive for nearly 25 per cent of the acquisitions. And intangible assets - capabilities and knowledge - are important in some of the cases, knowledge about markets being the most relevant motive.

H_{1a} is partially confirmed and H_{1b} is confirmed. As Table 11.9 shows, the regression analysis allows us to affirm that integration level is positively related to a firm trying to buy knowledge and abilities and is negatively related to a firm trying to buy financial assets. The impact of tangible resources, such as physical assets, is in the expected direction but is not significantly correlated with the integration level.

H_{2a} is partially confirmed. As Table 11.10 shows, buying tangible resources is more relevant in absorption acquisitions than in preservation and symbiotic ones. Post-hoc analysis allows us to say only that the difference from the preservation group is statistically significant. H_{2b} is contrasted. Table 11.10 shows that the importance of intangible resources is higher in symbiotic acquisitions than in absorption and preservation ones. Those differences are statistically significant. Post-hoc Bonferrony analysis shows that the symbiotic group is different from the other two groups.[7] H_{2c} is only partially contrasted. Buying financial assets is more relevant in the preservation approximation than in the other groups, but differences are not significant.

Lastly, H_3 is contrasted. As Table 11.11 shows, the total synergies obtained after the integration process are positively related to the level of integration and the use of a symbiotic approximation to integration. As shown in Table 11.11, the regression analysis allows us to explain 13.2 per cent of variance, and the two variables were significant.

Table 11.8   Motives for buying the target firm

Motives	Not at all (1)	Very little (2)	A little (3)	A lot (4)	Totally (5)	Total	(4+5)
Brands assets	57.5	8.8	10.0	11.3	12.5	100.0	23.8
Physical assets	37.5	11.3	11.3	18.8	21.3	100.0	40.1
Creation and brand development capabilities	67.5	17.5	6.3	7.5	1.3	100.0	8.8
Creation and product development capabilities	62.5	6.3	18.8	10.0	2.5	100.0	12.5
Capabilities of process improvement	61.3	23.8	10.0	2.5	2.5	100.0	5,0
Distribution channels knowledge	55.0	15.0	12.5	11.3	6.3	100.0	17.6
Markets knowledge	42.5	15.0	11,3	18.8	12.5	100.0	31.3
Technological knowledge	55.0	18.8	13.8	6.3	6.3	100.0	12.6
Management capabilities	56.3	15.0	13.8	7.5	7.5	100.0	15.0
Financial assets of the acquired	50.0	5.0	11.3	15.0	18.8	100.0	33.8
Financial assets of the acquirer	56.3	5.0	10.0	11.3	17.5	100.0	28,8

Table 11.9   Regression analysis

Model	R	R^2	Corrected R^2	F	Sig.
1	.477a	.228	.175	4.359	.002a

a Predictor variables: (constant), financial assets, brands assets, physical assets, know-how assets, management capabilities.

	No standarized coefficients		Standardized coefficients	T	Sig.
	B	Error típ	Beta		
(Constant)	3.7780	.8700	.1630	4.3420	.0190
Physical assets	.2490	.1600	.0590	1.5610	.1230
Brand assets	.0097	.1750	.0590	.5600	.5770
Management capabilities	.0048	.2310	-.0250	-.2080	.8350
Know-how assets	.1540	.0580	.3330	2.6330	.0100
Financial assets	-.1880	.0850	-.2330	-2.1980	.0310

Note: a. dependent variable: integration level.

Table 11.10   Anova between motives and integration approximation

	Absorption	**Symbiotic**	**Preservation**	**F**
Brands assets	1.97	2.66	1.13	4.179*
Physical assets	3.03	2.72	1.25	4.444*
Know how assets	10.56	13.87	6.87	7.877**
Management capabilities	1.51	2.78	1.00	14.171**
Financial assets	4.40	4.56	6.25	1.293

Note: *<0.05; **<0.01.

Table 11.11   Regression analysis

Model	R	R^2	Corrected R^2	F	Sig.
1	.397a	.158	.132	6.190	.003a

a Predictor variables: (constant), integration level and symbiotic approximation.

	No standarized coefficients		**Standardized coefficients**	**T**	**Sig.**
	B	Error típ.	Beta		
(Constant)	11.104	6.427		1.728	.089
Integration level	2.366	.966	.279	2.449	.017
Symbiotic approximation	6.809	2.426	.319	2.807	.007

Note: a. dependent variable: Acquisition performance.

CONCLUSION

Research in mergers and acquisitions is abundant. It has studied multiple questions from a variety of perspectives. One of the objectives has been to understand merger and acquisition performance. However a great part of the research has focused on the formulation phase in an attempt to rationalize it.

The work being presented here has focused on implementation processes, trying to relate the bases of value creation in an acquisition with post-acquisition integration processes. We have analyzed the influence of the types of resources that a firm wants to buy in the choice of the integration process.

We have defined an acquisition integration process by the determination of at least two variables: the integration level and the integration approximation. In this sense, integration level is based on the degree of interaction of the firms and integration approximation is based on the perspective used in integration; integration level looks at the number of functional areas and systems that are integrated, while integration approximation looks to see whether one of the firms dominates the integration process.

In this chapter we demonstrate that the integration level is high in symbiotic acquisitions as well as in absorption ones. Those two approximations do not differ in their level of integration but in the way they are done. Absorption acquisitions have been defined as those in which the vision of the acquirer is prevalent or, in some few cases, as those in which the vision of the acquired firm is prevalent. We have demonstrated that these imply a high integration level and that they are chosen when tangible physical resources are wanted for acquisition. Symbiotic acquisitions have been defined as those in which the acquirer does not dominate the integration process. In this case, sometimes the acquirer's way of doing things is used; at other times the acquired firm's way of doing things is used, and sometimes autonomy between functions and systems is the solution or a new way of doing things in that functional area or system is created.

The literature has proposed that the integration level in symbiotic acquisitions has to be measured with respect to the need for autonomy that the preservation of capabilities requires. In this chapter we show that the capabilities and knowledge transfer demands the integration of many functions and systems a high level of integration but that it also needs a non-domination perspective. So, in symbiotic acquisitions the level of integration is as high as in absorption ones; the difference arises out of the way in which functions and systems are integrated. The symbiotic type is used fundamentally when intangible resources are wanted for purchase.

Lastly, the study allows for affirming that acquisition performance is positively related to the integration level and to the use of a symbiotic integration. These results seem clearly coherent with the knowledge-based view of the firm and the research in knowledge transfer in multinational firms. These research works show that close interaction, formal and informal communication, the development of functional and social codes, and the motivation of the units are related to knowledge transfer (Ghoshal and Barlett, 1988; Kogut and Zander, 1992; Szulanski, 1996; Zander and Kogut, 1995). Acquisition research has not taken into account those findings until very recently (Bresman et al., 1999; Birkinshaw et al., 2000; Ranft and Lord,

2002). In our work we have only shown the role of a close integration and the perspective used in the acquisition performance. More studies are needed for developing the role that other integration issues play in acquisition performance.

New studies in the area must deal clearly with the issue of the level of analysis. We have shown in this chapter that integration is not a firm-level choice, but that firms choose different answers for different functional areas and systems.

The number of firms used in this study reveals the need for more studies to confirm, or refute, some of our hypotheses. Working with integration processes in mergers and acquisitions in European firms is difficult. Those studies that try to work with primary data and do not use a case study approximation are rare. It seems as if firms and their managers do not want to talk about their problems in handling their acquisitions, so from our point of view more work in this area would be welcome.

NOTES

1. In some cases they are done using for all the functions the way of doing things of the acquired. But in both cases there is a dominant or a one-way approximation to the integration.
2. See Trautwein (1990) for a review of merger motives.
3. The role played by this status bestowal was shown earlier by Cannella and Hambrick (1993) but for the top management team.
4. CNAE codes are the Spanish industrial classification system similar to SIC codes in the USA.
5. The tests of variance homoskedasticity were significant for $p<0.05$ in all cases beside the financial motives, so we can say that the difference did not come from difference in the size of the groups.

REFERENCES

Ahuja, G. and R. Katila (2001), 'Technological acquisitions and the innovation of acquiring firms: a longitudinal study', *Strategic Management Journal*, 22, 197–220.

Birkinshaw, J., H. Bresman and L. Hakanson (2000), 'Managing the post acquisition integration process: how the human integration and task integration processes interact to foster value creation', *Journal of Management Studies*, 37 (3), 395–425.

Bresman, H., J. Birkinshaw and R. Nobel (1999), 'Knowledge transfer in international acquisitions', *Journal of International Business Strategy*, 30(3), 439–462.

Bower, J. (2001), 'Not all M&A are alike and that matters', *Harvard Business Review*, March, 93–101.

Buono, A. and J. Bowditch (1989), *The Human Side of Mergers and Acquisitions: Managing Collisions between People and Organizations*, San Francisco: Jossey-Bass.

Cannella, A. and D. Hambrick (1993), 'Effects of executive departure on the performance of acquired firms', *Strategic Management Journal*, 14, 137-152.

Capron, L. (1999), 'The long term performance of horizontal acquisitions', *Strategic Management Journal*, 20, 987–1018.

Capron, L., P. Dussage and W. Mitchell (1998), 'Resource redeployment following horizontal acquisitions in Europe and North America, 1988 1992', *Strategic Management Journal*, 19, 631–661.

Capron, L., W. Mitchell and A. Swaminathan (2001), 'Asset divestiture following horizontal acquisitions: a dynamic view', *Strategic Management Journal*, 22, 817–844.

Chatterjee, S. (1986), 'Types of synergy and economic value: the impact of acquisitions on merging and rival firms', *Strategic Management Journal*, 7, 119-139.

Chatterjee, S., M. Lubatkin, D. Schweiger and Y. Weber (1992), 'Cultural differences and shareholder value in related mergers: linking equity and human capital', *Strategic Management Journal*, 13, 319-334.

Coff, R.W. (1997), 'Human assets and management dilemmas: coping with hazards on the road to resource-based theory', *Academy of Management Review*, 22 (2), 374–402.

Datta, D. (1991), 'Organizational fit and acquisition performance: effects of post-acquisition integration', *Strategic Management Journal*, 12, 281–297.

Eisenhardt, K. and J.A. Martin (2000), 'Dynamic capabilities: what are they?', *Strategic Management Journal*, 21, 1105–21.

Fowler, K. and D. Schmidt (1989), 'Determinants of tender offers post-acquisition financial performance', *Strategic Management Journal*, 10, 339–50.

Goshal, C.A. and C.A. Barlett (1988): 'Creation, adoption and diffusion of innovations by subsidiaries of multinational corporations', *Journal of International Business Studies*, Fall, 365–88.

Hakanson, L. (1995), 'Learning through acquisitions: management and integration of foreign R&D laboratories', *International Studies of Management and Organization*, 25 (12), 121–57.

Hall, R. (1992), 'The strategic analysis of intangible resources', *Strategic Management Journal*, 13, 135–44.

Hall, R. (1993), 'A framework linking intangible resources and capabilities to sustainable competitive advantage', *Strategic Management Journal*, 14, 607–18.

Hambrick, D. and A. Cannella (1993), 'Relative standing: a framework for understanding departures of acquired executives', *Academy of Management Journal*, 36 (4), 733–62.

Hansen, M.T. (1999), 'The search transfer problem: the role of weak ties in sharing knowledge across organization subunits', *Administrative Science Quarterly*, 44 (1), 82–111.

Haspeslagh, P. and D. Jemison (1991), *Managing Acquisitions: Creating Value through Corporate Renewal*, New York: Free Press.

Hunt, J. (1990), 'Gestionar la adquisición con éxito: una cuestión humana?' in COS (ed.), *Fusiones y Adquisiciones: Aspectos Culturales y Organizativos*, Barcelona: Gestión 2000, pp. 31–65.

Hunt, J., S. Lees, J. Grumbar and P. Vivian (1987), *Acquisitions: the Human Factor*, London Business School: Ego Zehnder International.

Iborra, M. (2000), 'La rotación de la alta dirección en los procesos de fusión y adquisición: el caso de la banca privada española 1987 1993', *Revista de Trabajo y Seguridad Social*, Centro de Estudios Financieros, 208, 153–80.

Jansen, A. (2002), 'Pre-and post merger-integration in cross border transactions, European M&As, corporate restructuring and consolidation issues', Barcelona: IESE.

Karim, S. and W. Mitchell (2000), 'Path dependent and path breaking change: reconfiguring business resources following acquisitions in the US medical sector, 1978 - 1995', *Strategic Management Journal*, 21, 1061–81.

Kesner, I. and D. Dalton. (1994), 'Top management turnover and CEO succession: an investigation of the effects of turnover on performance', *Journal of Management Studies*, 31 (5), 701–13.

Kitching, J. (1967), 'Why do mergers miscarry?', *Harvard Business Review*, Nov–Dec, 84–101.

Kogut, B. and U. Zander (1992), 'Knowledge of the firm, combinative capabilities, and the replication of technology', *Organization Science*, 3 (3), 383–97.

Krug, J.A. and W.H. Hegarty (2001), 'Predicting who stays and leaves after an acquisition: a study of top managers in multinational firms', *Strategic Management Journal*, 22, 151–69.

Kusewitt, J.B. (1985), 'An exploratory study of strategic acquisition factors relating to performance', *Strategic Management Journal*, 6 (2) 151–159.

Larsson, R. and S. Finkelstein (1999), 'Integrating strategic, organizational and human resource perspectives on mergers and acquisitions: a case survey of synergy realization', *Organization Science*, 10 (1), 1–25.

Larsson, R. and M. Lubatkin (2001), 'Achieving acculturation in mergers and acquisitions: an international case survey study', BPS Division of the 2001 Academy of Management Meetings, Washington, DC.

Lubatkin, M, D. Scheweiger and Y. Weber (1999), 'Top management turnover in related M&A s: an additional test of the theory of relative standing', *Journal of Management*, 25(1), 55–73.

McCann, J. and R. Gilkey (1990), *Fusiones y Adquisiciones de Empresas*, Madrid: Diaz de Santos.

Marks, M. and P. Mirvis (2001), 'Making mergers and acquisitions work: strategic and psychological preparation', *Academy of Management Executive*, 15 (2), 80–94.

Martinez Serrano, J.A., S. Gil, A.J. Picazo, M. Rochina and J.A. Sanchis (1995), 'Fusiones y adquisiciones en la economía española durante el periodo 1986–91', *Economía Industrial*, 306, 95–115.

Mascareñas, J. and G. Izquierdo (2000), 'Por qué se compran y se venden las empresas en España?', Instituto de Estudios Económicos, Informes.

Nahavandi, A. and A. Malekzadeh (1988), 'Acculturation in mergers and acquisitions', *Academy of Management Review*, 13 (1), 79....90.

Neira, E. (1992), 'Un modelo para evaluar el impacto sobre los recursos humanos de las fusiones y adquisiciones', *Revista Europea de Dirección y Economía de la Empresa*, 1, 91–98.

Pablo, A. (1994), 'Determinants of acquisitions integration level: a decision making perspective', *Academy of Management Journal*, 37 (4), 803....36.

Porter, M. (1987), 'From competitive advantage to corporate strategy', *Harvard Business Review*, May–June, 3, 43–59.

Pritchett, P. (1985), *After the Merger: Managing the Shockwaves*, New York: Dow Jones-Irwin.

Ranft, A.L. and M.D. Lord (2000), 'Acquiring new knowledge: the role of retaining human capital in acquisitions of high-tech firms', *The Journal of High Technology Management Research*, 11 (2), 295–319.

Ranft, A.L. and M.D. Lord (2002), 'Acquiring new technologies and capabilities: a grounded model of acquisition implementation', *Organization Science*, 13 (4), 420–41.

Seth, A. (1990), 'Value creation in acquisitions: a re-examination of performance issues', *Strategic Management Journal*, 11, 90–115.

Shelton, L. (1988), 'Strategic business fits and corporate acquisitions: empirical evidence', *Strategic Management Journal*, 9, 279....87.

Szulanski, G. (1996), 'Exploring internal stickiness: impediments to the transfer of best practice within the firm', *Strategic Management Journal*, 17, 27–43.

Trautwein, F. (1990), 'Mergers motives and mergers prescriptions', *Strategic Management Journal*, 11, 283–295.

Vermeulen, F. and H. Barkema (2001), 'Learning through acquisitions', Academy of Management Journal, 44 (3), 457–76.

Von Krogh, G. (1994), 'Implementing strategy in a newly acquired firm', in G. Von Krogh, A. Sinatra and H. Singh (eds), *The Management of Corporate Acquisitions: International Perspectives*, London: Macmillan, pp. 307–36.

Walsh, J. (1988), 'Top management turnover following mergers and acquisitions', *Strategic Management Journal*, 9, 173–83.

Zander and Kogut (1995), 'Knowledge and the speed of the transfer and imitation of organizational capabilities: an empirical test', *Organization Science*, 6 (1), 76–92.

12. Acquisition integration at Siemens Mobile Phones: applying a resource-based perspective

Denise Sumpf

INTRODUCTION

Mergers and acquisitions (M&A) have been a fact of organizational life and a constant managerial challenge over recent decades. After a slow-down in M&A activity in the late 1990s, takeover activities have recently regained momentum (for example, the bid of Sanofi Synthelabo for Aventis in Europe and the Comcast bid for Disney in the US in early 2004). Nevertheless, according to a PriceWaterhouseCoopers' study, less than 20 per cent of the transactions in the last five years yielded returns that exceeded the cost of capital involved (PriceWaterhouseCoopers 2001: 1). These alarming results imply that it is decisive for organizations to revise and improve M&A transaction processes in order to generate value and growth. Part of the problem is the integration phase, which has been identified as most critical, owing to the acquirer's and the acquiree's differences in several areas such as culture, leadership style and vision (Gerds 2000; Picot 2000; Fischer and Wirtgen 2000; Habeck et al. 2000; Haspeslagh and Jemison, 1991; Lajoux, 1998). Especially in knowledge-intensive industries (such as the telecommunication or biotechnology industries), where 'the knowledge you think you are buying may walk out the door' (Davenport and Prusak 1998: 55), careful integration management is a must. Otherwise valuable resources, and with them their contribution to the achievement of sustained competitive advantage, might be lost. This chapter examines the integration process in the case of Siemens Mobile Phones from the perspective of the resource-based theory and assesses whether the applied integration strategies qualify as unique capabilities of Siemens ICM.

The resource-based view (RBV) enables the examination of the cause–effect relationship between a firm's unique resources and capabilities (including physical, human and organizational capital[1] and its performance (cf. Peteraf 1993; Barney 1991; Wernerfelt 1984)[2]. The RBV can be applied to study the acquirer–acquiree-specific resources and capabilities generated in M&A transactions, but also to test the specific elements of an integration strategy and their impact on a firm's competitive positioning. Owing to the heterogeneity of firms within a certain industry, as assumed in the RBV, acquired resources and individual integration strategies have different values for different companies.

The analysis of the present single case study 'Siemens Mobile Phones' (SMP) sheds light on integration processes in knowledge-intensive industries. Furthermore it provides insight into Siemens' integration strategy, to determine its uniqueness, rareness and value. Siemens aimed to become one of the top three in the market of mobile telecommunications. For this reason the major acquisition purpose was to grow. Until 2000 the market share of Siemens Mobile Phones was low, compared to the market leaders Nokia, Motorola and Ericsson.[3] Consequently Siemens ICM acquired Bosch Telecom to gain access to valuable know-how (for example, multi-band technology) and human resources in the form of 350 R&D engineers. The chapter continues with an overview of the theoretical foundations, which build the basis of the case analysis later on.

CONCEPTUAL FOUNDATIONS

Research Streams

Four streams of M&A research can be differentiated with the help of criteria such as 'objective function of M&A transaction', 'theoretical frame of reference', and 'central propositions for the acquirer and acquiree'. Firstly, the *financial economics* research stream explains wealth creation for shareholders and the economy in general. Among others, the 'efficient market hypothesis',[4] 'agency theory,'[5] and the theory on 'market for corporate control' serve as theoretical underpinnings for the research body. As a result, the researchers' propositions are enhanced efficiency in the market for corporate control' and impact on shareholder value. Secondly, *organizational behavior* research focuses on the impact of acquisitions on individuals and organizational culture, which is theoretically reflected in the 'acculturation theory'. The central proposition states that employee satisfaction and effective integration are a function of the congruence between the cultural aspects of the acquirer and the acquiree. Thirdly, proponents of the *process perspective* emphasize value creation after acquisitions as their objective function and their theoretical frame of reference is the behavioral theory of the firm. According this view, management activities and the process of integration determine to what extent potential synergies can be realized. Fourthly, the objective function of strategic management research focuses on the prediction of the performance of the acquiring and acquired firms. On the one hand, the 'industrial organization' research body (Harvard School, Chicago School) concentrates on economies of scale and scope, while on the other hand the RBV directs its research to unique synergies within the new entity (Birkinshaw et al., 2000: 397–99).

Strategic management literature in the 1970s and 1980s was dominated by the examination of a firm's environment and its influence on a firm's competitive positioning. According to industrial organization, industry structure determines the conduct of a firm, and consequently its performance (for example, Porter's five forces of competition and profit impact of market strategy–PIMS).[6] The role of internal resources in determining a firm's strengths and weaknesses was left aside in strategic research. However military strategy adopted a resource-based perspective at all times (Grant 1998: 106–7).

The RBV benefits from the fact that a market-focused strategy provides insufficient stability of vision and strategic intent when faced with volatile customer preferences and permanently changing technologies. Hence the RBV focuses on the understanding of a firm's internalized sources of sustained competitive advantage[7] and explains the inter-firm performance disparity that cannot be attributed to industry conditions (Peteraf, 1993: 186). The choice of resources, their combination and the building of capabilities are considered as successful ways to create economic rents. (Makadok, 2001: 387; Conner, 1991: 132). Central to the RBV is a knowledge-based perspective, stating that knowledge is the basic source of competitive advantage. Knowledge acts as an important isolating mechanism, which renders resources inimitable. Here it is used in the sense of learning and development augmenting causal ambiguity (Hoopes et al., 2003: 891). The theory also suggests that the organizational mode (firm organization versus market contracting) has a strong impact on the generation of above-average returns and the achievement of competitive advantage (Conner and Prahalad 1996: 477).

With regard to M&A transactions, the resource-based approach favors the firm organization mode and identifies two efficient acquisition strategies: a supplementary and a complementary strategy (Wernerfelt, 1984:175). Both acquisition strategies seek justification through an increase in valuable tangible and intangible resources. Competitive advantage based on tangible resources (for example, machines), which can be purchased in open markets, cannot be considered as sustainable since imitation is easy. For this reason it is, rather, intangible resources and capabilities that fulfill the requirements of strategic assets,[8] despite the fact that they are difficult to identify. Not all intangibles are strategic assets, but intangibles such as product reputation or company reputation, know-how and organizational culture are strategic assets or possess the potential of becoming strategic assets (Michalisin et al., 1997: 364–65). Abstract concepts such as learning, strategy formulation, motivation and strategic leadership also embody valuable capabilities. Actual research conceptualizes such capabilities as dynamic, because constant adaptation and change is involved. Eventually capabilities complete a life-cycle (Helfat, 2000; Helfat and Peteraf, 2003; Teece et al., 1997). Within the constraints of the book, the present chapter continues the line of argument of the traditional RBV, but the author keeps in mind the ideas of the dynamic RBV.

According to Peteraf (1993: 179), the value of resources derives from the fulfillment of four conditions, which are the 'cornerstones of competitive advantage'. Each cornerstone has a different impact on the realization of economic rents. Firstly, *heterogeneity* mirrors the existence of productive factors which are limited in supply; for example special engineers. The scarcity of production factors creates rents, since competitors may not gain access. Secondly, to preserve the heterogeneity among organizations, *ex-post limits of competition*, such as property rights or quasi-rights like information asymmetries or time lags, must exist. Ex-post limits of competition entail imperfect imitability and imperfect substitutability, which contribute to the sustaining of rents from an external point of view. Thirdly, exposure to *ex-ante limits of competition* (imperfections in strategic factor markets) implies that there is, a priori, no equally distributed access to certain resources. In this situation, one firm possesses either superior knowledge regarding the resource's value or a better strategic fit to already owned resources. A firm can earn above-average returns owing to the absence of competition. Ex-ante limits of competition ensure that costs associated with the acquisition of necessary resources are excessively compensated by the ex-post value. Fourthly, *imperfect factor mobility* expresses the fact that a resource is more valuable in one firm than in another. The imperfect factor mobility contributes within a firm to the sustaining of rents as they are isolated from imitation or substitution (Hoopes et al., 2003: 890; Peteraf, 1993: 185–7).

To examine the value of resources it is necessary to analyze a capability's or resource's characteristics in the context of its generation process. Resources can be generated either through organizational learning or through asset accumulation. The focus of the present chapter is on accumulation by successful integration of acquired resources, which lead to the further evolution of idiosyncratic resources within the firm's organization. Nevertheless the impact of learning, namely 'learning to integrate', is considered as a fundamental. The important characteristic of a resource is its *social embeddedness*. For example, reputation and culture are socially embedded resources, because they cannot be separated from the organization. Social embeddedness also means that capabilities, for example organizational routines, are uniquely created through the social organization and its knowledge base (Godfrey and Gregersen, 1999: 46). The chosen resource-generation process and the social complexity determine the *path dependency* of a firm, which assumes internally evolved resources to be inherently non-tradable and non-imitable. It is based on the explanation that the characteristics of a firm's internal resources and the generating process of resources depend on behavioral and cognitive constraints within this firm, because consistent decision-making affects the vision pursued and influences asset accumulation. Moreover the unique historical conditions determine a firm's actual set of capabilities and its position among competitors (Barney, 1991: 107). The firms are forced to renew the value and uniqueness of their resources and capabilities in the course of constant self-transformation (Medcof, 2000: 61) in order to avoid any rigidities (Leonard-Barton, 1992: 112). As mentioned at the beginning, only a firm's resources and capabilities provide the reliable basis needed for a long-term strategy. Besides path dependency and social complexity, *causal ambiguity* strongly supports inimitability and non-substitutability of resources, since the term describes the impossibility of an explicit cause effect relationship between a specific resource and the firm's sustained competitive advantage (Barney, 1991: 107).

Linking Post-merger Integration to the Resource-based View

There are two alternative ways to link the RBV and post-merger integration:[9] the *process-oriented perspective* examines whether the entire integration strategy is a firm-specific capability, whereas the *element-oriented perspective* studies whether the individual elements or sub-strategies of an integration strategy are unique capabilities. From a process-oriented perspective the sustained competitive advantage of a firm results from the implementation of a value-creating strategy that current or potential competitors cannot implement. Additionally the competitors must be unable to duplicate the benefits of this strategy (Barney, 1991: 102). Obviously the post-merger integration strategies of companies like General Electric and Cisco are value-creating strategies that cannot be duplicated, because specific intra-firm constellations exist, which make each transaction unique. For example, General Electric Capital seizes the 'pathfinder model' to diminish the degree of improvization, but it is unlikely to completely avoid improvization in an acquisition transaction (Ashkenas et al., 1998: 167).[10]

Concentrating on value creation rather than on value capture, successful post-merger integration emphasizes the transfer of capabilities and the collaboration of people from both the acquirer and the acquired company

(Haspeslagh and Jemison, 1991: 11). A company's dynamism and flexibility depend strongly on the political and cultural willingness of the human beings within a firm, because their behavior and action control the evolution of rent-producing resources (Oliver, 1997: 706). Hence, especially in knowledge-intensive M&A transactions, the integration of unique and valuable human capital is the critical success factor. The RBV suggests that these human resources are best developed and maintained internally. Internal employment or development modes encompass own development and acquisition, while contracting and alliances represent external modes (Lepak and Snell, 1999: 33–6). The integration of the acquired capabilities leads to the evolution of firm-specific resources through combination with already existing ones, while the preceding acquisition decision, in favor of firm organization and against market contracting,[11] is based on due diligence, which never captures the full potential in advance. In knowledge-intensive industries, the advantages of a firm organization, for example the Siemens ICM research and development (R&D) network, are far-reaching. Basically communication and coordination costs diminish, while knowledge-transfer is facilitated, because the drain to competitors is diminished. According to Kogut and Zander (1996: 503), 'the advantage of a firm is more than just economizing on costs, but is also the creation of a context of discourse and learning that promotes innovation and motivated behavior'. The specific context of learning, experience, and decision-making symbolizes the path dependency of a firm, making technical capabilities as well as knowledge capabilities inimitable. Post-merger integration processes in knowledge-intensive industries have to pursue business transformation strategies that should focus primarily on people, not on products. For example, in the mobile phones industry, the speed of innovation has increased dramatically due to product life cycles that last merely a year. For instance, Siemens brought 26 mobile phone models to the market in the fiscal year 2003 (Siemens Mobile, 2004: 1).

The RBV and the post-merger integration process can also be linked from an *element-oriented perspective*, as not only does the whole process allow rent generation, but also the individual elements of an integration strategy qualify as unique resources. Barney (1986) exemplarily discusses the potential of organizational culture as a source of sustained competitive advantage. Besides a strong organizational culture, capabilities of individuals or groups are considered sources of competitive advantage; for example, excellent communication, leadership and/or vision creation, but also organizational routines and interactions that coordinate resources. Communication capabilities are interaction-based, owing to their specific combinations of sender, message and recipient, which are embedded in a social context and causally ambiguous. Leadership skills are highly tacit, which makes them specific to a person and thus neither substitutable nor imitable (Fahy, 2000: 98). Thus the post-merger integration process must enable a knowledge transfer in both directions, from the acquirer to the acquiree and vice versa. The transfer of tacit and explicit knowledge during the integration process is only possible when the participants share a sense of identity or belonging with their colleagues. Hence the integration process must focus on the psychological reasoning behind people's behavior (Bresman et al., 1999: 441).

RESEARCH METHODOLOGY

The case study approach is chosen to support the arguments of this chapter, since it is appropriate for assessing the explanatory power of the theoretical foundations for contemporary phenomena embedded in a real-life context (Yin, 1994: 13). The Siemens Mobile Phones case provides fine-grained detail on the measures taken during acquisition integration. Hence it constitutes the basis with which future acquisition integration strategies can be compared in order to substantiate the argument that the chosen integration approach allows Siemens a competitive advantage.

Site Selection and Unit of Analysis

The research site is Siemens Mobile Phones A/S (SMP) in Aalborg (Denmark), since it offers fine-grained details on integration in knowledge-intensive industries. The case study's unit of analysis is the post-acquisition integration process of a transnational acquisition.

Data Collection

The author collected empirical evidence for this study at different levels and through a variety of methods: semi-structured interviews with employees and the integration manager, direct observations, and reviews of corporate documents (for example, annual reports). The data triangulation ensured construct validity by providing multiple perspectives for the issues under study and allowed for a crosschecking of existing and emerging concepts (Eisenhardt, 1989: 537–8; Pettigrew, 1990: 277–9). Also publicly available information about post-merger interventions at SMP was of special interest. The reliability of the case study is ensured with a case study database allowing for replication.

SIEMENS MOBILE PHONES – INTEGRATION IN KNOWLEDGE-INTENSIVE INDUSTRIES

Introduction

On May 3 2000 Siemens ICM acquired the mobile communications development operations of Robert Bosch GmbH (Siemens, 2000: 21–2, 40). About 50 engineers in Salzgitter (Germany) and 250 in Aalborg (Denmark) embodied the valuable human capital, which became the new company called Siemens Mobile Phones (SMP). The Bosch Group wanted to exit the mobile phones business and divest its locations in Germany and Denmark. Parallel to the sale of the R&D facilities to Siemens ICM, it pursued the sale of the production facilities in Aalborg to Flextronics International, an American company specialized in large-scale high-tech manufacturing.

Consulting companies partially accompanied the acquisition process. The due diligence evaluation of the R&D work in progress turned out to be a tricky subject, since the actual R&D status at Bosch Telecom (former Dancall) was not as advanced as presented in the acquisition negotiations. No external consultants had been involved during the integration phase. The integration of the Salzgitter site proceeded without major complications, since the site became a satellite of the Munich R&D department and continued work complementary to the tasks in Munich. In contrast, the integration of the Danish facility was challenging (assumed reasons had been size, management styles and cultural issues). SMP was expected to deliver substantial gains to the Siemens ICM R&D network within 12 to 15 months.

Discussion

By the end of 2001 Siemens was listed in third place in the ranking of mobile phone producers worldwide. The set acquisition goal was reached quickly. The question that therefore arises is: how did Siemens ICM integrate its acquisition so successfully that it refuted all M&A failure statistics? A thorough look at the applied integration strategy allows a determination of how Siemens achieved a competitive advantage. Constantly involved in portfolio optimization, Siemens is considered to be experienced in M&A transactions. According to the behavioral learning theory, Siemens might benefit from learning-curve effects. Both individual and organizational learning, with regard to integration expertise, is considered a unique, firm-specific capability contributing to sustainable competitive advantage. The relationship between an organization's acquisition performance and its acquisition experience has been examined in a recent study. Haleblian and Finkelstein (1999) use a simple matrix to predict the success of acquisitions as a function of organizational behavioral response to antecedent conditions. Table 12.1 illustrates the four possible scenarios on the dimensions of generalization and discrimination towards similar and dissimilar preceding experience.

The SMP case is based on appropriate discrimination from antecedent experiences, because the acquisition of knowledge-intensive R&D functions was a first-time experience for the business unit ICM Devices (ICM D). However the managers involved had already gained expertise in the field of acquisition integration, which enabled them to perceive dissimilarities and manage these new conditions without generalizing thoughtlessly. The study stresses that best performance results are due either due to no acquisition experience or to appropriate discrimination through experienced people (Haleblian and Finkelstein, 1999: 51). The appropriate discrimination in the SMP case, as a consequence of perceived inexperience, could present a successful basis for the implementation of the chosen integration approach.

Table 12.1 Effects of acquisition experience on performance

	Acquisition perceived as **similar** to previous experience	Acquisition perceived as **dissimilar** to previous experience
Organization's response: **Generalization**	Appropriate generalization => positive experience effects	Appropriate generalization => negative experience effects
Organization's response: **Discrimination**	Appropriate discrimination => neutral experience effects	Appropriate discrimination => neutral experience effects

Source: Author, with reference to Haleblian and Finkelstein (1999: 33).

Various integration aims are differentiated: preservation, symbiosis, holding and absorption (Haspeslagh and Jemison, 1991: 145). *Absorption*, meaning a high need for strategic interdependence and a low need for organizational autonomy, was the aim of ICM in the integration of SMP. The R&D facilities in Aalborg and Salzgitter were supposed to function as part of a global R&D network. An absorptive integration is very susceptible to time-critical issues; however ICM executives opted for the slower process of human integration over task integration, since the knowledge-intensive R&D functions require such an approach in order to avoid substantive conflicts and power-based conflicts leading to the loss of valuable human capital (Mirvis and Marks, 1992: 162). Usually such human resources are used to a high degree of creative independence, and consequently they are very susceptible to changes or limitations in their work environment. By February 2001 it seemed that the acquisition of Bosch Telecom and its integration had contributed successfully to the extension of R&D capacity and knowledge. Siemens more than doubled its mobile phone sales from 4.4 million units in 2000 to 9.3 million units in the first quarter of the fiscal year 2001 (Süddeutsche Zeitung, 2001: 26). Figure 12.1 displays a comprehensive post-merger integration strategy with a portfolio of several independent strategic elements that enable successful acquisitions in knowledge-intensive industries. It is important to understand that they have to go hand in hand to ensure a successful integration. For example, leadership, visionary and communicative capabilities are strongly interrelated.

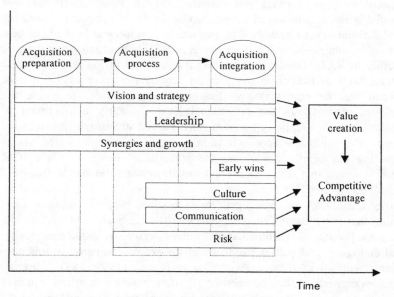

Source: Author, with reference to Haspeslagh and Jemison (1991: 12) Habeck et al. (2000: 13).

Figure 12.1 Integrative model of PMI elements

Vision and Strategy

The development of a sound vision and strategy is a key success factor in major change processes (Kotter, 1996: 21). The ICM vision: 'innovating the mobile world', served as the foundation of the multi-site R&D strategy. The multi-site approach allows knowledge to be captured which emerges across the globe. Ideally it allows facilitated access to knowledge workers (due to internal organizational structures), and also control of competitors (since no interfaces become active as in external networks). The literature differentiates two global R&D strategies (Kuemmerle, 1997: 63): *home-base-augmenting* sites, located in regional clusters of scientific excellence aiming at employing new sources of knowledge–the SMP case follows this approach by choosing an acquisition target geographically based in the telecommunications cluster in North Jutland–and, *home-base-exploiting sites*, focusing mainly on the proximity to large markets and manufacturing facilities. SMP was not interested in the acquisition of the production facilities, because this was not part of their interest or strategy. The aim was to outsource at least 30 per cent of the equipment production to Flextronics in order to concentrate on the core capability of R&D. Generally it appears that a sound vision and a strategic roadmap, well defined in advance of an acquisition, serve as a frame of reference for the managers and the employees in order to guide the integration process. On the operational level the early achievement of milestones and the creation of a team spirit proved supportive. Whereas the strategy of a multi-site approach is not unique, the implemented vision 'innovating the mobile world' has the potential of being a unique ICM capability, given that this vision continues to create solid bonds (Siemens Mobile, 2004: 3).

Visions can only be developed in an organic process within a firm, meaning that there are no interchangeable labels (Habeck et al., 2000: 35). An organic process of 'vision creation' is characterized by social complexity, causal ambiguity and path dependency of the whole company: in this case Siemens, with all its history. According to Barney (1999: 139), visionary companies outperform their competitors. A strong vision symbolizes a unique resource and its psychological effects on employees are evident in the Siemens case, because the powerful vision 'innovating the mobile world' has been successfully established and supports the changes during integration. Although the words of the slogan can be duplicated, its meaning is socially embedded into the ICM organization and it can only be transformed voluntarily to acquired entities. To inject the vision into a newly acquired entity, leadership qualities are mandatory in order to induce buy-in of employees.

Leadership

Leadership is a unique individual capability decisive for successful change management processes (Kotter, 1996: 175). Especially in the post-merger integration process, employees and external partners focus on managers' leadership capabilities, which include a favorable risk attitude, the decision-making approach, preferred mode of control, and communication patterns. The managers in integration phases should fulfill the role of 'guiding stars' navigating through the turmoil by managing conflicts and shaping norms (Heifetz and Laurie, 1997: 128). They have to set direction and push for change and adaptation, while giving the employees a sense of involvement[12] and protection. A manager's role includes the continuum from an 'influencer' to a 'visionary champion', thus responding to the environmental context (Collinson, 2000: 217). In the SMP case, the main task during integration was the preservation of existing human capital as well as further recruitment. Being an integration manager is a special situation, which requires the ability to adjust quickly to complex situations, profound project management skills and understanding of the parent company. Their tasks encompass the injection of speed, the creation of structure, networking and the engineering of early wins in addition to the transfer of capabilities and processes (Ashkenas and Francis, 2000: 110–5; Kotter, 1996: 21).

The two managers installed in Aalborg (one as integration general manager and one as R&D director) were chosen because of their long tenure within Siemens. The integration manager's personality and his leadership style, shaped by the Siemens' organizational culture, could be described as goal-oriented. The social embedding and the path-dependent development of this manager made him an idiosyncratic resource of Siemens. The R&D manager, with his ten-year career within Siemens, developed a more people-oriented leadership style, which seemed to fit best to the knowledge-intensive R&D department. As it turned out, the R&D integration had problems with bottlenecks in the rollout of new products and above-average loss of valuable engineers. Possibly a balanced leadership style would have been more supportive.

Leadership style or management style is part of the managerial or subjective culture of an organization; as a result it is unique to organizations and important in reaching performance goals (Datta, 1991: 283). As mentioned above, leadership capabilities are subject to social complexity (for instance, reputation and networks) and path dependency (learning within a certain environment). Both phenomena cause inimitability. Leadership is the key leverage point for cultural changes aiming at a 'culture by design' and not 'culture by default'. Especially in the case of SMP, where cultural assimilation was intended, strong leadership capabilities were required to reframe the employees' mental models to facilitate buy-in and acculturation, decreasing uncertainty avoidance (Marks and Mirvis, 1998: 226–8). An unambiguous evaluation of the leadership at SMP seems difficult, as the two managers were not equally successful. Wright et al. (1994: 305–14) discuss in detail how human capital fulfills the criteria of human resources.

Synergies and growth

Synergies are the most common M&A promises (Campa and Hernando, 2004: 47–8), occurring in various forms, such as financial synergies (lowering the cost of capital), operating synergies (economies of scale) and strategic synergies (shared know-how) (Goold and Campbell, 1998: 133). In the present case strategic synergies were desired, since the range of product platforms was expanded and a significant number of engineers were added to the human capital base of ICM. The tri-band and UMTS technological knowledge permitted synergies in the development of third- and fourth-generation mobile phones. Owing to integration difficulties concerning the R&D functions in Aalborg, the development of new products time-lagged and synergies could not be realized in the short term to yield an increase of market share more quickly. To become one of the top three players in the market for mobile phones requires an enlarged knowledge base and far more R&D engineers than ICM had before the acquisition.

The realization of synergies or the achievement of growth goals is fundamental. However, successful integration requires – in addition to task-orientation – a focus on the associated psychological issues. Managers have to be aware of 'synergy traps', which are expressed by four managerial biases (Goold and Campbell, 1998: 134–6). Firstly, *synergy bias* represents the overestimation of benefits in relation to an underestimation of costs. The cost estimation in the SMP case predicted that the costs of own development would exceed the acquisition and integration costs. But the synergies expected could not be achieved immediately, since benefits had been overestimated, as the factual state of R&D work in progress proved. Secondly, the *parenting bias* describes a situation where corporate level decisions concerning M&A transactions are made without consulting business level managers. Usually the business level managers are better able to judge the fit of their business with other businesses than the corporate level managers. Corporate level managers might not have sufficient insight to appraise negative synergies. In the case of SMP, parenting bias was reduced, because the business unit identified the acquisition target independently. Thirdly, the *skills bias* compounds the parenting bias, as corporate level managers are less strong in the required practical skills to integrate the concerned units. And lastly, the *upside bias* describes the managerial neglect of possible negative synergies. Managers act overconfidently, their optimism overpowers their judgment and the personnel bias tends to concentrate on supporting evidence instead of reflecting on possible pitfalls (Russo and Schoemaker, 1990: 236). To reduce managerial biases, a disciplined approach to synergy evaluation is mandatory. The SMP case suggests that such a disciplined approach was adopted. From a resource-based perspective, the ICM process of synergy evaluation qualifies as a unique capability.

Early wins
Early wins have to be harvested quickly in the integration phase. They demonstrate that the acquisition made sense and prevent people from building up feelings such as change resistance, capitulation/resignation, and/or a rise of discomforting uncertainty among external stakeholders. Most companies focus on internal accomplishments, while they ignore early wins through the integration of their customers. Early wins generally include new value propositions, improvements in work environment and the achievement of milestones (Habeck et al., 2000: 63). The transition of the Bosch extranet facilities to the new SMP homepage took place very early, to satisfy business and service partners. Internally, the knowledge transfer concerning the mobile phones' software packages to other R&D sites was achieved. The integration manager succeeded in negotiations with the local government about a new office building as well as for advertising and sponsoring (Siemens Mobile Phones sponsored the local soccer team AaB Aalborg). SMP's early integration results increased the presence of the new entity within and beyond the organization. The ability to identify and exploit low-hanging fruits may not be considered unique, but undoubtedly it is valuable. The author consequently proposes that this ability does not qualify to sustain competitive advantage, which is partly due to the short-term consumptive character of these early wins.

Culture
Culture may be defined as the "software of the mind... which distinguishes the members of one group or category of people from another (Hofstede, 1997: 4-5). International integration projects face cultural issues from two perspectives: national culture and organizational culture clashes must be avoided. Organizational culture or corporate culture" is a peculiar blend of an organization's values, traditions, beliefs, and priorities. It is a sociological dimension that shapes management style as well as operating philosophies and practices' (Pritchett et al., 1997: 10). Besides influence by the demographics of its members, the industry and the market, and the nationality, an organizational culture incorporates unique and idiosyncratic elements (Hofstede and Neuijen, 1990: 311). Assumedly non-significant

cultural differences between Bosch and Siemens led to an underestimation of difficulties concerning national and organizational cultural differences.

Hofstede (1997, 1985: 347–8) differentiates national cultures along four dimensions: (1) *Power distance* defines the degree to which less powerful members of an organization within a country expect and accept unequally distributed power. The score difference indicates that Danish people think less hierarchically than Germans. (2) The *degree of individualism* within a society refers to the distinction between individualists, who care about themselves and their immediate family, and collectivists, who are integrated lifelong in enduring and cohesive groups. Both Germany and Denmark score high as individualistic cultures. (3) The *dimension of masculinity versus femininity* captures the impact of gender roles in national cultures. The strong score difference implies that Germans are more masculine (career-oriented, competitive), whereas Danish people emphasize the feminine side by being concerned with care of their relationships and living environment. (4) The *uncertainty avoidance index* measures the extent to which uncertain or unknown situations discomfort members of a certain culture. Again a large score difference suggests that Germans have a significantly higher need for rules and their anxiety level rises when they are faced with unpredicted changes, whereas Danish people worry much less.

Although the integration efforts in the SMP aimed at the absorption of the newly acquired entity and the transformation into a pure Siemens company, the integration manager realized the differences in national culture and limited the integration to issues regarding organizational culture. The diversity of national cultures has been accepted as an asset and not as a liability in order to emphasize the international character of Siemens as a multinational company. Organizational cultures are more adaptive than national cultures, because organizations continuously develop whereas the impact of national culture cannot be changed easily (Schein, 1992: 12). A cultural profile along Hofstede's six-dimensional model (Hofstede, 1994: 4–8) had not been developed during acquisition preparation, thus the cultural integration has been handled situationally. The differences in organizational culture became evident (see Figure 12.2), but the SMP integration efforts concentrated on changing the visible elements of culture (symbols and corporate identity). From today's point of view, the *laissez-faire* approach was very successful, although the differences in organizational culture could have been assessed earlier.

Barney states 'that firms are idiosyncratic social inventions' which are path-determined by the unique personalities and experiences of their employees and founders as well as the unique circumstances of their foundation and growth (Barney, 1986: 660).

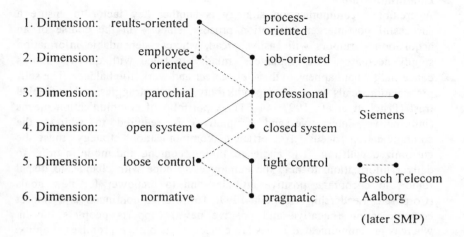

1. Dimension: reults-oriented — process-oriented

2. Dimension: employee-oriented — job-oriented

3. Dimension: parochial — professional

4. Dimension: open system — closed system

5. Dimension: loose control — tight control

6. Dimension: normative — pragmatic

Siemens ●——●

Bosch Telecom
Aalborg ●------●

(later SMP)

Source: Author, with reference to Hofstede 1994.

Figure 12.2 Organizational culture profiles of Bosch Telecom and Siemens

The foundation of Siemens in Berlin in 1847 by the charismatic Werner von Siemens shaped the organizational culture of the firm and led to strong employee identification (Siemens, 2001: 1). The inimitability of the Siemens corporate culture leads to sustainable competitive advantage, but the SMP integration showed that the transmission to the Aalborg unit was a lengthy process which could only be guided, not forced. The Salzgitter unit with its German national culture and the true Bosch corporate culture assimilated more easily. The Bosch corporate culture is closer to the Siemens culture owing to its foundation by Robert Bosch in 1886, whereas the Dancall culture, which still influenced the Aalborg site, resembled more that of a start-up company (Bosch Group, 2001). The cultural integration strategy was not exactly planned in the SMP case, but the strong corporate culture of Siemens contributed positively to the situational handling. The SMP case indicates that such a situational cultural integration strategy applied by a different company would not yield positive results, since the causal ambiguities (for instance, situational decisions and behavior by the ICM managers in SMP) and the social complexity of any organizational culture prevent the copying of the cultural integration approach applied at SMP.

Communication
A credible[13] communication strategy is another key factor to ensure a successful post-merger integration process, since – in the course of an acquisition – rumors will easily spread, whereas dependable information supply decreases. The employees' minds are filled with question marks concerning what happens to their job, career and work–life balance. The self-preservation leads to reduced productivity, power struggles and enfeebled trust (Pritchett et al., 1997: 44–51). A portfolio of communication means (informative, interactive and facilitative) is required to address the communication needs. An efficient communication strategy must be customized with regard to audience, timing, content, and mode in order to deliver information, to help the employees to cope with change, to dispel rumor, to encourage positive attitudes and to empower for new goals (Corporate Leadership Council, 1999: 16). Early, continued and honest communication (negative and positive news) supports people's buy-in, whereas uncommunicated issues are conceived as broken promises (Lajoux, 1998: 370–71).

In the SMP case, the top management level dealt with communication issues during the first months. Later even a special communication officer was installed. Informative one-way communication included presentations by the top management team from ICM and articles in the employee magazines *MAGIC* (ICM-wide) and *Magic Moments* (SMP only). The transfer of extranet pages had priority to avoid business interruption, but the new SMP homepage that broadcast information for employees and customers started as late as July 2001. Multi-directional (interactive) communication included workshops about changes in R&D processes, IT and marketing as well as social events such as the local summer party in Aalborg and the global ICM m-day party. Unfortunately the communication strategy lacked emphasis on the task integration. The communicated attempt to achieve an absorptive integration with a focus on human integration strategy was confusing. The reason for this was that in December 2000 the integration strategy changed from people integration to a focus on task integration that had not been explicitly communicated. The R&D engineers believed that they continued to be an independent entity, whereas ICM aimed to optimize its R&D network and cut back some core competencies in Aalborg. This eventually caused some R&D engineers to leave SMP. The communication strategy is embedded in the social context of the managers, employees and customers involved. Firm-specific characteristics of the audience imply that each communication strategy must be unique and valuable in an integration process. Causal ambiguity, due to individually different reception of messages and information processing, results in unfeasible duplication or imitation by another company. Nevertheless the communication strategy at SMP left room for improvement.

Risk management

The pursuit of effective financial and strategic risk management must be already initiated in the pre-combination phase, which is time, attention and resource consuming. On the other hand it enables short-term and long-term gains. Three categories of risk are differentiated: the *stakeholder risk* comprises the loss of key human resources, the *execution risk* concerns the timely transfer of capabilities, and *synergy risk* includes difficulties to benefit from the transaction (Habeck et al., 2000: 119–25). The different risks must be identified, evaluated and prioritized according to their urgency and impact. A high level of uncertainty is associated with knowledge-intensive transactions, which leads to estimation biases. Acquirers in knowledge-intensive industries may exercise three risk management strategies to cope with uncertainty, but the more the acquirer's business is perceived as related to the acquiree's business, the less coping strategies are implemented. The first strategy used is the decrease of the bid premium. Secondly, the acquirer augments the use of non-cash payments in order to shift risk. Lastly, it prolongs the negotiations and seeks extensive information from the target (Coff 1999: 145–8).

The SMP case does not indicate a special risk management program or any specific strategy to anticipate uncertainty, only that the R&D integration roadmap addressed uncertainty by evaluating work in progress and appraising the knowledge base. Despite this, problems occurred owing to the biased view regarding the factual stage of progress and the degree of difficulty in transferring key human resources. In the context of the SMP case, insufficient information about risk management inhibits an analysis as to whether the ability to manage risks is a capability in the sense of the RBV.

CONCLUSION

The discussion of the applicability of the RBV to integration strategies in the Siemens Mobile Phones case prepared the ground for future quantitative research. Seven basic elements of a comprehensive integration strategy have been analyzed in detail. Siemens' vision, leadership, culture and communication proved to be potential unique capabilities in the sense of the RBV. Risk management, the achievement of synergies, and 'early wins' may be considered as 'hygiene factors'[14] whereas the elements of vision, leadership, communication and culture are rather 'growth factors' or 'motivator factors', which enable value creation by successful integration.

Table 12:2 summarizes the research results. (A given 'yes' indicates that the condition is fulfilled, whereas a 'no' signifies that the individual strategy is unlikely to satisfy the conditions of the RBV.) The seven individual integration elements have been qualitatively tested as to whether they fulfill the conditions of the RBV and consequently represent a unique 'integration capability' of Siemens ICM.

Table 12.2 The seven elements and how they fulfill the requirements of the RBV

	Vision and strategy	Leadership	Synergy and growth	Early wins	Culture	Communication	Risk management
Rare	yes*	yes*	no	no	yes*	no	no
Valuable	yes	yes	yes	yes	yes	yes	yes
Inimitable	yes	yes	no	no	yes	yes	no
Non–substitutable	yes	yes	no	no	yes	yes	yes
Imperfect mobility	yes	yes	yes	yes	yes	yes	no

Note: *Rare in the sense that a sound vision, excellent leadership, and efficient cultural integration strategies seldom live up to dealing with the unpredictable situational problems arising in acquisition integration.

Source: Author.

The limitations of the explanatory power are based on the single-case research design. Furthermore, besides testing each element on the five categories given in Table 12.2, each element should also be tested for causal ambiguity, path dependency, and social complexity in order to substantiate the explanatory power. The seven integration elements discussed make up one possible frame of analysis covering the most important integration issues; nevertheless it could be complemented by more detailed categories to reflect the customized approach in integration strategies and to permit a facilitated comparison between cases. Integration, particularly the transfer of knowledge assets, is neither immediate nor easy; it is much more a process of mutual teaching and learning (Haspeslagh and Jemison, 1991: 109), therefore the dynamic nature of integration capabilities should be evaluated further. Barney (1999) hints that socially complex capabilities are generally beyond the ability of managers to change in the short term. Rather they evolve and change slowly over time. Thus long-term evaluation is necessary to judge an integration strategy's effectiveness. In February 2004 the SMP case can still be viewed as a successful example of post-merger integration in knowledge-intensive industries.

NOTES

1. A resource is an observable (but not necessarily tangible) asset that can be valued or traded 'such as a brand, a patent, a parcel of land, or a license. A capability, on the other hand, is not observable (and hence necessarily intangible) can not be valued, and changes hands only as part of its entire unit' (Hoopes et al., 2003: 890). The notion 'capabilities' comprise the organizational culture, core competencies and distinctive competencies, invisible assets as well as core skills (Fahy, 2000, p. 98).
2. Please refer to Hoopes et al. (2003: 890–91) for a review about the state of the art of research on the RBV and its integration with other theories, as well as to the special issue on 'Why is there a resource-based view? Toward a theory of competitive heterogeneity' in *Strategic Management Journal*, 24 (10).
3. The distribution of market shares (Siemens Mobile 2004: 4): For the year **1999**: Nokia (26.9%), Motorola (16.9%), Ericsson (10.5%), Samsung (6.2%), Panasonic (5.5%), **Siemens (4.6%)**, Alcatel (4.1%). For the year **2001**: Nokia (35%), Motorola (14.8%), **Siemens (7.4%)**, Samsung (7.1%), Sony Ericsson (6.7%), Panasonic (3.9%), NEC (3%). In 2001, Siemens was among the Top Three Mobile Phone companies. In the **first quarter 2004**: Nokia (35.5%), Motorola (14.4%), Samsung (10%), **Siemens (9.8%)**, LG Electronics (5.7%), Sony Ericsson (5.1%),
4. See Vasicek and McQuown (1972) for more information.
5. See Jensen and Meckling (1976) for more information.
6. See Anderson and Paine 1978 for more information.

7. The notion of competitive advantage is here defined as the differential between two competitors on any conceivable dimension that allows one to better create customer value than the other (Ma, 2000: 21).
8. An asset is something that is available to and/or owned by the firm (for example reputation, organizational culture), and/or it might be the way something is done (for example, specific technology, team experience) under the condition that it is valuable for corporate purpose. Assets are perceived to be strategic if they build the basis for competitive advantage (Martens et al., 1997: 7).
9. The use of the term 'post-merger integration' also includes post-acquisition integration.
10. Actual research assumes improvization as an organizational virtue. See, for example, the special issue of *Organization Science* on 'Jazz improvisation and organizing', 1998, *9* (5).
11. According to Conner and Prahalad (1996) firm organization represents a higher capability to control a given set of resources than does market contracting.
12. Current research investigates the relative importance of both positive and negative effects of involvement on the process of developing strategy (Collier et al., 2004).
13. For more information about credibility in organizations and management please refer to Thommen (1996, 2003).
14. Hertzberg (1968) introduces the notion of 'hygiene factors' defined as factors that avoid dissatisfaction, but do not generate satisfaction.

REFERENCES

Anderson, C.R. and F.T. Paine (1978), 'PIMS: a reexamination', *Academy of Management Review*, *3* (3), 602–3.

Ashkenas, R.N. and S.C. Francis (2000), 'Integration managers: Special leaders for special times', *Harvard Business Review*, *78* (6), 108–15.

Ashkenas, R.N., L.J. DeMonaco and S.C Francis (1998), 'Making the deal real: how GE Capital integrates acquisitions', *Harvard Business Review*, *76* (1), 165–78.

Barney, J. (1986), 'Organizational culture: can it be a source of sustained competitive advantage', *Academy of Management Review*, *11* (3), 656–65.

Barney, J. (1991), 'Firm resources and sustained competitive advantage', *Journal of Management*, *17* (1), 99–120.

Barney, J. (1999), 'How a firm's capabilities affect boundary decisions', *Sloan Management Review, 40* (3), 137–45.

Birkinshaw, J., H. Bresman and L. Håkanson (2000), 'Managing the post-acquisition, integration process: how the human integration and task integration processes interact to foster value creation', *Journal of Management Studies, 37* (3), 395–425.

Bosch Group (2001), *The Bosch Business World,* www.bosch.de, February 14.

Bresman, H., J. Birkinshaw, and R. Nobel (1999), 'Knowledge transfer in international acquisitions'. *Journal of International Business Studies, 30* (3), 439....62.

Campa, J.M. and I. Hernando (2004), 'Shareholder value creation in European M&As', *European Financial Management, 10* (1), 47–82.

Coff, R.W. (1999), 'How buyers cope with uncertainty when acquiring firms in knowledge-intensive industries: caveat emptor', *Organization Science, 10* (2), 144–61.

Collier, N., F. Fishwick and S.W. Floyd (2004), 'Managerial involvement and perceptions of strategy process', *Long Range Planning, 37* (1), 67–85.

Collinson, S. (2000), 'Knowledge networks for innovation in small Scottish software firms', *Entrepreneurship & Regional Development* (12), 217–44.

Conner, K.R. (1991), 'A historical comparison of resource-based theory and five schools of thought within industrial organization economics: do we have a new theory of the firm?', *Journal of Management, 17* (1), 121....54.

Conner, K.R.and C.K. Prahalad (1996). 'A resource-based theory of the firm: knowledge versus opportunism', *Organization Science, 7* (5), 477–501.

Corporate Leadership Council (1999), *Preparation for Merger Integration,* London: Corporate Leadership Council, Corporate Executive Board.

Datta, D.K. (1991), 'Organizational fit and acquisition integration performance: effects of post-acquisition integration', *Strategic Management Journal, 12,* 281–97.

Davenport, T.H. and I. Prusak (1998), *Working Knowledge: How Organizations Manage What They Know,* Boston, MA: Harvard Business School Press.

Eisenhardt, K. M. (1989), 'Building theories from case study research', *Academy of Management Review, 14* (4), 532....50.

Fahy, J. (2000), 'The resource-based view of the firm: some stumbling-blocks on the road to understanding sustainable competitive advantage', *Journal of European Industrial Training, 24* (2/3/4), 94–104.

Fischer, J. and J. Wirtgen (2000), *Post Merger Integration Management,* Berlin: Berlin Verlag.

Gerds, J. (2000), *Post Merger Integration: eine empirische Untersuchung zum Integrationsmanagement*, Wiesbaden: Gabler.

Godfrey, P.C. and H.B. Gregersen (1999), 'Where do resources come from? A model of resource generation', *The Journal of High Technology Management Research, 10* (1), 37–60.

Goold, M. and A. Campbell (1998), 'Desperately seeking synergy', *Harvard Business Review, 76* (5), 131....43.

Grant, R.M. (1998), *Contemporary Strategy Analysis*, Malden, MA: Blackwell.

Habeck, M.M., F. Kröger and M.R. Träm (2000), *After the Merger,* London: Pearson Education (*Financial Times*–Prentice Hall).

Haleblian, J. and S. Finkelstein (1999), 'The influence of organizational acquisition experience on acquisition performance: a behavioral learning perspective', *Administrative Science Quarterly, 44* (1), 29–56.

Haspeslagh, P.C. and D.B. Jemison (1991), *Managing Acquisitions: Creating Value Through Corporate Renewal*, New York: Free Press.

Heifetz, R.A. and D.L. Laurie (1997), 'The work of leadership', *Harvard Business Review, 75* (1), 124–34.

Helfat, C.E. (2000), 'Guest editor's introduction to the special issue: the evolution of firm capabilities', *Strategic Management Journal, 21* (10–11), 955–60.

Helfat, C.E. and M.A. Peteraf (2003), 'The dynamic resource-based view', *Strategic Management Journal, 24* (10), 997–1010.

Herzberg, F. (1968). 'One more time: how do you motivate employees?', *Harvard Business Review, 46* (1).

Hofstede, G. (1985), 'The interaction between national and organizational value systems', *Journal of Management Studies, 22* (4), 347–57.

Hofstede, G. (1994), 'The business of international business is culture', *International Business Review, 3* (1), 1–15.

Hofstede, G. (1997), *Cultures and Organizations: Software of the Mind,* New York: McGraw-Hill.

Hofstede, G. and J.A. Neuijen (1990), 'Measuring organizational cultures: a qualitative and quantitative study across twenty cases', *Administrative Science Quarterly, 35* (2), 286–316.

Hoopes, D.G., T.L. Madsen and G. Walker (2003), 'Guest editors' introduction to the special issue: why is there a resource-based view? Toward a theory of competitive heterogeneity', *Strategic Management Journal, 24* (10), 889–902.

Jensen, M. and W. Meckling (1976), 'Theory of the firm: managerial behavior, agency costs and ownership structure', *Journal of Financial Economics, 3* (4), 305–60.

Kogut, B. and U. Zander (1996), 'What firms do? Coordination, identity, and learning', *Organization Science, 7* (5), 502–18.

Kotter, J.P. (1996), *Leading Change*, Boston, MA: Harvard Business School Press.

Kuemmerle, W. (1997), 'Building effective R&D capabilities abroad', *Harvard Business Review, 75* (2), 61–71.

Lajoux, A.R. (1998), *The Art of M&A Integration*, New York: McGraw-Hill.

Leonard-Barton, D. (1992), 'Core capabilities and core rigidities: a paradox in managing new product development', *Strategic Management Journal, 13* (5), 111–26.

Lepak, D.P. and S.A. Snell (1999), 'The human resource architecture: toward a theory of human capital allocation and development', *Academy of Management Review, 24* (1), 31....48.

Ma, H. (2000), 'Competitive advantage and firm performance', *Competitiveness Review, 10* (2), 16–33.

Makadok, R. (2001), 'Toward a synthesis of the resource-based view and a dynamic-capabilities view of rent creation', *Strategic Management Journal, 22* (5), 387–401.

Marks, M.L. and P.H. Mirvis (1998), *Joining Forces: Making One Plus One Equal Three in Mergers, Acquisitions, and Alliances*, San Francisco: Jossey-Bass Inc.

Martens, R., I. Bogaert and A. Van Cauwenbergh (1997), 'Preparing for the future as a situational puzzle: the fit of strategic assets', *International Studies of Management and Organization, 27* (2), 7–20.

Medcof, J.W. (2000), 'The resource-based view and transnational technology strategy'. *Journal of High Technology Management, 11* (1), 59–74.

Michalisin, M.D., R.D. Smith and D.M. Kline (1997), 'In search of strategic assets', *International Journal of Organizational Analysis, 5* (4), 360–88.

Mirvis, P.H. and M.L. Marks (1992), *Managing the Merger: Making it Work*, Paramus, NJ: Prentice Hall.

Oliver, C. (1997), 'Sustainable competitive advantage: combining institutional and resource-based views', *Strategic Management Journal, 18* (9), 697–713.

Peteraf, M.A. (1993), 'The cornerstones of competitive advantage: a resource-based view', *Strategic Management Journal, 14* (3), 179–91.

Pettigrew, A.M. (1990), 'Longitudinal field research on change, theory and practice', *Organization Science, 1* (3) 267–92.

Picot, G. (2000), *Handbuch Mergers & Acquisitions: Planung, Durchführung, Integration*, Stuttgart: Schäffer-Pöschel.

PricewaterhouseCoopers (2001), *The Accelerated Transition*, www.pwcglobal.com, January 15.

Pritchett, P., D. Robinson and R. Clarkson (1997), *After the Merger: the Authoritative Guide for Integration Success,* New York; McGraw-Hill.

Russo, J.E. and P.J.H. Schoemaker (1990), 'The overconfidence quiz', *Harvard Business Review, 68* (5), 236.

Schein, E.H. (1992), *Organizational Culture and Leadership,* San Francisco; Jossey-Bass.

Siemens (2000), *Annual Report 2000,* Munich: Publicis MCD Werbeagentur GmbH.

Siemens (2001), *History* www.siemens.de/de2/html/about/history/index.html, February 14.

Siemens Mobile (2004), 'Siemens Mobile company profile', Siemens Mobile Press, www.siemens-mobile.com/press, February 2.

Süddeutsche Zeitung (2001), 'Siemens erzielt hohen Zuwachs'; 26 January.

Teece, D.J., G. Pisano and A. Shuen (1997), 'Dynamic capabilities and strategic management', *Strategic Management Journal, 18* (7), 509–33.

Thommen, J.-P. (1996), '*Glaubwürdigkeit: die Grundlage unternehmerischen Denkens und Handelns*', Zurich: Versus.

Thommen, J.-P. (2003), '*Glaubwürdigkeit und Corporate Governance*', Zurich: Versus.

Vasicek, O.A. and J.A. McQuown (1972), 'The efficient market model', *Financial Analysts Journal, 28* (5), 71–5.

Wernerfelt, B. (1984), 'A resource-based view of the firm', *Strategic Management Journal, 5,* 171–80.

Wright, P.M, G.C. McMahan and A. McWilliams (1994), 'Human resources and sustained competitive advantage: a resource-based perspective', *International Journal of Human Resource Management, 5* (2), 301–26.

Yin, R.K. (1994), *Case Study Research,* Thousand Oaks: Sage.

13. The determinants of inter-partner learning in alliances: an empirical study in e-commerce

Miguel Rivera Santos, Pierre Dussauge and Will Mitchell

INTRODUCTION

One of the main motivations for companies to form inter-firm alliances is learning, that is, the integration of a resource, a routine, or, more generally, knowledge into a firm. To explain learning in alliances, most research has used firm-level concepts, among which we can cite the absorptive capacity of the firm (Cohen and Levinthal, 1990), its experience in dealing with alliances, its knowledge base, its intent to learn (Hamel, 1991), the alliance content and governance, and the relative scope of an alliance (Khanna et al., 1998). We argue that these concepts are partially redundant and a shift to the micro-level of analysis shows that they are based on overlapping components. In this chapter, we propose that these micro-level components of inter-partner learning in alliances determine two essential abilities: a learning ability and a protection ability, which in turn influence the actual transfer of resources between the partner firms.

LITERATURE REVIEW

Learning is one of the main motivations for a firm to enter an alliance: it provides a way to gain access to missing competencies, to combine resources in order to create new resources, or to concentrate scarce resources on an existing business (Hamel et al., 1989; Hamel, 1991). In order to gain access to resources and competencies, alliances are an alternative to acquisitions, which often involve acquiring unrelated assets (Hennart, 1988), and to a lengthy internal development. In the case of information asymmetry, a joint venture also limits the risks of adverse selection in the acquisition process (Kogut, 1991; Balakrishnan and Koza, 1993).

Two types of factor have been identified which influence the transfer of resources or knowledge between partners in alliance. The type of resource targeted is one of them: acquiring tacit, as opposed to explicit, resources (Nonaka, 1994; Baughn et al., 1997; Inkpen, 1998) or ambiguous resources (Simonin, 1999) is more difficult and requires more effort. The second type of factor identified in the literature is firm-level, partner-level or alliance-level characteristics, which explain why some firms learn more easily than others. They can be divided into eight major groups of characteristics: the firm's absorptive capacity (Cohen and Levinthal, 1990; Lane and Lubatkin, 1998), the firm's learning intent (Hamel et al., 1989; Hamel, 1991), its experience in alliances (Anand and Khanna, 2000), the governance structure of the alliance (Hennart, 1988), the scope of the alliance (Khanna et al., 1998; Dussauge et al., 2000), the type of partner in the alliance (Khanna et al., 1998; Lane and Lubatkin, 1998; Mowery et al., 1996; Baum et al., 2000), the firm's ability to interact with its partner (Lorenzoni and Lipparini, 1999), and the trust between partners (Kale et al., 2000).

In addition to learning benefits, though, alliances also present dangers to the learning firm. The idea that learning races can be dangerous to the loser (Hamel et al., 1989; Hamel, 1991) and that joint-venture (JV) instability can be explained by such races is present throughout the literature, although the argument is sometimes considered extreme (Hennart et al., 1999). The debate as to whether alliances are dangerous or beneficial still goes on (Mitchell and Singh, 1996), although recent research tends to argue that it is possible to protect and learn at the same time. Kale et al. (2000), for instance, argue that relational capital, in conjunction with an integrative approach to managing conflict, is a key factor in achieving both learning and protection.

Research on learning in alliances has therefore shown that learning is a major concern in most alliances, and that the characteristics of the resource combined with firm-level, alliance-level and partner-level characteristics, have an impact on the success or failure of learning. Building on these findings and shifting the analysis from the firm as a whole (a macro-level of analysis) to the resource transfer proper (a micro-level of analysis), this chapter explores which micro-level determinants and which factors have a direct impact on the transfer itself.

THE LEARNING AND PROTECTION ABILITIES AND THEIR COMPONENTS

In simple terms, to learn means to acquire new knowledge. In an organizational setting, learning means acquiring a piece of knowledge, a resource, or a routine. We therefore define and analyze learning as a resource transfer, and include what the firm wants to learn as well as what the firm wants to protect from its partner.

The factors identified by previous research all include, or assume, at least implicitly, the necessity to enhance learning and protection at the same time. The intent to learn (Hamel et al., 1989; Hamel, 1991), for instance, is implicitly mirrored by the intent to protect. The experience in dealing with alliances (Anand and Khanna, 2000) will logically create a capacity both to learn and to protect better. What's more, these factors tend to overlap. For example, alliance experience will influence the choice of the partner, of the governance structure, and of the scope of the alliance. The identity of the alliance partner will influence the relative absorptive capacity of the firm, trust, and the scope of the alliance. Similarly trust will influence, or be influenced by, the alliance governance structure, specifically by its control mechanisms.

There is therefore a need to disentangle protection from learning in those factors and understand how and why they overlap. We propose that the factors highlighted in prior research are actually facets of two core factors: the firm's ability to learn on the one hand, and its ability to protect on the other hand, which we call the learning and the protection abilities. We define the learning ability as the ability to utilize a given resource by combining it with a pre-existing set of resources in a value creating way (Karim and Mitchell, 2000). It includes the identification of a relevant resource or routine, in order to coordinate it with existing resources or to replicate it (March, 1991; Szulanski, 1996), the adaptation of a resource or a routine to a new environment (Nelson and Winter, 1982; Chandler, 1992), the joint use of complementary resources or routines (Prahalad and Hamel, 1990), and the actual transfer of a resource or routine (Nelson and Winter, 1982; Szulanski, 1996). We define the protection ability as the ability to prevent the replication of the company's resources and routines by potential competitors (Hamel et al., 1989) and prevent the appropriation of the value of one of the company's resources and routines by potential competitors. It must be pointed out that, in our framework, the analysis is made at the alliance level, since we are trying to explain a transfer between an alliance and a focal partner. The abilities we consider are therefore specific to a firm in a given alliance.

In order to understand the relationship between the learning and protection abilities of the firm, and the factors described in the literature, we need to change the level of analysis. Most research so far has concentrated on firm-level concepts: the alliance experience of the firm, the absorptive capacity of the firm, or the type of partner. We argue that it is necessary to go down to the level of the resource transfer itself to uncover the building blocks for the firm-level concepts, and thus resolve the problems raised by the overlap in firm-level factors. For instance, the concept of alliance experience can be broken down into two elements. On the one hand, we find the firm-level experience, which, as Anand and Khanna (2000) argue, creates capabilities which help the organization manage alliances better over time. On the other hand, going down to the micro-level, the alliance experience can also be found among the employees involved in the alliance. A firm can have a broad alliance experience and yet send people who never participated in an alliance before to work with their alliance partner. Applying the same reasoning to all the factors found in the literature, a series of building blocks, which are components of the firm-level factors, are identified. The relationship between the components and the factors is shown in Appendix 1. We argue that these components are the building blocks for the learning and protection abilities we defined earlier, and explain why firm-level factors tend to overlap and to include both learning and protection facets.

We have divided the components into two types to simplify their presentation. The first group includes those components that are firm-specific, which means that they are independent of any given alliance. The second group includes those components specific to a given alliance. A table summarizing the learning-protection (LP) hypotheses can be found in Appendix 2.

Firm-specific components

Firm-specific components are unique to a firm and independent of any particular partner, and can potentially be common to all the alliances of a given firm. We have identified three major firm-specific components: interface, experience, and intent.

Interface

The interface is the structure (or structures) inside the firm in charge of dealing with alliances. It is the point(s) of contact between a firm and its alliances, and constitutes the 'membrane' through which alliance knowledge enters the firm (Hamel, 1991). Two dimensions characterize this interface: its degree of centralization and its knowledge base.

Degree of centralization captures the degree to which the interface is centralized, or decentralized. At the decentralized extreme, there is one interface per alliance with no central authority over the alliances within the focal firm. By contrast, at the centralized extreme, there is a corporate interface that controls relationships between the firm and its alliances. The influence of centralization on the learning ability is ambiguous. On the one hand, centralization is expected to have a positive impact on the firm's learning ability. A centralized firm-alliance interface provides easier coordination of the alliance portfolio and facilitates the sharing of experience across alliances, which is crucial when firms use their alliances as learning tools (Koza and Lewin, 1998). Kale et al. (2002) show that firms that create a dedicated alliance function, that is, firms that centralize their firm-alliance interface, achieve higher alliance performance than firms that manage alliances independently. In parallel with their findings, we therefore expect that a centralized firm-alliance interface will enhance the firm's learning ability. On the other hand, decentralized interfaces allow more flexibility in the firm's relationships with its partners. A centralization of decisions reduces the diversity of people taking part in the decision process and leads to a greater path dependence, thereby hindering the search routines for new resources (Nelson and Winter, 1982; Cohen and Levinthal, 1990; March, 1991). Overall we expect centralization to have both a positive and a negative impact on the firm's learning ability, which leads to two hypotheses.

Hypothesis 1a: The higher the degree of interface centralization, the higher the learning ability.
Hypothesis 1b: The higher the degree of interface centralization, the lower the learning ability.

The centralization of the firm-alliance interface also impacts n the firm's protection ability. A centralized structure diminishes the risks of leakage from micro-bargaining (Hamel et al., 1989), facilitates control with the establishment of standardized procedures, and overall allows an accumulation of experience in protecting from partners (Cohen and Levinthal, 1990; Anand and Khanna, 2000). A centralized structure is thus expected to enhance protection.

Hypothesis 1c: The higher the degree of interface centralization, the higher the protection ability.

Interface knowledge base captures the knowledge base of the group of employees in contact with the firm's alliances, in terms of their diversity or homogeneity. The greater the knowledge base on which this search is based (Cohen and Levinthal, 1990; Baughn et al., 1997), the higher the ability to identify relevant resources is expected to be, especially when exploration processes are involved. The greater the diversity of people working at the firm's interface, the greater the knowledge base on which the search for new routines when dealing with alliances will be. The employees working at the firm's interface are in charge of identifying resources transferred back from the alliance as being relevant or not, and thus deciding whether a resource will be integrated into the firm's bundle of resources or not. Therefore the greater the diversity of the firm's interface, the higher the ability to identify relevant resources and, consequently, the higher the learning ability.

Hypothesis 2: The greater the diversity at the firm's interface level, the higher the learning ability.

Experience
This captures a firm's previous accumulated experience in learning and protecting through alliances. Scholars have long recognized the role of experience as a factor enhancing learning in alliances. Experience in dealing with alliances reduces the adaptation time needed to operate with a partner, enhances the search routines to identify new resources, and helps transfer the resources back to the firm in an easier and quicker way (Cohen and Levinthal, 1990; Anand and Khanna, 2000). Although not stated as clearly in the literature, the same reasoning applies to the relationship between experience and protection: dealing repeatedly with alliance partners helps to identify the sources of leakage and diminish them. Therefore experience will enhance the learning and protection abilities of a firm.

Hypothesis 3a: The greater a firm's alliance experience, the higher the learning ability.
Hypothesis 3b: The greater a firm's alliance experience, the higher the protection ability.

Intent
This is the deliberate intent to learn/protect developed inside the firm. Intending to learn has been shown to be a major aspect of actual learning (Hamel et al., 1989; Hamel, 1991), and the search for new resources and routines itself involves intent in the form of search routines (Nelson and Winter, 1982; March, 1991). This intent to learn can be achieved in two major ways. First, the firm can have a focus on learning developed in its dominant logic system (Prahalad and Bettis, 1986; Bettis and Prahalad, 1995), or it can create the alliance with the intent to learn, making it co-evolve with their exploration or exploitation strategy (Koza and Lewin, 1998). Second, the firm can incite employees to focus on learning. This can be done either by specific training (which can be formalized with training sessions, or informal, as would be verbally explaining the importance of learning from partners) or by specific incentives aligned with the firm's

learning needs (Williamson, 1994). Although not stated as clearly in the literature, the same reasoning can be applied for protection.

Hypothesis 4a: The more training and/or incentives to learn from alliances a firm gives its employees, the higher the learning ability.

Hypothesis 4b: The more training and/or incentives to protect resources from alliances a firm gives its employees, the higher the protection ability.

Hypothesis 5a: The more focused on learning a firm is, the higher the learning ability.

Hypothesis 5b: The more focused on protecting a firm is, the higher the protection ability.

Alliance-specific components

Alliance-specific components are those components which are specific to each alliance. They can be the result of a negotiation between the firm and its partner or the result of the partner's characteristics. We have identified three groups of alliance-specific components: alliance characteristics, personnel characteristics, and governance structure.

Alliance characteristics

These are the characteristics of the alliance which might affect learning. Two main dimensions can be found: the similarity between the partners, and the potential opportunism of the partner.

Partner similarity is the similarity between the partner and the firm. Overlaps in knowledge bases have been shown to facilitate learning between partners (Cohen and Levinthal, 1990; Mowery et al., 1996): the closer the knowledge a firm wants to acquire from its partner is to its own knowledge base, the easier it will be for the firm to identify and understand new relevant pieces of knowledge. Lane and Lubatkin (1998) have shown that, in addition to similar knowledge bases, similar organizational structures and dominant logics facilitate learning. More generally, the more similar the partners are, the easier the learning processes will be. Partners that work in the same industry and have similar activities will be able to identify and understand valuable knowledge in each other, because their experience in the industry will make the search for new knowledge less extensive (Nelson and Winter, 1982). Partners with a similar size or coming from the same country will be able to overcome in an easier way the differences in management styles or cultures, which, being Type II differences (Parkhe, 1991), can endanger the very survival of the alliance. Finally, partners that have been involved in alliances together for some time develop collaborative experience, which can include knowledge-sharing routines, and trust in the relationship (Dyer and

Singh, 1998), thus facilitating future learning. Following a symmetric reasoning, learning is expected to be easier for the partner as well, thus decreasing the protection ability of the focal firm.

> *Hypothesis 6a: The higher the degree of similarity between partners, the higher the learning ability.*
> *Hypothesis 6b: The higher the degree of similarity between partners, the lower the protection ability.*

Potential opportunism of the partner captures the probability of the partner in an alliance having opportunistic behaviors. The potential opportunistic behaviors of its partners are a major concern and a source of danger for a firm involved in alliances (Hamel et al., 1989). Williamson (1994) argues that assuming zero-opportunism impoverishes the analysis of a company's behavior, but that assuming it does not mean celebrating it and, as noted earlier, one of the assumptions behind this framework is the existence of opportunism. We therefore expect the potential opportunism of the partner to impact on both the learning and the protection abilities of a company negatively.

> *Hypothesis 7a: The higher the potential opportunism of the partners, the lower the learning ability.*
> *Hypothesis 7b: The higher the potential opportunism of the partners, the lower the protection ability.*

Personnel characteristics
These are the characteristics of the firm's employees working in the alliance. Three major dimensions can be identified: employees' alliance experience, slack, and location.

Employees' alliance experience is the number of alliances in which the personnel assigned to the alliance have been involved, prior to the focal alliance. The role of experience as a factor enhancing learning through alliances has been discussed at the firm level in a previous section: experience reduces adaptation times, enhances search routines, and facilitates transfers (Cohen and Levinthal, 1990; Anand and Khanna, 2000). However the experience of a firm in dealing with alliances is not the same thing as the alliance experience of individuals assigned to a specific alliance: a firm can be involved in many alliances, but might still assign to a given alliance individuals who have no alliance experience and who will have to adapt to the new environment and develop specific search routines. The reasoning used at the firm level can be brought down to the individual level to argue that the more alliance experience individuals working in a given alliance have, the easier it will be for them to identify and understand resources in alliances and to protect valuable resources from the partner.

Hypothesis 8a: The greater the experience of employees assigned to the alliance, the higher the learning ability.
Hhypothesis 8b: The greater the experience of employees affected to the alliance, the higher the protection ability.

Slack is the amount of time that employees working in the alliance can potentially spare, in the course of day-to-day work, in order to learn from the partner. Hannan and Freeman (1977, 1984) have argued that organizations can be split into specialists and generalists: specialists are organizations which have little excess capacity, because they use their resources efficiently, and generalists are organizations with greater excess capacity, which use their resources less efficiently, as shown by the mere fact that they have excess capacity, but are also better prepared for unexpected changes in the environment. A similar reasoning applies at the team level: the more excess capacity a team has, the more easily the team is expected to identify changes in the environment and react to them. We therefore expect a positive relationship between slack and both the learning and protection abilities.

Hypothesis 9: Greater slack in the number of employees assigned to the alliance will have a positive influence on learning ability.

Location is the physical location of the personnel of the firm working in the alliance before being transferred back to the firm. Although a strategic resource cannot be possessed by a given individual, since it would then be acquirable by hiring personnel and would thus not be a resource on which competitive advantage can be based (Wernerfelt, 1984; Amit and Shoemaker, 1993), resources are embodied in individuals and resource transfers require sharing knowledge between individuals. Depending on the type of resource or routine involved, the need for interaction between individuals varies: if the knowledge is explicit, it can be transferred in the form of a blueprint and the individuals involved do not have to interact, but the more tacit the knowledge becomes, the more day-to-day interactions between individuals are necessary in order to transfer it (Nonaka, 1994; Inkpen, 1998). The rotation of employees between the alliance and the learning firm is thus required to ensure that resources and routines acquired in the alliance are transferred back to the learning firm. The higher the rotation rate is, the more learning is expected to take place. However, if rotation is necessitated by the need for alliance employees to interact with employees inside the firm, rotation will also have a negative effect if the rate becomes too high. Indeed, in order for employees to acquire resources inside the alliance, day-to-day interactions over longer periods are also needed (Inkpen, 1998): if the time spent in contact with the partner is reduced by a high rotation rate, no learning can occur inside the alliance anymore, especially when resources are tacit. We therefore expect that the location of the employees inside the learning firm will diminish its learning ability, because it reduces the day-to-day interactions with the partner and makes acquiring tacit resources more difficult, but will also increase it, because it eases the transfer of the resource from the alliance to the learning firm. The employees' location will also have an impact on protection: a day-to-day interaction with the partner increases the probability of micro-leakage (Hamel et al., 1989; Baughn et al., 1997), and having the employees located outside the firm reduces the firm's ability to control them (Geringer and Herbert, 1989 ; Kumar and Seth, 2000). Keeping the employees inside the company should therefore increase the protection ability of the firm.

> *Hypothesis 10a: The location of the employees working in the alliance inside the company will reduce the learning ability.*
> *Hypothesis 10b: The location of the employees working in the alliance inside the company will increase the learning ability.*
> *Hypothesis 10c: The location of the employees working in the alliance inside the company will increase the protection ability.*

Structure
This is the governance structure of the alliance. It has been widely tested in the literature, which suggests three dimensions: independent structure, financial and non-financial hostages, and type of contract. In our model, we argue that those components actually impact on the abilities to coordinate and protect, instead of directly impacting on the transfer itself.

Independent structure captures whether or not the alliance has an independent existence. Note that a joint–venture structure does not necessarily imply an independent structure. One of the major hurdles to cooperation is the lack of trust due to potential opportunism (Hamel et al., 1989). Opportunism arises from the misalignment of incentives between employees coming from different partners: Williamson (1994) argues that, as opposed to a market, a firm has the ability to align incentives, and thus drastically reduce opportunism. By creating a firm-like structure, alliances with an independent structure may be able to align the employee incentives better than alliances without independent structures. Moreover locating alliance employees in a single location increases the opportunities of repeated interactions and thus facilitates learning and creating (Nonaka, 1994; Inkpen, 1998). However, if learning inside the alliance can be enhanced by an independent structure, learning between the alliance and the learning firm is expected to be hindered for the same reasons: creating a firm-like structure for the alliance reduces the interaction opportunities between the alliance and the learning firm. Because of these two opposite influences, we formulate two contradictory hypotheses.

Hypothesis 11a: The existence of an independent structure increases the learning ability.

Hypothesis 11b: The existence of an independent structure decreases the learning ability.

Financial and non-financial hostages are the partners' investments in the alliance or in each other. The transaction-cost theory stream of research on alliances has emphasized the problem of appropriability hazards due to potential opportunism (Hennart, 1988; Kogut, 1988; Oxley, 1997). One of the solutions to deal with opportunism in alliances is to have financial hostages (Kogut, 1988): by possessing a share of its partner or by ensuring that the partner has a financial stake in the alliance, a firm can increase the cost of 'betrayal' for the partner. Thus the greater the financial hostages a firm holds in its partner, the costlier it will be for the partner to break the collaborative deal, which increases the protection ability of a firm. The same reasoning can be applied to non-financial investments, such as a patent brought to the alliance.

Hypothesis 12: The greater the financial and non-financial hostages, the higher the protection ability.

Contract captures the characteristics of the alliance contract and their impact on the learning and protection abilities of the focal company. An important section of research literature focuses on the way contracts can protect or fail to protect companies in alliances. Williamson (1994), with others, argues that a contract cannot provide complete protection, because contracts are by definition incomplete; that is, they cannot take into account all the possible evolutions of a given agreement over time. Although contracts cannot be complete, they do provide some protection through 'protection clauses' to the partners in alliances–as the wide use of non-disclosure agreements before starting alliance negotiations seems to show– and should therefore be present in our model, as having an impact on the protection ability of a company. Following a symmetric reasoning, the existence of 'learning clauses' in the contract is also expected to enhance learning between the partners.

Hypothesis 13a: The more learning clauses in the contract, the higher the learning ability.
Hypothesis 13b: The more protection clauses in the contract, the higher the protection ability.

THE RESOURCE TRANSFER PROPOSITIONS

In the previous section, we discussed the learning and protection abilities of the firm in an alliance, and also their components. In this section we introduce our set of resource transfer propositions, which are the propositions linking the learning and protection abilities of the firm and the actual resource transfer. The basic model is depicted in Figure 13.1 (dotted arrow shows negative relationship).

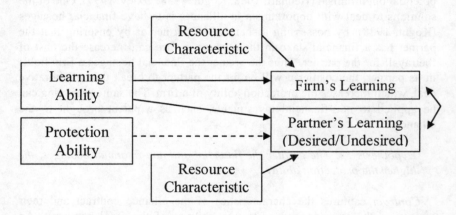

Figure 13.1 The basic model

The core proposition of this chapter states that success in learning from a partner (modeled as a resource transfer) and preventing undesired partner learning (modeled as an undesired resource transfer to the partner) is influenced by a firm's learning and protection abilities, as well as by the characteristics of the resources at stake. The successes in learning and in preventing undesired partner learning are linked together and not necessarily antagonistic (Kale et al., 2000). Moreover the learning/leakage dichotomy, which is implicit in many studies of learning in alliances, assumes that there cannot be desired learning by the partner. However a firm might want its partner to learn the resources needed to make the alliance work. In this study we therefore shift the dichotomy to learning/partner's desired learning and partner's undesired learning, and we argue that, if the partner's learning is desired, the firm's learning ability will have a positive impact on it. Each of the arrows in the previous model corresponds to a core proposition in our model.

The learning ability of a firm encompasses the four dimensions described above, and all of them influence learning. The first dimension is identification, which is the first step before any adaptation, joint use of resources or transfer. Identification of relevant resources is as crucial internally (March, 1991; Szulanski, 1996) as it is externally (March, 1991; Cohen and Levinthal, 1990). The greater the ability of a firm to identify relevant resources in an alliance, the more successful the actual transfer will be. The second dimension found in learning is resource adaptation. Resources being a bundle of routines, the ability to adapt them for new uses (Nelson and Winter, 1982) should increase the perceived value of an identified resource, and thus make the actual transfer of that resource likelier. The third dimension in learning is the complementary use of resources. Following a similar reasoning, the ability to use resources jointly (Penrose, 1959; Prahalad and Hamel, 1990) should increase the perceived value of a resource, and thus make the actual transfer of that resource likelier. The fourth dimension in learning is the ability to transfer a resource. The easier it is for a firm to transfer a resource, the likelier the actual transfer is expected to be. In addition, the ability to coordinate resources implies that the resource transfer can be somehow controlled, through the identification of specific routines (March, 1991), their adaptation (Nelson and Winter, 1982), and their complementary use (Penrose, 1959; Prahalad and Hamel, 1990). We can therefore expect that the better a firm can coordinate resources, the more able it will be to transfer resources voluntarily to its partner if it decides to do so.

Core hypothesis 1a: The greater the learning ability of a firm in an alliance, the more successful the resource transfer to the firm.
Core hypothesis 1b: The greater the learning ability of a firm in an alliance, the more successful the desired resource transfer to the partner.

The protection of valuable assets has been argued to be a major incentive to internalize transactions (Williamson, 1994), and firms have been considered mechanisms of protection of knowledge (Porter Liebeskind, 1996). In an alliance, the potential leakage of valuable information is a major danger, because of the ability that this governance structure gives to potential competitors to access the firm's resources (Hamel et al., 1989). In the same way that learning from external sources requires a specific ability that is unique to each firm (Cohen and Levinthal, 1990), protecting resources from a partner requires a specific firm-specific ability as well.

Core hypothesis 2: The greater the protection ability of a firm in an alliance, the less the undesired resource transfer to the partner.

A firm's learning and protection abilities depend on a series of components, which we analyzed in detail in the previous section. Some components are common to both abilities, and others only influence one of them. Most of those components are explicit strategic choices, such as choosing the characteristics of the employees who participate in the alliance or choosing the frequency with which these employees are transferred back to the parent company, and will jointly affect learning and protecting. Because of the possibility of a company to set up those factors in an alliance, and to combine them efficiently, a firm can consider the potential for desired learning and the danger of undesired partner learning jointly.

Core hypothesis 3a: The greater the resource transfer to the firm, the less the undesired resource transfer to the partner.
Core hypothesis 3b: The greater the resource transfer to the firm, the greater the desired resource transfer to the partner.

A resource transfer will be influenced by the learning and protection abilities of a firm but, as the literature discusses in some detail, will also depend on the characteristics of the resources at stake. The literature suggests four main characteristics influencing the ease or difficulty of resource transfer: their tacitness, their similarity with existing resources, the fact they might be patented or filed, and the partner's agreement on their transfer.

Core hypothesis 4a: The easier it is to transfer a resource, the more successful the learning by the firm.
Core hypothesis 4b: The easier it is to transfer a resource, the more successful the learning by the partner.

The model we introduce in this study is therefore a two-stage model: micro-level components influence the firm's learning and protection abilities in the alliance, and these abilities, in turn, determine the learning and protection abilities of the firm in the alliance.

METHODOLOGY

The empirical setting chosen to test our model is e-commerce alliances, defined as alliances created between companies in order to conduct activities on the internet. After several rounds of interviews with managers of e-commerce companies and industry experts, a web-based questionnaire was developed, and 124 usable responses were collected. Our sample's descriptive statistics can be found in Appendix 3.

The measures for the variables used in this study were all based on one or more items of the questionnaire. Interface centralization, diversity at the interface, experience in learning and protecting, partner potential opportunism, the employees' alliance experience, and slack are measured by seven-point Likert questions. The general firm-specific alliance experience is also measured by the number of alliances the firm was involved in prior to the current one (in numbers). The intent to learn and protect is measured by two series of three questions: the incentives of training given to employees participating in the alliance (seven-point Likert), the perception of the importance of the learning/protective culture of the firm (7-point Likert), and whether the alliance had been created in order to learn (7-point Likert). The similarity between partners is measured by two variables: a constructed variable and a questionnaire variable. For the constructed variable, the respondent was asked to describe its activity and the activity of the partner. On the basis of these descriptions, each firm and each partner was placed in a general activity category. A dichotomous variable was then created, with a value of 1 when the general category was the same for both the firm and the partner, and of 0 when not. This measure is completed by a seven-point Likert question asking the respondent to assess the similarity of its employees' and its partners' employees' backgrounds. Rotation is measured by three questions: two dichotomous questions asking whether the management and the engineers work in the alliance and the firm at the same time, and one dichotomous question asking whether the employees are still located in the firm's facilities. The independent structure and the existence of financial hostages are measured by dichotomous questions. The existence of non-financial hostages is measured by a constructed variable: respondents were asked to check any non-equity investment they made to the alliance. The variable is constructed as the number of non-equity investments made. Finally, the type of contract is measured by three seven-point Likert questions asking whether the firm and the partner are efficiently protected by the contract, and whether the contract enhances resource transfers.

To test for the existence of the learning and protection abilities and for their relationship with the micro-level components we have identified, we have conducted a factor analysis. If the two abilities exist, we should find two major factors underlying the measured components, and the loadings of the components on these two factors should be consistent with our propositions.

The resource transfer propositions between the factors extracted with the EFA and the actual learning are tested with linear regression techniques. The dependent variables, the firm's learning and the partner's learning, are measured with a questionnaire item each, in the form of a seven-point Likert question. The learning and protection abilities are the scores of the extracted factors. Five characteristics of the transferred resource are measured through seven-point Likert questions: the agreement on the transfer, the difficulty to copy the resource, the fact that it is patented or filed, its closeness to resources already possessed, and its complementarity to resources already possessed. Six control variables are also introduced in the model: the activity of the partners (1 if both partners are software or service providers, 0 if not), the year in which the alliance was created (1 if created in 2000 or after, 0 if before), whether the alliance is in the firm's core business (seven-point Likert question), whether the industry is competitive (seven-point Likert question), and the geographical location of the alliance activities (two dummy variables to capture whether the alliance is active in the US or in Europe).

RESULTS

The results of the factor analysis are provided in Appendices 4 and 5. Several methods exist to choose which factors to keep in a factor analysis (Kim and Mueller, 1978). In this study, we use Cattell's scree-test (1965). This method plots the different factors' eigenvalues in decreasing order, and instructs to stop factoring at the point where the eigenvalues begin to level off. The scree plot (Appendix 4) shows a very clear drop after the third factor. We therefore keep the first three factors for the rest of the analysis. The factor loadings of each variable on the three factors after an orthogonal rotation are shown in Appendix 5. It should be noted here that using principal factor analysis instead of principal component analysis as the method to extract factors, or using an oblique rotation instead of an orthogonal rotation after the factors are extracted, does not drastically change the factor loading pattern. In the rest of this analysis we follow Kim and Mueller (1978) and consider factor loadings of less than .3 as not substantial.

The analysis of the factor loadings on each of the three factors shows that, although the factor analysis finds three factors instead of the two hypothesized, the interpretation of the factors is straightforward. Starting with the interpretation of factor 2, we find that the firm wanted to have access to its partner's resources from the very beginning (obj3=.4, obj5=.5, objlat=0), creates incentives to learn for its employees (incacq=.5), and gives them time to do so (slack=.5); it has experience in dealing with alliances (nball=.5), especially in the acquisition of resources through alliances (acqpast=.4), and so do its employees (empexp=.5); it tends to centralize at the business level (centrb=.4, centr=.1) and people working at the interface have a broad knowledge base (backg=.4); its partner is a potential competitor (pcomp=.4) and is relatively similar (smpart=.3); however it feels it does not need protection by contract (fcntprt=-.3, pcntprt=-.3), by financial or non-financial hostages (equity=.1, xneqf=.2), or by any intent to protect (incprt=.2, cultp=.2). This factor therefore clearly represents a firm's ability to learn without protection. Factor # 3 seems to be the exact opposite: the firm did not intend to use the alliance to learn (obj3=-.3, obj4=-.4, objlat=.4, incacq=-.1), considers that it could not learn from alliances in the past (acqpast=-.4) and does not give time to its employees to learn (slack=-.3), but is clearly preoccupied by its protection (incprt=.3), and centralizes the management of its alliances at the corporate level (centr=.3), although the partner is surprisingly not really perceived as a potential competitor (pcomp=.2) while being similar (xsimac1=.4); the employees working in the alliance tend to stay within the company (xmgtro2=.7, xengro2=.6, locall=.5, indep=-.3). This factor clearly represents a firm's ability to protect, without any intent to learn. After analysing factors -2 and -3, the meaning of factor #1 becomes clear: the firms creates incentives to both learn and protect for its employees (incacq=.3, incprt=.6), and has a culture focused on both learning and protection (cultl=.3, cultp=.5); it centralizes the management of its alliances (centr=.4), but has a broad knowledge base at the interface (backg=.4); it has experience in alliances, especially in protecting valuable resources (prtpast=.5); and it relies on contracts for enhancing both protection and learning (fcntprt=.8, pcntprt=.7, cnttrs=.4). This factor clearly represents the combination of learning and protecting in an alliance. Thus, while we find support for the hypothesized existence of the learning and protection abilities, we also observe the existence of a third distinct ability: the ability to coordinate and protect simultaneously.

In Appendix 2 we present a summary of the learning-protection hypotheses. Following the .3 cut-off rule-of-thumb for factor loadings (Kim and Mueller, 1978), we can see that most hypotheses have at least partial support. H1 hypothesized that interface centralization could have either a positive (H1a) or a negative (H1b) impact on learning, and a positive impact (H1c) on protection. We find that corporate-level centralization enhances the protection ability as well as the ability to both learn and protect, while business unit-level centralization enhances the learning ability. H2 hypothesized that interface diversity would enhance learning. It is supported. H3 hypothesized that the firm's experience would enhance both learning and protection. It is supported. H4 hypothesized that the learning and the protecting intents would enhance both learning and protection. It is supported. H6 hypothesized that the similarity between partners would enhance learning and hinder protection. It is only partially supported: similarity does not seem to hinder protection, quite the opposite. This might be due to the fact that the more similar the partner is, the easier it is for the firm to anticipate and adjust for its moves. H7 hypothesized that the partner's potential opportunism would hinder both learning and protection. This hypothesis is not supported. Surprisingly, having a potential competitor for a partner seems to enhance learning. This might be related to the fact that measuring the degree to which a partner is also a competitor captures the similarity between the two firms. H8 hypothesized that employee experience would enhance both learning and protection. It is partially supported: it seems to enhance learning, but not protection. H9 hypothesized that slack would enhance learning. It is supported: slack seems to enhance learning. This might be due to the phrasing of the question, which does not allow for a response stating that too much slack was given to employees in the alliance. H10 hypothesized that the location of employees inside the focal firm could either enhance or decrease its learning ability, and that it would enhance its protection ability. We find that the location of employees does not have a significant effect on the learning ability, which suggests that the negative impact on identification and the positive impact on internalization cancel each other. As hypothesized, the location of employees inside the focal firms enhances its protection ability. H11 hypothesized that an independent structure could either enhance or hinder learning. We find that the existence of an independent structure does not have a significant effect on the learning ability, which suggests that the postive impact on learning inside the alliance and the negative impact on learning between the alliance and the focal firm cancel each other. H12 hypothesized that financial and non-financial hostages would enhance protection. It is not supported. H13 hypothesized that contractual clauses could enhance both the learning and protection abilities. Our results show that contractual clauses only impact on the ability to coordinate and protect simultaneously. It is interesting to note that protective contractual clauses seem to reduce the firm's learning ability.

We tested our resource-transfer hypotheses with linear regression techniques. Two regressions were conducted: one with the firm's learning as the dependent variable, and one with the partner's learning as the dependent variable. The results of the regressions are provided in Appendix 6. Both regression models are significant. Tolerance tests on each independent variable showed no multicollinearity problems. We find that the ability to learn and protect simultaneously as well as the learning ability, extracted from the micro-level components, have a positive and significant effect on the focal firm's learning, as hypothesized in our core hypothesis 1a. Moreover, we find that the protection ability, which is the ability to protect without learning, reduces the focal firm's learning significantly. This is consistent with the idea that learning will occur only if a company develops an ability to learn (Hamel et al., 1989; Cohen and Levinthal, 1990). Among the five characteristics of the transferred resource, two have significant parameters: the perceived difficulty to acquire a resource, because it is embedded or tacit, reduces a firm's learning, while the complementarity of the targeted resource with resources already possessed by the learning firm increases its learning, which is consistent with the idea drawn from the resource-based view literature that resources can be more or less easy to learn, and with our core hypothesis 4a. We do not find support for the hypothesized impact of the protection ability on the partner's ability to learn, as stated in our core hypothesis 2, although the sign is in the hypothesized direction. This result might be due to the fact that the measure used for the partner's learning is a perception by the focal firm, which is less reliable. However we find support for our core hypothesis 1b, which states that the learning ability of a firm can increase its partner's learning, although we do not find support for our distinction between desired and undesired learning. Finally, we find partial support for our core hypotheses 3a and 3b, stating that a firm can increase its learning and its protection at the same time: the EFA does extract a factor representing the combination of the learning and protection abilities of the firm, but this factor only has a positive impact on the focal firm's learning.

DISCUSSION AND CONCLUSION

Building on previous research, we propose in this chapter that a firm's capacity to learn in alliances without losing valuable knowledge to its partners is driven by two essential abilities, a learning ability and a protection ability. We propose that these two abilities rely on a set of micro-level components derived from the literature, which can be either firm-specific or alliance-specific. Firm-specific micro-components, which are those components independent of any specific alliance or partner, include the characteristics of the firm-alliance interface, the firm's alliance experience, and the firm's intent to learn and protect in its alliances. Alliance-specific micro-components include the characteristics of the alliance partner, the characteristics of the employees assigned to the alliance, and the alliance governance structure.

The empirical test of our model on a sample of e-commerce alliances supports our theoretical model. We find support for the existence of two distinct abilities, an ability to learn and an ability to protect in alliances. We show that both the firm's ability to learn from its alliances and its ability to protect in its alliances rely on a blend of firm-specific and alliance-specific micro-components. In addition to these two hypothesized abilities, we empirically show the existence of a third ability, the firm's ability to simultaneously learn and protect in alliances. We find support for most of the hypotheses regarding the impact of specific micro-level components on one or both abilities, and, while we do not find a significant impact of the firm's protection ability on its partner's learning, we show that the firm's learning ability impacts on both the firm's and its partner's learning patterns.

We believe this research to have both theoretical and managerial implications. The major theoretical contribution we hope to have made is the integration of the rather diverse set of factors identified in prior studies into an overarching theory of learning and protection in alliances. While building on previous research, the learning and protection ability model we propose is more parsimonious, more detailed, and more comprehensive than previous models. Eight major determinants of learning and protection in alliances have been identified in the literature: the firm's absorptive capacity (Cohen and Levinthal, 1990; Lane and Lubatkin, 1998), the firm's learning intent (Hamel et al., 1989; Hamel, 1991), its experience in alliances (Anand and Khanna, 2000), the governance structure of the alliance (Hennart, 1988), the scope of the alliance (Khanna et al., 1998, Dussauge et al., 2000), the type of partner in the alliance (Khanna et al., 1998; Lane and Lubatkin, 1998; Mowery et al., 1996; Baum et al., 2000), the firm's ability to interact with its partner (Lorenzoni and Lipparini, 1999), and the trust between partners (Kale et al., 2000). These factors, as we discussed earlier in this chapter, come from different theoretical streams and tend to overlap conceptually. By identifying, within each of these factors, their learning and protection micro-components, and by exploring how they converge to create two abilities, as opposed to eight factors, the model we propose is significantly more parsimonious than what is found in the literature. Our approach is also more detailed than prior studies, as we incorporate within the same model two levels of analysis, a micro-level with the learning and protection micro-components, and a macro-level with the learning and protection abilities. Finally, our model is more comprehensive, as we take into consideration both the firm's learning goals and its protection needs in alliances. Moreover the empirical identification of a third ability, the firm's ability to simultaneously learn and protect in its alliances, suggests that learning and protection in alliances are not contradictory goals and that both can be simultaneously achieved by firms. This result is consistent with several recent studies (Kale et al., 2000; Das and Teng, 2001), and provides a better understanding of the interactions between learning opportunities and the danger of leakage in alliances.

From a managerial perspective, these results show that it is possible for firms to put into place mechanisms that can influence learning and protection outcomes in their alliances. We stress that, among the micro-components, which are the building blocks of the firm's learning and protection abilities in alliances, many are choices that can be adjusted more or less instantaneously, suggesting that top management can significantly impact on a firm's learning in alliances.

Building on this study's results, several lines of future research can be identified: while this chapter proposes an overarching theory of learning and protection in alliances, several of its components need to be further explored. For instance, the relationship between firm-specific and alliance-specific micro-components requires more attention. Koza and Lewin (1998) suggest that the alliance portfolios of firms co-evolve with their learning needs. Similarly, Lorenzoni and Lipparini (1999) argue that firms can deliberately construct a network of alliances for learning purposes. If such a strategy of learning through alliances is indeed possible, firms must be able set up mechanisms independent of their partners to improve their learning and protection abilities in alliances. Exploring which firm-specific micro-components identified in our model can support this strategy seems to be a necessary step towards understanding how firms can use their alliances to learn in a systematic way. In addition, the study of the interactions between different micro-components would help firms identify which alliance-specific components, which are the result of interpartner negotiations, can potentially be replaced by firm-specific micro-components, over which the focal firm has full control, in order to fulfill their learning and protection needs. Finally, an exploration of regional differences in the use of learning and protection micro-components would improve our understanding of how firms increase their alliance learning and protection abilities in different environments.

APPENDIX 1

Figure 13.A.1   From firm-level factors to micro-level components

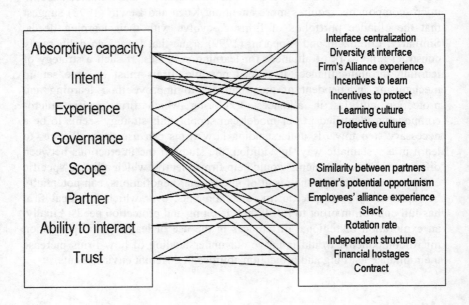

APPENDIX 2

Table 13.A.1   Learning-protection hypotheses

Hypotheses	Components	Learning	Protection
I. Firm-specific Components			
A. Interface			
1	Interface centralization	+/-	+
2	Diversity at interface	+	
B. Experience			
3	Alliance experience	+	+
C. Intent			
4a	Training or incentives to learn	+	
4b	Training or incentives to protect		+
5a	Learning culture	+	
5b	Protective culture		+
II. Alliance-specific Components			
A. Alliance characteristics			
6	Similarity between partners	+	-
7	Partner's potential opportunism	-	-
B. Personnel characteristics			
8	Employees' alliance experience	+	+
9	Slack	+	
10	Employee location	+/-	+
C. Governance structure			
11	Independent structure	+/-	+/-
12	Financial and non-financial hostages		+
13	Contract	+	+

APPENDIX 3

Table 13.A.2 Sample description

Characteristics of the Responses

Questionnaires Sent:	1211
Responses:	148
Usable Responses:	124
Response Rate:	12.22%
Language of Response:	
English	58.9%
French	41.1%
Respondents:	
Ceo	45.0%
VP for Business Development	15.8%
VP for Marketing	15.0%
VP for Alliances	14.2%
Manager	6.7%
Cto	1.7%
Communication/PR	1.7%

Characteristics of the firms

Size (number of employees):	
Mean	382
Min	1
Max	10000
Type of activity of Firm:	
Hardware	7.26%
Software	35.48%
Service	57.26%
Type of activity of Partner:	
Brick & Mortar	12.90%
Hardware	16.13%
Software	41.13%
Service	29.84%

Characteristics of the alliances

Date of Creation:	
Mean	1999
Median	2000
Min	1993
Max	2001
Location of Activity:	
Europe	78.23%
North America	39.52%
Asia	12.90%
Level of competition with Partner:	3.85/7
Learning:	
Both tried to learn	52.42%
Only Firm tried to learn	13.71%
Only Partner tried to learn	14.52%
None tried to learn	19.35%

APPENDIX 4

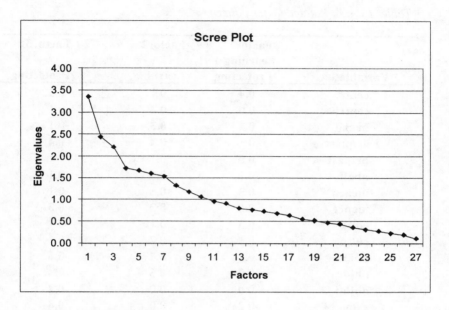

Figure 13.A.2   Scree plot

APPENDIX 5

Table 13.A.3   Rotated factor pattern

Variable	Factor1 Learning + Protecting	Factor2 Learning	Factor3 Protecting
centr	**0.4**	0.1	**0.3**
centrb	0.0	**0.4**	0.1
backg	**0.4**	**0.3**	-0.1
acqpast	0.1	**0.4**	**-0.4**
prtpast	**0.5**	0.1	-0.1
nball	-0.1	**0.5**	0.1
incacq	0.3	**0.5**	-0.1
incprt	**0.6**	0.2	**0.3**
cultl	0.3	0.1	-0.1
cultp	**0.5**	0.2	0.1
obj3	0.2	**0.4**	**-0.3**
obj4	0.0	**0.5**	**-0.4**
objlat	0.0	0.0	**-0.4**
xsimac1	-0.2	0.0	**0.4**
smpart	0.3	0.3	0.1
pcomp	0.0	**0.4**	0.2
empexp	0.1	**0.5**	-0.1
slack	0.2	**0.5**	**-0.3**
xmgtro2	0.1	0.1	**0.7**
xengro2	0.1	0.1	**0.6**
locall	-0.1	0.2	**0.5**
indep	0.2	0.0	**-0.3**
equity	0.0	0.1	**-0.3**
xneqf	0.0	0.2	0.1
fcntprt	**0.8**	**-0.3**	-0.1
pcntprt	**0.7**	**-0.3**	-0.1
cnttrs	**0.4**	0.0	-0.2

APPENDIX 6

Table 13.A.4 Regression results

Model 1

Dependent Variable: firm's learning

F: 2.48 — Pr. > F: 0.0044
R²: 0.2412 — Adj. R²: 0.1438

Parameter	Estimates	t	Pr > |t|
Intercept	1.665	0.730	0.467
Learn.-Prot. Ability	**0.408**	1.700	0.093
Learning Ability	**0.458**	1.760	0.081
Prot. Ability	**-0.854**	-3.210	0.002
Agreement	0.037	0.220	0.827
Difficulty to Copy	**-0.348**	-2.040	0.044
Patent	-0.017	-0.110	0.912
Closeness	0.229	1.130	0.260
Complementarity	**0.491**	2.080	0.040
Activity	**1.510**	2.570	0.012
Year	-0.210	-0.410	0.679
Core	0.001	0.010	0.992
Competitiveness	-0.291	-1.400	0.165
North America	-0.414	-0.650	0.514
Europe	-0.317	-0.410	0.679

Model 2

Dependent Variable: partner's learning

F: 1.96 — Pr. > F: 0.0272
R²: 0.2015 — Adj. R²: 0.0989

Parameter	Estimates	t	Pr > |t|
Intercept	-2.676	-1.320	0.189
Learn.-Prot. Ability	0.078	0.360	0.722
Learning. Ability	**0.608**	2.710	0.008
Prot. Ability	-0.099	-0.410	0.686
Agreement	0.116	0.790	0.433
Difficulty to Copy	0.206	1.350	0.178
Patent	-0.042	-0.350	0.729
Closeness	**0.348**	1.910	0.059
Complementarity	0.187	0.740	0.460
Activity	-0.461	-0.850	0.397
Year	0.639	1.420	0.158
Core	0.045	0.370	0.711
Competitiveness	0.015	0.080	0.937
North America	0.937	1.600	0.111
Europe	0.845	1.260	0.210

REFERENCES

Ahuja, G. (2000), 'The duality of collaboration: inducements and opportunities in the formation of interfirm linkages', *Strategic Management Journal*, 21, 317- 43.

Almeida, P. (1996), 'Knowledge sourcing by foreign multinationals: patent citation analysis in the U.S. semiconductor industry', *Strategic Management Journal*, 17 (Winter Special Issue), 155- 65.

Amit, R. and P. Schoemaker (1993), 'Strategic assets and organizational rent', *Strategic Management Journal*, 14, 33- 46.

Anand, B. and T. Khanna (2000), 'Do firms learn to create value? The case of alliances', *Strategic Management Journal*, 21, 295- 315.

Appleyard, M. (1996), 'How does knowledge flow? Interfirm patterns in the semiconductor industry', *Strategic Management Journal*, 17 (Winter Special Issue), 137- 54.

Baker, W. (1984), 'The social structure of a national securities market', *American Journal of Sociology*, 89, 775- 811.

Baker, W. (1990), 'Market networks and corporate behavior', *American Journal of Sociology*, 96, 589- 625.

Balakrishnan, S. and M. Koza (1993), 'Information asymmetry, adverse selection and joint-ventures: theory and evidence', *Journal of Economic Behavior and Organization*, 20, 99- 117.

Baughn, C., J. Stevens, J. Denekamp and R. Osborn (1997), 'Protecting intellectual capital in international alliances', *Journal of World Business*, 32 (2), 103- 17.

Bettis, R.A. and C.K. Prahalad (1995), 'The dominant logic: retrospective and extension', *Strategic Management Journal*, 16, 5- 14.

Burt, R. (1992), 'The social structure of competition', in Nohria and Eccles (eds), *Networks and Organizations: Structure, Form, and Action*, Boston, MA: Harvard Business School Press, pp. 57- 91.

Burt, R. (1997), 'The contingent value of social capital', *Administrative Science Quarterly*, 42, 339- 65.

Chandler, A. (1992), 'Organizational capabilities and the economic history of the industrial enterprise', *The Journal of Economic Perspectives*, 6 (3), 79- 100.

Cohen, W. and D. Levinthal (1990), 'Absorptive capacity: a new perspective on learning and innovation', *Administrative Science Quarterly*, 35, 128- 52.

Das, T.K. and B.S. Teng (2001), 'Trust, control, and risk in strategic alliances: an integrated framework', *Organization Science*, 22 (2), 251- 84.

Doz, Y. (1996), 'The evolution of cooperation in strategic alliances: initial conditions or learning processes?', *Strategic Management Journal*, 17, 55-83.

Dussauge, P., B. Garrette and W. Mitchell (2000), 'Learning from competing partners: outcomes and durations of scale and link alliances in Europe, North America, and Asia', *Strategic Management Journal*, 21, 99- 126.

Dyer, J. and H. Singh (1998), 'The relational view: cooperative strategy and sources of interorganizational advantage', *Academy of Management Review*, 23 (4), 660-79.

Gulati, R. (1998), 'Alliances and networks', *Strategic Management Journal*, 19, 293- 317.

Gulati, R., N. Nohria and A. Zaheer (2000), 'Strategic networks', *Strategic Management Journal*, 21, 203- 15.

Hamel, G. (1991), 'Competition for competence and interpartner learning within international strategic alliances', *Strategic Management Journal*, 12 (Special Issue), 83-103.

Hamel, G., Y. Doz and C.K. Prahalad (1989), 'Collaborate with your competitors - and win', *Harvard Business Review*, 67, 133- 39.

Hannan, M. and J. Freeman (1977), 'The population ecology of organizations', *American Journal of Sociology*, 82, 929- 64.

Hannan, M. and J. Freeman (1984), 'Structural inertia and organizational change', *American Sociological Review*, 49, 149- 64.

Hennart, J.F. (1988), 'A transaction cost theory of equity joint ventures', *Strategic Management Journal*, 9, 361-74.

Hennart, J.F., T. Roehl and D. Zietlow (1999), 'Trojan horse or workhorse? The evolution of US–Japanese joint ventures in the United States', *Strategic Management Journal*, 20, 15- 29.

Inkpen, A. and P. Beamish (1997), 'Knowledge, bargaining power and the instability of international joint ventures', *Academy of Management Review*, 22 (1), 177- 202.

Inkpen, A. (1998), 'Leaning, knowledge acquisition, and strategic alliances', *European Management Journal*, 16 (2), 223- 29.

Kale P., J. Dyer and H. Singh (2002), 'Alliance capability, stock market response, and long-term alliance success: the role of the alliance function', *Strategic Management Journal*, 23 (8), 747-67.

Kale, P., H. Singh and H. Perlmutter (2000), 'Learning and protection of proprietary assets in strategic alliances: building relational capital', *Strategic Management Journal*, 21, 217- 37.

Karim, S. and W. Mitchell (2000), 'Path-dependent and path-breaking change: reconfiguring business resources following acquisitions in the US medical sector, 1978–1995', *Strategic Management Journal*, 21, 1061- 81.

Khanna, T., R. Gulati and N. Nohria (1998), 'The dynamics of learning alliances: competition, cooperation, and relative scope', *Strategic Management Journal*, 19, 193-210.

Kogut, B. (1988), 'Joint ventures: theoretical and empirical perspectives', *Strategic Management Journal*, 9, 319-32.

Kogut, B. (1991), 'Joint ventures and the option to expand and acquire', *Strategic Management Journal*, 37, 19-33.

Kogut, B. (2000), 'The network as knowledge: generative rules and the emergence of structure', *Strategic Management Journal*, 21, 405-25.

Koza, M.P. and A.Y. Lewin (1998), 'The co-evolution of strategic alliances', *Organization Science*, 9 (3), 255-64.

Lane, P.J. and M. Lubatkin (1998), 'Joint venture formations and stock market reactions: an assessment in the information technology sector', *Academy of Management Journal*, 34, 869-92.

Lorenzoni, G. and A. Lipparini (1999), 'The leveraging of interfirm relationships as a distinctive organizational capability: a longitudinal study', *Strategic Management Journal*, 20 (4), 317-37.

March, J.G. (1991), 'Exploration and Exploitation', *Organization Science*, 21, 71-87.

Milliken, F. and L. Martins (1996), 'Searching for common threads: understanding the multiple effects of diversity in organizational groups', *Academy of Management Review*, 21 (2), 402-33.

Mitchell, W. and K. Singh (1996), 'Survival of business using collaborative relationships to commercialize complex goods', *Strategic Management Journal*, 17, 169-95.

Mowery, D.C., J. Oxley and B.S. Silverman (1996), 'Strategic alliances and inter-firm knowledge transfer', *Strategic Management Journal*, 17, 77-91.

Nelson, R.R. and S.G. Winter (1982), *An evolutionary Theory of Economic Change*, Boston, MA: Harvard Business School Press.

Nohria, N. and R. Gulati (1999), 'What is the optimum amount of organizational slack? A study of the relationship between slack and innovation in multinational firms', *Academy of Management Proceedings*, 32-6.

Nonaka, I. (1994), 'A dynamic theory of organizational knowledge creation', *Organization Science*, 5 (1).

Oxley, J. (1997), 'Appropriability hazards and governance in strategic alliances: a transaction-cost approach', *Journal of Law, Economics, and Organization*, 13 (2), 387-409.

Parkhe, A. (1991), 'Interfirm diversity, organizational learning, and longevity in global strategic alliances', *Journal of International Business Studies*, 22, 579-601.

Penrose, E.T. (1959), *The Theory of Growth of the Firm*, London, UK: Basil Blackwell.

Porter Liebeskind, J. (1996), 'Knowledge, strategy, and the theory of the firm', *Strategic Management Journal*, 17 (Winter Special Issue), 93- 107.

Powell, W., K. Koput and L. Smith-Doerr (1996), 'Interorganizational collaboration and the locus of innovation networks of learning in biotechnology', *Administrative Science Quarterly*, 41, 116- 45.

Prahalad, C.K. and H. Hamel (1990), 'The core competence of the corporation' *Harvard Business Review*, may-june, 71-91.

Schulze, W.S., M.T. Lubatkin, R.N. Dino and A. Buchholtz (2001), 'Agency relationships in family firms: theory and evidence', *Organization Science*, 12 (2), 99-116.

Simonin, B. (1999), 'Ambiguity and the process of knowledge transfer in strategic alliances', *Strategic Management Journal*, 20, 595- 623.

Szulanski, G. (1996), 'Exploring internal stickiness: impediments to the transfer of best practice within the firm', *Strategic Management Journal*, 17 (Winter Special Issue), 27- 43.

Wernerfelt, B. (1984), 'A resource based view of the firm', *Strategic Management Journal*, 5, 171- 80.

Williamson, O. (1994), 'Transaction cost economics and organization theory', in Smelser and Swedberg (eds), *The Handbook of Economic Sociology*, Boston, MA: Princeton University Press, pp. 77- 107.

14. Deliberate learning in corporate acquisitions: post-acquisition strategies and integration capability in US bank mergers[*]

Maurizio Zollo and Harbir Singh[°]

INTRODUCTION

The performance of corporate acquisitions has long been a topic of interest to researchers in several disciplines, such as industrial economics, management, and finance. Considerable heterogeneity still exists, however, with respect to the definition of performance (for example, benefit to the acquiring firm, the acquired firm, the combined entity) as well as to its measurement (accounting returns, stock price reactions, and so on). Overall evidence shows that stockholders of the acquired firms make positive economic returns, while acquirers' abnormal returns (in either financial or accounting terms) are not statistically distinguishable from zero. Whereas the evidence on the average magnitude of value created for the various counterparts involved is relatively uncontroversial, the explanation of the variance around the mean is still very much in need of both theoretical and empirical work.

In this chapter, we focus on acquirers' variation in performance and examine how learning processes specific to the management of the post-acquisition phase affect it. We also provide a theoretical argument and an empirical test for the performance implications of post-acquisition integration decisions, as well as the interaction between these decisions and some resource- and capability-based antecedents. Our focus on the acquiring firm, instead of the target or the combined entity, is influenced by the observation that learning processes and post-acquisition decisions are housed primarily within the acquirer's corporate development department or its relevant business unit.

[°] This chapter appeared originally in *Strategic Management Journal*, vol. 25, no. 13, December 2004, pp.1233-1256.

The US banking industry, where the study is positioned, is a good example of a particularly turbulent environment, where the tight coupling of deregulation, disintermediation, and technological evolution have generated an unprecedented wave of acquisitions in a relatively short amount of time. It thus provides a good laboratory for testing whether different acquirers' approaches to post-acquisition management and different levels of expertise in managing the integration process are systematically associated with different performance outcomes.

The section below summarizes relevant prior research. Afterwards, we introduce a knowledge-based perspective, which we apply to the management of acquisition processes, and advance testable hypotheses. The following section then describes the research design, some of the key findings in our fieldwork, and the operationalization of the most important theoretical constructs. Finally, we discuss the results of our analyses and conclude by noting several implications of our findings for theories of corporate strategy and organizational learning.

THE PERFORMANCE OF CORPORATE ACQUISITIONS

In this section , we examine how scholars in financial economics, strategic management, and organizational theory have discussed and tested the performance implications of corporate acquisitions.

The Market for Corporate Control and the Resource-based Views of Acquisitions

Research in financial economics has examined returns to acquirers and targets in large samples of acquisitions. In general, it views acquisitions as transactions that reflect the market for corporate control, in which management teams vie for the control of firms' productive assets. If one management team underperforms, then a more competent team takes its place (Manne, 1965; Jensen and Ruback, 1983). Empirically, this research has found that although there are positive gains from the combination of the acquiring firm and the target's assets, most of these gains accrue to shareholders of the target firm. More recently, it has shown that *average* abnormal returns to the acquiring firm are either statistically equivalent to zero (Jarrell et al., 1988, Franks et al., 1991; Loderer and Martin, 1992; Shleifer and Vishny, 1994; Agrawal and Jaffe, 2000) or lower (Agrawal et al., 1992). This result is confirmed in the literature on acquisitions in the banking industry developed by financial economics scholars (Hawawini and

Swary, 1990; Rhoades, 1994). Rhoades' review of 39 bank merger studies, in particular, showed that changes in acquiring firms' accounting and financial returns around the acquisition event are not statistically significant.

The strategic management field, on the other hand, has focused on several factors that might influence the post-acquisition performance of acquirers. Most prominently, it has used the resource-based view of the firm (Wernerfelt, 1984; Rumelt, 1984: Barney, 1986; Dierickx and Cool, 1989) to test the impact of resource relatedness on such performance (Chatterjee, 1986; Singh and Montgomery, 1987; Lubatkin, 1987; Shelton, 1988; Seth, 1990, Healy, Palepu, & Ruback, 1992, Chatterjee *et al.*, 1992). The evidence, however, suggests that no clear relationship links resource relatedness and performance. This variation in results may be explained in several ways. First, there might be several mechanisms that can influence the post-acquisition performance of the combined entity, but that do not rely on the exploitation of economies of scale and scope, and that therefore would not benefit from higher degrees of relatedness between the two firms. Seth (1990), for example, found evidence for coinsurance effects, which allow the combined entity to obtain higher leverage by combining uncorrelated streams of cash flows to yield higher tax shields. Additionally, Baker and Montgomery (1994) observed that LBO firms and 'enlightened conglomerates' can consistently create significant rents by developing idiosyncratic capabilities in the structuring of highly powered incentive systems (LBO firms) and in restructuring, turnaround, and control processes.[1] Second, Barney (1988) argues, consistent with evidence shown by Lubatkin (1987) and Singh and Montgomery (1987), that an acquirer has to create a uniquely valuable and inimitable combination of its assets with those of the acquired firm to earn positive abnormal returns on its investment. Although many acquirers may possess resources related to those of a target, the uniqueness condition provides a much more stringent criterion for value creation. Third, although relatedness may sometimes directly and significantly impact performance, as in the context of consolidating and declining industries (Anand and Singh, 1997), these conditions might not be generalizable to other industry conditions. Thus, relatedness may be a necessary but not sufficient requirement for superior performance. Generally, it might be possible to achieve synergy only when firms carefully design and execute integration processes focused on extracting the gains associated with the combination of the two organizations. Accordingly, when resource relatedness is used to explain how economic rents may accrue to acquirers, it is important to include as explanatory variables the activities necessary to extract such rents.

This chapter intends to improve our understanding of the predictors of acquisition performance by exploring the explanatory roles of pre-acquisition resource characteristics, learning from prior acquisitions, and key elements of the post-acquisition integration process. By design, however, it restricts the scope of the strategic intent that could potentially be pursued through acquisitive growth by focusing on horizontal acquisitions among commercial banks, where the economic logic can be defined in terms of either cost efficiencies derived from larger scale in the same geographic markets, or by a combination of (more limited) cost efficiencies and revenue enhancement potential from the expansion of activities in new geographic markets. Hence product diversification strategies (for example, the acquisition of an investment bank or insurance business) and new product development objectives (for example acquisitions of financial 'boutiques' specialized in the structuring or trading of innovative products) are excluded from the scope of the study.

Also, in this study, acquisition performance is defined as the variation in the acquiring firm's overall performance and measured as the deviation from competitors' long-term variation in return on assets.[2] The choice of the accounting measure to proxy the performance construct is forced by the relative unobservability of post-acquisition decisions, as well as learning processes, from the financial market standpoint. Because financial markets are unlikely to be able to anticipate and incorporate information relative to our key explanatory variables in the acquirer's stock price at or around the time of the acquisition announcement, event-study models that focus on cumulative abnormal returns to stock prices are not appropriate for our analysis. The next section reviews the extant literature that focuses on how firms manage the post-acquisition phase.

Research on the Management of Integration Processes

The process acquiring firms use to manage their acquisitions is substantially more complex to study empirically, compared to the relatedness studies reviewed above, because of the lack of process level data typically available for a sufficiently large number of observations. As a result, prior research in this area has established few definitive findings.

Jemison and Sitkin (1986) indicate that it is useful to think about acquisitions in terms of both their strategic and organizational fit, which generally do not correspond neatly to each other. Thus, the organizational complexity of an acquisition can be quite different from the strategic considerations driving the transaction. Building on this insight, Haspeslagh and Jemison (1991) highlight the relevance of the processes firms use to select their acquisition targets, negotiate the agreement to purchase or to merge, decide how to manage the post-acquisition transition phase, and interact with the acquired firm to implement the selected integration strategy.

They also indicate some critical dimensions of the post-acquisition decision-making process, such as the extent of functional integration and the timing of its implementation. Their work was an important step in understanding the dimensions of the integration process and in relating the strategic objectives driving the acquisition to key managerial decisions made in the post-acquisition phase of the transaction.

Subsequent work has attempted to understand post-acquisition processes by focusing on one decision at a time. Consequently, it trades off rich contextual descriptions of the interdependencies among integration decisions for analytical precision and theoretical rigor. For example, Pablo (1994) examined the antecedents of the decision about the level of integration, whereas Datta and Grant (1990) and Shanley (1994) attempted to test the performance implications of this decision and found some support for a positive influence on performance. All these authors define the construct 'level of integration', drawing on Thompson's (1967) pioneering work, as the extent to which the functions of the acquired unit are linked to, aligned with, or centralized in, the equivalent functions of the acquiring organization, and we make no exception in this study.[3] More recently, Capron (1999) focused her attention on a related phenomenon, the extent of resource redeployment and knowledge transfer between the two organizations, and found that it is significantly related to increased performance. This provides additional evidence that achieving some degree of integration between the two organizations offers economic benefits.

Another important dimension of the post-acquisition integration process involves the degree to which pre-existing resources within the acquired firm are replaced with the equivalent resources of the acquirer, or are simply dismissed. Chief among these resources is the human and social capital embedded in the acquired firm's employees, particularly in its top management team. Contrary to the predictions of the 'market for corporate control' perspective, Cannella and Hambrick (1993) found that managerial turnover was harmful to acquisition performance and that the impact increased in magnitude when more senior managers were replaced. More recently, Krishnan et al. (1997) reached similar conclusions, and noted that the degree of complementarity between the two top management teams positively influences performance and should be protected when possible.

Other studies have researched the antecedents of the decision to replace the target's top management team. Walsh (1988) examined top management turnover rates by comparing post-acquisition turnover in a sample of firms to that of a control group. He found that turnover rates could not be explained by the product market relationship between the acquirer and the target firm. In subsequent work, Walsh and Ellwood (1991) found that post-acquisition turnover is influenced by the pre-acquisition profitability of the *acquirer*, rather than that of the target, as one would expect. In particular, the higher the acquirer's pre-acquisition performance, the lower the post-acquisition turnover of the acquired company's management.

In sum, this research has emphasized the potential benefits and the complexities involved in creating value through acquisition processes. Striking the right balance between achieving the necessary level of organizational integration and minimizing the disruptions to the acquired firm's resources and competencies is a fundamental challenge that affects the success of not only the integration process but also the entire acquisition. Because of these managerial trade-offs, it is important to understand better whether and how firms develop processes and capabilities specific to the management of corporate acquisitions.

The empirical work that explicitly considers the relationship between the acquiring firm's experience and acquisition performance shows that simple 'learning curve' explanations are of limited relevance. Although some studies have found that such experience positively impacts performance (Fowler and Schmidt, 1989; Bruton *et al.*1994), others have found no such relationship (Lubatkin, 1987; Baum and Ginsberg, 1997). Haleblian and Finkelstein (1999) reported evidence for a non-linear, U-shaped, relationship, which highlights possible negative learning effects (Gick and Holyoak, 1987) for the first few acquisition experiences, during which acquirers might inappropriately apply lessons learned in past experiences to contexts that seem superficially similar but are inherently different, thereby reducing the probability of success. In a similar vein, Hayward (2002) finds no linear impacts of prior acquisition experience on short-term stock price reactions, but a number of non-linearities in the quality of such experience (such as the average success of prior acquisitions). Finally, evidence of non-linear experience effects in multi-task contexts (that is, spillovers of alliance experience on acquisition performance) was found by Zollo and Reuer (2003).

In the next section, we present a knowledge-based perspective on the management of acquisition processes and show that the lack of consistency in empirical tests of the learning curve hypothesis might be owing to incomplete theoretical treatment of the underlying organizational learning processes, rather than to anomalies of the M&A context or broader unobserved heterogeneity.

A KNOWLEDGE-BASED PERSPECTIVE ON MANAGING ACQUISITIONS

The knowledge-based view of the firm (Nelson and Winter, 1982; Kogut and

Zander, 1992; Grant, 1996) suggests that the outcome of the acquisition process is influenced by the degree to which the acquiring firm develops a capability specific to managing the acquisition process. Prior literature has highlighted this capability as a key prerequisite for completing these complex organizational endeavors successfully (Haspeslagh and Jemison, 1991; ch. 2). Building on their initial insight, we intend to first develop a theoretical understanding of the mechanisms that might underlie this collective learning process. We then apply these notions to the development of one specific type of acquisition-related capability, that is managing the process through which the acquired firm is, partially or totally, integrated within the structures and processes of the acquiring firm. We note that the integration capability is not the only one of relevance to the success of the post-acquisition phase. The ability to identify the appropriate acquisition candidate, for example, is just as important as the ability to integrate it once acquired. Whereas acquirers can develop competence related to different aspects of the acquisition process, in this chapter we focus on the integration capability since this is likely to be a crucial antecedent to the performance of the acquisition, and has not received so far specific attention from a theoretical standpoint. We therefore consider other competencies unrelated to the integration process outside the scope of this chapter and indicate them as promising areas for future research.

Organizational Knowledge and Capability-building Mechanisms

Previous literature on acquisitions has used research on learning curves originally developed to understand manufacturing processes (Yelle, 1979; Dutton and Thomas, 1984; Epple *et al.*, 1991; Lapre *et al.*, 1998) to test whether learning processes exist within acquirers. It linked the accumulation of experience in prior acquisition processes with improvements in acquisition performance as measured by either financial variables or survival (Lubatkin, 1987; Fowler and Schmidt, 1989; Bruton, *et al.*, 1994; Pennings, *et al.*, 1994; Baum and Ginsberg, 1997; Haleblian and Finkelstein, 1999; Hayward, 2002). Firms might be able to learn how to manage acquisition processes by simply doing more of the same, and thereby tacitly forming and refining organizational routines that might directly (that is, without explicit knowledge articulation or codification) impact the performance of subsequent acquisitions. This 'learning-by-doing' hypothesis can be more formally stated and submitted as follows:

H1: The greater the acquiring firm's previous acquisition experience, the better the economic performance of the focal acquisition.

The accumulation of prior experience, however, is not the only way in which firms can develop collective capabilities in handling organizational tasks (Zollo, 1998; Kale *et al.*, 2002; Zollo and Winter, 2002). We argue that one reason why the received literature on learning effects in acquisitions has not derived consistent results is that it has failed to account for mechanisms different from 'learning-by-doing' to explain how firms improve in their understanding of the ways acquisitions should be managed. We therefore intend to leverage on, and possibly extend, the work produced by scholars interested in the strategic implications of organizational knowledge to discuss the role of more refined mechanisms in explaining organizational learning processes in contexts such as corporate acquisitions.

Rogers (1980), Winter (1987), and Kogut and Zander (1992) propose several dimensions of organizational knowledge that influence how practices evolve and transfer within and across firms. These dimensions include the degree to which knowledge is articulable, teachable, and codifiable, or the extent to which the individuals and the groups which possess the knowledge are actually aware of it, can describe it, and therefore communicate it using oral or written media (Polanyi, 1962, 1966). These dimensions are clearly interrelated. For example, the degree of articulability and teachability will influence the degree of codifiability. In the context of acquisition management, it is likely that the knowledge underlying any given organizational process can accumulate in both explicit forms, such as manuals, blueprints, and information systems, and implicit forms, such as human memory.

Given the same level of codifiability of knowledge necessary to perform a certain task, however, firms might choose to codify the amount of accumulated experience to different degrees. For instance, firms with equivalent levels of experience might develop different kinds of written tools or information systems related to the management of the acquisition processes. Not all codifiable and teachable knowledge is actually codified and taught. Because the costs of creating and updating tools and systems are likely to be high, the proportion of codified knowledge to what is potentially codifiable might be quite small. The decision to invest scarce managerial resources in knowledge codification processes might therefore be interpreted as a strategically relevant activity, which could significantly affect the development of explicit task-related competence.

As a group produces tools and systems to execute a given task, it will have to evaluate how and why its past decisions and actions for similar situations have influenced performance. This effort will likely improve the quality of the group's understanding of the causes of successes and failures in the task at hand. It will, in other words, increase a firm's capability to plan and manage that particular process. Weick's (1995) work on retrospective sensemaking evokes well how we believe capability building happens in the context we observed. Nevertheless, we do not assume that the group that develops and refines these codes learns intentionally. Firms, or groups of individuals, might very well learn about the drivers of performance in their acquisitions without realizing that they are doing so. For example, the development of an integration manual is normally motivated by the need to coordinate the execution of the huge number of virtually simultaneous activities necessary to align processes in the two organizations. In doing so, however, the acquirer might develop a theory of what decisions are most appropriate in what conditions, therefore unintentionally contributing to the improvement of the understanding of the performance implications of those decisions.

If these arguments are correct, the degree to which past experience is reflected upon, articulated, and codified into *ad-hoc* tools should influence how effective organizational practices evolve. Both tacit knowledge accumulation and explicit knowledge codification might precede the development of organizational capabilities, at least in the context of infrequent and heterogeneous processes, such as corporate acquisitions (Zollo and Winter, 2002).

We view these two mechanisms as linked, in that the effectiveness of knowledge codification as a learning process depends, to some extent, on the magnitude of accumulated experience (Levitt and March, 1988). Yet they are also theoretically distinguishable because they assume different underlying behavioral and cognitive processes. Although learning-by-doing occurs without explicit resource commitment and intense cognitive effort, articulating and codifying knowledge requires firms to deliberately attempt to improve the odds of success in future repetitions of the task. They can do so only by dedicating time, money, and managerial attention to grasp the causal mechanisms between decisions, actions, and performance outcomes.

This argument suggests that the effects of the *process* of knowledge codification, not necessarily its outcomes, are of strategic relevance. Our argument focuses on the development and refinement of these tools, rather than on these tools' usefulness as repositories of collective memory (Cohen and Bacdayan, 1994; Cohen et al., 1997) or as diffusers of organizational knowledge (Nonaka, 1994; Nonaka and Takeuchi, 1995). The process/outcome distinction is important for understanding the source of sustainable advantages firms can derive from their efforts to codify. Although the codification of knowledge reduces the ability of firms to protect their rents from imitation and replication (Winter, 1995) and might induce phenomena of superstitious learning (Levitt and March, 1988), the superior understanding of the action-performance linkages derived from the creation of those tools will not diffuse with the tools. Just as it is not sufficient to send a manual of explanations in order to transfer superior practices (Szulanski, 1997), so it will not be easy for competitors to reproduce the performance of the initial codifier even if they can obtain access to the tools.

Our approach complements the 'recombinatory' (Kogut and Zander, 1992; Grant, 1996, Teece, *et al.*, 1997) and modular (Henderson and Clark, 1990, Clark and Fujimoto, 1991; Sanchez and Mahoney, 1996) views of organizational capabilities, which emphasize the manipulation of competence already residing within the organization. Recombining, integrating, or 'harnessing' (Grant, 1996) current knowledge can and should be distinguished from creating new organizational competence in tasks that bear little relationship with established firm activities. The effectiveness of vicarious learning mechanisms for such tasks is limited by the very nature of the organizational knowledge necessary for their execution: sticky (Winter, 1995; Szulanski, 1997), system-dependent (Winter, 1987), and causally ambiguous (Lippman and Rumelt, 1982). Finally, our approach offers the non-trivial advantage of enhanced measurability, with respect to the notions of combinative and architectural capabilities because experience curves and the existence of codification outputs can be easily quantified with the appropriate methodology.

As do partnering, reengineering, and reorganization processes, acquisitions present a formidable challenge for the firm attempting to develop a specific capability in handling them. First, they occur relatively infrequently and unpredictably, thereby reducing a firm's ability to accumulate large amounts of 'observations' necessary to capitalize on learning-by-doing mechanisms (March *et al.*, 1991). Second, when they do occur, they present themselves in highly heterogeneous forms and usually a number of unique challenges to be tackled (Haspeslagh and Jemison, 1991). Third, this activity is inherently causally ambiguous (Lippman and Rumelt, 1982), as the number, simultaneity, and interdependence of the decisions and the actions entailed, particularly in the context of the post-acquisition integration phase, imply an endemic lack of clarity with respect to their performance implications.

Under these conditions, the extent to which acquiring firms codify the knowledge accumulated through past experiences might be a necessary pre-condition for the development of the ability to manage the acquisition process. By creating and updating tools for executing the different phases of the acquisition (that is, negotiation, due diligence, integration planning, and implementation), the acquiring firm might be able to form and refine its understanding of the determinants of performance outcomes. If it can, the quality of its decisions and implementation steps should be positively related to the degree to which it codifies knowledge from prior experiences in *ad-hoc* tools. Based on the above arguments, we propose the following hypothesis:

H2: The higher the degree of knowledge codification from previous acquisition experiences, the better the economic performance resulting from the focal acquisition.

Integration Capability and Task Complexity

Supporting our hypothesis about the causal link between knowledge codification and acquisition performance is our observation that intense cognitive efforts are necessary to develop and update acquisition-specific tools that lower the degree of causal ambiguity between decisions and performance outcomes. If our argument is true, then the effectiveness of the investments in deliberate learning processes should increase, relative to the process of accumulating tacit experience, at increasing levels of task complexity (Zollo and Winter, 2002). In other words, the more complex the task at hand, the higher its causal ambiguity, and the more necessary it will be for the firm to invest in deliberate learning efforts in order to counteract the steeper barrier to the understanding of cause–effect relationships.

A second argument in support of a possible interaction of knowledge codification processes with the degree of complexity of the organizational task has to do with the cognitive simplification entailed by the production of these tools. As Gavetti and Levinthal (2000) show, investments in forward-looking, off-line learning efforts should reduce the cognitive complexity of the task at hand by simplifying decision-making and facilitating the coordination of the implementation sub-tasks.

This second point supplements the argument Adler and Borys (1996) make in their analysis of the conditions under which formalization might be productive. The degree of formalization might therefore represent a key to managing complex contexts if it is enacted within a capability-building approach, thereby *enabling* the achievement of higher levels of understanding rather than *coercing* the actions of the individuals involved. The former approach is more likely to be taken, however, when the learning challenge is greater. Easier tasks might be more frequently approached with coercive, bureaucratic attitudes.

In the acquisition context, the level of post-acquisition integration of the acquired unit within the acquiring firm is inherently tied to the complexity of the organizational task. The higher the level of integration the larger the number of organizational units and functional departments in both firms that need to coordinate and cooperate in order to achieve the desired structural, operational, and cultural unity. The number, the frequency, and the interdependence of decisions and actions increase correspondingly, perhaps even non-linearly, at increasing levels of intended integration between the two organizations.

Based on the above arguments, we present the following hypothesis:

H3: The impact of the degree of knowledge codification on performance will be stronger when the focal acquisition is managed with a high, as opposed to a low, level of integration.

Performance Implications of Post-acquisition Integration Strategies

Knowledge accumulation mechanisms do not, however, solely determine the development of acquisition-specific capabilities; this development is obviously connected to, and is dependent on, the type of integration approach selected by the acquiring firm. Given the system-dependent and causally ambiguous nature of the organizational knowledge necessary to manage an acquisition, acquirers will be able to develop competence only in a fairly narrow knowledge domain, which will likely correspond to the management of a specific kind of acquisition process. When the characteristics of this process, particularly the post-acquisition integration phase, change substantially, the acquirer should be considered a novice, regardless of its accumulated experience in substantially different types of acquisition. It thus has to start accumulating new competencies specific to the new challenges it faces. It is therefore very important to understand the performance implications of post-acquisition integration decisions (Haspeslagh and Jemison, 1991) and to relate them to the capability-development process described above.

As discussed in the section on the 'Performance of Corporate Acquisitions', there appear to be at least two key dimensions of the integration process: the level of organizational integration between the two firms involved in the acquisition, and the extent to which the target's resource endowments, with particular emphasis on the target's top management team, is replaced.

The Level of Integration

To the extent the acquired firm is integrated within the structures and operations of the acquirer, a number of outcomes are likely to occur. First, consistent with established results on the effects of organizational change on firm survival (Amburgey *et al.*, 1993; Haveman, 1992, 1993), a more extensive integration results in greater disruption of the pre-existing resources and routines in both firms. This disruption is likely to lead to declines in the performance of the combined entity (Marks and Mirvis, 1985; Schweiger, *et al.*, 1987; Buono and Bowditch, 1989, Astrachan, 1990; Empson, 2001).

A second negative consequence of the integration decision relates to its effect on the complexity of the integration process. As argued above, an extensive integration entails a large number of highly interdependent and virtually simultaneous decision-making processes, involving increasing levels of interaction between parts and functions of the two organizations (Kitching, 1967; Jemison and Sitkin, 1986; Pablo, 1994). Consequently, extensive integration makes it harder for acquirers to assess the performance outcomes of the integration process and implies higher levels of risk in the selection of the correct integration approach, as well as in the implementation of the selected approach (Pablo *et al.*, 1996). Finally, high integration levels translate into increasing explicit and hidden costs relative to the expenses (for example, training, lay-offs, information systems conversion, and so on), to the time and to the degree of managerial attention (Ocasio, 1997) required to design and implement the integration process.

Nonetheless, a higher level of integration between the two firms is necessary in order for the acquirer to realize the potential value of the transaction (Datta and Grant, 1990; Haspeslagh and Jemison, 1991; Shanley, 1994; Capron, 1999). In particular, the positive performance implications of the degree of resource relatedness (Rumelt, 1974, 1984; Chatterjee, 1986; Lubatkin, 1987; Singh and Montgomery, 1987; Chatterjee et al., 1992) imply that related acquisitions should be managed with at least a minimum level of organizational integration.

Unfortunately, prior empirical work that has attempted to link the level of integration to performance has not yielded definitive results. Datta and Grant (1990) did not find statistically significant results for either their overall sample or their sub-sample of related acquisitions, although their sample of unrelated acquisitions did seem to benefit from lower levels of integration. In contrast, Shanley (1994) found some evidence that positive performance was related to the level of integration. As our study focuses on horizontal and market extension acquisitions, thereby excluding strategic logics related to product diversification, we expect the benefits from economies of scale and scope to emerge only when the operations of the two organizations are integrated extensively, and that these benefits outweigh the negative impacts of organizational disruptions, process complexity, and implementation costs outlined above. Following Datta and Grant (1990) and Shanley (1994), we therefore propose the following hypothesis for empirical testing:

H4: The higher the degree of integration of the acquired firm within the acquirer, the better the economic performance of the acquisition.

The Degree of Resource Replacement

We now consider the relationship between resource replacement and acquisition performance. Of particular interest, given the attention it has received in prior work, is the replacement of the top management team of the target firm. This variable might be also considered a proxy, however, for a more general construct of firm-wide replacement of resources, such as brand names, distribution channels, and physical assets, as an acquiring firm opting for a quick, aggressive, integration process is likely to replace other pre-existing resources within the acquired business that it considers non-vital.

We expect that when more extensive integration is pursued, resource redundancy between the activities of the two organizations is more likely. Nevertheless, given the decisions made on the degree of integration, acquirers still have considerable latitude in deciding *how* to achieve the desired level of integration. For instance, the top management team can be either retained and motivated to cooperate, or replaced with a new team sent from the acquiring firm, regardless of how much autonomy is given to the acquired organization. Also, if the acquisition is primarily motivated by the access to undervalued or underexploited assets, such as brands or location, the decision on the retention of top management is only loosely connected to the one on the degree of integration of the productive assets.

According to proponents of the 'market for corporate control' hypothesis, the better team gains control of the productive assets of the acquired firm by displacing the less competent team (Manne, 1965; Jensen and Ruback, 1983). The acquiring team, according to this argument, needs to believe that it is more competent than the one currently in place in the target firm. As reviewed in the section on the 'Performance of Corporate Acquisitions', however, prior research suggests that replacing the acquired firm's top management will result in reduced economic performance because it entails the loss of human and social capital caused by the departure of top executives. Empirical studies have found that managerial turnover reduces acquisition performance (Cannella and Hambrick, 1993; Krishnan *et al.*, 1997), lending support to a negative sign of the causal link.

In an effort to find an integrative solution to this debate, we are interested in identifying a moderating variable that might function as 'switch' in the sign of the relationship and that might have been left out of the theoretical discourse so far. To this end, an obvious moderator of the impact of top management on performance is the quality of the assets of the acquired firm. Replacing the target's top management might be connected with enhanced performance if the acquired firm is characterized by poor quality of its resources (and presumably of its pre-acquisition performance), since the advantages of establishing a better management team might outweigh the potential disruptions to routines and motivations within the acquired organization. Conversely, replacing the management team of better performing acquired firms is likely to be detrimental to the performance of the combined entity. If this is the case, then we can propose the following hypothesis based on the interaction between the replacement decision and the quality of the pre-acquisition performance of the acquired firm:

H5: The higher the pre-acquisition performance of the acquired firm, the worse the impact of the replacement of top management in the acquired firm on the economic performance of the acquisition.

Figure 14.1 summarizes the causal relationships discussed and the research hypotheses advanced.

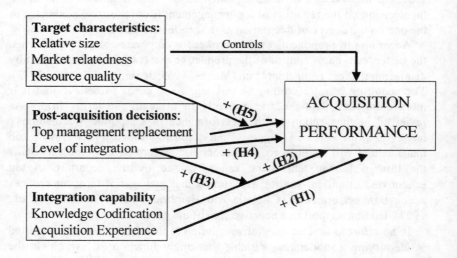

Figure 14.1   Model and hypotheses

RESEARCH METHODOLOGY AND MEASURES

The Research Setting

We tested these hypotheses on a large sample of acquisitions in the US commercial banking industry. This setting was deemed to be particularly well suited for our research purposes for several reasons. First, by holding the industry constant, we ensured that the population of firms from which we drew our sample was relatively uniform in the environmental conditions that it faced. Of course, the price paid was a reduction in the degree of generalizability of our results, at least beyond the banking sector. Second, this industry underwent a period of rapid consolidation in response to changes in regulation that allowed banks to cross state lines in the early 1990s. This institutional change created a sufficiently large universe of potential observations in a relatively compact time frame. Third, given the relevance of acquisition-driven growth in the industry, it was easier to find firms that would grant us access and participate in our survey. Finally, banking has been the most active industry in terms of acquisition volumes since the beginning of the 1990s; its share of the total domestic volume of acquisitions was estimated to be about 25 per cent during the first half of the decade.

The research design involved two phases: initial fieldwork to gain a deeper understanding of the integration process in this industry, and a larger questionnaire-based sample study of post-acquisition practices and performance. For the initial field research, we obtained access to twelve banks, all of which were active acquirers. We interviewed 45 decision-makers in these banks to obtain a better understanding of how they handle integration challenges and attempt to distill useful lessons from their prior acquisition experiences. In analyzing the content of these interviews, we made the following observations:

1. Most acquisitions made prior to 1990 were managed as virtually autonomous affiliates. Acquired firms' information systems were not changed significantly, and their top management teams were typically not replaced.
2. During the 1990s, acquiring banks have increasingly sought to obtain cost efficiencies by integrating the operations of the acquired bank into their own, by standardizing products of the combined organizations, and by converting information systems. Acquirers varied in how they managed acquisitions not only longitudinally (increasing levels of integration over time) but also cross-sectionally. Some acquirers allowed the acquired units to remain relatively autonomous, and

typically retained their top management. Banc One was an example of this approach to managing acquisitions. On the other hand, equally experienced acquirers used substantially different approaches to manage essentially the same types of task by integrating and/or replacing existing resources to a much greater extent. Nationsbank (now Bank of America) was considered one of the champions of this more aggressive approach.

3.   Finally, we were surprised to witness how extensively some acquirers had codified the integration process, and the large cross-sectional variation that different acquirers exhibited along this dimension. Experience levels seemed to explain part, but not all, of this variation, as we found several inexperienced acquirers with highly sophisticated integration tools and highly experienced ones with only average levels of codification. Also, the development of integration-specific tools went beyond the predictable, industry-specific challenges related to the conversion of the IT systems, and spanned issues of human resources management, customer communication and retention, and general project management systems.

The large sample study was then conducted in 1996, with a survey of the 250 largest bank holding companies in the US, covering more than 95 per cent of the industry's assets. The asset size of the smallest institution was about $400 million, which implies very rare acquisition activity and very small transaction sizes (usually one or two branches). Further extensions of the sample to smaller institutions would probably have resulted in very few responses because of the scarcity of acquisitions in such firms' histories, and low comparability among the observations in the sample due to the large size differentials.

The survey consisted of two parts: 1) the Acquisition History Profile and 2) the Acquiring Bank Questionnaire. The Acquisition History Profile was a list of all acquisitions conducted by the bank, with basic information about each of them, such as their asset size, the degree of market overlap, pre-acquisition profitability, level of integration, and the replacement of the top management team. The Acquiring Bank Questionnaire described characteristics of the acquisition process at the firm (rather than the transaction) level of analysis, including the type and the time of creation of acquisition support tools such as integration manuals, system conversion manuals, product mapping models, training packages, and other items. Of the 250 bank holding companies contacted, 70 did not make any acquisitions after 1985, and 16 were acquired during the survey process. Of the remaining 164 banks, we obtained responses from 51, translating into a response rate of 31.7 per cent. This response rate is satisfactory given the complexity of the survey and the involvement of top management in responding to the survey.

The respondents to the survey were senior executives at the acquiring bank with direct experience in the coordination of the acquisition process. Due to variation in how firms were organized, we contacted each potential respondent before the mailing in order to identify the best respondent within the bank. The respondents included the manager responsible for corporate development and acquisitions (26 institutions), the coordinator of post-acquisition integration processes (14 institutions), the CFO (8 institutions), and the CEO (in three cases of smaller institutions).

Four responses had to be excluded from the analysis because the data they supplied were seriously incomplete. The remaining 47 institutions had completed 577 acquisitions, for an average of 12.3 each. Standard mean comparison tests were used to check for response bias. The responding organizations were not significantly different from the original set of 250 organizations in terms of return on assets, return on equity, or efficiency ratios, although they tended to be larger in terms of asset size (p <.05).

Measures

Dependent variable: performance. Acquisition performance is measured as the difference between return on assets (ROA) of the acquiring bank three years after the acquisition versus the same measure one year before the acquisition. The acquired banks in our study were very often consolidated, from an accounting standpoint, into the acquiring banks, leaving us unable to analyze the target's post-acquisition performance. Also, the vast majority of acquired firms were privately held community banks, whose accounting returns were not publicly available even before the acquisition. We therefore resolved to utilize a measure based solely on the acquiring bank's pre- and post-acquisition performance, and then collect a qualitative assessment of the target's pre-acquisition performance to use as control variable.[4]

In addition to these measurement problems, our interest in the performance implications of integration decisions and learning processes in the acquiring firm meant it was appropriate to use performance measures related to the acquirer. The influence of pre-acquisition performance and size of the acquired unit are explicitly controlled for in the multiple regression model. In order to control for competitive conditions in the acquirer's market, we adjusted the acquiring bank's return on assets against the performance of its peers in the same geographic area.[5]

The change in performance over time is then expressed as:

Change in ROA = $(ROA_{i,t+3} - ROA_{c,t+3}) - (ROA_{i,t-1} - ROA_{c,t-1})$ where $ROA_{i,t+3}$ and $ROA_{i,t-1}$ = return on assets of acquiring bank i in years t+ 3 and t-1 respectively, and $ROA_{c,t+3}$ and $ROA_{c,t-1}$ = average return on assets in the same geographic area as that of the acquiring bank i at years t+ 3 and t-1 respectively.

The accounting data were collected from 1985 to 1997 with the use of three different databases (Compustat, Compact Disclosures, and Moody's) in order to maximize the coverage of the banking sector. The coverage of the banking sector (for both respondents and non-respondents) was significantly lower for the years prior to 1985. Extending the data set would have implied a significant loss of comparability among the institutions surveyed as well as consistency among the observations between the first and the last years of the period. Given the construction (three–year average) of the dependent variable, the years 1985, 1995, 1996, and 1997 were lost, thus restricting the period of observation to acquisitions completed between 1986 and 1994.

Explanatory variables
Knowledge codification This is measured as the sum of acquisition tools developed by the acquiring firm at the time of the focal acquisition. The tools are specific to different parts of the acquisition process, including financial evaluation, due diligence, conversion of information systems, human resources integration, and sales/product integration. The information was gathered through the Acquiring Bank Questionnaire, which asked whether the following items were developed and, if so, when they were developed:

Documents/manuals Due diligence checklist, Due diligence manual, Systems conversion manual, Affiliation/integration manual,[6] Systems training manual[7], Products training manual[8],

Quantitative models Financial evaluation, Staffing models, Product mapping,[9] Training/Self-training packages, Project management.[10]

Acquisition experience is computed as the number of acquisitions completed by the acquiring firm before the focal acquisitions. The Acquisition History Profile collected the list of all the acquisitions completed by the responding institution since founding or since a merger of equals. The oldest acquisitions in the data set were completed in 1968 (by Banc One and Crestar Bank). Although the analysis is based on the observations between 1986 and 1994 (see above), the History Profile allowed us to construct the complete stock of prior acquisition experience for each of the observations in the analysis. The measurements of the two capability-building mechanisms, as well as of the dependent variables, are therefore comparable across firms.

Integration was measured with a single scale collected with the Acquisition History Profile instrument. For each acquisition they completed since their founding, respondents answered the following question: To what extent were the systems, procedures and products aligned or centralized?

Possible answers were: '**0**' (few or no features were aligned or centralized), '**1**' (if only selected systems, procedures or products were aligned or centralized), '**2**' (many but not all systems, procedures and products were aligned or centralized), and '**3**' (all systems, procedures and products were completely integrated).

Replacement was measured with a similar four-point scale, where respondents answered the following question:[11] To what extent has the executive leadership of the acquired bank been changed after the acquisition?

Alternative answers were: '**0**' (no substantial change), '**1**' (some changes), '**2**' (many changes), and '**3**' (virtually all the top management team was changed).

Controls
Relatedness The research design called for limiting the variation in the degree of relatedness between the two organizations to the geographic dimension. The construct was therefore measured with a dummy variable identifying either horizontal acquisitions (or 'in-market' in the banking terminology), coded as '1', or market extension acquisition (or 'out-market'), coded as '0'. This measure is a good proxy for market relatedness in the banking industry, given the importance of geographic location as a key competitive factor and the importance of rationalizing the branch network in order to create value from acquisitions through cost efficiencies. In terms of value creation mechanisms, in-market acquisitions generally prioritize cost efficiencies driven by economies of scale, whereas 'out-market' acquisitions tend to rely more on cross-selling opportunities and economies of scope since many of the cost-efficiencies derivable from the rationalization of the two branch networks are not available.

Resource quality In order to isolate the effect of the resource replacement variable, we assessed the pre-acquisition quality of the acquired firm's resource endowment. The construct was measured by asking about the performance level of the target bank prior to the acquisition. The scale anchors were:"**-2**" (the acquired institution was bankrupt), '**-1**' (it was a poor performer), '**0**' (it was an average performer), '**+1**' (it was a good performer) and '**+2**' (it was an outstanding performer).

Other controls included the asset size of the acquiring firm, the relative asset size of the acquired firm with respect to the acquirer, and the number of acquisitions completed by the responding bank during the same year of the focal acquisition.

Construct validity
We tested the validity of our measures of integration, replacement, relatedness, and resource quality using multiple item scales we developed for a sub-sample of 57 acquisitions. For this sub-sample, we had multiple indicators for resource relatedness (8 items), resource quality (11), managerial replacement (9), and the degree of integration both as product and process alignment (8) and as functional centralization (7, with a total of 15 items for the integration construct). Comparisons of the mean between this sub-sample and the entire database of acquisitions did not indicate any bias for these constructs. We used three tests to check the validity of our measures: (1) Cronbach alphas of the multiple items, (2) correlation between the scale used in the study and the sum of the z-scores of multiple items, and (3) correlation between the scale used in the study with the main factor extracted from the multiple items.

Results indicate that the measures used in the empirical analysis are generally valid representations of the underlying constructs utilized in the theoretical treatment of acquisition performance. For our measure of top management replacement, the Cronbach alpha, correlation of the scale with the sum of the z-scores for the multiple items, and the correlation between the scale and the main factor are 0.826, 0.606 ($p<.01$), and 0.549 ($p<.01$), respectively, all of which indicate that our scale for the replacement of top management is valid. For the degree of integration, the same statistics are 0.950, 0.521 ($p<.01$), and 0.542 ($p<.01$), all of which indicate that our integration scale is valid. We also validated our resource quality construct (Cronbach alpha = 0.853; correlation with the sum of the z-scores for the multiple items = .463, $p<.01$; correlation with the main factor = .482, $p<.01$). The only item that was not validated was the approximation of resource relatedness with the single measure of market overlap (in-market versus out-market acquisitions). Nonetheless, the single measure does correlate strongly with a more focused set of items related to the degree of overlap in terms of branch network and customer base (.520, $p<.01$). Consequently, we replaced the general notion of resource replacement with the narrower concept of market relatedness in our interpretations of the results of this analysis.

The Model
The model being tested in this study is specified as follows: change in ROA = a + b*integration - c*replacement + d*codification + e*experience + f*codificationXintegration + g*replacementXquality + controls + ε. The error term is distributed according to the standard normality assumptions.

The estimation method used is ordinary least squares. All variables utilized to construct the interaction terms were standardized so as to eliminate the initial multicollinearity problem in the estimated model. With this correction, the maximum variance inflation factor (VIF) across the co-variates was 2.591, which is significantly below the rule of thumb of ten used to detect multicollinearity problems (Neter *et al.*, 1985). We also checked the stability of the coefficients to different specifications of the model, dropping one of the post-acquisition decisions or one of the (highly correlated) resource characteristics of the acquired firm, and found no important variations to the magnitude and statistical significance of the coefficients. Four observations were identified as outliers (> 3 standard deviation) and were excluded from the analysis. The only other violation of standard normality assumptions that we could find was related to a possible correlation of the error terms stemming from the multiple observations for each responding institution. We dealt with this concern through a specific set of analyses reported in the next section.

RESULTS

Table 14.1 reports descriptive statistics and the correlation matrix for the data used in this study. Consistent with the prior literature on mergers and acquisitions, we find that the mean for the performance variable (-0.004) is not statistically distinguishable from zero. The correlation table indicates that the dependent variable is significantly correlated with virtually all of our explanatory variables, with the notable exception of acquisition experience. Many of our explanatory variables are also correlated with each other. We thus used a multivariate analysis to identify the net influence of each variable on acquisition performance.

The results of the regression analysis of the model described earlier are reported in Table 14.2. The six nested models presented allow the effect of each group of variables on acquisition performance to be identified. The models fit with the data reasonably well, as shown by the strongly significant F-statistics (p<.001) and by the increasing adjusted R^2 statistic (.165 in the full model). The incremental F-statistic (not reported) is statistically significant in each model, with the exception of the one introducing the level of acquisition experience. The two focal post-acquisition decisions appear to impact the variation in acquisition performance more strongly than any of the other sets of explanations. We enter the two decisions simultaneously in model 3 because of their relatively high correlation ratio; a sequential entry would not have changed the results in a substantive way, but would have shown a biased estimate of the coefficient of the first decision entered, since part of the variation of the second decision would have been picked up. The organizational learning variables, as well as the pre-acquisition resource characteristics, which we entered separately because of their theoretical relevance, show mixed results, with only one of the two variables significantly influencing performance. The stability of the coefficients across the models, as well as customary controls of VIF and tolerance ratios, shows that multicollinearity problems, which could arise from high correlations among groups of variables, are not present in this sample.[12]

The analysis indicates that hypothesis 2, which posits a positive relationship between knowledge codification and performance, is strongly supported ($p<.01$). In addition, the interaction between knowledge codification and the level of integration is also statistically significant at the 5 per cent level, supporting hypothesis 3. The fact that the creation of these tools shows increasing influence on acquisition performance at increasing levels of integration (that is, task complexity) empirically supports our argument about the role of deliberate learning efforts in the development of integration capabilities.

In contrast, the accumulation of tacit knowledge through acquisition experience turns out to be a non-significant predictor of performance, failing to support hypothesis 1. This finding confirms the mixed results of the received literature on the performance implications of accumulating acquisition experience. The data analyzed suggest that in the context of relatively infrequent, heterogeneous, and causally ambiguous tasks,[13] organizations develop competence primarily by articulating and codifying knowledge derived from previous acquisition experiences. Simple exposure to acquisition processes does not seem to suffice.

Hypothesis 4, suggesting that the level of integration is positively associated with changes in performance, is supported at the 1 per cent significance level. Regarding the performance implications of top management replacement, we first note that the direct effect is negative and significant at the 1 per cent level, lending further support to the 'organizational disruption' view (Cannella and Hambrick, 1993) versus the 'market for corporate control' perspective (Manne, 1965; Jensen and Ruback, 1983). The strength of the result was surprising, given theoretical arguments supporting both a positive and a negative impact for this decision. However, this result could be explained by the presence of a larger number of good performing targets in the sample analyzed. According to Hypothesis 5, in fact, the pre-acquisition performance levels of the acquired firm should moderate the relationship between replacement and acquisition performance.

In order to probe this, we added the interaction term between replacement and the resource quality assessment of the acquired bank. In addition, we split the dataset in three sub-samples by separating our observations into low (that is, response = -2 or −1), average (response = 0), and high (response = +1 or +2) resource quality. Table 14.3 reports the results of OLS estimates with the full model including the interaction term, as well as for three sub-samples. As Hypothesis 5 proposes, the interaction term is strongly significant and negatively related to performance, indicating that top management replacement is increasingly correlated with poorer performance when the resource quality of the acquired unit increases. More interestingly, though, the strongest negative effect of the replacement decision is found for observations with an average quality of resources, though it would be logical to expect a stronger negative effect for observations with the highest quality of resources. At low, quality levels, the replacement decision takes on a positive sign, as per the 'market for corporate control' hypothesis, but does not reach statistical significance.[14]

One possible explanation for this non-linearity in the TMT replacement coefficients could be provided by the fact that the uncertainty about the performance implications of replacement is highest at intermediate levels of pre-acquisition performance. Also, the model seems to fit the data very well for low–and average–performing targets, but not for high–quality ones. This might be a consequence of the paucity of degrees of freedom (only 55 observations) and a possible overspecification of the model. It might also be, though, that some of the prescriptions valid for the acquisition of 'normal' targets might not transfer to high–quality ones. Cost efficiencies from the integration of high–quality targets, for example, might be effectively counterbalanced by higher hazards of disruption of superior routines. In terms of learning, the advantages of knowledge codification might be reduced outside the more routinizable case of restructuring poorly performing targets.

Compared to post-acquisition decisions, and knowledge codification, the characteristics of the pre-acquisition resources of the target, resource quality, and market relatedness show weaker explanatory power, with the market relatedness measure showing no statistically significant effect. This finding is puzzling from a theoretical standpoint, as the potential for economies of scale should be significantly superior for horizontal acquisitions than for market extension ones, as the overlap of two branch networks typically allows efficiency gains from rationalization. One interpretation might be that acquirers can create or destroy value equally well through cost rationalizations, typically prioritized in 'in-market' acquisitions, or through revenue enhancement processes, which become the priority in market extension acquisitions.

Resource quality consistently impacts performance negatively, indicating that the acquisition of well-performing targets is less likely to enhance acquirers' performance than is the acquisition of poorly performing ones. This result can be interpreted in two ways: first, in terms of directionality of the knowledge flows between the acquiring and the acquired firm. Consistent with Capron (1999)'s results on the performance implications of resource redeployment to and from the target, our finding can be interpreted as showing that the transfer of resources and capabilities from the acquirer to the target (that is, the cases in which the target quality is low) outperforms the opposite mechanism, through which the acquirer 'learns' from the (highly performing) acquired entity. The second interpretation refers to increasing levels of resistance to change that can be expected to occur as the levels of pre-acquisition performance of the acquired firm grow. The better the acquired firm performed before the acquisition, the stronger the confidence its managers will have in the superior quality of its processes and the less willing they will be to accept the changes required to align processes and procedures across the two organizations. Interestingly, this result also replicates findings in prior finance literature on US bank mergers studying short-term stock price reactions to merger announcements (Hawawini and Swary, 1990).

None of the other variables entered as controls in the model: acquirer's size, acquisition relative size, and the frequency of simultaneous acquisitions, significantly influences performance, further suggesting that the variables considered in our theoretical discussion are meaningful and relevant to the explanation of acquisition performance.

Robustness of results
As we noted in the previous section, the error terms for our results may not be independently distributed because we have multiple observations from the same responding institution. In order to address this problem, we replicated the analysis by aggregating the data in two different ways: the firm/year level of analysis, where all acquisitions in the same year by the same firms were averaged, and the firm level of analysis, where all the acquisitions completed by the same firm were aggregated. Weighted least squares estimations (where weights are assigned by the number of acquisitions completed by the same bank over the period of observation) at these two levels of analysis yield results that are consistent with the ones described above, in spite of the significantly lower number of degrees of freedom.[15] The result offers further evidence that the estimated model accurately characterizes this sample (see Table 14.4). Using firm level dummies to control for firm effects was not appropriate, as they would have picked up the measurement errors of our main theoretical variables (experience accumulation and knowledge codification). Also, although firm controls might alleviate this problem, the aggregation of the data eliminates it by making only one observation available for each respondent.

Another issue of concern was related to our measurement of the dependent variable, which did not include the ROA of the acquired bank before the acquisition, while the post-acquisition value included the acquired unit. In response to one of the reviewers' suggestions, we collected pre-acquisition

ROA data for all the acquired banks we could find (only 79 complete observations) and constructed a measure of acquisition performance, which included the asset-weighted average of ROA for the two banks one year before the acquisition. The correlation of the resulting measure with the one utilized in the reported analysis is .972 (p<.0001), confirming that the two approaches provide almost identical estimates of the dependent variable.

Table 14.1 Correlation matrix

	VARIABLES	Av.	Std	1	2	3	4	5	6	7	8	9	10
1	Acquisition Perf. Ch. In ROA (3 yrs)	-.004	.3518										
2	Acquirer's size	23.137	23.08	.084									
3	Relative acquisition size	6.108	11.45	-.013	-.075								
4	Simultaneous acquisitions	3.589	2.836	*.235*	*.481*	-.223							
5	Resource quality	-.017	1.06	-.070	-.048	.052	.051						
6	Market relatedness	.61	.49	.040	*.178*	-.08	*.144*	*-.201*					
7	Level of integration	2.635	.703	*.115*	.089	-.09	*.172*	*-.213*	*.396*				
8	Degree of replacement	1.76	1.28	*-.23*	-.067	.019	*-.210*	*-.309*	*.352*	*.417*			
9	Acquisition experience	11.34	10.17	.026	*.502*	-.09	*.515*	.036	*.17*	*.118*	-.057		
10	Knowledge Codification	4.877	3.676	*.146*	*.436*	-.052	*.36*	*.175*	.026	.078	*-.109*	*.455*	
11	Codification x Integration	.173	1.155	*.143*	-.023	.072	.047	.063	-.009	*-.154*	*-.111*	-.066	*-.176*

Notes: Pearson's correlation. Bold numbers are significant at the 5 per cent level. Bold and italic ones are significant at the 1 per cent level.

Table 14.2 *Acquisition performance: transaction level of analysis*

	Model 1	Model 2	Model 3	Model 4	Model 5	Model 6
Controls						
Acquirer's size	-.031	-.044	-.064	-.054	-.127	-.118
Relative acquisition size	.072	.065	.080	.077	.096	.072
Simultaneous acquisitions	.298***	.308***	.129	.149	.155	-.113
Target quality		-.136**	-.18***	-.179***	-.221***	-.227***
Market relatedness		.001	.062	.064	.068	.061
Post-acquisition Decisions						
Level of integration			.181**	.174**	.176**	.185**
Degree of replacement			-.344***	-.339***	-.338***	-.336***
Integration Capability						
Acquisition experience				-.037	-.098	-.081
Knowledge codification					.198**	.207***
Codification x Integration						.142**
F statistic	6.024***	4.544***	5.976***	5.234***	5.455***	5.506***
Adjusted R²	.062	.072	.133	.129	.150	.165
N	228	228	228	228	228	228

Notes: Ordinary Least Squares estimation. Standardized beta coefficients: significant at the 1% (***), 5% (**) or 10% (*) level. Dependent Variable: Change in ROA years after the acquisition versus the year before, minus same variation in local competitors' ROA.

Table 14.3   Test for interaction between TMT Replacement and Target Quality

	Interaction	Low Quality	Average	High
Controls				
Acquirer's size	-.061	-.031	-.152	-.031
Relative acquisition size	.061	.032	-.034	.193
Simultaneous acquisitions	.044	-.022	-.041	.064
Target quality	-.151**			
Market relatedness	.082	-.122	.133	.183
Post-acquisition Decisions				
Level of integration	.309***	.397***	.365***	.091
Degree of replacement	-.401***	.144	-.621***	-.359**
Integration Capability				
Acquisition experience	-.095	-.140	-.037	.013
Knowledge codification	.151**	.226*	-.014	.153
Codification x Integration	.168***	.255**	.081	.263*
Replacement x quality	-.228***			
F statistic	7.131***	2.61***	5.963***	1.253
Adjusted R^2	.221	.148	.314	.040
N	238	83	98	55

Notes: Ordinary Least Squares estimation. Standardized beta coefficients: significant at the 1% (***), 5% (**) or 10% (*) level. Change in ROA years after the acquisition versus the year before, minus same variation in local competitors' ROA.

334

Table 14.4 *Acquisition performance firm level of analysis*

Variable	Model 1	Mmodel 2	Model 3	Model 4
Resource-based factors				
Quality of assets (average)	-.259	-.310	-.315	-.549***
Market relatedness	.250	-.013	-.031	.109
Post-acquisition decisions				
Integration		.559***	.546***	.518**
Replacement		-.292	-.259	-.292
Integration capability				
Acquisition experience				-.068
Knowledge codification			.066	.515***
F statistic	3.068*	4.368***	3.408**	5.364***
F improvement	3.068*	4.853**	.130	9.546***
Adjusted R^2	.118	.303	.280	.458
N	31	31	31	31

Notes: Weighted Least Squares Estimations. Standardized Beta coefficients. Significant at the 1% (***), 5% (**) or 10% (*) level.
Dependent Variables: Average change in ROA over the period of analysis.
Due to the low N, variables that had no significant effect in previous analyses were omitted in order to save d.f.

CONCLUSION

This chapter has discussed how post-acquisition decisions and capability-building processes affect the economic performance of corporate acquisitions. We proposed a knowledge-based perspective of acquisitions, which builds on the intuition that in order to enhance acquisition performance acquiring firms need to not only select the appropriate mix of integration decisions but they have to simultaneously develop the organizational capability to implement it. We drew upon multiple theoretical traditions, using resource-based, process-based, and evolutionary economics arguments to enrich the existing literature on the knowledge-based view of the firm (Kogut and Zander, 1992; Grant, 1996). One crucial insight, which seems to be supported by our data, is that firms develop collective competence by not only accumulating experience but also investing time and effort in activities that require greater cognitive effort in order to produce enhanced awareness of action-performance linkages.[16] Firms learn directly by articulating and codifying the lessons they learned from previous experiences, even if they might not be aware of the positive learning spillovers from these activities. At an extreme, the benefit in creating and fine-tuning acquisition-specific tools might lie more in the learning achieved through the creative process itself than in the use of the outputs as coordination and implementation support devices.

The results of the analysis also suggest that the 'process view' of acquisitions (Jemison and Sitkin, 1986; Haspeslagh and Jemison, 1991; Pablo, 1994; Pablo *et al.*, 1996), which emphasizes the role of the integration phase, is relevant to consider in understanding the performance of the entire acquisition process. Although the results of prior attempts to relate the level of integration to performance are equivocal, our finding suggests that, at least in the banking industry, which has a trend of efficiency-driven consolidation, the benefits from cost efficiencies gained through higher levels of integration might be greater than the costs inherent to the integration process (for example, routine and competence disruptions, increased process complexity, and hidden implementation costs). Thus, in this setting, the negative consequences typically attributed to post-acquisition integration processes within the human resources management and organizational behavior literature do not systematically occur (Marks and Mirvis, 1985; Schweiger, *et al.*, 1987; Buono and Bowditch 1989; Astrachan, 1990).

In addition, we tested for the direct effect of the replacement of top management in the acquired firm on acquisition performance, as well as the influence that the pre-acquisition performance of the acquired firm has on the strength of the relationship. Our results show that the main effect of the replacement decision in the context studied is negative and significant, and that pre-acquisition performance impacts the relationship in the hypothesized sense but in a non-linear way. The negative impact of top management replacement on performance is maximum at intermediate levels of pre-acquisition performance, rather than at high levels. Moreover, the sign of the impact switches to positive with low–performing targets, but does not reach statistical significance. Taken together, these results confirm the value of searching for an integrative solution to the debate in the literature on the view of acquisitions as policing mechanisms for agency problems in the 'market for corporate control'. Results seem to indicate that this view might be applicable only to the case of underperforming targets, but applying its tenets to cases of average (as well as superior) performers might lead to lower performance for the combined organization.

The knowledge-based variables in the model show interesting effects. The degree of codification has a strong and positive influence on acquisition performance; as the first of its type, this finding merits subsequent research to test for its generalizability. In contrast, the impact of experience accumulation is non-significant. This latter result adds to a series of mixed findings on experience accumulation in these types of tasks. Learning curve effects in the context of highly infrequent and heterogeneous events such as those studied[17] might be heavily attenuated as the hazards of erroneous generalization from the lessons it learned in past contexts to seemingly similar but inherently different ones are correspondingly high (Cormier and Hagman, 1987; Cohen and Bacdayan, 1994; Haleblian and Finkelstein, 1999; Levitt and March, 1988).

Importantly, and central to our arguments on the co-evolution of integration decisions and capability-building processes, the interaction between the degree of codification and the level of integration positively and significantly influences acquisition performance. At increasing levels of complexity, the benefits of explicitly extracting lessons learned from previous experiences appear to exceed the costs connected to codification activities (for example, investment in time, effort, and managerial attention). This result is important because it is direct evidence of the relationship between acquisition capabilities and the management of more complex integration decisions, and may explain why a large number of integrations (even simpler ones) are not successful. Recent related research is examining the role of post-acquisition organizational decisions in influencing product performance in knowledge-intensive acquisitions, another domain replete with instances of post-acquisition failure (see, for example, Puranam, *et al.*, 2004).

We also introduced the type of acquisition (horizontal or market extension) as an important control variable in the analysis. The lack of significant performance implications for this variable is interesting. Ex ante, one could argue that acquiring a competitor in the same geographic area would create higher potential for efficiency-driven cost reductions. Such acquisitions might, however, require more complex integration efforts in terms of the number of potential overlaps of resources and activities across the organizations and the consequently large array of simultaneous, interdependent decisions and actions necessary to accomplish this integration. Therefore the characteristics of pre-acquisition resources might not necessarily predict post-acquisition performance. Instead, the set of post-acquisition decisions about manipulating those resources, the capability to do so that the acquiring firm eventually develops, and the fit between these two factors, seem to matter most. It is important to note, however, that our sample deliberately excludes product extensions and unrelated acquisitions, so the range of variation on acquisition type is less extensive than it is in most other studies.

This study has other limitations. It is a single industry study, focusing on US bank mergers. Its applicability to other industries and other geographic and institutional contexts needs to be, therefore, closely examined. This problem might be particularly relevant for the generalizability of the performance implications of integration decisions. The results related to the capability-building mechanisms might be more safely extended to other types of acquisitions, and in fact to similarly complex organizational tasks, such as alliances and internal restructuring processes, as long as they maintain comparable levels of (in)frequency, heterogeneity and causal ambiguity. Importantly, the study is also based on a limited definition of acquisition performance, which emphasizes the variation in performance of the acquiring firm. The measurement of the dependent variable, based on accounting data, could also be effectively corroborated with other proxies.

This study of acquisitions attempts to bridge and integrate different theoretical approaches to the highly visible phenomenon of corporate acquisitions. In spite of the economic relevance of the phenomenon, when firms turn to academia for some guidance on how to improve their chances of creating value from their investments, they are typically met with a set of highly segmented recommendations. Finance scholars point to the fact that acquisitions on average do not create abnormal returns for the acquirers, raising questions of acquirers' motives for engaging in these transactions. Strategy scholars are slightly more optimistic, distinguishing between more sensible (for example, related) and less sensible (for example, unrelated) types of investments. Finally, scholars in organization studies emphasize the hardships connected with the effective management of the integration phase, the disruption of existing resources and competencies, and the loss of managerial and operational talent.

We hope this study will help to signal the advantages of leveraging different theoretical perspectives in offering managers a more clearly defined and useful account of the conditions under which competitive advantage can be gained or destroyed in acquisition activities. Acquisitions, like any other challenging organizational task, can be effectively managed in a consistently value-creating way, if the conditions enabling performance enhancement are correctly identified and understood. Even more importantly, firms seem to be capable of developing specific capabilities that allow them to improve their chances of success over time. The data analyzed in this study shows that deliberate learning processes, as opposed to semi-automatic (for example learning-by-doing) ones, play an important role in predicting acquisition performance, providing some indications of the way an acquisition capability may develop.

More studies will be necessary in order to test our hypotheses in different contexts and to achieve a more fine-grained understanding of the conditions under which distinct integration strategies work and how integration capabilities develop. We believe that the results of the analyses presented above can guide future scholars in promising directions towards increasing understanding of the antecedents of merger performance. This work also has implications, more broadly, for the creation of organizational capabilities. Further research on the processes used by firms to develop capabilities in other contexts, such as restructuring, alliances and new product development, will strengthen our understanding of these important phenomena. In addition, such research will provide additional settings in which to apply and extend the knowledge and capability based view of the firm.

NOTES

*Generous funding from the Sloan Foundation and support from the Wharton Financial Institutions Center, the Mack Center for Technological Innovation, and the R&D Department at INSEAD are gratefully acknowledged. Many useful comments on previous versions of this chapter were received from Sea-Jin Chang, Philippe Haspeslagh, David Jemison, Prashant Kale, John Kimberly, Dan Levinthal, Phanish Puranam, Jeff Reuer, Jose Santos, Anju Seth, Gabriel Szulanski, and Sid Winter. All remaining errors are our responsibility. Note that previous versions of this manuscript were entitled 'Post-acquisition strategies, integration capability and the economic performance of corporate acquisitions'.

1. For another example of how acquirers can consistently create value without recourse to synergistic potential from resource relatedness, see the case of Hanson Plc (Taubman and Haspeslagh, 1992).
2. Please see the 'Measures' paragraph in the section on 'Research Methodology and Measures' for details on the measurement of the dependent variable in this study
3. In the context observed, acquisitions in the banking industry, the concept of 'level of integration' translates into a set of fairly discrete choices related to decisions

such as the conversion of information systems, the alignment of loan approval processes, or the rationalization of the two networks of bank branches.

4. See also our discussions in the section presenting the 'Results' for the robustness checks of our results, where we validate this measure with a smaller sub–sample of observations for which we could construct a weighted average of both banks' ROA before the acquisition. The two measures are essentially equivalent for all practical purposes.

5. Seven geographic areas in the US (New England, North Atlantic, South Atlantic, Mid-west, South, Rocky Mountains, and Pacific) and one in Canada were used to benchmark performance.

6. Such manuals describe all the procedures necessary to accomplish the desired level of integration between the two organizations. They usually covers issues such as human resources, accounting, audit, CRA, etc.

7. These manuals describe how to train the DP users at the acquired company. They are 'train-the-trainer' tools.

8. These manuals describe how to train the sales–force at the acquired company.

9. These packages allow thorough comparison of the features of the acquired bank's products with those of the acquirer.

10. These models assign tasks, requirements, and deadlines, allowing careful planning and control of complex projects.

11. The use of the word 'replacement' was deemed too negative. We therefore substituted the word 'change' without significantly altering the meaning of the question. Note that the use of the phrase 'has been changed', rather than 'has changed', implies an active role of the acquirer in substituting the top management of the acquired bank. We are likely to capture, therefore, deliberate lay-offs by the acquirer as opposed to retention problems.

12. Particularly important is the stability of the coefficients across models 4, 5, and 6 despite the significant correlation between acquisition experience and knowledge codification.

13. Note that the assessment of acquisitions as infrequent and homogeneous tasks needs to be viewed in comparative terms with respect to more standard organizational activities, such as operating or administrative tasks.

14. These results are confirmed by a Chow test analysis on the replacement coefficient as well as on the entire model. For the entire model, the average level of resource quality changes the slope significantly *vis-à-vis* the other two levels ($F=6.595$, $p<.001$), the high-quality model adds some additional shift but is only marginally significant ($F=1.661$, $p<.10$), whereas the low–quality coefficients do not differ from the others in a statistically significant way ($F=1.235$). Similarly, the single coefficient of TMT replacement shows the strongest negative impact in the interaction with the average quality dummy ($t=-5.134$, $p<.0001$), followed by the high-quality one ($t=-2.113$, $p<.05$), with the one with the low-quality resources indeed switching sign but failing to reach statistical significance ($t=+0.466$). We wish to acknowledge that the results on the interaction effect between replacement and resource quality were the consequence of one reviewer's insightful comments and generous advice, for which we are particularly grateful

15. Our sample size dropped from 47 to 31 banks because a lot of institutions completed their acquisitions only in the last 3 years of the observed period (1985– 1997), and therefore are missing from the analysis. Also, the aggregation process was restrictive, in the sense that any bank with one missing value in any one of

the acquisitions completed was removed from the analysis.
16. As Zollo and Winter (2002) noted, deliberate learning efforts are not to be viewed as systematically warranted as superior mechanisms for capability development. In tasks more frequent, less heterogeneous and less causally ambiguous than the type studied, the costs connected with knowledge articulation and codification processes may overcome the benefits firms derive from them.
17. Again, note that the characterization of acquisitions as infrequent and heterogeneous tasks is made in comparative terms, *vis-à-vis* normal operating or administrative activities, the typical subject of received studies in learning curves.

REFERENCES

Adler P. and Borys, B. (1996), 'Two types of bureaucracy: enabling and coercive', *Administrative Science Quarterly*, 41: 61–89.

Agrawal, A., Jaffe, J.F. and Mandelker, G.N. (1992), 'The post-merger performance of acquiring firms: a re-examination of an anomaly', *Journal of Finance*, 47(4): 1605-1621.

Agrawal, Anup and Jaffe Jeffrey F. (2000), 'The post merger performance puzzle', in and Cary Cooper (eds), *Advances in Mergers and Acquisitions*, pp. 7-41, New York: JAI.

Amburgey, T.A., Kelly, D. & Barnett, W.P. (1993), 'Resetting the clock: the dynamics of organizational change and failure', *Administrative Science Quarterly*, 38: 51-73.

Anand, J. and Singh, H. (1997), Gregory Alan 'Asset redeployment, acquisition and corporate strategies in declining industries', *Strategic Management Journal*, 18 (Summer Special Issue): 99-118.

Astrachan, J.H. (1990), *Mergers, Acquisitions, and Employee Anxiety: A Study of Separation Anxiety in a Corporate Context*, New York, NY: Praeger.

Baker, G. and Montgomery, C.A. (1994), 'Conglomerates and LBO associations: a comparison of organizational forms, Unpublished Manuscript, Harvard Business School.

Barney, J.B. (1986), 'Strategic factor markets: expectations, luck, and business strategy', *Management Science*, 32(10): 1231-1241.

Barney J.B. (1988), 'Returns to bidding firms in mergers and acquisitions: reconsidering the relatedness hypothesis', *Strategic Management Journal*, 9 (Special Issue): 71-78.

Baum J.A.C. and Ginsberg, A. (1997), 'Acquisition experience and profitability: exploring the value of learning by doing, Unpublished manuscript, New York University.

Bruton, G.D., Oviatt B.M. and White M.A. (1994), 'Performance of acquisitions of distressed firms', *Academy of Management Journal*, 37: 972-989.

Buono, A.F. and Bowditch, J.L. (1989), *The Human Side of Mergers and Acquisitions*, San Francisco, CA: Jossey-Bass.

Cannella, A.A. Jr. and Hambrick, D.C. (1993), 'Effects of executive departures on the performance of acquired firms', *Strategic Management Journal*, 14: 137-152.

Capron, L. (1999), 'The long-term performance of horizontal acquisitions', *Strategic Management Journal*, 20(6).

Chatterjee, S. (1986), 'Types of synergy and economic value: the impact of acquisitions on merging and rival firms', *Strategic Management Journal*, 7: 119-139.

Chatterjee, S. and Lubatkin, M., Schweiger, D.M. and Weber, Y. (1992), 'Cultural differences and shareholder value in related mergers: linking equity and human capital', *Strategic Management Journal*, 13: 319-344.

Clark, K. and Fujimoto, T. (1991), *Product Development Performance*, Boston, MA Harvard Business School Press.

Cohen, W. M. and Bacdayan, P. (1994), 'Organizational routines are stored as procedural memory: evidence from a laboratory study', *Organization Science*, 5(4): 554-568.

Cohen, W. M., Burkhart R., Dosi G., Egidi M., Marengo L., Warglien M. & Winter S. (1997), 'Routines and other recurring action patterns of organizations: contemporary research issues', *Industrial and Corporate Change*, 5: 653-698.

Cormier, S. and Hagman, J. (1987), *Transfer of Learning: Contemporary Research and Applications*, Academic Press Inc: San Diego.

Datta, D.K. and Grant, J.H. (1990), 'Relationships between type of acquisition, the autonomy given to the acquired firm, and acquisition success: an empirical analysis', *Journal of Management*, 16(1): 29-44.

Dierickx, I. and Cool, K. (1989), 'Asset stock accumulation and sustainability of competitive advantage', *Management Science*, 35(12): 1505-1513.

Dutton, J.M. and Thomas A. (1984), 'Treating progress functions as a managerial opportunity', *Academy of Management Review*, 9: 235-247.

Empson, L. (2001), 'Fear of exploitation and fear of contamination: Impediments to knowledge transfer in mergers between professional service firms', *Human Relations*, 54(7): 839-862.

Epple, D., Argote L. and Devadas R. (1991), 'Organizational learning curves: a method for investigating intra-plant transfer of knowledge acquired through learning by doing', *Organization Science*, 2: 58-70.

Fowler, F.K. and Schmit, D. (1989), 'Determinants of tender offer post-acquisition financial performance', *Strategic Management Journal*, 10: 339-350.

Franks, J., Harris R. and Titman, S. (1991), 'The post-merger share price performance of acquiring firms', *Journal of Financial Economics*, 29: 81-96.

Gavetti, G. and Levinthal, D. (2000), 'Looking forward and looking backward: cognitive and experiential search', *Administrative Science Quarterly*, 45: 113-137.

Gick, M.L. and Holyoak, K.J. (1987), 'The cognitive basis of knowledge transfer', in S.M.Cormier and J.D.Hagman, (eds.), *Transfer of Learning: Contemporary Research and Applications,* New York: Academic Press . pp.9-47.

Grant, R.M. (1996), 'Toward a knowledge-based theory of the firm', *Strategic Management Journal*, 17 (Winter Special Issue): 109-122.

Haleblian, J. and Finkelstein, S. (1999), 'The influence of organization acquisition experience on acquisition performance: a behavioral learning theory perspective', *Administrative Science Quarterly*, 44: 29-56.

Haspeslagh, P.C. and Jemison, D.B. (1991), *Managing Acquisitions*, New York: Free Press.

Haveman, H.A. (1992), 'Between a rock and a hard place: organizational change and performance under conditions of fundamental environmental transformation', *Administrative Science Quarterly*, 37: 48-75.

Haveman, H.A. (1993), 'Organizational size and change: diversification in the savings and loans industry after deregulation', *Administrative Science Quarterly*, 38: 20-50.

Hawawini G. and I. Swary (1990), *Mergers and Acquisitions in the U.S. Banking Industry: Evidence from the Capital Markets*, Amsterdam: North Holland Publishing.

Hayward M. (2002), 'When do firms learn from their acquisition experience? Evidence from 1990–1995', *Strategic Management Journal*, 23(1) 21-40.

Healy, P.M., Palepu, K. and Ruback, R.S. (1992), 'Does corporate performance improve after mergers?', *Journal of Financial Economics*, 31: 135-175.

Henderson, R.M. and K.B. Clark (1990), 'Architectural innovation: The reconfiguration of existing product technologies and the failure of established firms', *Administrative Science Quarterly*, 35: 9-30.

Jarrell, G.A., Brickley, J.A. and Netter, J.M. (1988), 'The market for corporate control: the empirical evidence since 1980', *Journal of Economic Perspectives*, 2: 49-68.

Jemison, D.B. and Sitkin, S.B. (1986), 'Corporate acquisitions: a process perspective', *Academy of Management Review*, 11: 145-163.

Jensen, M.C. and Ruback, R.S. (1983), 'the market for corporate control: the scientific evidence', *Journal of Financial Economics*, 11: 5-50.

Kale, P., Dyer, J. and Singh, H. (2002), 'Alliance capability, stock market response, and long-term alliance success: the role of the alliance function', *Strategic Management Journal*, 23: 747-768.

Kitching, J. (1967), 'Why do mergers miscarry?', *Harvard Business Review*, 45(6): 84-102.

Kogut, B. and Zander, U. (1992), 'Knowledge of the firm, combinative capabilities and the replication of technology', *Organization Science*, 3(3): 383-397.

Krishnan, H.A., Miller, A. and Judge, W.Q. (1997), 'Diversification and top management team complementarity: is performance improved by merging similar or dissimilar teams?', *Strategic Management Journal*, 18: 361-374.

Lapre, M.A., Mukherjee, A.S. and Van Wassenhove, L.N. (2000), 'Behind the learning curve: linking learning activities to waste reduction', *Management Science*, 46(5): 597-611.

Levitt, B. and March, J.G. (1988), 'Organizational learning', *Annual Review of Sociology*, 14: 319-340.

Lippman, S. and Rumelt, R. (1982), 'Uncertain imitability: an analysis of inter-firm differences in efficiency under competition', *Bell Journal of Economics*, 13 (Autumn): 418-438.

Loderer, C. and Martin K. (1992), 'Post-acquisition performance of acquiring firms', *Financial Management*, 21: 69-79.

Lubatkin, M. (1987), 'Merger strategies and stockholder value', *Strategic Management Journal*, 8: 39-53.

Manne, H.G. (1965), 'Mergers and the market for corporate control', *Journal of Political Economy*, 73-74: 110-120.

March J.G., Sproull L.S. and Tamuz M. (1991), 'Learning from samples of one or fewer', *Organization Science*, 2(1): 1-13.

Marks, M.L. and Mirvis, P.H. (1985), 'Merger syndrome: stress and uncertainty', *Mergers and Acquisitions*, Summer: 50-55.

Nelson, R.R. and Winter, S.G. (1982), *An Evolutionary Theory of Economic Change*, Cambridge, MA: Harvard University Press.

Neter, J., Wasserman, W., and Kutner, M. H. (1985), *Applied linear statistical models*, Homewood, IL: Irwin, 2nd edn.

Nonaka, I (1994), 'A dynamic theory of knowledge creation', *Organization Science*, 5(1), 14-37.

Nonaka, I. and Takeuchi, H. (1995), *The Knowledge-creating Company*, New York, NY Oxford University Press.

Ocasio, W. (1997), 'Towards an attention-based view of the firm', *Strategic Management Journal*, 18 (Summer Special Issue): 187-206.

Pablo, A.L. (1994), 'Determinants of acquisition integration level: a decision-making perspective', *Academy of Management Journal*, 37(4): 803-836.

Pablo, A.L., Sitkin, S.B. and Jemison, D.B. (1996), 'Acquisition decision-making processes: the central role of risk', *Journal of Management*, 22(5): 723-746.

Pennings, J.M., Barkema, H. and Douma, S. (1994), 'Organizational learning and diversification', *Academy of Management Journal*, 37(3): 608-640.

Polanyi, M. (1962), *Personal Knowledge: Toward a Post-critical Philosophy*, New York: Harper Torchbooks.

Polanyi, M. (1966), *The Tacit Dimension*, New York: Anchor Day Books.

Puranam, P., Singh, H. and Zollo, M. (2004), 'The coordination-autonomy tradeoff in technology grafting acquisitions', Working paper, Mack Center for Technological Innovation, Wharton School.

Rhoades, S.A. (1994), A summary of merger performance studies in banking, 1980-93, and assessment of the "operating performance" and "event study" methodologies, *Federal Reserve Bulletin*, 80(7): 589-596.

Rogers, E. (1980), *Diffusion of innovation*, New York, Free Press.

Rumelt, R.P. (1974) Strategy, structure and economic performance, Division of Research Graduate School of Business Administration, Harvard University.

Rumelt, R.P. (1984) 'Towards a strategic theory of the firm', in Lamb R.B. (ed.), *Competitive Strategic Management*, Englewood Cliffs, NJ: Prentice Hall 556-570.

Sanchez, R. and Mahoney, J.T. (1996), 'Modularity, flexibility and knowledge management in product and organization design', *Strategic Management Journal*, 17 (Winter Special Issue): 63-76.

Schweiger, D.M., Ivancevich, J.M. and Power, F.R. (1987), 'Executive actions for managing human resources before and after acquisition', *Academy of Management Executive*, 1: 127-138.

Seth, A. (1990), 'Sources of value creation in acquisitions: an empirical investigation', *Strategic Management Journal*, 11: 431-446.

Shanley M.T. (1994), 'Determinants and consequences of post-acquisition change', in G. Von Krogh, A. Sinatra and H. Singh (eds), *Managing Corporate Acquisitions: A Comparative Analysis* London, UK: Macmillan pp.391-413.

Shelton, L.M. (1988), 'Strategic business fits and corporate acquisitions: empirical evidence', *Strategic Management Journal*, 9(3): 279-88.

Singh, H. and Montgomery, C.A. (1987), 'Corporate acquisition strategies and economic performance', *Strategic Management Journal*, 8(4): 377-86.

Szulanski, G. (1997), 'Exploring internal stickiness: Impediments to the transfer of the best practice within the firm', *Strategic Management Journal*, 17 (Winter Special Issue): 27-44.

Taubman C. and Haspeslagh P. (1992). *Hanson Plc*, INSEAD Business School case, 393-004-1, Fontainebleau, France: INSEAD.

Teece D.J., Pisano, G. and Shuen, A. (1997), 'Dynamic capabilities and strategic management', *Strategic Management Journal*, 18(7): 509-533.

Thompson J.D. (1967), *Organizations in action* , New York, NY McGraw Hill

Walsh, J.P. (1988) 'Top management turnover following acquisitions', *Strategic Management Journal*, 9(2): 173-183.

Walsh J.P. and Ellwood, J.W. (1991), 'Mergers, acquisitions and the pruning of managerial deadwood', *Strategic Management Journal*, 12(3): 201-217.

Weick, K. (1995), *Sensemaking in Organizations*, Thousand Oaks, CA: Sage Publications.

Wernerfelt, B. (1984), 'A resource-based view of the firm', *Strategic Management Journal*, 5(2): 171-180.

Winter, S. (1987), 'Knowledge and competence as strategic assets', in D.J. Teece (ed.), *The Competitive Challenge: Strategies for Industrial Innovation and Renewal*: Cambridge, MA: Ballinger, pp.159-184.

Winter, S. (1995), 'Four Rs for profitability: rents, resources, routines and replication', in C.A. Montgomery (ed.), *Resource-based and Evolutionary Theories of the Firm: Towards a Synthesis*: Norwell, MA: Kluwer, pp.147-178.

Yelle, L.E. (1979), 'The learning curve: historical review and comprehensive survey', *Decision Sciences*, 10; 302-328

Zollo M. (1998), *Knowledge codification, process routinization and the creation of organizational capabilities: post-acquisition management in the US banking industry*, Unpublished doctoral dissertation, University of Pennsylvania.

Zollo M. and Reuer J. (2003), 'Experience spillovers across corporate development activities', INSEAD Working Paper 03-98-SM.

Zollo M. and Winter S.G. (2002), 'Deliberate learning and the evolution of dynamic capabilities', *Organization Science*, 13(3): 339-351.

15. Beyond this book: a proposed research agenda

Arturo Capasso, Giovanni Battista Dagnino and Andrea Lanza

Some centuries ago Francis Bacon, the grand English philosopher and empiricist, was the originator of the expression '*knowledge is power*'. Bacon argued that the only knowledge of importance to man was empirically rooted in the natural world; and that a clear system of scientific inquiry would assure man's mastery over the world. Paraphrasing Bacon's expression, we can contend that '*knowledge transfer is power*' for firms engaged in a modern-day knowledge race where the only possession of knowledge that can guarantee a strategic advantage is the possession of an unremittingly renewing base of knowledge. In this collective endeavor, we have tried to underscore why and how intra- and inter-organizational knowledge transfer is an synonym of power.

Stemming from the systematic investigation of the multifaceted relationships between strategic capabilities and knowledge transfer in complex environments, this book provides management studies with several interesting insights from both the theoretical viewpoint and the empirical stance, spanning from heterogeneity management to inter-organizational best practice transfer, from capabilities development to learning and innovation in networks and to the management of the acquisition and post–acquisition processes. It also provides us with several intriguing underpinnings for managerial practice.

The fourteen chapters contained heretofore in this book do not cover the entire spectrum of research on strategic capabilities and knowledge transfer; rather, we have tried to endeavor those research streams which appear to be relevant in the fields of strategy and organization. Nor can this book claim to present a comprehensive review of the full gamut of these issues. A number of relevant questions remain open and embryonic, waiting for future researchers and investigations in the years to come. Notwithstanding, we are confident that the contributions contained in this book will be an *inspiration* to others to join these scholars in advancing our understanding of the crucial links between strategic capabilities and knowledge transfer within and between organizations. We are also positive that it is going to remain a crucial topic for the future.

The costs and difficulties of transferring knowledge will undoubtedly continue to decline. New information technologies, such as the Internet, promise to continue lowering the cost of unraveling and conveying information and knowledge bits and pieces. Accordingly, advances in computers and telecommunications should bring new forms of transmitting higher bandwidth information electronically. In a foretaste of things to come, communities will span throughout organizations in virtual teams work, connecting unremittingly individuals from a firm 'X' with individuals from other firms and institutions among the five continents using multimedia collaboration software. Community members will learn to work together without ever meeting face to face.

To present an actual example in this vein, one of the most important results achieved with this book is definitely the gathering of several scholars who focus their research interest on strategic capabilities and knowledge transfer in the attempt to continue shaping and growing a scientific mini-community dedicated to this topic. Some of these scholars have only met once or twice, but this has not prevented them in interacting relentlessly and actively. We are thus confident that we may render this community increasingly established and carry out further research activity.

Because of these advances, strategic capabilities for knowledge transfer will continue to matter in managerial arenas. People and organizations will continue to use them more intensely and develop their capabilities to enhance the knowledge transfer processes, not only within, but also across organizational boundaries. Similarly, cheap access to knowledge offers at best an imperfect substitute for intra- and inter-organizational transfer. Indeed, the two differ in at least one respect: both intra- and inter-organizational transfer require premeditated action, but the logic of transfer can transcend arrangements made in the vein of Williamson-like free-riding behaviors and opportunistic reasons.

As far as the methodological crux is concerned, the book provides the reader with a pretty good mix of quantitative and qualitative studies. Both of them help us to refine our understanding of the critical knowledge transfer processes which typically occur within and between organizations. Therefore, we do believe that studies advancing a fruitful *combination* of both, qualitative and qualitative methodologies, are better suited to disentangle these topics. Given the dynamic nature of knowledge, this intriguing association of methods could ensure the required consistency between the nature of the issues under investigation and the method employed. By coupling longitudinal field methods and cross-sectional studies, management researchers could account for the mutual relationships among actors, contexts and processes at different levels of analysis and for prolonged time periods, deepening farther our comprehension of the mechanisms that facilitate and prevent strategic knowledge dynamics.

In the next section, we discuss some issues that, in our opinion, are expected to inform a substantial part of the future research agenda on strategic capabilities and knowledge transfer.

THE RESEARCH AGENDA

The past decade has witnessed a rapid increase of interest in and research relating to the development of strategic capabilities and their influence in transferring knowledge. There is a growing consensus of the need to develop, nurture and guide specific firm capabilities explicitly directed to transfer knowledge both within and between organizations. Pertinent to this fundamental connection are the following observations and proposals that, taken cumulatively, shape an agenda for prospective research in strategy and management.

A. The strategic theory of the firm

(1) *Governance of capabilities*

If the firm is a structure to govern people, activities, systems and processes, then the boundaries of the firm should be set with reference to the capacity of the firm to provide advantageous knowledge transfer mechanisms. The governance of capabilities and knowledge is likely to affirm in order to provide appropriate guidance to the application and execution of firm capabilities and knowledge transfer.

(2) *The evolution of firm capabilities*

We have learned that firms' capabilities are dynamic in nature and scope. They exhibit a sort of capabilities lifecycle (Helfat and Peteraf, 2003). Dynamic resource-based and evolutionary analyses may be supportive in explaining how capabilities evolve over time and change their shape and structure accordingly.

(3) *The elusive and sticky nature of knowledge*

Knowledge displays an elusive nature in that it is embedded in individuals and organizations and is therefore extremely *sticky* in nature (Szulanski, 2003). It is thus generally difficult to transfer. Knowledge is also codifiable (Zollo, 1998; Zollo and Winter, 2002). The codification of knowledge enables its reification and routinization; hence it enhances transferability. Nonetheless, codified knowledge is less appropriable by the firm and, at the same time, once codified, it is difficult to change. It inescapably loses flexibility and adaptability thereby reinforcing its stickiness.

(4) *The knowledge-based view of the firm*

The knowledge-based theory of the firm (Eisenhardt and Santos, 2002; Grant, 2003; Nonaka et al., 2000) contends that a firm's ability to integrate the knowledge efforts of different actors is an essential prerequisite for achieving superior performance. Although firms are generally thought superior to markets and alliances in integrating knowledge to produce goods and services, Hayekian knowledge production occurs at different levels and throughout the economic system. Firms need to recognize the bits and pieces of knowledge that are distributed in the system, capture them and proceed to an idiosyncratic integration of this knowledge.

(5) *Systems and networks considerations*

The ways and the reasons why the firm as a whole is larger (or thinner) than and different from the sum of its parts need to be explicated. New analytical and conceptual tools need to be worked out and devised. Because of its systemic nature, research on networks, clusters, districts, and more generally on interorganizational arrangements, may be of particular help in this regard.

(6) *The limits of strategic capabilities*

Strategic capability literature suffers from limitations. Even firm capabilities suffer from limitations. Capabilities are essentially based on learning and are therefore subject to aging processes (Helfat and Peteraf, 2003). It is often difficult to replicate a capability inside a firm or to simply repair it when needed.

(7) *The limits of knowledge transfer*

The transfer of knowledge has limitations as well. For instance, it is almost impossible to transfer the knowledge possessed by a firm (of a firm subpart, such as an office, a factory plant or a department) in its entirety and so rapidly to immediately access sources of competitive advantages.

B. Applications to management functions

(1) *Finance*

Mergers and acquisitions (M&A) may be described in financial terms. They are in fact financial instruments. But it is misleading to think of M&A only in financial terms if the critical economic difference between these two instruments turn also on their knowledge transfer characters and the capabilities needed to manage both pre-acquisition, acquisition and post–acquisition (that is, integration) processes. A combined theory of corporate finance and corporate capabilities are needed. Work on these matters is still in its infancy but do not lack of promises and hopes.

(2) *Marketing*
A capability-based approach to marketing should lead to understand better the nature and scope of reputation building and branding. It may also be beneficial to studies such as the transfer of knowledge in alliances. Work of this kind and evidence are coming along.

(3) *Operations management*
As it has been noted, knowledge transfer within organizations will be characterized by decreasing costs, at least for codified knowledge and information. This may affect operation costs not only in an efficiency-based perspective, but also from the viewpoint of the effectiveness of knowledge leveraging within the context of multidivisional and networked firms. This research topic may deserve further attention by scholars.

(4) *R&D management*
Given the huge amount of investments required to keep the pace of innovation in a growing number of industries, the management of R&D in an inter–organizational perspective, shaped by complementarity, can lead several firms to increasing specialization on focused activities, yet raising concerns about the risks and costs of cospecialization.

C. Applications to managements areas and related fields
(1) *Firm strategy*
Strategic thinking has been extremely appealing to academics and managers since its inception. Nonetheless, strategizing may also be costly and can be misguiding. A theory of strategizing via capabilities and knowledge is affirming mostly at the expenses of the older economizing and contractual approaches. The inception of knowledge transfer issues and insights bears the potential of igniting more comprehensive frameworks of firm strategizing via capabilities deliberate evolution. A strategy paradigm knowledge-capability-performance is on its way to establish.

(2) *Organization theory*
Organization theory is concerned with both organizational and inter-organizational relationships and learning. A conceptual approach solidly rooted in organization theory can help developing significant extensions of such perspectives as inter–partner learning in alliances, learning in acquisition processes, knowledge and practice transfer and the ensuing development of structures, systems and processes for knowledge transfer.

(3) *Management of multinational firms*
In the last two decades, the management of multinational companies has progressively become a field of studies *per se*. This field has much to exchange in a dialogue with capabilities and knowledge transfer. For their territorial ramifications and geographical diffusion, multinationals are (and have always been) an ideal environment to study knowledge transfer via

capabilities and may benefit greatly from the introduction of the knowledge-capability-performance approach.

(4) *Entrepreneurship and family business*

Since there is a widespread concern on the relative lack of highly specialized competencies (mainly related to top–and middle–management) in small firms and family businesses, studies in entrepreneurship and family business may greatly benefit from adopting a strategic capability approach. Researches on these issues, expressly from an inter–organizational basis, may shed additional light on crucial issues such as the small firms' actual ability to absorb and integrate external competencies.

(5) *Innovation and technology management*

The relevance of innovation in the contemporary competitive landscape is ascertained. What may deserve further investigation is the role of absorptive capabilities and knowledge integration once innovation is carried out on an inter–organizational basis.

(6) *Business history*

Business history has progressed in the last fifteen years all over the world. In our view, it needs to inform and be informed by the combined study of strategic capabilities and knowledge transfer. Business history research can in fact provide intriguing and inspirational insights in the firm-, network- and industry-level evolution of the links between strategic capabilities and knowledge transfer. It can also receive theoretical grounding from dialogue and exchange and offer historical–longitudinal support.

D. Policy considerations

(1) *Economic development via capabilities*

It is widely recognized that knowledge affects economic development by means of innovation and the commercial application of technology. Given the mushrooming relevance of science-based industries, not only in Western countries but also in Eastern countries, this is even more appropriate nowadays. The leverage of scientific and technological capabilities on an international and global basis may be the source of economic and social development for nations and national blocks (i.e., NAFTA, ASEAN, Mercosur and the European Union) in the 21st century.

(2) *Regulation*

The two deregulation waves of the 1980s and 1990s, respectively in the USA and Europe, have allowed more interfirm interaction and transfer of knowledge. Regulation must not prevent the development of firm and inter–firm capabilities of knowledge absorption and transfer. It should favor the market-driven interchange of knowledge protecting the breaking of legal rights. But it should also prevent the establishment of business monopolistic behaviors in the appropriation and protection of knowledge.

(3) *Antitrust policy*
Public policy toward business needs to be informed and reformed accordingly. Antitrust has already been reshaped especially with respect to vertical integration in the industry value chain and more in prospect, joint ventures and alliances being an example. However additional work in this area needs to be done.

E. Managerial implications

(1) *Toward a more holistic view of business management*
In the vein of some forerunners, such as Chester Barnard and Herbert Simon, a more holistic view of management is required by managers and entrepreneurs who wish to cope with the current hypercompetitive and fast-changing environments. Managers are increasingly called to recognize that today the received view of the firm as a fragmented entity made up of dispersed parts and functions that are hardly communicating is neither sufficient nor adequate. A firm is like a social fabric made up of parts that are different but highly complementary, ineradicably intertwined and dependent one to another. Managerial decisions at all levels should be taken in the light of this more comprehensive and holistic framework.

(2) *Transfer of practices*
Best practice transfer is the subject of managerial purposive design both within and between organizations. Best practice inter–organizational transfer could be enhanced by structuring and managing a number of inter–organizational arrangements: benchmarking teams, best practices teams and knowledge and best practices networks and/or communities (Dagnino, 2005). If skillfully planned and implemented, these elements of organizational design may help to guarantee the selection, replication, and enhancement of best practices throughout the firm.

(3) *The role of communities of practice*
Since relevant communities of practice (Brown and Duguid, 1991; Wenger, 1998) are repositories where capabilities are embedded, they are concurrently capability *enhancing* (Leonard-Barton, 1992) and knowledge barriers *lowering* (Szulanski, 2003). Accordingly, they become a relevant moderating mechanism affecting the speed of knowledge generation and utilization at the level of the firm as a whole (Zander and Kogut, 1995). Communities are repositories of an important potential for the exploitation of existing capabilities, for increasing their efficiency by exploiting the best practices. They are able to articulate bits and pieces of (unarticulated and tacit) knowledge emerging from current practices so as to increase their efficiency (Cohendet and Llerena, 2003: 288; Amin and Cohendet, 2004).

(4) *The role of innovation and technology*
We underscore the role that innovation and technology (and especially computer-, network- and Internet-based technologies) play in today's business environments. In order to survive the current multiple intertwined innovation processes, firms needs to forge, identify and introduce new technology incessantly and transfer them most rapidly inside their organizations.

REFERENCES

Amin A. and P. Cohendet (2004), *Architectures of Knowledge*, Oxford: Oxford University Press.

Brown, J.S. and P. Duguid (1991), 'Organizational learning and communities-of-practice: toward a unified view of working, learning, and innovation', *Organization Science*, 2 (1): 40–57.

Cohendet, P. and P. Llerena (2003), 'Routines and incentives: the role of communities in the firm', *Industrial and Corporate Change*, 12 (2): 271–97.

Dagnino, G.B. (2005), 'Coupling combinative and relational capabilities in interorganizational best practice transfer: an evolutionary perspective', chapter 6 in this volume.

Eisenhardt, K.M. and F.M. Santos (2002), 'Knowledge-based view: A new theory of strategy?', in Pettigrew A., H. Thomas and R. Whittington (eds), *Handbook of Strategy and Management*, Thousands Oak, CA: Sage.

Grant, R.M. (2003), 'The knowledge-based view of the firm', in Faulkner D.O. and A. Campbell (eds), *The Oxford Handbook of Strategy*, New York: Oxford University Press.

Helfat, C.E. and M.A. Peteraf (2003). 'The dynamic resource-based view: capability lifecycles', *Strategic Management Journal*, Special Issue, **24** (10): 997–1010.

Leonard-Barton, D. (1992), 'Core capabilities and core rigidities: a paradox in managing new product development', *Strategic Management Journal*, 13: 111–25.

Nonaka, I., R. Toyama and A. Nagata (2000), 'A firm as a knowledge-creating entity: a new perspective on the theory of the firm, *Industrial and Corporate Change*, **9** (1):

Szulanski, G. (2003), *Sticky Knowledge*, London: Sage.

Wenger, E. (1998), *Communities of Practice: Learning, Meaning, and Identity*, Cambridge University Press: New York.

Zander, B. and B. Kogut (1995) 'Knowledge and the speed of transfer and imitation of organizational capabilities: an empirical test', *Organization Science*, 1 (6): 76–92.

Zollo M. (1998), *Knowledge codification, process routinization and the creation of organizational capabilities: post-acquisition management in the US banking industry*, Unpublished doctoral dissertation, University of Pennsylvania.

Zollo M. and Winter S.G. (2002), 'Deliberate learning and the evolution of dynamic capabilities', *Organization Science*, 13 (3): 339–51.

Index